So has Ptah come to rest…
having set the gods in their cult places,
having made sure their bread offerings,
having founded their shrines…

From the Memphite Theology

The Complete
Temples of Ancient Egypt

RICHARD H. WILKINSON

With 535 illustrations, 173 in colour

Thames & Hudson

Cover: *(front) Interior of the hypostyle hall, temple of Dendera
(© Könemann Verlagsgesellschaft mbH, Köln/photo: Andrea Jemolo); (back)
The temple of Hatshepsut, Deir el-Bahri (© Thames & Hudson Ltd/photo:
Heidi Grassley).*

Half-title: *Entrance pylon of the Temple of Luxor as depicted on the
temple wall.*

Title page: *David Roberts' depiction of the Temple of Philae, from his*
Egypt and Nubia, *1846–50.*

Contents pages: *The ruins of the Temple of Karnak, from the*
Description de L'Égypte, *1809, commissioned by Napoleon.*

First published in the United Kingdom in 2000 by Thames & Hudson Ltd,
181A High Holborn, London WC1V 7QX

First paperback edition 2017

British Library Cataloguing-in-Publication Data
A catalogue record for this book is available from the British Library

ISBN 978-0-500-28396-7

Printed in China by Hing Yip Printing Company

To find out about all our publications, please visit
www.thamesandhudson.com. There you can subscribe
to our e-newsletter, browse or download our current catalogue,
and buy any titles that are in print.

CONTENTS

Introduction:
Temple, Land and Cosmos

The ruins of the mortuary temple of Nebhepetre Mentuhotep, Hatshepsut and Tuthmosis III at the foot of the cliffs at Deir el-Bahri, western Thebes, a site long considered sacred to the goddess Hathor.

The temples of Egypt are without doubt among the most impressive monuments to have survived from the ancient world. Once-shining cities whose towers and gates 'pierced the sky' and whose gold and bronze-capped monuments shone 'like the sun in its rising', many of these structures still rank among the greatest architectural accomplishments of human history.

Already ancient and a source of wonder in Greek and Roman times, Egypt's temples continued to amaze conquerors, explorers and travellers long after the civilization which created them had vanished. For centuries, monuments such as the Great Temple of Amun at Karnak – the largest religious structure the world has ever known – have continued to astound those who have seen them, through the richness of their architectural design and decoration, their colossal statues and obelisks, and often through the sheer vastness of their scale alone.

But there is more than this. Beyond the physical stone of Egypt's temples we may still sense much of the symbolic nature of these structures, the deeper reasons for their construction. So well-fitted to their purpose were these buildings that even now, thousands of years since the chanting processions of priests were halted and the music of singers stilled, it is difficult to walk through the great courts, pillared halls and porticoes of some of these structures and not sense once more something of their original life and presence.

No other ancient culture produced temples in such numbers, and although the remaining monuments may represent perhaps only a fraction of the

hundreds of temples built throughout Egyptian history (including many of which we doubtless have no record), they offer a unique view into the lives and minds of the ancient Egyptians. This is because Egyptian temples were far broader in relevance and importance than those of many other cultures. As a result, they have been described in widely varying ways: as mansions of the gods, models of Egypt and of the universe itself, focal points of Egyptian worship, portals to the divine, and perhaps most colourfully, as islands of order in a cosmic ocean of chaos. In reality, as will be seen in this book, Egyptian temples never functioned exclusively as any of these things. Rather, despite the seeming hyperbole of some of these descriptions, Egyptian temples were all of these things and much more.

Some temples served primarily as houses of the gods, built and expanded over the millennia to serve their patron deities, while others were mortuary monuments built to serve the spirit of deceased kings and to ensure their comfort and rule in the hereafter. Still other temples served different purposes, some doubling as fortresses, administrative centres and even as concrete expressions of propaganda or royal retreats.

Within the walls of most of these monuments, sanctuaries and treasuries, offices and palaces, slaughterhouses and schools might be found. Not only were many of the religious complexes centres of government, economy and commerce, but also within these temples ancient science and scholarship thrived and the nature of existence itself was pondered by generations of learned priests.

The Ramesseum – temple of the cult of the deified Ramesses II – from the west. Behind the temple proper lie the extensive mud-brick buildings of the temple's storehouses.

As the interface between the divine and human spheres, the Egyptian temple served as a theatre in which symbolic ritual dramas were enacted. Here the myriad gods of Egyptian belief were fed, clothed and reassured that justice, order and balance were being preserved through the ritual services performed by the pharaoh and the priests who functioned as his appointed agents. In return, the gods gave life to the land and upheld Egypt's ordained place in the cosmos. In one sense, the Egyptian temple was the source of power by which all of Egyptian society ran.

Thus, it was the prerogative of Egypt's kings not only to serve, but also to adorn and enrich the domains of the gods: the spoils of military conquest, the tribute of foreign nations and much of

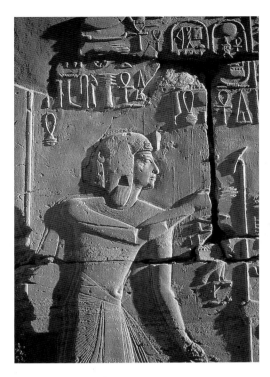

the wealth of Egypt itself were brought to the temples. The ancient texts describe – and archaeology confirms – the magnificence of some of the great wonders created on behalf of the gods of Egypt. Vast edifices set within even vaster estates, the largest of the temples of Egypt grew into institutions which rivalled, and sometimes even came close to surpassing, the power of pharaoh himself.

Although the physical treasures of these great monuments vanished as history enveloped them, many of the architectural wonders of Egypt's temples are still extant. Much of their art remains to impress and to instruct us, and temple texts still inform us of wide-ranging historical matters and of the deepest spiritual and philosophical concerns of the ancient Egyptian mind. Shattered though they may be, as remnants of profound religious machinery, the temples of Egypt remain – and are still accessible – as eternal symbols in stone.

(Opposite) Luxor Temple, with the obelisk and pylon of Ramesses II, and, beyond, the colonnade of Amenophis III.

(Below) The prostrate head of Ramesses II, from one of his colossal statues in the Temple of Luxor. Ramesses, together with Amenophis III, was largely responsible for building much of the temple that we see today.

(Above left) Relief of Sethos I from the Great Hypostyle Hall of the temple of Amun at Karnak. Sethos and Ramesses II decorated the hall, and their military campaigns in Syria and Palestine are shown on the exterior walls.

(Above) The forest of columns with papyrus-bud capitals supporting the roof of Karnak's Great Hypostyle Hall.

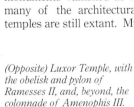

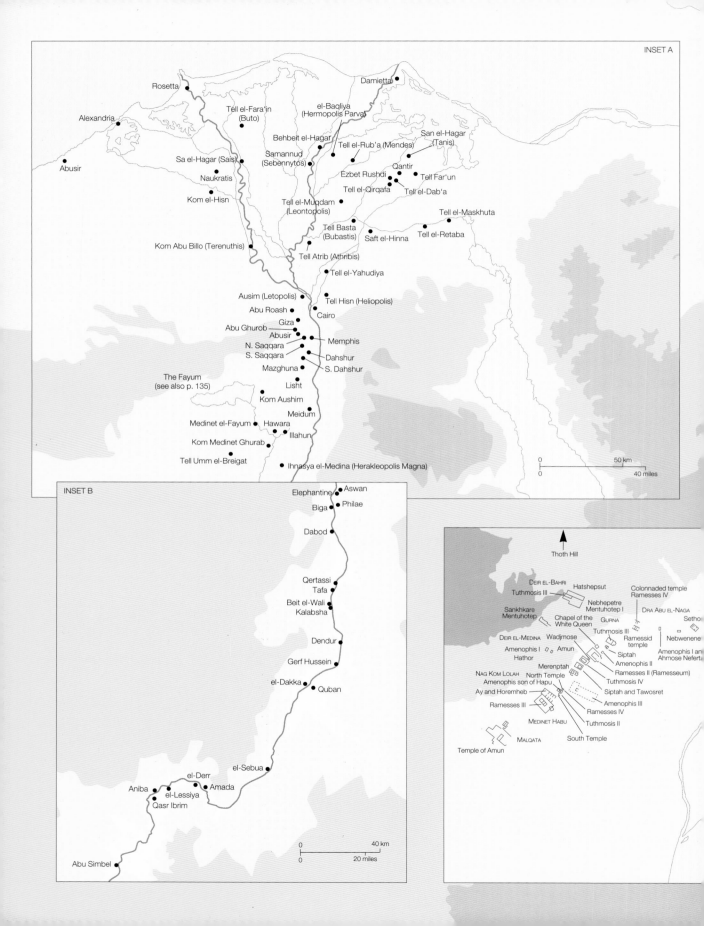

INSET A

Rosetta
Damietta

Alexandria

Tell el-Fara'in
(Buto)
el-Baqliya
(Hermopolis Parva)

Abusir

San el-Hagar
(Tanis)
Behbeit el-Hagar
Tell el-Rub'a (Mendes)

Sa el-Hagar (Sais)
Samannud
(Sebennytos)
Qantir

Naukratis
Ezbet Rushdi
Tell Far'un

Kom el-Hisn
Tell el-Qirqafa
Tell el-Dab'a

Tell el-Muqdam
(Leontopolis)
Tell el-Maskhuta

Kom Abu Billo (Terenuthis)
Tell Basta
(Bubastis)
Tell el-Retaba
Saft el-Hinna

Tell Atrib (Athribis)

Tell el-Yahudiya

Ausim (Letopolis)
Tell Hisn (Heliopolis)

Abu Roash
Cairo
Giza
Abu Ghurob
Abusir
Memphis
N. Saqqara
S. Saqqara
Dahshur
Mazghuna
S. Dahshur

The Fayum
(see also p. 135)
Lisht

Kom Aushim
Meidum

Medinet el-Fayum
Hawara

Kom Medinet Ghurab
Illahun

Tell Umm el-Breigat
Ihnasya el-Medina (Herakleopolis Magna)

0 _____ 50 km
0 _____ 40 miles

INSET B

Elephantine
Aswan
Biga
Philae
Dabod

Qertassi
Tafa
Beit el-Wali
Kalabsha
Dendur
Gerf Hussein
el-Dakka
Quban

el-Sebua
el-Derr
Aniba
Amada
el-Lessiya
Qasr Ibrim

Abu Simbel

0 _____ 40 km
0 _____ 20 miles

Thoth Hill

DEIR EL-BAHRI
Hatshepsut
Colonnaded temple
Ramesses IV
Tuthmosis III
Nebhepetre
Mentuhotep I
DRA ABU EL-NAGA
Sankhkare
Mentuhotep
Chapel of the
White Queen
GURNA
Setho
Tuthmosis III
Ramessid
temple
Nebwenene
DEIR EL-MEDINA
Wadjmose
Amenophis I and
Ahmose Nefert
Amenophis I
Amun
Siptah
Hathor
Amenophis II
NAG KOM LOLAH
Merenptah
Tuthmosis IV
Amenophis son of Hapu
North Temple
Ramesses II (Ramesseum)
Ay and Horemheb
Siptah and Tawosret
Amenophis III
Ramesses III
Ramesses IV
MEDINET HABU
Tuthmosis II
MALQATA
South Temple
Temple of Amun

INSET A

Alexandria

Tell el-Fara'in (Buto)
Tell el-Rub'a (Mendes)
Sa el-Hagar (Sais)
San el-Hagar (Tanis)
Tell el-Dab'a
Tell Basta (Bubastis)
Tell Hisn (Heliopolis)
Cairo
Mit Rahina (Memphis)

The Fayum
Ihnasya el-Medina (Herakleopolis Magna)

Serabit el-Khadim

Timna

Siwa

Bahariya

el-Hiba

Tihna el-Gebel
Beni Hasan
el-Ashmunein (Hermopolis)
el-Sheikh 'Ibada (Antinoopolis)
el-Amarna

Asyut

Qaw el-Kebir (Antaiopolis)
Akhmim

Wannina (Athribis)

el-Dakhla

Abydos
Dendera
Hiw
Qift (Koptos)
Tukh (Ombos)
Qus (Apollinopolis Parva)
Shenhur
Medamud
Armant
Thebes
Gebelein
Tod
Esna
el-Kab
Wadi Mia
Kom el-Ahmar (Hierakonpolis)
Edfu
Gebel el-Silsila
Kom Ombo

el-Kharga

INSET B

Aswan
FIRST CATARACT

Dendur

Amada
Aniba

Abu Simbel

Nabta Playa
Abahuda
Faras
Aksha (Serra West)
Buhen
Mirgissa
SECOND CATARACT

Semna
Uronarti Island
Kumma (Semna East)

Amara West
THIRD CATARACT
Sedeinga
Gebel Dosha
Soleb
Sesebi

Island of Argo

Kawa
FOURTH CATARACT

Gebel Barkal
Sanam
FIFTH CATARACT

Precinct of Montu
Precinct of Amun
Karnak
Precinct of Mut
Luxor

0   2 km
0   1 mile

0   150 km
0   100 miles

Chronology of the Temple Builders

The precise dates of the Egyptian dynasties and of individual reigns are still the subject of much scholarly debate. The dates employed here are based on the chronology developed by Professor John Baines and Dr Jaromir Málek and put forward in their *Atlas of Ancient Egypt*.

Late Predynastic	**c. 3000 BC**

Early Dynastic Period

1st dynasty	**2920–2770**
Menes (Hor-Aha); Djer; Wadj; Den; Adjib; Semerkhet; Qa'a	
2nd dynasty	**2770–2649**
Hetepsekhemwy; Raneb; Ninetjer; Peribsen; Khasekhem(wy)	
3rd dynasty	**2649–2575**
Nebka	2649–2630
Djoser (Netjerykhet)	2630–2611
Sekhemkhet	2611–2603
Khaba	2603–2599
Huni	2599–2575

Old Kingdom

4th dynasty	**2575–2465**
Sneferu	2575–2551
Khufu (Cheops)	2551–2528
Djedefre	2528–2520
Khafre (Chephren)	2520–2494
Menkaure (Mycerinus)	2490–2472
Shepseskaf	2472–2467
5th dynasty	**2465–2323**
Userkaf	2465–2458
Sahure	2458–2446
Neferirkare	2446–2426
Shepseskare	2426–2419
Raneferef	2419–2416
Niuserre	2416–2388
Djedkare-Isesi	2388–2356
Unas	2356–2323
6th dynasty	**2323–2150**
Teti	2323–2291
Pepi I	2289–2255
Merenre	2255–2246
Pepi II	2246–2152
7th/8th dynasties	**2150–2134**
Numerous ephemeral kings	

First Intermediate Period

9th/10th dynasties	**2134–2040**
11th dynasty (Theban)	**2134–2040**
Intef I	2134–2118
Intef II	2118–2069
Intef III	2069–2061
Mentuhotep	2061–2010

Middle Kingdom

11th dynasty (all Egypt)	**2040–1991**
Mentuhotep I	2061–2010
Mentuhotep II	2010–1998
Mentuhotep III	1998–1991
12th dynasty	**1991–1783**
Amenemhet I	1991–1962
Senwosret I	1971–1926
Amenemhet II	1929–1892
Senwosret II	1897–1878
Senwosret III	1878–1841?
Amenemhet III	1844–1797
Amenemhet IV	1799–1787
Sobekneferu	1787–1783

13th dynasty	**1783–1640**
About 70 kings, including	
Ameny-Qemau	c. 1750
Khendjer	c. 1745
14th dynasty	
Probably contemporary with the 13th or 15th dynasty	

Second Intermediate Period

15th dynasty (Hyksos)	
16th dynasty	
Minor Hyksos rulers, contemporary with 15th	
17th dynasty	**1640–1532**
Numerous Theban kings, ending with	
Kamose	c. 1555–1550

New Kingdom

18th dynasty	**1550–1307**
Ahmose	1550–1525
Amenophis I	1525–1504
Tuthmosis I	1504–1492
Tuthmosis II	1492–1479
Tuthmosis III	1479–1425
Hatshepsut	1473–1458
Amenophis II	1427–1401
Tuthmosis IV	1401–1391
Amenophis III	1391–1353
Amenophis IV/Akhenaten	1353–1335
Smenkhare	1335–1333
Tutankhamun	1333–1323
Ay	1323–1319
Horemheb	1319–1307
19th dynasty	**1307–1196**
Ramesses I	1307–1306
Sethos I	1306–1290
Ramesses II	1290–1224
Merenptah	1224–1214
Sethos II	1214–1204
Siptah	1204–1198
Tawosret	1198–1196
20th dynasty	**1196–1070**
Sethnakhte	1196–1194
Ramesses III	1194–1163
Ramesses IV	1163–1156
Ramesses V	1156–1151
Ramesses VI	1151–1143
Ramesses VII	1143–1136
Ramesses VIII	1136–1131
Ramesses IX	1131–1112
Ramesses X	1112–1100
Ramesses XI	1100–1070

Third Intermediate Period

21st dynasty	**1070–945**
Smendes	1070–1044
Amenemisu	1044–1040
Psusennes I	1040–992
Amenemope	993–984
Osorkon I	984–978
Siamun	978–959
Psusennes II	959–945

22nd dynasty	945–712
Sheshonq I	945–924
Osorkon II	924–909
Takelot I	909–
Sheshonq II	–883
Osorkon III	883–855
Takelot II	860–835
Sheshonq III	835–783
Pami	783–773
Sheshonq V	773–735
Osorkon V	735–712

23rd dynasty	c. 1070–712
Various contemporary lines of rulers in Thebes, Hermopolis, Herakleopolis, Leontopolis, Tanis	

24th dynasty (Sais)	724–712

25th dynasty	770–712
(Nubian and Theban Area)	
Kashta	770–750
Piye	750–712

Late Period	712–332
25th dynasty	712–657
Shabaka	712–698
Shebatko	698–690
Taharqa	690–664
Tantamani	664–657
26th dynasty	664–525
Necho I	672–664
Psammetichus I	664–610
Necho II	610–595
Psammetichus II	595–589
Apries	589–570
Amasis	570–526
Psammetichus III	526–525
27th dynasty	525–404
(Persian)	
Cambyses	525–522
Darius I	521–486
Xerxes I	486–466
Artaxerxes I	465–424
Darius II	424–404
28th dynasty	404–399
Amrytaios	404–399
29th dynasty	399–380
Nepherites I	399–393
Psammuthis	393
Hakoris	393–380
Nepherites II	380
30th dynasty	380–343
Nectanebo I	380–362
Teos	365–360
Nectanebo II	360–343

2nd Persian Period	343–332
Artaxerxes III	343–338
Arses	338–336
Darius III	335–332

Graeco-Roman Period	332 BC–AD 395
Macedonian dynasty	332–304
Alexander the Great	332–323
Philip Arrhidaeus	323–316
Alexander IV	316–304

Ptolemaic dynasty	304–30
Ptolemy I Soter I	304–284
Ptolemy II Philadelphus	285–246
Ptolemy III Euergetes I	246–221
Ptolemy IV Philopator	221–205
Ptolemy V Epiphanes	205–180
Ptolemy VI Philometor	180–164
	163–145
Ptolemy VIII Euergetes II	170–163
	145–116
Ptolemy VII Neos Philopator	145
Cleopatra III and	
Ptolemy IX Soter II	116–107
Cleopatra III and	
Ptolemy X Alexander I	108–88
Ptolemy IX Soter II	88–81
Cleopatra Berenike	81–80
Ptolemy XI Alexander II	80
Ptolemy XII Neos Dionysos	80–58
	55–51
Berenike IV	58–55
Cleopatra VII	51–30
Ptolemy XIII	51–47
Ptolemy XIV	47–44
Ptolemy XV Caesarion	44–30

Roman emperors	
Augustus	30 BC–AD 14
Tiberius	14–37
Caligula	37–41
Claudius	41–54
Nero	54–68
Galba	69
Otho	69
Vespasian	69–79
Titus	79–81
Domitian	81–96
Nerva	96–98
Trajan	98–117
Hadrian	117–138

Temple Highlights

c. 4500–4000 BC
Standing stones at Nabta Playa

c. 3500 BC
Earliest shrine at Hierakonpolis

c. 2900–2700 BC
Mud-brick royal funerary enclosures at Abydos

c. 2600 BC
Stone shrines and temple of Djoser's pyramid complex

c. 2500 BC
Mortuary and valley temples of Khafre

c. 2400 BC
Sun temple of Niuserre

2060–2010 BC
Mortuary temple of Nebhepetre Mentuhotep at Deir el-Bahri

1971–1926 BC
'White Chapel' of Senwosret I at Karnak

1844–1797 BC
'Labyrinth' of temple of Amenemhet III at Hawara

1473–1458 BC
Mortuary temple of Hatshepsut at Deir el-Bahri

1391–1353 BC
Mortuary temple of Amenophis III in Western Thebes

1306–1290 BC
Great Hypostyle Hall at Karnak

1290–1224 BC
Rock-cut temple of Ramesses II at Abu Simbel

1194–1163 BC
Mortuary temple of Ramesses III at Medinet Habu

750–664 BC
Napatan temple building at Gebel Barkal in Upper Nubia

664–525 BC
Great Temple enclosure at Sais

246–51 BC
Temple of Horus at Edfu

380 BC–AD 300
Temple of Isis at Philae

Development, Glory and Decline

*'He made it as a monument for his father Amun ... making for him a
splendid temple ... a monument of eternity and everlastingness.'*

Stela of Amenophis III

From ancient ritual structures built before the dawn of human history to the great mansions of the gods which towered above the Nile, Egypt's temples developed over thousands of years. At the behest of generations of kings, they grew ever larger and more glorious until, for a time, they threatened to eclipse the wealth and power of the very rulers who were their patrons and high priests.

Even after their eventual fall and dissolution, the influence of the temples of Egypt continued to be felt – as heirs to sacred space they were numinous loci replete with traditions and associations which often served later religions well, and which shaped the youthful faiths in many ways as they grew. Christianity and even Islam did not escape their sway, and the saints and festivals of today are sometimes surprisingly rooted in some temples' ancient past.

In secular history, kings and emperors of Persia, Greece and Rome visited Egypt's temples or sought knowledge of them, Greek philosophers studied in them and countless explorers, travellers and scholars from Renaissance times to the present century have been drawn to visit and study these buildings and to try to unlock their secrets. With the savants of Napoleon's great Egyptian Expedition, disciplined recording and study of Egypt's temples began; and almost all the great names of Egyptology – from Champollion down to the present day – studied and worked in one or more of Egypt's temple sites.

The Temple of Isis, Philae.

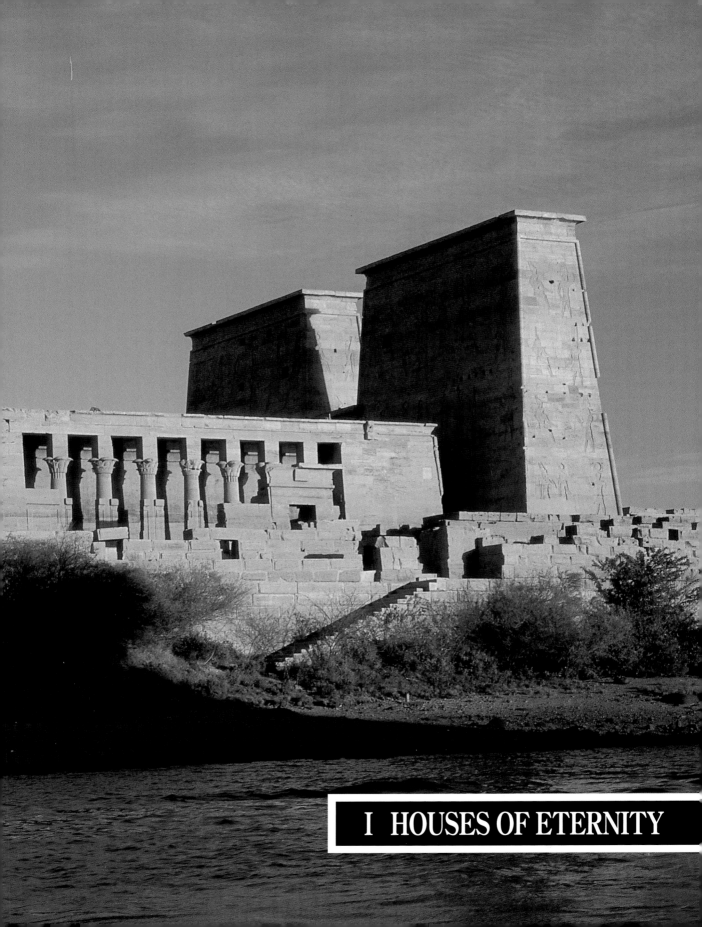

I HOUSES OF ETERNITY

Temple Origins

The beginnings of the temple in Egypt are as shrouded in mystery as any aspect of that civilization's ancient origins. Working backwards from the historical period when temples dotted the Egyptian landscape and were present in virtually every town, we arrive eventually at the proto-historic and pre-historic periods when it becomes far more difficult to label the remains of architectural structures. In this formative period of Egyptian society it is not always possible to tell which structures had sacred functions, or were regarded as sacred space, and which did not. We are also faced with questions regarding the nature of the sacred itself, such as what did sacred mean to this most ancient people and at what point did specific physical areas assume sacred status. We will probably never know the precise answers to these questions, but archaeologists have recovered evidence which at least suggests the path along which the earliest temples may have developed.

Nabta Playa: standing stones

Ancient remains only recently discovered in the Sahara Desert about 100 km (60 miles) west of Abu Simbel in southern Egypt may represent the earliest existing evidence for religious structures in Africa. They may also provide a possible starting point for the evolution of what would become, in time, the temples of Egypt.

The ancient site now known as Nabta Playa is between 6,000 and 6,500 years old and was discovered by an international archaeological team led by Professor Fred Wendorf of the Southern Methodist University of Dallas, Texas. The site stands on the shores of what was once an ancient lake which existed in the now parched landscape. It contains standing stones as much as 2.75 m (9 ft) high, dragged to the site from a mile or more away. Several of the stones are lined up in an east–west direction and appear to have been used as vertical sighting stones aligned with the sun at the summer solstice. During summer and autumn, other stones would have been partially submerged in the lake and may have served as markers for the onset of the rainy season.

While the carefully arranged stones of this site seem to have served as a simple calendric observatory, Nabta Playa is also believed to have had symbolic and ceremonial functions. It may thus have integrated the temporal cycles of the sun with the recurrent cycles of the life-giving waters as a kind of cosmic clock tied to the underlying principles of life and death. As such, the site might even be called a proto-temple, and while the people of this region may or may not have been among the ancestors of the ancient Egyptians of pharaonic times, these same factors of life and death, water and the sun certainly lie at the symbolic core of all later Egyptian temples.

It is impossible to know exactly what the religious functions of the stones of Nabta were, or if they represent a type of religion which predated the worship of tribal fetishes and gods which is evident in later predynastic Egyptian history. But the climate of North Africa was changing during the period in which the Nabtans began carefully to follow the cosmic cycles and, as the region of the Sahara became increasingly dry, various nomadic

(Below and below right) The stone circle at Nabta Playa in southern Egypt is the earliest astronomically aligned site (possibly with cultic significance) ever discovered. It is between 6,000 and 6,500 years old.

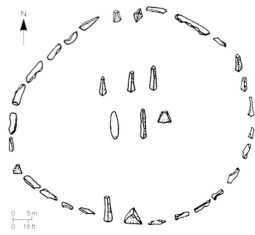

0 5 m
0 15 ft

peoples – perhaps including the Nabtans themselves – began to move down from the Libyan and Arabian highlands and to construct settlements along the banks of the River Nile. At this time, gods which were already ancient were probably given homes which were the precursors in their basic plans of later Egyptian temples.

Hierakonpolis: the shrine in the south

Not until the Early Dynastic period, however, do we gain a fairly clear picture of what these earliest temples may have looked like. The first example of a cult temple of this period known to us is that of Nekhen or Hierakonpolis – 'city of the falcon' as the Greeks called it – in southern Egypt (Kom el-Ahmar; p. 203). Recent excavations in this area indicate that by 3500 BC Hierakonpolis was perhaps the most important settlement in the Nile Valley and may have acted as a kind of national shrine for Upper Egypt in this early period. Archaeological evidence uncovered since 1985 shows that the earliest temple complex at the site consisted of a large, parabolic-shaped court over 32 m (105 ft) long and some 13 m (43 ft) wide. The court was bounded by a mud-covered reed fence and contained a large mound of sand and, near the court's apex, a tall pole which, judging by later representational evidence, bore a flag or totem, possibly an image of the falconiform deity of Hierakonpolis. On the north side of the court were a gateway and a number of small rectangular buildings – evidently workshops associated with the cult – while on the court's south side stood the shrine itself.

From the evidence of the excavated post holes and trenches, combined with early representations of the shrine on surviving seal impressions, we know that it was a rectangular structure fronted by huge wooden pillars 1–1.5 m (3 ft 3 in–4 ft 11 in) in diameter and as much as 12 m (39 ft 4 in) high. The

(Above) Modern excavation of area HK 29 at Hierakonpolis has discovered much information about this very early temple. The post holes that once held the great wooden pillars that fronted the shrine are visible.

(Below) A reconstruction of Egypt's oldest known temple at Hierakonpolis.

Horus as subduer of the Delta peoples: a detail from the Narmer Palette from the so-called 'Main Deposit' at Hierakonpolis. This dates to c. 3000 BC, demonstrating the antiquity of the falcon god in Egyptian symbolism.

curved roof rose to the front of the structure, giving it a form sometimes said to resemble of a crouching animal but also not unlike the shape of the archaic fetish represented as a bandage-wrapped bird of prey and later used as a determinative in writing the words *akhem* 'divine image' and *Nekheny* '(the god) of Nekhen [i.e., Hierakonpolis]'. This latter similarity should be considered seriously because it appears that it was the falcon god assimilated with Horus, the patron god of kingship – as depicted on the Narmer Palette and other artifacts found at this site – which was worshipped here. In any event, the sloping roofline of the shrine may possibly be reflected in the gradually lowering levels – front to back – of the later Egyptian temple.

Buto: Delta cult centre

In historical times the site of Buto, or Pe, in the Delta functioned as the Lower Egyptian counterpart of Hierakonpolis, in that this settlement was used symbolically to represent all northern Egypt, just as Hierakonpolis represented the south. But a scarcity of archaeological evidence of very early occupation in the area had previously led many Egyptologists to doubt that Buto had been a central Early Dynastic site. Recent excavations, however, have revealed that Buto was perhaps as important as Egyptian tradition claimed.

Beginning in 1983, drill core samples obtained and studied by researchers of the German Archae-

ological Institute have revealed evidence of the earliest settlements of the area some 7 m (23 ft) below the current surface and well beneath the water-table which has long hampered archaeological investigation in the Delta region. This new evidence shows that Buto was indeed inhabited for some 500 years within the Early Dynastic period. The archaeological findings also show that the pottery types of this northern culture were first influenced by, and then superseded by, southern Egyptian styles, thus also giving weight to the ancient tradition that the Lower Egyptian area was subjugated by southern, Upper Egypt in an expansion which led to the united 'two kingdoms' of Egyptian history.

While nothing has yet been found of the earliest shrine or temple of Buto, representational evidence depicts a somewhat different shrine type from that of Hierakonpolis, with tall side poles and a distinctive arched roof. The two shrines – representing Upper and Lower Egypt – were depicted in the hieroglyphic signs 🏠 and 🏛, and in many representations made throughout Egyptian history. Large models of the two shrine types were also part of the ritual complex of the Step Pyramid of Djoser in the early 3rd dynasty (p. 126).

Abydos: fortresses of gods and kings

At Abydos a number of walled enclosures located about 1.6 km (1 mile) from the tombs of the 1st-dynasty kings seem to represent funerary

Evolution of the Egyptian Temple

The early temple enclosure (1) and 'palace' (2) at Hierakonpolis, as well as the enclosures of Khasekhemwy at Abydos (3) and Djoser at Saqqara (4), together with others, show a common plan.

Our understanding of the development of the Egyptian temple has been guided by the researches of a number of archaeologists. Recently, the British Egyptologist Barry Kemp developed a model which suggests that the classical Egyptian temple evolved through distinct developmental stages which he termed 'preformal', 'early formal', 'mature formal' and 'late formal', with a distinction being made between royal funerary temples – which Kemp believes were already constructed in early formal style in the Early Dynastic and Old Kingdom periods – and provincial temples, which he believes were smaller and persisted in preformal mode until Middle Kingdom times. Only then, according to Kemp, did the provincial temples reach the levels of complexity of comparable royal monuments, and from that point they kept pace, with both types of monument developing through the

mature formal phase during the New Kingdom and late formal in Graeco-Roman times.

The American Egyptologist David O'Connor's subsequent study of the evidence for Egyptian temple development has reached somewhat different conclusions. O'Connor points to indications that provincial temple complexes at Hierakonpolis, Abydos and perhaps elsewhere were actually in the mainstream of evolving monumental architecture in Early Dynastic times and that royal and provincial temples developed more synchronously. O'Connor has also shown that the plans of many Early Dynastic and early Old Kingdom formal enclosures follow essentially the same pattern. Though the size of the enclosures may vary, comparison of the Hierakonpolis temple enclosure (1) and so-called 'palace' (2) with the enclosures of Djer, Khasekhemwy (3) and Peribsen at Abydos, and Djoser (4) at Saqqara (not shown to scale) reveal common traits of proportion and axial layout. In all these structures, for example, one entrance is located at the southeast corner of the enclosure and another at the northeast corner. There is also some evidence that the position of the mound in the Hierakonpolis temple enclosure may well have been matched in others of these structures, and it is also approximated by the pyramid of Djoser – indicating the utilization of a common plan for early Egyptian temple, cenotaph and pyramid enclosures.

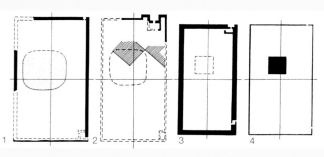

The site of Buto (Tell el-Fara'in) in the northwestern Delta is an ancient one, extending from Predynastic times to the Ptolemaic and Roman periods. Nothing has been found of the earliest shrine, but symbolically it represented all Lower Egypt.

tures with sacral functions relating to the gods. David O'Connor has linked the structures to the 'fortresses of the gods' mentioned in early Egyptian inscriptions. These seem to have been ceremonial gathering places for the gods known as the *shemsu-her*, the 'entourage of Horus', who were associated with the king as the manifestation of the falcon god Horus – probably regarded as the same deity worshipped at Hierakonpolis. According to a reconstruction by O'Connor and others, in Early Dynastic times the cult gods of various regions made symbolic journeys to the fortresses of the gods for the celebration of important ritual events. The gathering of the gods in these enclosures may have been connected with the annual gathering of taxes, but in any event, the fortified aspect of the structures seems to have been symbolic of royal or religious power, or both.

At least ten of these enclosures have been found in varying degrees of completeness at Abydos, dating from the first two dynasties and from the period termed Dynasty 0. Consisting of large rectangular brick walls measuring about 65 × 122 m (213 × 400 ft), with two still standing to heights of over 10 m (32 ft 9 in), the enclosures are inset with niches along three of their four sides and are deco-

rated with more elaborate panels on the east. This style of building has been called 'palace façade' because it is commonly believed that the structures imitated the walls of the living king's palace.

The open courts of these enclosures may have contained a sacred mound similar to that found in the shrine of Hierakonpolis as well as in other later temples and shrines. This mound is of particular significance as it may have been regarded as a symbol of the original mound of creation in Egyptian mythology, from which the primordial falcon god was said to have surveyed the world from his perch or standard.

The 'followers' or 'entourage' of Horus also played an important role in the enactment of the regenerative Sed festival, an ancient series of rituals involving the periodic recoronation of the king on the thrones of Upper and Lower Egypt. This festival was ideally held 30 years after the king's accession and was very probably performed within the court of the fortress of the gods. Because the ceremonies could renew the king's powers in this life and the next, they were assimilated into the funerary complexes of Old Kingdom rulers, as may be seen in the famous Sed-festival courts and shrines of Djoser's Step Pyramid at Saqqara.

(Below) The royal enclosures of the 2nd dynasty at Abydos seem to have mimicked in brick architecture the wood and reed structures of some of the earliest cultic complexes. At the top left in the diagram is the funerary enclosure of king Khasekhemwy, the great ruin of which, known as the Shunet el-Zebib, is seen below.

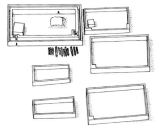

Old and Middle Kingdom Development

Pyramid temples, sun temples and provincial temples of the Old Kingdom

In its developed form the Old Kingdom pyramid complex contained, in addition to possible various minor chapels, two structures which are referred to as temples. A valley temple – which provided an entrance to the complex from the Nile or its canal – was connected by a long, walled causeway to the second structure, a mortuary temple, where sacrifices and other rituals were conducted for the deceased king.

In the earlier pyramids the mortuary temple usually stood on the north or south side of the pyramid in a north–south oriented enclosure. Later pyramid enclosures, from the 4th dynasty, positioned the mortuary temple at the base of the eastern face of the pyramid superstructure and were oriented on an east–west axis – the orientation of most later temples of all types.

By the time of Khafre/Chephren (2520–2494 BC) the plan of the royal mortuary temple was established, with certain fixed areas: an entrance hall was followed by a broad columned court, which gave access to the rear section of the temple containing an enclosed area with five shrines or niches for statues of the king, as well as storage chambers, and an inner sanctuary. Essentially, most of these elements are also found in later temple design. While many of the details are clearly different, a very real transition may be seen in the Old Kingdom mortuary temple from the simple plans of the Predynastic and Early Dynastic shrines to the more complex Middle and New Kingdom forms of the developed Egyptian temple.

An important variant of the pyramid temple is found in the sun temples constructed by a number of kings of the 5th dynasty at various sites in the general area of the Memphite necropolis. Specifically intended to establish an eternal cult of the king 'in the domain of Re' they were additional to the pyramid cult complex.

Six of these structures were built, though only that of Niuserre (2416–2388 BC) at Abu Ghurob survives to any recognizable extent. In fact, four of the sun temples known to have been built have not been located; but it is likely that all these temples shared a fairly common plan and function. Judging by the temple of Niuserre, the sun temples of the 5th dynasty were similar to the standard pyramid complex in having a valley temple with a causeway leading up to the main enclosure with its focal structure – in this case, an obeliskoid monument rather than a pyramid – and ancillary buildings.

The so-called valley temple of the standard Old Kingdom pyramid complex was built with access to water and functioned primarily as an elaborate entrance to the complex and also served as a symbolic portal to the world of the afterlife. A long, enclosed causeway linked the valley temple with the mortuary temple at the base of the pyramid itself.

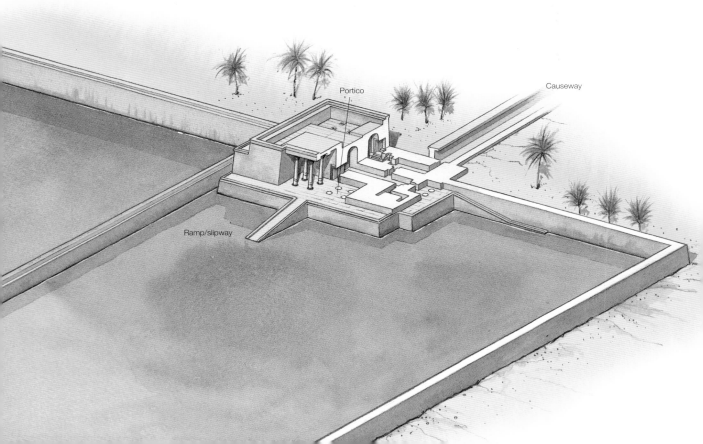

Portico

Causeway

Ramp/slipway

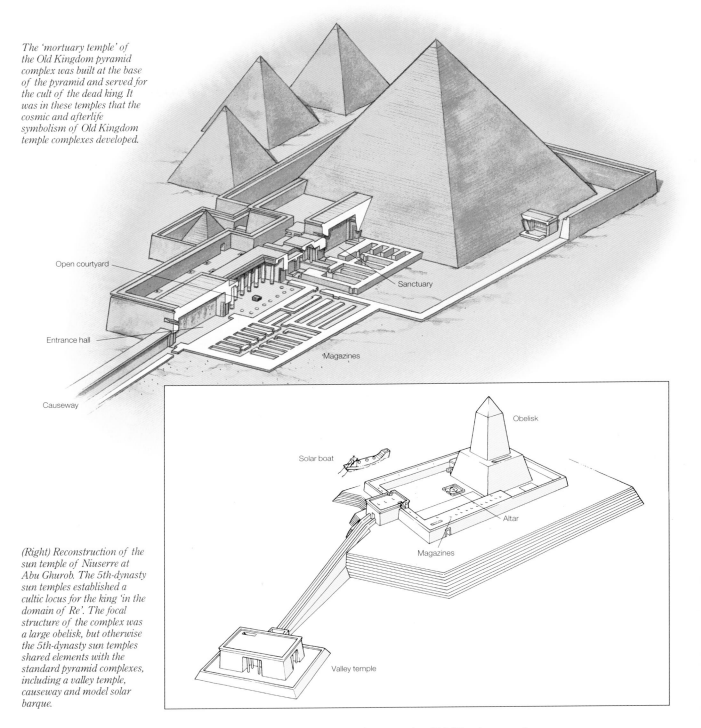

The 'mortuary temple' of the Old Kingdom pyramid complex was built at the base of the pyramid and served for the cult of the dead king. It was in these temples that the cosmic and afterlife symbolism of Old Kingdom temple complexes developed.

Open courtyard

Sanctuary

Entrance hall

Magazines

Causeway

Obelisk

Solar boat

Altar

Magazines

Valley temple

(Right) Reconstruction of the sun temple of Niuserre at Abu Ghurob. The 5th-dynasty sun temples established a cultic locus for the king 'in the domain of Re'. The focal structure of the complex was a large obelisk, but otherwise the 5th-dynasty sun temples shared elements with the standard pyramid complexes, including a valley temple, causeway and model solar barque.

Like the pyramid complexes of the period, the sun temple of Niuserre was oriented on an east–west axis, and again like the standard pyramid complex it contained a brick model of the sun barque positioned just to the side of the complex. Given that the underlying symbolism of the pyramid is also largely solar-related, the connection between pyramid and sun temple complexes seems clear.

The contrast between the Old Kingdom royal mortuary temples and sun temples on the one hand, and provincial cult temples of the same period on the other could hardly be greater. Often distant from the major settlement centres and ultimately on the fringes of royal concern, provincial cult temples developed without the constraints of the royal architectural tradition. And although these structures may have displayed ancient and distinctive

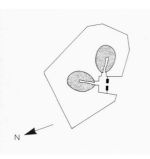

The dual mounds of the temple at Medamud are an example of the unusual plans found in Old Kingdom provincial temples.

characteristics, ultimately they represent dead ends in the long-term development of the temple. The irregularly shaped Archaic and Old Kingdom temple at Medamud, a little to the north of Thebes, provides an excellent example. Although we do not know what deity was worshipped at the site in Old Kingdom times (later it was the falcon-headed god Montu), the unusual twin mounds of this temple are doubtless rooted in ancient mythic traditions similar to those which inspired the mounds of Hierakonpolis and other early Egyptian sites.

Separate from the provincial temples, yet in some ways falling alongside them, the cult temple built for the *ka* or 'life force' of the 6th-dynasty king Pepi I (2289–2255 BC) at Bubastis (Tell Basta) in the eastern Delta and the special chambers built in the temple area at Hierakonpolis – in one of which was found the famous life-sized copper statue of this king along with a statue of his son (or possibly also of Pepi) – are hard to classify. Not physically con-

nected with the pyramids of this king, the *ka* temple at Bubastis and the chapel – if that is what it was – at Hierakonpolis may represent smaller royally commissioned provincial religious structures of which we still have little knowledge.

Middle Kingdom developments

Although the Middle Kingdom witnessed the widespread building of religious structures – including many more royally commissioned provincial temples than in early times – a great many of these structures were later demolished or substantially rebuilt when they were incorporated into more elaborate structures erected on the same sites (p. 51). The extant evidence for Middle Kingdom temples is thus paradoxically scarcer than for some other periods in which fewer temples were constructed.

One of the earliest examples of Middle Kingdom temple architecture and one of the few not substantially destroyed in later rebuilding is the combined

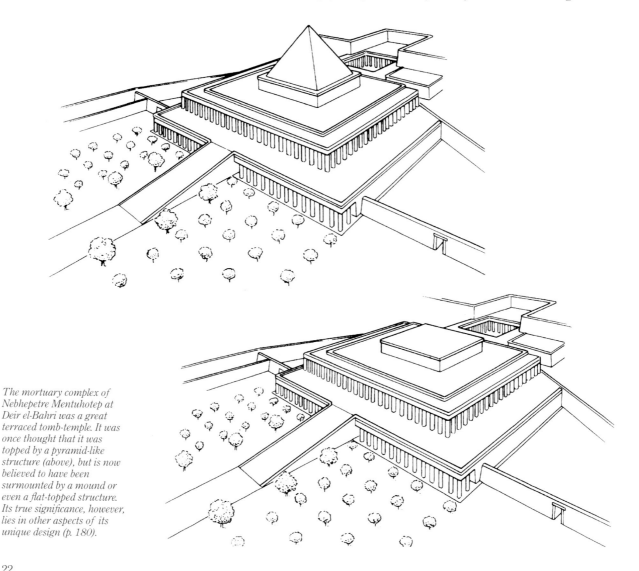

The mortuary complex of Nebhepetre Mentuhotep at Deir el-Bahri was a great terraced tomb-temple. It was once thought that it was topped by a pyramid-like structure (above), but is now believed to have been surmounted by a mound or even a flat-topped structure. Its true significance, however, lies in other aspects of its unique design (p. 180).

mortuary temple and tomb of Nebhepetre Mentuhotep (2061–2010 BC) at Deir el-Bahri in Thebes. This innovative, terraced building with its colonnades and central monumental superstructure (the exact form of which is not known) was set at the back of the natural 'bay' in the Theban mountains and was the inspiration for several later mortuary temples of the same type – including the famous and much better preserved temple of Hatshepsut in the same location.

Senwosret (Sesostris) I (1971–1926 BC), the second king of the 12th dynasty, was the first monarch of the Middle Kingdom to institute an extensive building programme, constructing a number of temples from the Delta to at least as far as Elephantine in the south. At Thebes, he constructed a monolithic shrine and massive limestone shrine walls, as well as the beautifully decorated 'White Chapel' which provides a fine example of the expanded use of hieroglyphic inscription and representational art in Middle Kingdom temples.

The solitary obelisk bearing Senwosret's name is now all that remains of what may have been an extensive temple complex at Heliopolis, but the foundations of a number of smaller temples of this king and his successors remain to show a temple style which incorporated a pillared court before a sanctuary with separate – frequently tripartite – shrines at the temple's rear. Sometimes, as in the small temple of Amenemhet I and Senwosret III at Ezbet Rushdi, near Qantir in the eastern Delta, the pillared hall is fronted by an open courtyard so that we see an incipient grouping of the three elements of court, pillared hall and sanctuary which form the basis of later New Kingdom temple design.

While there were many archaizing tendencies in the architecture of this period, developments in certain aspects of temple design and structure can be seen throughout the Middle Kingdom. For instance, building in stone became increasingly common. While some temples contained only a few elements (such as doorways and pillars) of stone, the temple of Amenemhet III and Amenemhet IV at Medinet Madi in the Fayum, although only a little more than 8 by 11 m (26 × 36 ft) in size, consisted of a sanctuary with multiple chambers and a small pillared court, all of which were constructed of stone.

Architectural symmetry also increased in the Middle Kingdom, and the temple of Montu built by Senwosret I at Tod provides one of the clearest examples of the developed Middle Kingdom temple, with its precisely symmetrical design and the incorporation of various cult chambers adjacent to the main sanctuary. And as well as being beautifully decorated, Senwosret's 'White Chapel' on the processional route from the Great Temple of Amun at Karnak provides an example of an equally symmetrical and exquisitely fashioned barque chapel or way-station of this same period.

The richly decorated 'White Chapel' of Senwosret I at Karnak shows the expanded use of inscriptions and representational art which developed in Middle Kingdom temples. The detail shows Senwosret before Amun.

Plan of Senwosret I's symmetrically designed temple of Montu at Tod.

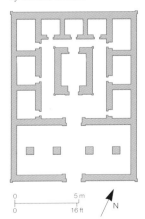

New Kingdom Temples

The expansion of Egypt's political and economic power during its New Kingdom age of empire led to both the building of numerous new temples and the expansion of many which already existed. Individual kings strove to outdo their predecessors, not only in the construction of their own mortuary temples but also in the further development of major cult centres and in the building of temples dedicated to established deities as well as those that had not previously enjoyed formal cults.

Temple construction in the New Kingdom reached its high points under Amenophis III in the 18th dynasty and Ramesses II in the 19th, and did not really decline until several hundred years later. In terms of development also the Egyptian temple may be said to have reached its apogee in this period. Costly and magnificent religious structures were produced on a regular basis, and many if not most temples were constructed almost entirely of stone. The so-called 'standard' temple plan was established, in which an entrance pylon gave access to an open court followed by a columned hall and finally the sanctuary itself. Although it might be varied, and was certainly elaborated in many cases, this standard form persisted all the way through the Graeco-Roman Period, and is the plan of most of the Egyptian temples that have survived relatively intact till modern times.

The standard plan was used, in fact, not only for the divine cult temples but also for the mortuary temples of the rulers of the New Kingdom. The kings of this period abandoned the pyramid complex of earlier ages and – doubtless for the purposes of security – constructed their tombs in the

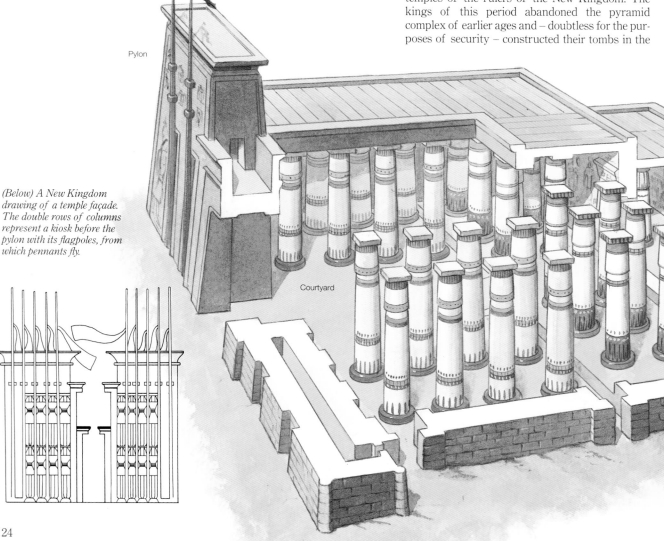

(Below) A New Kingdom drawing of a temple façade. The double rows of columns represent a kiosk before the pylon with its flagpoles, from which pennants fly.

Pylon

Courtyard

Valley of the Kings, in the hidden reaches of the Theban mountains well away from their mortuary temples. This move eliminated the pyramid itself – the focal point of the earlier funerary complexes – and as a result the royal mortuary temples of the New Kingdom were free to follow the standard plan already utilized for the divine temples.

A number of scholars now feel that the traditional division of temples into the categories of 'mortuary' and 'divine' is a false one, arguing that the functions and symbolic characteristics of all Egyptian temples were both too varied and too intertwined to support this distinction. Certainly, it would be a mistake to ignore the common elements which underlie the wide variety of temple structures which existed in Egypt; and *hut* or 'mansion' was the common term used by the Egyptians for all types of temple. Also, because it was believed that the Egyptian king became a god in the afterlife, any distinctions between divine and mortuary spheres necessarily blur in both theory and practice. 'Divine' temples often had mortuary significance and 'mortuary' temples often had divine associations. Nevertheless, the distinction is perhaps too established to shake off easily and in some ways it may still be a useful one.

The Egyptians themselves followed it to the extent that divine cult temples were usually referred

temples was simply one of tenure. Although in theory they were established as temples of millions of years, many of the mortuary temples of the New Kingdom monarchs did not, in fact, fare well in that regard: a number were deserted and used as quarries for stone even before the New Kingdom was over. The cults of the gods tended to enjoy more continuity, but they too were not immune to turmoil and, sometimes, disaster.

During the Amarna Period the heretic king Akhenaten (1353–1333 BC) not only severely curbed the power of the burgeoning cult of Amun but also promulgated a system of worship in which the Aten solar disc was intended to supersede all other deities. Not even the gods were safe from the agents of this king, and while the temple closures and suppressions of other deities may have been short lived, the scars of desecration are still visible in most of the major temples which have survived from the New Kingdom. In the years after Akhenaten's death thousands of names and images of Amun and other deities had to be recut into the temple walls from which they had been expunged, and thousands more remain in only hacked and chiselled outline.

If the Amarna Period can only be seen as a decisive downturn for the fortunes of most of Egypt's cults, the following Ramessid era was characterized by recovery and unprecedented growth. Ramesses II (1290–1224 BC) is credited with building more

The tripartite layout of the classic Egyptian temple – open courtyard, columnar hall and inner sanctuary – had begun to develop in the Old and Middle Kingdoms but became standard in the New Kingdom and later periods. It is the form found in most temples surviving today.

Inner sanctuary

Hypostyle hall

to as 'mansions of the gods' and mortuary temples as 'mansions of millions of years' – an allusion perhaps to the desired continued cult of the deceased king. In practical reality, one of the greatest differences between the divine and mortuary

temples than any other monarch in Egyptian history. Although none of his successors completed anything like the number of his monuments, temples continued to be built throughout the later New Kingdom. Perhaps more importantly for the cults themselves, the power and relative autonomy of the major temples – especially that of Amun at Karnak – recovered and grew steadily.

A Glorious Decline

The Third Intermediate and Late Periods

The shift of power from Thebes to the Delta region that took place during the 19th and 20th dynasties left the Theban high priests of Amun essentially in control of Upper Egypt. There was certainly inter-action between the two areas: the Theban priests acknowledged the northern kings and married into their families; the royal 'Libyan' line in the north was evidently related to Libyan elements at Thebes; and a number of northern kings left evidence of their activities in the Theban area. Nevertheless, for much of the Third Intermediate Period, Upper and Lower Egypt existed as functionally independent regions.

The most important temple remains of the period 1070–712 BC are thus those of the Delta cities of Tanis, Mendes, Sais and Bubastis. This trend continued into the succeeding Late Period (712–332 BC); the temple enclosure of Sais in the 26th dynasty, for example, was well over 450,000 sq. m (4,845,000 sq. ft) in area and its buildings, according to Herodotus,

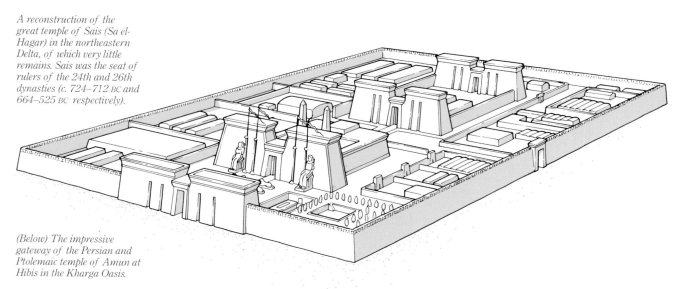

A reconstruction of the great temple of Sais (Sa el-Hagar) in the northeastern Delta, of which very little remains. Sais was the seat of rulers of the 24th and 26th dynasties (c. 724–712 BC and 664–525 BC respectively).

(Below) The impressive gateway of the Persian and Ptolemaic temple of Amun at Hibis in the Kharga Oasis.

were as splendid as any in Egypt. A number of the kings of this period constructed their tombs within the precincts of these temples and doubtless embellished them considerably.

During much of the Late Period, however, Egypt was ruled successively by a number of outside powers. Beginning with the 25th dynasty, Nubian or 'Kushite' kings controlled most of the country – and constructed many fine monuments. This period of rule by Egypt's southern neighbour was cut short by Assyrian invasion, followed eventually by the forces of Achaemenid Persia, which threatened or controlled Egypt to some extent for the best part of 200 years. Some of the earlier Achaemenid emperors adopted the pharaonic style of rule and built or elaborated upon a number of Egyptian temples. Darius I, for example, built the impressive temple of Hibis in the Kharga Oasis and repaired others, from Busiris in the Delta to el-Kab in southern Upper Egypt. Persian rule was never popular, however, and revolts and other problems also led to the Persian destruction of a number of Egyptian temples during this period.

Unfortunately, comparatively little evidence survives of the temples built during the Third Intermediate and Late Periods, and in many cases less is known of them than the structures built both before and after this epoch. It seems clear, however, that it was towards the end of the Late Period, in the 30th dynasty, that the architectural style usually considered typical of the Graeco-Roman era in fact developed.

After Alexander: the Ptolemaic Period

When Alexander the Great entered Egypt in 332 BC he was hailed as a saviour from the hated Persians. On his orders, repairs were carried out to temples

damaged in the Persian devastation of 343, and his legacy to Egypt was to prove both extensive and lasting. After Alexander's death and the dissolution of his empire, rule of Egypt fell to Ptolemy I, one of Alexander's generals; and with Ptolemy began the dynasty of naturalized foreigners which would rule for almost 300 years.

The pious construction of temples to Egyptian deities was an obvious method for these foreign kings to legitimize their rule, and one which they exercised to the full. Following the architectural styles of the temples only recently established in the preceding period, the Ptolemaic rulers constructed temples throughout Egypt. Many of these are today among the best preserved of all Egypt's religious structures.

The relative smoothness of the transition from the Late Period temples to those of the Graeco-Roman era may be clearly seen in the ruined temple of Behbeit el-Hagar in the Delta (p. 104). Dedicated to Isis, and functioning as a northern centre for her worship, the temple was begun in the latter part of the 30th dynasty but completed by Ptolemy II and Ptolemy III in a manner which shows a clear continuity of decoration and design. As the kings who preceded them had done, the Ptolemies built on a large scale, using great quantities of granite and other hard stones which were often decorated with reliefs of particularly fine quality. The representations and inscriptions utilized in the decorative programmes of these Ptolemaic temples became increasingly obscure, however, as the details of the ancient religion became the special domain of a diminishing priestly elite. Eventually, obscurity became a goal in itself, and the inwardly focused and exclusive nature of the later Ptolemaic and Roman period temples would have much to do with the ultimate demise of Egyptian religion.

Pharaohs from afar: the Roman Period

The latter part of the Ptolemaic dynasty was plagued by internal power struggles, and as the contesting factions turned to Rome for assistance Egypt fell increasingly under the influence of the emerging Mediterranean power. Finally, the victory of Octavian (later Augustus) over his rival Mark Antony and Cleopatra VII spelled the end of Egyptian independence, and Egypt was declared a Roman province under imperial control.

Like the Ptolemaic kings, the Romans who followed them desired to adopt Egyptian models both for the purposes of their own legitimation and acceptance with the Egyptian priesthoods and people, and perhaps more importantly to preserve the social and economic stability within the area which provided much of Rome's grain supply. Roman emperors were thus depicted in pharaonic guise and continued to restore and in some cases elaborate Egypt's temples. One of the

(Far left) Carved block from the sanctuary of Isis at Behbeit el-Hagar, which flourished in the north-central Delta in the 30th dynasty and Ptolemaic period.

(Below) Statue of Augustus Caesar depicted as a pharaoh wearing the nemes headdress, found at Karnak.

The Romans displayed great interest in Egyptian civilization, and several emperors commanded the removal of sculptures and monuments from Egypt's temples (though these were perhaps already abandoned structures, such as at Heliopolis) which were to be set up in Rome. An example is the obelisk which today stands in the Piazza San Giovanni in Laterano and which was taken to Rome in the 4th century AD by Constantius II.

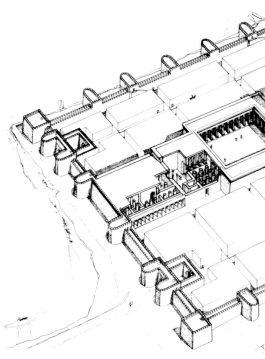

(Above) In the late 3rd century AD the Temple of Luxor at Thebes was used as a garrison and administrative centre by the Romans and was adapted to serve the cult of emperor worship.

Overall, the continued decline in the importance of Egypt's temples is evident, however, and by the early 4th century AD we find no less a structure than Luxor Temple incorporated into a permanent Roman military camp and adapted to serve the cult of emperor worship. Arguably, as Stephen Quirke has suggested, this could be seen as a Roman interpretation of Amenophis III's concept of Luxor Temple as a statement of the divine nature of kingship – now in the form of the emperor. But in any event, the fate of Egypt's temples was finally sealed by the acceptance of Christianity as the official religion of the Roman empire.

Trajan's Kiosk on the island of Philae is a good example of the kind of building accomplished by the Romans in Egyptian temples, in addition to the embellishment of existing structures.

most distinctive structures in Egypt, Trajan's Kiosk, on the island of Philae, was constructed as a monumental entrance to the temple of Isis at that site, though the structure was never completed. Entirely new temples were also built, in many cases following the old styles. The temple of Esna, for example, reflects the design of the earlier Ptolemaic temple at Dendera and is decorated with representations of several emperors in motifs which were by this time thousands of years old.

The coming of Christianity and Islam

In AD 383 pagan temples throughout the empire were closed by order of the emperor Theodosius. A number of further decrees and edicts, culminating in those of Theodosius in AD 391 and Valentinian III in AD 435, sanctioned the persecution of pagans and

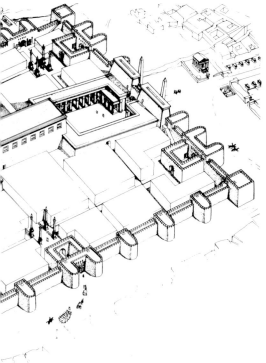

destruction of their religious structures, and soon Egypt's temples were shunned and empty. The ancient shrines were quarried for stone, or in some cases overgrown by surrounding areas of housing or even purged of much of their decoration and utilized as chapels and basilicas of the new faith (p. 194). For the most part, however, the early Christians rejected the pagan buildings and many were destroyed by austere figures such as Shenute, a 5th-century monk whose fortress-like monastery in Middle Egypt was built from the stone of nearby temples.

Eventually Christianity itself was challenged by Islam. In AD 639 an Arab army crossed Sinai and entered Egypt, wresting the country from Byzantine control. For a time the caliphs, Muhammad's successors as rulers of Islam, were content to run Egypt through a Coptic administration, but eventually the majority of Egyptians converted to the new religion. Sometimes existing temple structures were used as the setting for festivals in the new era or were adapted, as at Luxor Temple, where a mosque was built atop the earlier Christian and pagan structures (p. 167). But, by and large, the processes of dissolution continued.

The few temples which were abandoned and which were distant from major population centres fared best and remain today as the most perfectly preserved examples of Egypt's ancient religious structures. Eventually, Egypt's temples and other monuments of her pharaonic past became as mysterious to the Egyptians themselves as they were to the outside world. Whether covered by drifting sands or standing in full view, Egypt's temples were lost and would have to wait to be rediscovered.

In Roman times the entrance to the inner temple area at Luxor was sealed and a niche and flanking columns built as a focus for the Roman religious use of the temple.

Early Travellers and Modern Rediscovery

The beginning of rediscovery: explorers and travellers

'I did not travel for any useful purpose, but only to see so many superb edifices, churches, statues, colossi, obelisks and columns.'
Anonymous Venetian traveller to Egypt, c. 1589

Even as Egypt's temples fell into disuse their legend was already in the making. Many Greeks and Romans travelled to the Nile Valley where not only the pyramids and Sphinx but also some of the great temples were considered 'wonders'. Especially notable was the Greek historian Herodotus who visited Egypt around the middle of the 5th century BC and who described much of what he saw in the second book of his famous *History*. Although many of Herodotus' claims are questioned by modern scholars, much of what he recorded was clearly based on fact, and his writings preserve a great many details which would otherwise have been lost. The later Greek historian Strabo (*c.* 63 BC) also described monuments which, in many cases, are now greatly ruined or no longer exist, as did the Roman writer Diodorus Siculus, an older contemporary of Strabo who visited Egypt between 60 and 56 BC. The Greek writer Plutarch (AD 46–120), who may have had only limited first-hand knowledge of Egypt and who evidently drew on sources of varying levels of value, has nevertheless left us a wealth of detail on cult practices and the various temple festivals celebrated in Egypt.

These and other early writers who compiled accounts of their Egyptian travels – or those of others – recorded the details of what they were told by the members of the temple priesthoods they interviewed, leaving us much useful information on the temples, their festivals and personnel. But within a few hundred years of the advent of Christianity, the knowledge of the ancient hieroglyphic script was com-

Herodotus, the Greek scholar and renowned 'father of history', travelled in Egypt in the mid-5th century BC. He recorded in detail everything he saw and was told, and his work contains much of value concerning Egyptian temples.

pletely lost. The ancient spoken language of Egypt was replaced by Coptic and then Arabic, and as the old religion died, so too did knowledge of the old culture. During the ensuing Middle Ages Egypt was thus a source of little more than stories and legends which grew ever more fabulous as they spread, though many Egyptian sites were visited by medieval European crusaders and pilgrims for their supposed Christian associations. Interpretations of Egyptian monuments and artifacts by European scholars of the Renaissance were often no less fanciful, yet the period did see the beginnings of a growing interest in Egypt and its antiquities which would lead to increased travel and exploration.

Although dangerous and sometimes restricted by law, some of these early travels by Europeans were extensive indeed. Although his identity is not known, one Italian tourist (quoted above) who travelled to Egypt in 1589 shows in his anonymous writings that he visited most of the major sites – and many minor ones – from Cairo as far south as el-Derr in Nubia. It was not until the 19th century and the rule of Muhammad Ali, however, that increasing numbers of Europeans began to visit Egypt purely for pleasure, and from this period we have several records giving impressions and descriptions of specific temple sites.

One of the most significant advances in rediscovery was made by the Jesuit Claude Sicard

18th-Century Visitors

(1677–1726) who was commissioned by the French regent to investigate the monuments of Egypt. Between 1707 and 1726 Sicard visited many ancient sites including 24 temples, among them the great temples of Thebes, which he was the first in modern times correctly to identify on the basis of classical descriptions. Most of Sicard's records were subsequently lost, though his travels rank high among those of a number of increasingly educated and careful observers. The writings of the Dane Frederik Norden (1708–1742) and the Englishman Richard Pococke (whose *Observations on Egypt* records his extensive travels in Egypt between 1737 and 1740) were highly influential at the time. Likewise, the account of the French traveller the Comte de Volney, published in 1787, is said to have inspired Napoleon Bonaparte's inclusion of trained scholars in his military campaign to Egypt in 1798.

Rediscovery in earnest: scholars and scientists

To say that Napoleon's Expedition was a turning point in the rediscovery of ancient Egypt is an understatement. Napoleon's scholars systematically studied and recorded monuments and artifacts in a manner which was truly unprecedented. For the first time, whole temples were measured, planned and painstakingly depicted in carefully executed drawings. In 1802, the artist and diplomat Vivant Denon who accompanied the expedition

published a succinct single volume account with records and sketches of temples and other monuments as far south as the area of the first cataract, and this was followed, between 1809 and 1830, by the 36 volumes of the official *Description de l'Égypte*. This work awakened nothing short of a mania for all things Egyptian, and adventurers, antiquarians, artists and scholars began to travel to Egypt in increasing numbers. So, eventually, did collectors and the agents of European museums

DESCRIPTION
DE L'ÉGYPTE
OU
RECUEIL
DES OBSERVATIONS ET DES RECHERCHES
QUI ONT ÉTÉ FAITES EN ÉGYPTE
PENDANT L'EXPÉDITION DE L'ARMÉE FRANÇAISE
SECONDE ÉDITION
DÉDIÉE AU ROI
PUBLIÉE PAR C. L. F. PANCKOUCKE

ATLAS GÉOGRAPHIQUE

PARIS
IMPRIMERIE DE C. L. F. PANCKOUCKE

(Above) Luxor Temple and title-page from the Description de l'Égypte, *which was the first modern scholarly attempt at the systematic recording of Egypt's monuments.*

Temple sites visited and described by some of the 18th-century European travellers to Egypt:

Site	Traveller	Approx. date
Abydos	sieur Granger	1731
Amada	Frederik Norden	1738
Antinoopolis	Claude Sicard	1715
Armant	Peter Lucas	1715
	Richard Pococke	1737
Behbeit el-Hagar	Claude Sicard	1710
Dabod	Frederik Norden	1738
Dendera	Paul Lucas	1716
Dendur	Frederik Norden	1738
	Richard Pococke	1737
el-Dakka	Frederik Norden	1738
el-Kab	Claude Sicard	1715
el-Sebua	Frederik Norden	1738
Heliopolis	Peter Lucas	1716
Kom Ombo	Richard Pococke	1737
	Frederik Norden	1737
Memphis	S. Villamont	1790
Meroe	James Bruce	1772
Philae	Claude Sicard	1715
Qertassi	Frederik Norden	1738
Speos Artemidos	Claude Sicard	1715
Tafa	Frederik Norden	1738
Thebes	Claude Sicard	1715

Frederik Norden

James Bruce

Many of the early travellers to Egypt wrote accounts of their journey, illustrated by vivid, if to modern eyes rather unscientific drawings, such as Pococke's engraving of one of the Colossi of Memnon.

Jean-François Champollion (1790–1832) is best known for his crucial decipherment of the hieroglyphic script but he did also travel to Egypt where he recorded many temples.

The Temple of Edfu by David Roberts, 1838. Roberts and other European artists stirred great interest in Egypt's past.

Giovanni Belzoni (1778–1823) in 1817 as part of this intense period of exploration.

The next great advance, however, was the decipherment of the hieroglyphic script in 1822–24 by Jean-François Champollion (1790–1832) and others, which led to the first real translations of temple texts and inscriptions. The decipherment itself was based in part, of course, on the Rosetta Stone discovered in 1799, with its trilingual (hieroglyphic, demotic and Greek) decree of Ptolemy V dating to 196 BC, and also on an inscription on an obelisk of Ptolemy IX and his wife Cleopatra IV from Philae. These and other temple monuments supplied the scholars who worked on the long-locked language with the necessary clues for the decipherment of hieroglyphs.

Following this massive breakthrough a new age of Egyptological scholarship became possible. Scholars such as the English pioneer John Gardner Wilkinson (1797–1875) – whose works, including his *Manners and Customs of the Ancient Egyptians* published in 1837, are still useful today – were able to begin to reconstruct ancient Egyptian civilization and to understand the significance of its treasures.

and libraries who began to purchase large quantities of antiquities. The Great Temple at Abu Simbel was rediscovered by J.L. Burckhardt in 1813 and opened by the famous procurer of antiquities

Foremost among a number of other European scholars of this period was the Prussian Carl Richard Lepsius (1810–1884), whose 12-volume *Denkmäler aus Aegypten and Aethiopien* stands as the earliest reliable publication of a large number of Egyptian temples and other monuments.

The complete recording of Egyptian monuments was begun in the later 19th century by Johannes Dumichen (1833–1894) and Maxence de Rochemonteix (1849–1891). Although neither man was able to come close to fulfilling their ambitious goal, the idea was continued by Jacques de Morgan (1857–1924), who began a *Catalogue des monuments* and produced a complete publication of the temple of Kom Ombo, and by the Egypt Exploration Fund (later Society) of England, which initiated its 'Archaeological Survey of Egypt', resulting in much valuable recording. The Franco-Egyptian Centre at Karnak also provides an example of excellent work done in a specific location.

The greatest advance in the recording of Egyptian temples would come about, however, as a result of the vision and planning of the American archaeologist James Henry Breasted (1865–1935). Founder of the University of Chicago's Oriental Institute, Breasted organized the Institute's Epigraphic Survey of Egyptian monuments which, beginning in 1924, has produced some of the finest and most complete recordings of Egyptian monuments ever made. He also developed his own methodology for the precise recording of texts and inscriptions on monuments (p. 241) which, in its essential form, is still in use today. Although interested in all aspects of Egyptology, Breasted was especially fascinated with Egypt's temples, and it was no coincidence that the first monument to receive the detailed attention of the Epigraphic Survey was the great mortuary temple of Ramesses III at Medinet Habu. Since then the Survey has turned its attention to a number of other temples, continuing to produce

complete documentation in the same painstaking tradition.

The Oriental Institute is only one academic institution which has worked in the temples of Egypt. Throughout the 20th century scholars from other universities, museums and archaeological institutes in many countries, as well as those of Egypt itself, have laboured in the painstaking excavation, recording and reconstruction of the ancient temples. Today, modern methods of scientific archaeology are being applied and we are in a position to understand these structures to a degree impossible in previous decades. But much remains to be learned, and much is only now coming to light. The story is a detailed and fascinating one which unfolds with the description of the various elements of the Egyptian temple, the actual functioning of the temple institutions, and the history of the individual temples themselves.

(Above left) Sir John Gardner Wilkinson (1797–1875), depicted here in native dress, conducted pioneering work in the study and recording of ancient Egypt and its monuments between 1821 and 1856.

(Above) The forecourt of the temple of Amun at Karnak in one of the British photographer Francis Frith's many views of Egyptian temple sites. He made three expeditions to the country between 1856 and 1860.

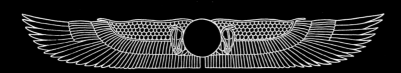

Construction, Growth and Change

'May you build a house, may you embellish a sanctuary, and may you consecrate my godly place.'

Words spoken by Amun to Hatshepsut

The Egyptian temple was rooted deep within the myths and memories of times ancient even to the Egyptians themselves. Each 'house of god' was thus planned, founded and constructed with the utmost care, according to traditions which had developed through extended historical time. Not only was the site for every temple carefully chosen, with the exact alignment of the new building often being precisely calculated, but it was also carefully prepared with complex and arcane rituals. Once the necessary rituals of foundation were enacted, actual construction could commence – with choice stone and other materials often being brought from great distances for the new house of the god.

Constructed with great skill, despite the simple tools available to the ancient craftsmen, the temples of Egypt were finely built and decorated to the degree that even minor shrines are sometimes architectural jewels and many of the larger temples ranked as wonders of the ancient world. As institutions, they stretched beyond the boundaries of their own walls in many ways and functioned as integral and vital parts of their communities' lives and economies.

Even long after they were initially built, Egypt's temples often continued to grow – with succeeding kings striving to outdo their predecessors in expanding, embellishing and enriching the gods' homes. But they were also robbed, torn down for their building materials or simply reinscribed by usurping monarchs who wished to claim them as their own exploits. Without an understanding of these changes – subtle and brutal alike – it is all but impossible to grasp the complex and tangled story of formation and transformation in many temple buildings.

The ornate screen wall of the Roman birth house at Dendera.

II BUILDINGS FIT FOR GODS

Selecting the Sacred Space

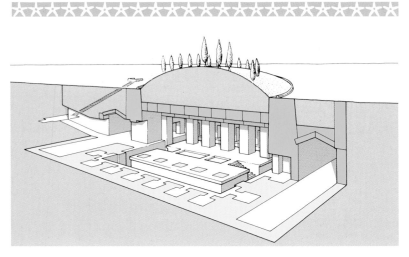

The 'Osireion' of Sethos I at Abydos was carefully located near a source of underground water in order to make it a model of the first mound rising from the primeval waters.

Egyptian temples were usually located and oriented according to some significant point – whether an important natural feature, a building or place, a cardinal direction or an astronomical point. In the broader sense, the choice of location might be governed by ancient myths and traditions – such as the supposed site of a god's 'birthplace' or 'grave', or some natural feature believed to have numinous power or associations. But in the narrower sense temple location was usually controlled by practical factors such as proximity to population centres, travel routes or necessary resources. Sometimes, exact temple location could be affected by the special needs of a particular cult. The location of the Osireion in the temple of Sethos I at Abydos, for example, is due to the proximity of a natural spring. This seems to have been used to provide a pool of water around the subterranean 'grave' in order to make it a model of the mythical mound of creation which the Egyptians believed rose from the primeval waters.

The orientation of temples

Orientation within a site or general location could be controlled by several factors. Most commonly, temples built along the Nile were oriented on an east–west axis (p. 172) according to local cardinal directions as determined by the river. Because the Nile flows from south to north it was fitting, according to the Egyptian sense of geographic space, to align temples at 90 degrees to the river – though variations in the river's course often caused temples aligned in this manner to be oriented only according to 'local' rather than true cardinal directions. While some of these alignments seem to have been made quite precisely, at other times temples were apparently oriented much more loosely. Many of the New

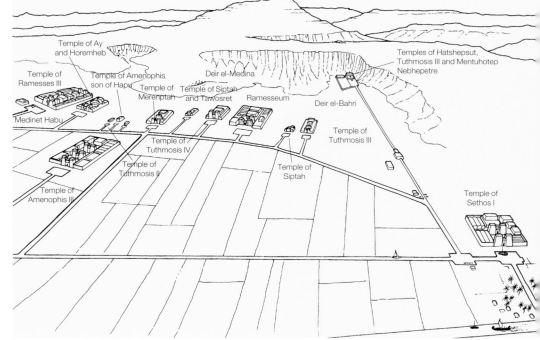

The mortuary temples of New Kingdom rulers at Thebes were situated on the Nile's left bank beneath the Theban massif – symbolic site of the setting sun. They were also oriented east to west on the axis of the solar journey, though there are some slight differences in orientation.

Kingdom mortuary temples of the Theban west bank which were built within a few generations of each other were given slightly different orientations, although all share a basic east–west alignment. Once built, temples were also given their own internal east–west orientation by means of solar images positioned along the temple's axis and by cardinally opposed decorative motifs – such as the various heraldic symbols of Lower and Upper Egypt, or scenes from those regions, which were placed on the respective 'north' and 'south' walls, columns, and other architectural features.

Less frequently, as at Luxor and Edfu, a temple's main axis might run north–south, though this kind of atypical orientation is usually dictated by the location of earlier structures (as was the case with these two temples), or by geographic and topographical factors. The orientation of Amun's temple in Luxor was towards the main Karnak temple, and the Ptolemaic temple at Edfu was oriented at right angles to the earlier east–west oriented New Kingdom temple on the same location.

On occasion, orientation towards the sun or important stars was definitely the priority, and this principle may be more important than is often recognized. In the Great Temple of Ramesses II at Abu Simbel (p. 226), for example, and in shrines of the solar-disc worshipper Akhenaten, alignment was clearly made to permit maximum or precisely controlled influx of sunlight. It is possible that some temples may have been oriented according to the summer solstice sun, but research in this area is at present only beginning.

There is also clear evidence of stellar alignment in temples such as that at Elephantine, the island opposite modern-day Aswan, which was oriented towards the star Sothis (Sirius) whose heliacal rising announced the annual flooding of the Nile. Stellar alignment could also be based on mythological factors. The 11th-dynasty mud-brick temple built by Sankhkare Mentuhotep atop the peak known as Thoth Hill in western Thebes was on a slightly different orientation from the earlier stone temple built on the same site in Archaic times. The Hungarian team excavating these structures believes that this difference may be attributed to the shift in astronomical alignments over the intervening centuries.

Their research indicates that the later brick temple was aligned towards the heliacal rising of the star Sirius. In the Archaic period the same star would have appeared just over 2 degrees further south in the eastern sky – exactly the difference visible in the orientation of the earlier building. Thus, rather than simply following the physical orientation of the early sacred structure, the Middle Kingdom architects had carefully adjusted the temple's orientation in order to align the new building once more precisely with Sirius – which was equated with Horus, the patron deity of the temple.

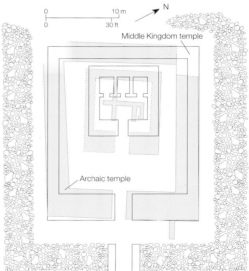

(Above) The lotus (left) and papyrus (right), the heraldic plants of Upper and Lower Egypt respectively, are cardinally aligned before the sanctuary of the temple of Amun at Karnak.

(Left) Plan of the Archaic and Middle Kingdom temples on Thoth Hill, western Thebes, showing the difference in orientation of the structures corresponding with changed astronomical alignments.

Middle Kingdom temple

Archaic temple

Rituals of Foundation

(Above) Stages in the rituals of foundation for an Egyptian temple. The king 'stretches the cord' to lay out the new temple site with the help of the goddess of writing and measurement, scatters purifying gypsum into the area and digs the foundation trenches – all symbolically.

(Right) An Egyptian drawing showing the placing of ritual deposits into a foundation pit (Old Kingdom).

'Laying out the foundation ground which was made in the Temple ... according to that which is in the book "The delineation of the sacred mounds..."'

– From the Edfu Inscriptions

Construction of all religious buildings in ancient Egypt began with ceremonies which were of very ancient origin. Comparison of texts and representations from many sites show that the complete foundation ceremonies consisted of as many as ten discrete rites, most of which were enacted before actual construction could begin. In theory, the rites were conducted by the king himself, assisted by various deities, and consisted of:

1 Fixing the plan of the building by 'stretching the cord'
2 Scattering gypsum on the assigned area to purify it
3 Digging the first foundation trench
4 Pouring sand into the foundation trench
5 Moulding the first brick or bricks
6 Placement of foundation deposits at the corners of the structure, etc.
7 Initiation of the work of building
8 Purification of the completed temple
9 Presentation of the temple to its intended deity/ies
10 Offering of sacrifices

Late texts, such as that found in the Ptolemaic temple at Edfu, include other aspects of the king's performance such as departing from the palace and arriving at the site of the new temple.

The ten elements set out here include all the essential rites of earlier lists such as that of Tuthmosis III depicted on the walls of the Small Temple

at Medinet Habu. Of all these rituals, the first – known as the *pedj-shes* or 'stretching the cord' – was of particular importance. Originally simply one of the foundation rites, *pedj-shes* became by extension the name of the whole group of foundation ceremonies, or at least those which preceded the actual work of construction. The rite involved the careful orientation of the temple by astronomical observation and measurement. Apparently this was usually accomplished by sighting the stars of a northern circumpolar constellation through a notched wooden instrument called a *merkhet*, and thus acquiring a true north–south orientation which was commonly used for the temple's short axis. According to the texts, the king was assisted in this ritual by Seshat or Sefkhet-Abwy, the scribal goddess of writing and measurement, though the actual alignment was probably ascertained by temple personnel at a time conducive to observation prior to the beginning of the ceremonies. It may thus only have been acted out symbolically by the king in the performance of the ritual.

While it is impossible without specific information to know how many of these foundation activities were actually conducted by the pharaoh in the building of a specific temple, in theory each was the king's prerogative. Indeed, all stages of temple construction were performed at least symbolically by him.

Foundation deposits

During or soon after the foundation ceremony, foundation deposits consisting of small votive plaques, bricks, models of building tools or food offerings, and often the head of a bull and a goose, were placed in shallow pits near the outer corners of the temple being built and sometimes also on the axis,

at the corners of individual halls and courtyards and shrines, along the main processional route of the temple, and beneath some pylons, columns and obelisks. These votive objects were usually models of a purely symbolic nature. On the whole they were made of clay, wood or some other simple material and only quite unusually of more expensive or rarer substances, though deposits of the Late Period sometimes include small samples of materials actually used in the building.

Interestingly, such foundation deposits are frequently uninscribed or inscribed with only the briefest of texts. When they are present, Middle and New Kingdom temple foundation inscriptions usually simply state the name of the king responsible for commissioning the building and, not uncommonly, the deity to whom the temple or feature was dedicated according to the formula: 'The good god (King X) beloved of (Deity Y) [Lord of (City or Temple Z)]'.

(Right) Vessels, plaques and other items from a foundation deposit of Nectanebo I at Tell el-Balamun.

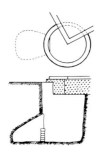

(Left) Plan and section of a foundation pit with niche.

(Below) An artist's reconstruction of a typical temple foundation deposit.

Examples of Foundation Deposit Contents

Although temple foundation deposits differed widely, it was especially common for tools, vessels and certain other items to be included. The following contents from selected deposit pits of Tuthmosis III show the range typical of many foundation deposits:

Temple	Tools	Vessels	Miscellaneous
Temple at Abydos (deposit 82)	4 tool blades	1 large dish 1 alabaster ointment jar	–
Temple at Koptos (deposit 7)	around a dozen model tool blades	1 saucer inside a larger vessel 1 alabaster saucer 12 alabaster ointment jars	2 grinders/ grindstones
Amun-Kamutef barque-station at Thebes (deposit 1)	–	2 model saucers	–
Mortuary temple (portico deposit)	–	–	166 carnelian beads
Temple at Deir el-Bahri barque-station (deposit 3)	4 examples each of wood brick mould, hoe, adze, axe, knife, chisel; various gravers, mallet, surveyor's stake	4 oval and circular baskets 4 basketwork sieves	4 grinders/ grindstones 1 string of carnelian beads
Temple at el-Kab (deposits 1 and 2)	–	small cups of brown clay	–

Building the 'God's House'

Once the foundation rituals were completed, the process of temple building could begin in earnest – though undoubtedly the logistical issues of manpower, material acquisition and construction work had already been addressed, with the necessary preparations made well in advance.

Obtaining the stone

Geologically, the Nile Valley is made up for the most part of massive beds of limestone and sandstone, which were the major building stones used by the ancient Egyptians. The sandstone deposits are primarily found in southern Upper Egypt while those of limestone are found throughout the rest of the Nile Valley as far as Cairo. Deposits of other stones such as granite, basalt and calcite tend to be more localized, and stones of these types were often transported great distances from specific quarries valued for the characteristics of their stone.

Stone was cut by different methods depending on its nature. Quarrymen working with the relatively soft limestone and sandstone would usually cut away small building-block sized sections from long shelf-like strips worked from outcroppings of the rock. Harder stones were mostly extracted in larger blocks, closer to the size of the finished monument or architectural feature, as this ultimately involved less work than the cutting of many smaller blocks from the parent rock. Only tools of stone, wood and softer metals were available to the workmen, consisting mainly of stone-tipped drills, metal saws (used with hard, abrasive sand slurry which actually performed the work of cutting) and simple stone pounders.

A large number of records have survived to tell us of the selection, cutting and transportation of monolithic stone blocks for the great colossi, obelisks and other monuments which were placed within temples; but in contrast, very little written evidence remains as to the procurement of the majority of the stone used for building the temples themselves. Instead, we must rely on the evidence of modern analyses of stone found in known pharaonic quarries and matching the stone types in the temples themselves. This line of research has shown that stone for different structures in the same area was often transported from widely different sources. During the Middle Kingdom, the limestone used in the construction of the 11th-dynasty temple of Mentuhotep at Deir el-Bahri in western Thebes came from Gebelein some 30 km (19 miles) to the south, while buildings of Senwosret I on the east bank were constructed of limestone from the quarries of Tura, some 800 km (500 miles) to the north. In the first part of the New Kingdom the stone used to construct the temples in the area of Thebes was limestone quarried at Gebelein, while later in the New Kingdom, most if not all the temples constructed in the capital city were built from sandstone cut from quarries at Gebel el-Silsila about 160 km (99.5 miles) to the south.

The switch from limestone to sandstone which occurred in the mid-18th dynasty at Thebes probably came about as a result of the depletion of the limestone quarries at Gebelein and perhaps also because it was believed (erroneously) that sandstone would prove more impervious to damage caused by flooding. In any event, sandstone often proved to be a stronger material and allowed longer

Stone Types

The most common stones used in temple building were sandstone, limestone and, to a lesser extent, granite and basalt.

Sandstone, the lightest and softest of the commonly used stones, was present in the northern Tura region and in the south at Gebel Silsila, Aswan and further south. Apparently regarded by the Egyptians as more impervious to flooding than limestone, sandstone was the major stone type used in temple construction from the mid-18th dynasty.

architraves and blocks to be utilized, to some degree facilitating the construction of the larger halls and courts of the later temples.

Methods of construction

By modern standards, the foundations for the Egyptian temple were often somewhat insubstantial and frequently consisted of little more than a trench filled with sand and a few courses of rough-hewn stones. It was not until the Graeco-Roman Period that temple foundations were made stronger by the use of courses of securely laid masonry. Yet the effectiveness of the Egyptians' building techniques is evident in the still-stable condition of massive pylons weighing thousands of tons, as well as many of the huge columns and obelisks which the Egyptians erected. Egyptian temples also often display an amazing degree of skill in the construction of complex architectural features such as the

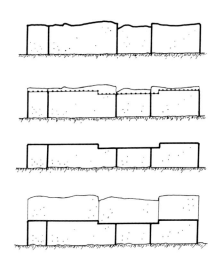

(Right) Stages in the building of temple walls: (from top to bottom) first a course of stones is laid, which are initially dressed only on their bases and sides. This course is then smoothed on the top and the stones of the next course are fitted to the shape of the ones below, and so on. The outer surfaces were only dressed once the wall had been completed.

Limestone, a slightly heavier sedimentary rock, but like sandstone relatively easy to quarry, was plentiful in the areas of Tura in the north and at Gebelein near Thebes and in a number of outcroppings along the Nile between these two points. Important quarries were located in the regions of Abydos and el-Amarna, for example, making large-scale building from this stone practical in these areas.

Granite, an igneous rock consisting of quartz, felspar and mica, was heavier and far harder to quarry, transport and carve. It was usually used only for specific features in temple construction such as obelisks, stelae, statues, column bases, door jambs and lintels. In the later periods, however, granite was employed exclusively in some temple structures. The Aswan area provided much granite though the stone was sometimes brought from more remote areas – not without massive effort. One inscription from the reign of Ramesses IV records a stone-quarrying gang of 8,362 men which was sent to the Wadi Hammamat in the Eastern Desert to cut the hard metasedimentary 'siltstone', also classed as 'granite' by the Egyptians.

Basalt, a heavy, black composite rock, is among the hardest of the stones used by the Egyptians. Employed from the earliest times, it was not only chosen for vases and other small objects, but in the Old Kingdom it was also used for temple pavements. Major outcrops of basalt occur at Aswan, Abu Za'bal, Bilbeis and Kirdasa. Most of the basalt used in pyramid temples seems to have been obtained from the sites in the Fayum.

Other hard stones such as **quartzite** (a variety of sandstone) and **calcite** (the so-called Egyptian 'alabaster') are also found in Egyptian temples, but these were used relatively infrequently and in far smaller quantities.

smoothly sloping walls of pylons and interlocking roofing elements. Despite the limitations of their tools and the methods of construction available to them, the Egyptian builders were clearly masters of their art.

In most periods mortar was used only sparingly in stone construction, and temple walls were built by laying down courses of blocks which were carefully fitted together at their joining surfaces and only dressed on their outer surface once the wall was completed. Wooden braces were often used within walls to support blocks until their mortar had dried or they were firmly locked together in the finished construction. Complex and sometimes rather strange-looking jointing techniques were utilized in corners and other areas which were perhaps necessary in some cases due to the size of the blocks

The large stone blocks of temples were manoeuvred into position using levers. Although a cement mortar was sometimes used, as seen here, stones were more usually laid without the use of a binding agent.

41

employed or in the building of additions to already existing structures.

The tools available to the ancient masons were simple but effective. Precut stone was dressed with metal chisels and hard stone pounders; and small, stick-like rods were run over the surface of blocks to level them and to check their smoothness. These 'boning rods' may have served as the builder's characteristic tool, somewhat like the scribe's palette, as their use is often depicted in ancient representations, while other tools known to have been commonly used are not. Wooden set squares were employed to lay out and check the angles of corners, and plumb bobs suspended from wooden frames were used to check the angles of features such as walls and column shafts. An 'A'-shape level was used for horizontal surfaces and an 'E'- or 'F'-shape level for checking vertical surfaces. With little more than these basic tools stone was cut from the quarries, shaped, fitted and finally decorated.

It seems fairly certain that the Egyptians did not use complex mechanical lifting devices for manoeuvring and positioning even the largest of the stone blocks found in temple architecture, at least before Graeco-Roman times, when the true pulley was first widely used. Before this, although simple devices such as levers, rollers, rockers and 'proto-pulleys' may have been employed, the usual method of raising stone blocks in pharaonic times was simply hauling them up the slopes of ramps built against the face of the wall under construction. Somewhat

(Above) In this painting from the tomb of Rekhmire at Thebes workmen prepare and lay bricks using a mould. Most of the outlying buildings and walls of Egyptian temples were made of mud-brick.

(Right and below) 'Boning rods' connected by a length of string were run over the surface of blocks as they were dressed to find protrusions or rough areas which needed further smoothing. The inscribed 'boning rod' (right) is from the temple of Amenophis III.

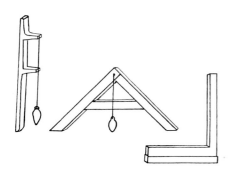

different methods were utilized for the erection of precut obelisks and statues. Walls were thus essentially buried in ever growing ramps of dirt, brick or rubble as building progressed, and these ramps were then removed on the completion of the structure. The remains of such a ramp or embankment built of mud-brick can still be clearly seen inside the first pylon of the Great Temple of Amun at Karnak, where it was left when construction of the pylon was halted.

Stone surfaces were left rough as the construction progressed from the ground up, and were then dressed and decorated from the top down as the building ramps were removed or, in some cases, by means of scaffolding erected for this purpose. Although some columns were made from large, monolithic blocks of stone, most were built up in sections which were then shaped and smoothed from the top down in the same manner, leaving a finely finished surface which – especially when painted – looked like a single shaft of stone. Unfinished columns in several temples provide examples of this construction procedure.

The advantages of this method of building are clear, for it enabled the Egyptians to cut, manipulate and erect large pylons, walls, columns and other features without damage to finished surfaces and also allowed walls and other broad areas to be dressed and decorated by large groups of workmen. That various operations in the building process were often conducted at the same time – with stone dressers, plasterers, carvers, and painters working in close proximity – is evident from the unfinished areas in various temples.

Despite the practical limitations of their building methods and tools, the ancient masons were able to produce huge areas of cut and decorated stone surface in relatively short periods of time, though many of the larger temple buildings must still have taken a considerable time to complete.

The physical and logistical manipulation of thousands of tons of stone, hundreds of shiploads of timber, and virtual mountains of sand and brick, as well as many other materials, in the creation of Egypt's monumental temple structures was an incredible work which doubtless occupied years and, in some cases, even the lifetimes of their builders.

(Far left) The ancient Egyptians utilized several types of squares and levels for accurate building. Plumb weighted 'F'-shaped levels were used to check vertical surfaces and 'A'-shaped levels for horizontal surfaces. Set squares were used to check both vertical and horizontal corners.

(Below) Remains of a mud-brick construction ramp are still visible against the inner surface of the first pylon of the Great Temple of Amun at Karnak. The ramp was not removed as this pylon was never completed. The unfinished column in the centre reveals the Egyptian masons' method of working: roughly hewn stones were placed one on top of another and then, when the structure was complete, were shaped and smoothed from the top down.

Decorating the Temple

Partially completed areas in several temples show that the decoration of pylons, walls and columns (as with that of obelisks and other monuments) was carried out as the building work progressed, often while construction continued in close proximity to the artisans engaged in this final work. The workmen used standard techniques consisting of the sketching and incising of the outlines of representations, which were then carved in detail and painted. Both raised (*bas*) reliefs and sunk (*en creux*) reliefs were found in temples, though the expense and time-consuming nature of raised relief (in which the entire backgrounds of represented figures had to be cut down) meant that it was always utilized to a much lesser extent than the simpler sunk relief style. The quality and depth of carving in both styles varies considerably from period to period, however.

By Ramessid times the practice of usurpation of royal monuments had become so common that sunk relief – especially royal cartouches – was carved at great depth in order to discourage or make impossible the recarving of the stone by future kings. In temples such as that of Ramesses III at Medinet Habu the carving of the king's names thus commonly extends several inches into the stone.

The various motifs used in particular temple decorations will be examined in detail later, but certain underlying principles of decoration should be noted here. Throughout the dynasties decorative programmes included the motif of the royal smiting scene and its variations, shown at the temple entrance – the origins of which may stretch back to the very beginnings of Egyptian history. Inner temple motifs showing the king before various gods also appear in almost all periods, along with

Temple decoration was carved in both raised (bas) and sunk (en creux) relief, as seen in these examples from the temple of Horus at Edfu. The more time-consuming raised relief (near right) was often reserved for inner surfaces, while incised carving (far right) was often used on outer surfaces where shadows helped define its forms in bright sunlight.

texts which also often reveal little change in their essential character through the ages. On the other hand, temple decoration did remain fluid in that variation could occur within fairly fixed overall parameters.

In the New Kingdom, however, we see certain quite radical, if short-lived, developments. Temples of the Amarna period were decorated with new or modified motifs according to the requirements of Akhenaten's religious beliefs, and there was also a stress on scenes from everyday life during this period, a genre which was highly unusual within

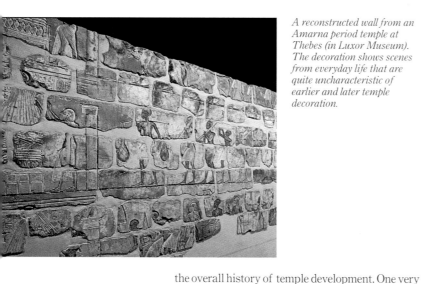

A reconstructed wall from an Amarna period temple at Thebes (in Luxor Museum). The decoration shows scenes from everyday life that are quite uncharacteristic of earlier and later temple decoration.

Cryptographic inscriptions

There is also a trait of increasing obfuscation which is evident in both the representations and texts of later temples. From the 19th dynasty on, New Kingdom temples often displayed royal protocols and dedications in ornamental cryptographic writing which utilized the figures and emblems of the gods, though these inscriptions were usually accompanied by transcriptions of the cryptic text in normal hieroglyphic writing. This cryptographic tradition may actually have begun as early as the Middle Kingdom or even before in certain

the overall history of temple development. One very fine example of this can be seen in a reconstructed Amarna period temple wall now exhibited in the Luxor Museum of Ancient Egyptian Art. The wall, with brightly painted decoration in sunk relief, depicts numerous scenes of everyday life in quite remarkable detail which can only be understood as replacing the detailed treatments of royal martial activity normally shown in New Kingdom temple decoration.

Throughout most of the New Kingdom as well as at other times, specific examples of the king's military and hunting exploits were represented in great detail on the outer walls and courts of royal and divine cult temples. In all periods, however, the function of these scenes is largely symbolic and apotropaic, providing visual examples of the defence of the temple against its enemies – the forces of chaos which existed beyond the sacred precinct.

(Below) Post-Amarna temple decoration displays some residual realism, as in this narrative scene of Ramesses II and the battle of Kadesh. The king, beset by enemy forces, is far more vulnerable than in pre-Amarna art.

types of inscriptions, but it became widespread in the Graeco-Roman Period, when many inscriptions were made more secret by the use of cryptic variants of normal hieroglyphic characters. The temple inscriptions thus became increasingly unreachable for any but the small and dwindling number of priestly initiates. Finally, after knowledge of the hieroglyphic script had long been lost to history these writings would confuse early explorers and scholars who read into them the erroneous idea that Egyptian writing employed a purely symbolic script.

Graffiti

Even after the formal temple decoration was completed, many other small inscriptions or scenes were often carved over the original decorations or in the spaces between them in the form of graffiti. Although certainly contrary to the intentions of the original temple builders and artists, these graffiti sometimes add considerably to our knowledge of ancient temple life, as well as events affecting the later history of the gods' houses.

Because the plaster into which they were carved is usually missing, very early graffiti can be especially difficult to reconstruct as only the lightest scratches may be left in the underlying stone. Even in well-preserved areas the low quality of writing or drawing frequently makes the task of interpretation difficult; nevertheless, a number of scholars have completed valuable work with this type of evidence and the recording of graffiti is now an established aspect of temple documentation and study (p. 221 and p. 236).

Temple graffiti range from crudely scratched names, dates and almost indistinguishable drawings to quite elaborate and sometimes extremely well-executed texts and representations. Pictorial graffiti include drawings of gods, kings, priests and other human figures as well as animals of various types – especially those species commonly used as sacrifices. Textual graffiti include both those contemporary with the active life of the temples – written in hieroglyphic script, Hieratic, Demotic, Greek or Latin – and those of later times written in Coptic, Arabic and various other languages.

The earlier texts often supply specific names and titles of temple personnel and can help us to understand the inner workings of a particular temple and the historical and social events which surrounded it. Later graffiti also add to our knowledge of temple use and dissolution, and the numerous travellers' names preserved on temple walls and columns help to construct the story of temple rediscovery in more recent centuries. A single graffito may, in fact, sometimes be all the evidence we have for the history of a given temple within a time frame of several centuries, yet that evidence may be particularly telling in the inferences it allows, and in linking the history of one temple with that of others in other regions.

(Above) Temple graffiti range from crudely scratched names and dates to lengthy texts such as this Greek inscription on the wall of the Ptolemaic temple at Deir el-Medina.

(Left) Cryptographic inscriptions, such as this text from the temple of Horus at Edfu, were written in a manner accessible only to a limited number of temple personnel.

Growth, Enhancement and Change

As time progressed, established temples grew through the benefactions of kings who added to and enlarged the original structures. The usual pattern discernible in the growth of the developed temple plan was for a king to add a new court and entrance pylon in front of the existing temple entrance. This type of addition would sometimes be repeated by numerous kings in the course of history, with each added unit growing larger and larger as kings strove to outdo their predecessors.

Karnak and Luxor temples in Thebes provide clear examples of the growth and development of individual Egyptian temples. These massive structures were built in a number of successive stages beginning with early 18th-dynasty cores (doubtless constructed around even earlier shrines) and culminating with massive additions by Ramesses II and later rulers. In fact, the ratio of growth found in Karnak Temple approximates that of the Fibonacci mathematical sequence in which each successive number is the sum of the two numbers preceding it: 1, 2, 3, 5, 8, etc. Because the Egyptians usually preferred measurements that were divisible by ten in their architectural planning and design, the lengths and widths of courts and pylons added to existing temples were quite often increased in multiples of ten 'cubits' (5.24 m, or about 17 ft).

While Karnak Temple shows the ever increasing scale of additions made by many rulers of different dynasties, Luxor Temple, somewhat differently, demonstrates the types of changes which could transform even the basic plan and appearance of a

(Above) A simplified plan of the fully developed Great Temple of Amun at Karnak, showing the complexity of the stages of its accretion and growth – in this case along two intersecting axes.

(Right) Luxor Temple: the main stages of development. The area of the initial Middle Kingdom core (1) was substantially enlarged by Amenophis III (2) and by Ramesses II (3), as well as by later rulers and Christian and Moslem inhabitants of the area (4).

(Opposite) Aerial view of Luxor Temple, showing the different areas of the successively expanded temple and, at the top, the sphinx-lined causeway which linked Luxor to the temples to the north.

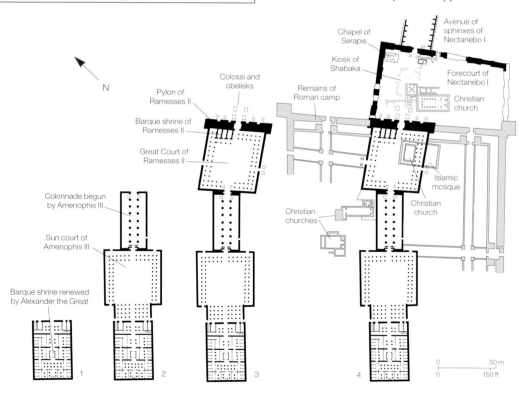

48

temple within a dynasty and even within the reign of a single king such as Amenophis III or Ramesses II.

The improvements endowed as benefactions to various temples by a king were not always simply ones of size in the form of expansion, however. Perhaps more often the improvements were of quality and consisted of the upgrading of already existing features – both in adding new adornment and decoration or simply in the replacing of inferior materials with more costly ones. Tuthmosis III, for example, records Amun's assessment of that king's gifts to the god's temple at Karnak. The god states both that 'You have built my temple as a work of eternity, made longer and wider than it had been' and also that 'Lo, my majesty found the southern pylon of mud brick, the southern gateway … stone in the lesser constructions, the double door leaves of cedar, the columns of wood. Then my majesty made of it … its gateway of granite, its great door leaf of copper ….My majesty dug for [Amun] the southern lake, freshened and extended [it].' Such additions and improvements were clearly seen as worthy of being recorded as demonstrations of the same level of royal piety as the construction of new temples.

Enhancement of existing temple features became especially common during stable and long-lasting dynasties, as individual kings had opportunity to complete works begun by their predecessors (especially when they were their own fathers) or even to repair and enhance monuments of earlier rulers of their own dynasty.

Temple economy

Once constructed, the Egyptian temple began to function and grow – not only in terms of the temple proper but also beyond its walls in the wider world with which it interacted. Most temples were supported by their own estates, given as sustaining gifts from the king or bequeathed by prosperous individuals who sought the favour of the gods through prayers purchased on their behalf. The amount of land accrued and controlled by temples through many generations is still astonishing, however. It is known that in the time of Ramesses III, for example, the Domain of Amun alone controlled well over 2,300 sq. km (900 sq. miles) of usable agricultural land, along with vineyards and gardens and other temple estates such as marshlands, quarries and mines. Temples thus grew into thriving enterprises at the heart of the economies of their local areas and also participated in trade with other regions. Some of the gods' houses had their own fleets of riverboats and even seaworthy ships capable of trade beyond the boundaries of Egypt.

The economic relationships between temples and their surrounding areas, as well as their relationships with other temples and various departments of the government, have been relatively well documented and provide a fascinating picture of economic power beneath ostensible dependency.

Much of a given temple's land was rented out to the peasant population who paid up to one third of the grain they harvested as rent. This provided the basis of regular temple income along with that obtained from the farms, gardens, etc, worked directly by temple employees. And in some periods – especially during the New Kingdom – a significant part of the spoils of war brought back to Egypt by the pharaoh's armies was also routinely paid as offerings to the great temples. Such plunder taken in military campaigns was followed by ongoing tribute from foreign areas paid in the form of raw materials such as gold, silver and wood as well as livestock, foodstuffs and finished products.

This situation led to the establishment of the particular kind of redistributive economy practised in the New Kingdom in which tribute and offerings (*baku(t)*) from lands conquered or controlled by the king were delivered to the temples. The various goods were then used not only for internal temple needs but also redistributed in the form of rations and also as payment of expenses for activities of the king such as the building of his tomb. Goods were thus cycled through the two most powerful and organized institutions of ancient Egypt – the monarchy and the temples – in a way in which each supported the other.

The balances of this economic arrangement were complex and shifting, however. A number of kings made reforms which curbed the various temple endowments. This is clearly documented in the New Kingdom, especially around the time of the Amarna heresy, when we find Amenophis III, Akhenaten, Tutankhamun, Merenptah and Ramesses III all making fairly major adjustments to temple endowments in the course of their reigns. On the other hand, decrees were often made to protect temples (especially the cult temples of the kings themselves) from the encroachment of taxation officers or other agents of the state involved in conscription of labour for corvée and other work. The Nauri decree of Sethos I provides just such a detailed list of prohibitions, whereby temple staff and even their wives and servants were protected from the requisitions of press-gangs or the organizers of the corvée. Thus, almost immune to the forces which might have restricted their growth, many of Egypt's temples burgeoned incredibly through the centuries. The more the gods favoured Egypt in the abundance of its crops and other resources, the more the Egyptians favoured the houses of the gods with enriching offerings.

Yet, even as the gods' houses grew, their great economic power would itself eventually trigger repercussions throughout society. A broken but interesting example of criticism of wealthy temples for not helping the poor seems to occur in the Late Period Papyrus Vandier, and such feelings may have been widespread at certain times. More importantly, Egypt's kings often found ways to limit

(Below) Personified estates bearing offerings to the pyramid temple of Sneferu at Dahshur. The income from farms and estates all over Egypt formed the basis of most temples' economies.

temple income and the practice of usurpation – where monarchs took the monuments of earlier rulers as their own – can sometimes be seen as arising from economic motives – this was cheaper by far than providing new materials for the temple enlargements and embellishments which were the usual duty of the king.

Usurpation and reuse of temples

Temples were often taken over for new use in the course of time; this might consist of the reuse of a sacred site, reuse of stone or other material from an existing temple in a new structure, or finally, reuse of an entire building for new purposes – often with recutting of decorated surfaces to express the new ownership or purpose.

Temple sites were thus sometimes transformed in order to utilize sacred space already hallowed to the gods' use for new structures – a frequent event in Egypt – and at other times in order to superimpose a new religion on an old one. This occurred in many ancient civilizations – sometimes more than once, as in the case of the Israelite Temple in Jerusalem. This was re-dedicated to Zeus Olympus by Antiochus Epiphanes (*c.* 165 BC) and again by Hadrian when he built a temple to the Capitoline Triad (*c.* AD 135) on the same temple mount after suppressing the Second Jewish Revolt.

In Egypt, however, this type of radical rededication of holy ground was uncommon, though it may have occurred in the Amarna Period and certainly in later times when Egypt fell to outside invaders. In the temple of Amun at Luxor, for example, a Christian basilica was built in the first court which was in turn itself replaced by an Islamic mosque on the same site. Even the temple of Isis on the island of Philae – which persisted as one of the last outposts of paganism – was finally rededicated, in AD 553, to St Stephen and the Virgin Mary.

More common throughout Egyptian history was the reuse of temple materials in new construction work. Egyptian kings would frequently dismantle earlier structures found to be blocking their own

planned expansions (see p. 196 and p. 243) and were also not averse simply to quarrying buildings of earlier monarchs as cheap and convenient sources of building materials.

When, as in the case of Akhenaten, an earlier king suffered a *damnatio memoriae,* the dismantling of that monarch's monuments could be almost complete. For example, more than 40,000 decorated sandstone blocks from destroyed structures belonging to Amenophis IV/Akhenaten have been recovered from within other monuments at Karnak, and the destruction of these early monuments was so thorough that they will never be completely reconstructed.

Temples, or parts of them, would also frequently be usurped by later monarchs simply through the recutting of their representations and texts. And even despite the excessively deep carving of royal names and inscriptions which was common by Ramessid times (p. 44), the practice of usurpation of standing monuments continued throughout Egyptian history.

Sometimes the same site, building or materials were reused on multiple occasions. The so-called 'Small Temple' within the precincts of the great temple of Ramesses III at Medinet Habu provides a classic case of this kind of repeated usurpation, addition and growth through cannibalization. Although the core of the monument was begun by Hatshepsut and Tuthmosis III, the queen's name was later replaced by those of her more 'legitimate' predecessors, Tuthmosis I and II. The original entrance to the structure was eventually supplanted by the pylon of the Nubian king Shabaka and later usurped in turn by his nephew Taharqa. A small fronting gateway was built at the site during the 26th dynasty and this too was usurped during the 30th dynasty by Nectanebo I. Even the stone-faced pylon and gateway constructed for the temple during the Ptolemaic Period, although not later usurped, were themselves constructed with numerous blocks taken from the mortuary temple of Ramesses II – the Ramesseum.

As part of Akhenaten's religious reforms the cartouches of Amenophis III in Luxor Temple were partly destroyed in order to remove the name of Amun. Most of Akhenaten's own temple structures were in turn comprehensively dismantled when the old religion was reinstated and the cult of Amun restored. The recut cartouche on the right is visibly lower than the left.

The so-called Small Temple at Medinet Habu (foreground) shows repeated usurpation and reuse by various monarchs who expanded and elaborated upon the temple's core.

The Parts of the Temple and their Meaning

'The King of Upper and Lower Egypt … [made a temple] … of fine sandstone, wide, very great, and exceedingly beautiful. Its walls are of fine gold, its pavements of silver. All its gates are worked with the pride of lands. Its pylons reach to the sky, its flagpoles to the stars.'

Stela of Amenophis III

Truly awesome structures in their developed forms, the temples of Egypt were not only magnificent homes fit for gods, they were also complex and carefully planned structures which functioned on many different levels. In the world of giant metaphors which the Egyptian temple represented, each element in the overall architectural programme played both a physical functional role and a metaphorical one in symbolizing some aspect of the temple's underlying meaning and purpose. Thus, the rich range of symbolism that lay behind a temple's appearance and its ramifications for Egyptian religion may be grasped only after the individual areas are examined and understood.

Every temple was divided into zones of increasing sacredness. First were the temple approaches and the area within the compound's enclosure – an area open to every Egyptian. Next came the pylon gateways and outer courts of the temple proper which were accessible to the priests and, on some occasions, to representatives of the populace. Finally there were the inner halls, which only the purified priests were allowed access to, and the sanctuary itself, which could be entered only by the king and by certain priests of the highest ranks. Beyond these areas central to every temple's form and role, other ancillary elements were often also present – administrative chambers, magazines and stores, sacred lakes, gardens, schools, libraries and areas dedicated to numerous other uses.

Many areas had their own distinctive temple 'furniture' – such as the great obelisks and statues which fronted entrance pylons – and each individual item of furniture had its own distinctive decoration and inscriptions so that the whole temple could be seen as an intricate mechanism of interacting parts. The monuments of the gods were in fact nothing less than models of creation and of the cosmos itself – parts within parts, worlds within worlds.

The sacred lake, Temple of Amun at Karnak.

The Temple Entrance

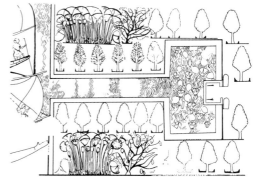

The one remaining obelisk and colossi of Ramesses II before the entrance pylon at Luxor Temple. Although temple pylons provided formal entrances to the gods' houses, the temple's precincts usually began well before these structures.

It is easy to think of the entrance to the Egyptian temple in terms of the huge pylon gateways which, in most cases, are the most visible parts of temples to have survived. In reality, however, the pylons usually lay well within the domain of the gods, and the actual temple entrances included elements such as the landing quays, kiosks, gates and processional ways which preceded the temple's outer walls – all of which stood before the pylon gateways themselves.

Temple landing quays

Because transportation was largely conducted by water in Egypt, from archaic times onwards most temples were located near the Nile or a canal connected to it. The landing quays of temples thus often served as the major, initial entrance to the religious structures even when, as at Karnak, the temple had several entrances. Many were built to accommodate boats of considerable size as they were required not only to receive boats holding large quantities of supplies but also in order to enable the docking of vessels of sufficient size for the transportation of the king or the images of the gods.

Often the quays were positioned at the end of a secondary watercourse cut back from the river in order both to get as close as possible to the temple and to provide a more stable water surface for loading and unloading the boats docked at the quay. The quays themselves also had to be built to cope with the rising and falling waters of the Nile's seasonal flood as much as possible, although all but the largest quays were usually covered by the swollen river in times of full flood.

It was at the temple quay that visiting or returning images of deities began their processional journeys to the temple proper, and it was there that they were usually greeted by crowds of common people, by high representatives of the temple, and in some cases by members of the royal family participating in the event (p. 171).

Protective sphinxes and divine images

The processional paths leading from the landing quays of temples to their main entrances – and in some cases connecting them by land routes – were delineated from quite early times by means of paving or some kind of marker. In the Old Kingdom pyramid complex the causeway which ran from the so-called valley temple to the mortuary temple at the base of the pyramid was also often roofed. From at least New Kingdom times, though rarely covered, the processional entry ways to temples were frequently decorated with sculptures which served as liminal entry markers and also as protective elements. The most common image of this type was the sphinx. Sphinxes might be human-headed, ful-

(Opposite) A New Kingdom representation of a landing quay at the Great Temple of Amun at Karnak. The quay itself is flanked by round-topped stelae which begin the processional path to the temple.

(Right) The avenue of human-headed sphinxes stretching from Luxor Temple to the area of Karnak is over 2 km (1.2 miles) long and originally contained hundreds of these statues which were carved with the features of Nectanebo I.

filling the role of the king as guardian of the temple and its approaches, or they might take theriomorphic form as fusions of the lion with some other animal, depending on the nature of the god with whose temple they were associated. Ram-headed sphinxes thus lined the processional way leading to the temple of the god Amun at Karnak, and elsewhere there were hawk-headed sphinxes for the god Re. A small image of the king was often placed between the outstretched paws of the recumbent animal and in such cases the sphinx was doubtless intended to represent an image of the god himself rather than the king, though the essentially protective function of the image remains the same. The use of fully theriomorphic types of sphinxes parallels the way in which statues of the gods themselves were sometimes erected along processional ways, for instance the many famous statues of the seated goddess Sekhmet which were placed along the processional way linking the precinct of Mut with the temple of Amun at Karnak.

In some instances such pathways were marked by large numbers of sphinxes or divine statues, and the amount of work involved in their production must have been considerable. The processional avenue which joins Karnak and Luxor temples, for example, is approximately 2 km (1.2 miles) in length and was furnished with literally hundreds of sphinxes combining the body of a lion with the head of Nectanebo I (380–363 BC). This late ruler rebuilt the line of sphinxes in the 4th century BC to replace the ruined New Kingdom examples which were erected along at least part of the avenue from as early as the time of Hatshepsut.

Way stations

Along the formal processional routes which linked either neighbouring temples or a temple and its river quay, one or more way stations were often constructed. These structures were usually only large enough to allow the entrance of the god's small portable barque (or barques when the stations were for the use of multiple deities) during its temporary halt. Although the image of the deity might be refreshed in these way stations, the buildings did not normally contain anything other than an altar-like base upon which the god's barque or image would be set. Of the way stations which have survived at least reasonably intact, the most

The way station of Sethos I in the forecourt of the Great Temple of Amun at Karnak. The tripartite station held the ceremonial barques of the Theban triad – Amun, Mut and Khonsu.

impressive is without doubt that of Senwosret I, which was reconstructed from the ninth pylon of the Great Temple of Amun at Karnak.

The enclosure walls

The temple domain proper was entered through the large enclosure walls which surrounded the core area of the god's estate. The function of these walls was twofold. Primarily, their role was one of containment in that they delineated the god's estate and sealed it from surrounding habitation or open areas. But the enclosure walls were also protective in that they were usually designed to protect the temple in times of civil strife or invasion.

These enclosure walls were invariably built of sun-dried mud-brick and constructed in sections which were sometimes built over a simple framework of wooden beams and reed mats. Such outer walls are particularly common from New Kingdom times, and at the beginning of that period a new word – *sebty* – was coined for this type of massive enclosure wall placed around both towns and

A reconstruction of the temple of Edfu, showing the construction of the massive enclosure walls which ringed the temple precincts.

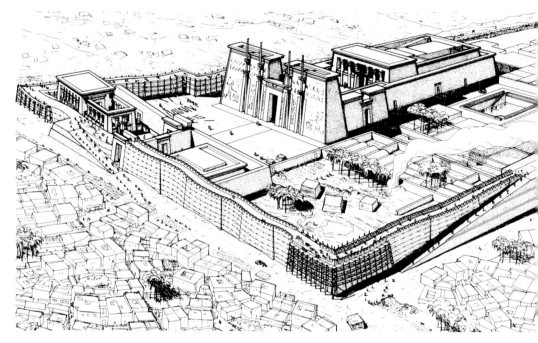

(Left) The partially surviving mud-brick enclosure walls of the temple of Soknopaios – a form of the crocodile god Sobek – at Soknopaiou Nesos (Dimai), in the Fayum.

(Opposite) The standing obelisks of Hatshepsut (at the rear) and Tuthmosis I in the Great Temple of Amun at Karnak. Each was originally one of a pair erected near what became the temple's core. The obelisk of Hatshepsut is 29.56 m (97 ft) high and weighs some 325 tonnes.

temples. Many of the temple walls were built to thicknesses of up to 10 m (*c.* 30 ft) or more to prevent their destruction, and were often crenellated with rounded 'battlements' to enhance their protective role. Occasionally, bastions or fortified gateways were also added as we find recorded in Papyrus Harris I: 'I surrounded the temple of Inhur with an enclosure-wall … with turrets, fortified gates and bastions on its every side' – though in reality, the number of entrances piercing the outer wall was usually kept to a minimum for defensive reasons.

There was also a symbolic element to these walls as the brick enclosure walls of temples were often built with alternating concave and convex sections apparently representing the waters of the mythical primeval ocean. It has been suggested, however, that this wave-like pattern had the purely practical purpose of preventing cracking in the walls due to shrinkage of the bricks when drying or the uneven swelling of the ground when flooded, etc, but none of these theories fits the evidence of the surviving walls which were usually built in this fashion only around temple precincts, or around areas apparently controlled by temples.

In the most complex type of undulating design the walls were not only built with alternating concave and convex sections along the length of the wall, but also in such patterns across their width. Often more simplified patterns were utilized, however, and in some enclosure walls undulating courses of brickwork were simply built in the upper sections of the walls above regular horizontally laid courses (as at Edfu), or above regular stone foundation courses (as at Philae).

Obelisks

The obelisk was one of Egypt's most ancient symbolic architectural forms. At first perhaps only an irregularly shaped upright sacred stone, in its developed form it consisted of an elongated tapering four-sided shaft, polished, inscribed and surmounted by a sharply pointed pyramidion.

Dating back to the earliest periods, the obelisk seems to have originated, or at least to have become established, in the sun cult of Heliopolis and spread from there around Egypt. Especially common in New Kingdom times, obelisks were often erected in pairs before the temple entrance proper (though at times single obelisks were placed on the central axis of some temples) and only came to be enclosed within the temple form as the precincts grew and new pylons were added. As major gifts to the gods, obelisks were important monuments commemorating royal jubilees, victories or other notable events and are frequently depicted on the walls of the temples in which they were erected to record their donor's piety.

In their fully developed form, obelisks were thus made as ornately inscribed objects, often rising

The Prerogative of Pharaohs: Hatshepsut's Donation of Obelisks to Amun

An inscribed block of Hatshepsut celebrating her donation of two obelisks 'for her father Amun' at Karnak.

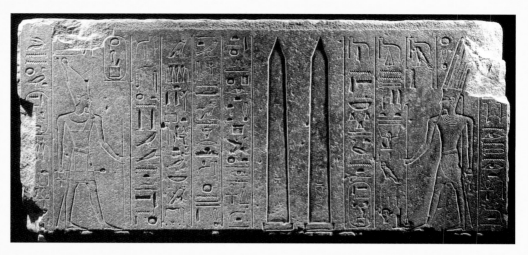

Temple obelisks were not commissioned or erected by the temple administrations but by the king himself in his capacity as son of the god and high priest of the cult. Queen–King Hatshepsut donated four obelisks to the god Amun at Karnak.

A decorated block (above) removed from the third pylon at Karnak late last century records the donation of these obelisks. The block was originally part of a small sanctuary named 'The august shrine and favourite place of Amun', and shows the queen as a male, with ceremonial beard and full kingly regalia, standing before the god Amun who pronounces blessings upon her for the gift.

On the block Hatshepsut is shown on the left wearing the double crown of kingship, but in other ways her appearance and attributes match those of Amun.

The inscription reads:

'The king himself [Hatshepsut] erected two great obelisks to her [note change of gender] father Amun-Re, before the chief columned hall, made with much electrum. Their [the obelisks'] heads pierce the sky and illuminate the two lands like the sun disc.'

Amun is depicted on the right of the block wearing the *shuty* or double-feather crown associated with the god and carries the *was* sceptre and *ankh* sign: symbols of power and life. Here the inscription reads:

'Words spoken by Amun lord of the thrones of the two lands [to] the daughter of [his] body, Hatshepsut. [I] gave to you kingship [of] the two lands [with] millions of years upon the throne [of] Horus, in stability like Re.'

The short inscriptions shown on the faces of the two engraved obelisks summarize the intent of the texts on the actual monuments – dedicating them to 'The beloved Amun-Re, king of the gods and lord of heaven.'

A drawing of a relief showing the erection of obelisks by Ptolemy XII. Although obviously symbolic, ropes were probably used.

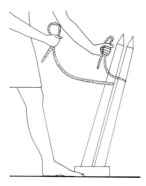

The probable method for erecting obelisks using a ramp and a sand-filled ditch. Ropes would have been used to control the movement of the stone.

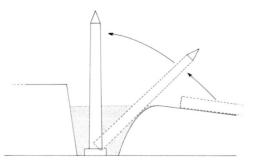

scores of feet above the sacred enclosures, their gilded pyramidions being the first and last points of the temple to catch the rays of the rising and setting sun. Monolithic in nature, they frequently weighed many hundreds of tons and represent some of the ancient Egyptians' greatest achievements of stone cutting and handling. Many were made from the red granite quarried at Aswan where, at over a thousand tons, the great Unfinished Obelisk – the largest ever attempted – still lies.

Despite the fact that dozens of obelisks were erected in the course of Egyptian history, the raising of these monolithic blocks must have presented a challenge for the Egyptians. The exact method used is not known and different ones may have been preferred at different times. The extant representational evidence only shows obelisks being transported in their upright state, though a

The 12 Largest Standing Obelisks

Of the hundreds of obelisks erected by the Egyptians, only 4 or so remain standing in Egypt and some 21 stand outside Egypt in the locations to which they were subsequently transported. The following are the largest obelisks currently standing, with their location.

King	Present Location	Height m/ft
Tuthmosis III	Rome, Piazza S. Giovanni	32.18 m / 105 ft 6 in
Hatshepsut	Karnak, Great Temple of Amun	29.56 m / 97 ft
Tuthmosis III	Istanbul, Atmeidan	28.95 m* / 95 ft*
Unknown**	Rome, Piazza S. Pietro	25.37 m / 83 ft 3 in
Ramesses II	Luxor Temple	25.00 m / 82 ft
Sethos I–Ramesses II	Rome, Piazza del Popolo	23.20 m / 76 ft
Ramesses II	Paris, Place de la Concorde	22.55 m / 74 ft
Psammetichus II	Rome, Monte Citorio	21.79 m / 71 ft 6 in
Tuthmosis III	New York, Central Park	21.21 m / 69 ft 6 in
Tuthmosis III	London, Thames Embankment	20.88 m / 68 ft 6 in
Senwosret I	Heliopolis, Midan el-Massala	20.41 m / 67 ft
Tuthmosis I	Karnak, Great Temple of Amun	19.50 m / 64 ft

* Estimated original height.
** May have been constructed by a Roman ruler of Egypt.

The eastern side of the obelisk of Ramesses II at Luxor.

relief depiction of the ritual or symbolic erection of obelisks by means of ropes exists from the time of Ptolemy XII. Almost certainly obelisks were dragged up artificial ramps and then lowered in some manner, base first, on to their socles. To prevent breakage some method of arresting or controlling the movement of the obelisk must have been employed, perhaps by lowering it into a funnel-shaped area filled with sand. A section of the Papyrus Anastasi I which deals with the erection of a royal monument seems to describe the removal of sand from this kind of erection 'chamber'.

Many of Egypt's obelisks were later removed to other locations (often with great difficulty, even much later in history). The Assyrian king Ashurbanipal removed two to Nineveh, and Roman emperors took a number to Rome and Constantinople. As late as the 19th century modern western states continued this trend, so that there now remain only four or five standing obelisks in Egypt itself, most famous being those of Luxor and Karnak temples, with that of Hatshepsut at Karnak now the largest remaining in its native land.

Colossi

From as early as Old Kingdom times and even before, great stone images of kings were carved from monolithic blocks of limestone, sandstone, quartzite and granite for erection in temples and shrines. These colossi functioned on several levels. Stationed along the temple approaches and in major processional areas they certainly acted in a protective role, but they also showed the inseparable relationship of the king with the gods at a level close to that of the divine. As manifestations of the

spirits of the pharaohs they represented, they were usually accessible to the people or in areas which were at least open on special occasions. Colossi could be given individual names such as 'Amenophis Sun of Rulers' or 'Ramesses-Montu in the Two Lands' and worshipped directly by the people, acting as intercessors with the gods or as gods in their own right.

The largest colossi made in Egypt were produced during the New Kingdom reigns of Amenophis III and Ramesses II and were of truly gargantuan proportions. The famous 'Colossi of Memnon' erected by Amenophis outside his mortuary temple at Thebes (p. 188) and the gigantic ruined statue of

The so-called Colossi of Memnon are great statues carved from single blocks of stone depicting Amenophis III. They stood at the entrance to the king's mortuary temple in western Thebes and are now virtually all that remains of this great monument.

A colossal seated statue of Ramesses II at the first pylon of Luxor Temple. A greater number of colossal statues were made of this king than of any other Egyptian monarch.

Ramesses II in that king's Theban mortuary temple (p. 184) are among the largest objects ever cut from single blocks of stone.

Ramesses II was especially enamoured of these colossal figures and had more, and larger, statues carved than any pharaoh before or after him. Although it is unknown exactly how many colossi were made for this prolific builder, fragments of his giant monuments are uncovered in the cultivation or the desert sands so frequently that Egyptian villagers often refer to any colossus as a 'Ramesses'. Certainly, dozens of his colossi were set up in temples throughout Egypt, and while many smaller statues of previous rulers were also usurped and reused by this king, most of his larger colossi appear to have been made directly at Ramesses' behest. It is recorded that one day Ramesses was walking on the hill known to the Egyptians as the 'Red Mountain' where he found a great block of quartzite 'the equal of which had never been found'. This block of red (a colour symbolic of solar divinity) stone was said to be taller than an obelisk and from it Ramesses immediately ordered that 'a great statue of Ramesses the god' should be made. The work on this single statue is said to have taken over a year to complete.

The skill involved in the construction of these behemoths was impressive. While the bodies of many free-standing colossi were carved from one block, with the statue body joined to the base at the feet, some – such as the colossi of Amenophis III erected to the south of Karnak Temple – were carved completely free so that they actually stood on the soles of their feet.

It might be expected that colossal statues would have been quarried and transported in recumbent position, and raised, like obelisks, on their bases once at their destinations. The well-known Middle Kingdom relief of Djehutihotep at Deir el-Bersha, however, depicts the transportation of a huge seated colossus in an upright position, and this seems unlikely simply to have been artistic licence. Perhaps for seated statues an upright position caused less drag. Nevertheless grooves visible on the bases of some statues (such as those on the southern side of the bases of the colossi of Memnon) show that erection in a method similar to that used for obelisks was almost certainly employed at least in some cases.

The pylon gateways

'Its pylons reach heaven and the flag poles, the stars of heaven.'

– Soleb Temple

The twin-towered pylon gateways of the developed Egyptian temple are without doubt the most distinctive architectural feature of these ancient religious structures. This type of pylon seems to have developed in Old Kingdom pyramid temples but may first have been regularly incorporated into temple design in the Middle Kingdom, though little archaeological evidence of these early mud-brick pylons remains.

Many later pylons were built with a casing of massive stones around an inner core of smaller, irregular and reused stones. Structures built by previous kings would often be used for this kind of filler, especially if the king had become discredited or if the location of the earlier structure interfered with planned expansions. Ironically, a number of temple structures consigned to oblivion in this manner were in fact protected from damage. The so-called White Chapel at Karnak is one of the most famous examples of this, along with the many decorated *talatat* blocks from Akhenaten's Aten temple at east Karnak which were used within the ninth pylon of the Great Temple of Amun when that structure was erected (p. 243). Sometimes reused stone was even employed for the outer casing of pylons, as is the case with the first great pylon that fronts the Amun temple. In later periods, pylons were often simply constructed of some combination of brick and stone. The Ptolemaic pylon built before the Small Temple at Medinet Habu was constructed in this way, for example, although it was given a stone façade on its outer face and plastered over on its inner side.

The massive structure of the completed pylons clearly served a defensive and apotropaic function, not only physically defending the gateway from intruders, but also symbolically standing as a bastion repelling the inimical forces of chaos and evil in the outer world. The pylon's usual Egyptian name, *Bekhnet*, appears with certainty only in the 18th dynasty and seems to be derived from a verbal form meaning 'to be vigilant' relating to the watchtower-like nature, if not actual function, of these structures.

Although we are unsure of the decoration on temple pylons in earlier times, in the developed temple of the New Kingdom and later periods the most common decorative motif is that of the king smiting enemies. This conventional motif has many variations, but in most the towering figure of the king raises a club or short *khepesh* sword above his enemies in the traditional 'smiting scene' known from the earliest dynasties. The very antiquity of this motif suggests that it may well have appeared on cult temples before the New Kingdom, though it is also possible that this particular use coincided with Egypt's period of greatest military expansion and empire. Symbolically, as will be seen, it is also axiomatic that the pylon mimicked the shape of the *akhet* or horizon hieroglyph, or at least was viewed as such, for it was here that the sun rose on the physical horizon between the outer world and the hidden, sacred landscape of the temple.

The flagpoles set into the face of the temple pylon mimicked the poles upon which fetishes and flags

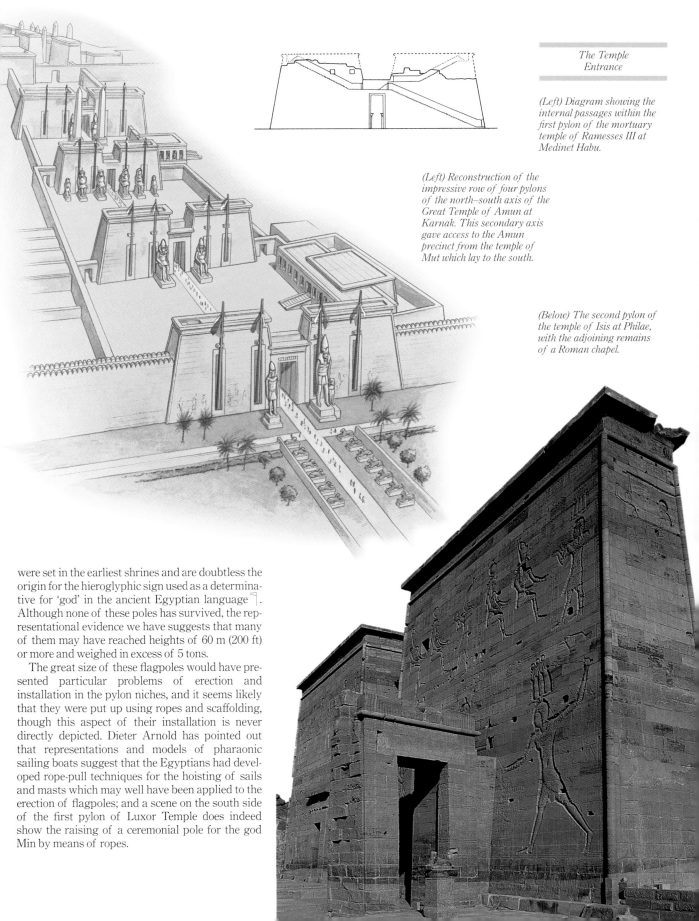

(Left) Diagram showing the internal passages within the first pylon of the mortuary temple of Ramesses III at Medinet Habu.

(Left) Reconstruction of the impressive row of four pylons of the north–south axis of the Great Temple of Amun at Karnak. This secondary axis gave access to the Amun precinct from the temple of Mut which lay to the south.

(Below) The second pylon of the temple of Isis at Philae, with the adjoining remains of a Roman chapel.

were set in the earliest shrines and are doubtless the origin for the hieroglyphic sign used as a determinative for 'god' in the ancient Egyptian language ⌐. Although none of these poles has survived, the representational evidence we have suggests that many of them may have reached heights of 60 m (200 ft) or more and weighed in excess of 5 tons.

The great size of these flagpoles would have presented particular problems of erection and installation in the pylon niches, and it seems likely that they were put up using ropes and scaffolding, though this aspect of their installation is never directly depicted. Dieter Arnold has pointed out that representations and models of pharaonic sailing boats suggest that the Egyptians had developed rope-pull techniques for the hoisting of sails and masts which may well have been applied to the erection of flagpoles; and a scene on the south side of the first pylon of Luxor Temple does indeed show the raising of a ceremonial pole for the god Min by means of ropes.

The Outer Courts

Two views of the peristyle court of the temple of Horus at Edfu: above, the rear of the pylon, and below looking the other way, towards the temple's great columned hall.

Behind the entrance pylon of the developed or 'standard plan' Egyptian temple there was usually an open peristyle court, partially or wholly surrounded by a colonnade. Several names were given by the Egyptians to this part of the temple, depending on its architectural style and the kind of columns it contained – as the columns were central both to the structure and symbolic function of the outer areas of a temple (p. 76). The major practical function of the temple's outer court, however, was transitional since the court frequently served as a zone of interface between the inner, sanctified areas of the god's domain and the outer, more public areas.

Between gods and mortals

Although contained within the temple proper, the outer court was often accessible to the common people, at least in part or on special occasions, as can be seen from the Ptolemaic name for the outer court, 'the court of the multitude', and by the large *rekhyt* hieroglyphs representing the people of Egypt which were often inscribed on the walls or columns of the court. These hieroglyphs indicated to those who were allowed into the court where they should stand while processions were enacted (p. 99).

Specially designated areas for 'making supplication and the hearing of petitions' were sometimes located within temple courts as well as on the temple's perimeters, and the populace doubtless was able to meet priests on personal matters or temple business and to deliver offerings in the open courts of many temples. A clear example of public presence is also seen in the statues which were set up in these areas.

Temple statuary

While not as obvious as the obelisks and colossi which often stood before a temple's pylon, the most important items of temple furniture found in the outer courts were the many royal and private statues placed there from Middle Kingdom times. The function of the royal statues was for the most part not essentially different from examples placed along the processional ways or before the pylon, but statues of non-royal individuals fulfilled several functions. In funerary contexts statues acted as potential 'hosts' in which the soul/*ka* could reside after death

as a physical alternative to the body itself, but temple statues were probably not intended to share this role. Temple statues certainly served as a memorial to the deceased individuals they portrayed and allowed their owners to be perpetually present in the sacred area – they were thus not only constantly in the close presence of the gods, but also might be noticed by the pious living who were often implored in the statues' inscriptions to pronounce the name of the deceased and to recite the offering formula on his or her behalf. Even when the statues stood unnoticed in the temple courts it is possible that they were believed to have participated magically in the 'reversion of offerings' by which the priests and temple staff received the sustenance of offerings once they had been presented to the gods. In Middle Kingdom times the statues were almost always of men – thus, for example, the only Middle Kingdom woman represented in the Karnak cachette was the mother of the vizier Ankhu of the 13th dynasty – though with the 'mature formal' temples of the New Kingdom and beyond, temple statues of women became more common.

Occasionally the statues of elevated individuals – as with royal statues – acted also as intermediaries between the people and the gods. A famous block statue of the 18th-dynasty sage Amenophis son of Hapu from Thebes confidently asserts in its inscription: 'people of Karnak who wish to see Amun: come to me and I will transmit your petitions'. But unlike the intermediary function of royal statues, this service was offered in return for pronouncing the name and reciting the offering formula on behalf of the son of Hapu, so that his

statue and others like it must be seen to have combined some of the functions of royal and private temple statuary.

Rather than being made to attract or seize attention, private temple statues were usually intended to be unobtrusive. The forms in which they were often carved – the 'block statue' showing the individual squatting on the ground or the kneeling figure presenting an offering before a deity – had low centres of gravity and were the most stable for positioning in the sometimes crowded courts, as well as symbolizing in their poses the humble and patient attendance of the individual before the gods.

(Above left) A seated statue of an 18th-dynasty ruler in the Great Temple of Amun, Karnak.

(Above) The Courtyard of the Cachette at Karnak, where hundreds of stone statues were found in 1903.

A statue of Amenophis son of Hapu, as a seated scribe, an example of a statue of a non-royal person who held elevated status.

Courtyard caches

Unobtrusive as they may have been individually, the temple statues gradually accumulated over the centuries until they seriously encroached on the space available and got in the way of new building projects. Temple personnel had to accept new statues, yet could not simply discard the older, hallowed dedications. The usual solution was to relegate the older statues to large pits or caches dug beneath the surface of the temple courtyard. Here, although buried and no longer visible to passers by, the ancient statues were at least still within the sacred precincts.

In 1903, while working in the north court of the seventh pylon of the Great Temple of Amun at Karnak, Georges Legrain made the sensational discovery of the so-called Karnak Cachette. In the course of the subsequent three years of excavations, over 900 stone statues and statuettes dating mainly from the 20th Dynasty to the Ptolemaic Period emerged from this deep pit. More recently, another cachette of this type was found in the court of Luxor Temple which, although smaller in size, has yielded many outstanding works of sculpture (see box below).

Amenophis III from the Karnak Cachette, the largest deposit of statues found in Egypt.

Statues of Ramesses II stand between the columns of the first court of Luxor Temple.

The Luxor Temple Cachette

On 22 January, 1989, while working on the western side of Amenophis III's colonnaded solar court in Luxor Temple, archaeologists and workers of the Egyptian Antiquities Organization discovered a deep pit containing a remarkable hoard of statuary now known as the 'Luxor Temple Cachette'. The deposit seems to have been made in the early 4th century AD to hold unwanted statuary during the installation of the cult of the deified Roman emperor which was established in Luxor Temple at that time.

A quartzite statue of Amenophis III from the Luxor Cachette which contained many fine items of temple statuary.

Once opened, the pit was found to contain a wide range of statues ranging in date from the mid-18th dynasty to the Ptolemaic Period. About half of the objects proved to be well preserved; now cleaned and repaired where necessary, many are regarded as among the finest artifacts to have been found in Egypt.

Some of the statues are of individual figures representing gods, goddesses, queens and kings, and kings as gods, while others are group statues – dyads and triads of divine and royal groups. Perhaps the most amazing single statue is the larger than life-sized, almost perfectly preserved 'statue of a statue' of Amenophis III which depicts a sledge-borne image of the king carved from a striking purple-red-gold quartzite. This and several others of the finest sculptures from the hoard are now on display in the Luxor Museum.

The Inner Halls and Sanctuaries

(Left) The inner halls of the temple of Hathor at Dendera. Beyond the main hypostyle hall lie subsidiary halls used in the practice of the cult and the sanctuaries of the goddess and those deities associated with her.

columns of the hypostyle hall can thus be seen as types of these cosmic pillars, so that statements such as that made by Amenophis III regarding the temple of Karnak, 'Its pillars reach heaven like the four pillars of heaven', contain a symbolic truth beyond the obvious hyperbole.

Decorated columns within the hypostyle hall of the temple of Khnum at Esna. The columns feature texts giving particularly full descriptions of events of the sacred year at this temple.

The hypostyle hall

Positioned directly beyond the temple's open court, the hypostyle hall was usually broader than it was deep and was filled with columns except along the central processional way which followed the temple's main axis towards the inner shrine. Although it is sometimes said that the hypostyle's dense forest of columns acted as a screen to block the view from the semi-public courtyard into the inner shrine, the open processional way along the temple's axis meant that this could not be so, and the privacy of the inner sacred areas of the temples was achieved instead by increasing darkness and by doors. In reality, the true functions of the hypostyle were more practical and also symbolic.

In the earlier stone-built structures of the Old Kingdom, chambers and passages rarely had a width of more than 3 m (9 ft 10 in) as this was about the maximum span that could be trusted with limestone architraves and roofing slabs. Once the sandstone quarries of Gebel el-Silsila began to be exploited and large quantities of this stone were made available, the use of architraves of 8 m (26 ft 3 in) or so became possible. Nevertheless, Egyptian architecture was usually conservative and the spans employed in the basic post-and-lintel construction were never great, so that large numbers of columns were needed to support the roofs of hypostyle halls.

The crowded halls of columns also held symbolic meanings. In Egyptian mythology the celestial realm of the sky was supported above the earth on columns – which are often shown as a framing device at the sides of temple representations. The

The columns of the hypostyle could also represent the marshland vegetation which sprang up around the primeval mound of creation – symbolized by the temple's inner shrine. Accordingly they were often decorated to reflect this symbolism; and the single papyrus stem column, while hardly a copy of a realistic building material, was particularly appropriate in this regard. The large variety of column types employed in hypostyle architecture was also appropriate to the metaphor of original creation; and despite the often massive size of the columns, the larger temples might contain great numbers of them in their hypostyle halls. No fewer than 134 columns – each some 24 m (79 ft) high – were erected in the great hypostyle hall of Karnak Temple alone.

Types of columns and pillars

Although some columns and pillars were made from large monolithic blocks of stone (especially in the earlier periods), most were built up in sections which were then shaped and smoothed from the top down (p. 43), leaving a finely finished surface which – especially when painted – looked like a single pillar of stone.

In most cases the shafts of Egyptian columns were copies in stone of supports made from plants – either trunks or bundles of stems of smaller diameter such as those of the papyrus plant. The shapes of column capitals were likewise derived from plant motifs, and the shafts and capitals were usually connected by five horizontal ties representing the lashings which held together the bundle of stems of which the earliest columns were composed. Above the shaft and capital a low abacus usually connected the column to the architraves placed upon it.

There was a great variety in column design and as many as 30 differing forms can be distinguished in temples of different periods. Generally, the exact form of a column was dictated by its location in the temple, with 'bud'-like capitals being found in the outer courts and away from the central axis of the inner temple and 'open' capital type columns being found in the temple's central areas. This practice was not always followed, however, and later temples especially may show great variation in the placement and style of their columnar forms. In the temples of the Graeco-Roman Period the columns are especially varied, yet even there most can be seen to be derivative of the major types (see below).

A great variety of different types of column capitals were used in ancient Egypt, sometimes within the same area, as seen here in the temple of Horus–Sobek at Kom Ombo.

Columns and Pillars

• *Fluted* columns of stone representing bundled reeds or plant stems first appear in the Step Pyramid enclosure of Djoser. Though they were no longer popular in Egypt by New Kingdom times, fluted columns continued to be used in temples in Nubia. In Egypt proper the fluted form was sometimes replaced by a somewhat similar version – the polygonal column shaft.

• *Palmiform* columns did not represent the palm tree itself but eight palm fronds lashed to a pole. This was one of the earliest column types used in Egyptian temple architecture, and the granite columns in the 5th-dynasty pyramid temples of Unas were palmiform. Although this type was not commonly used in succeeding periods, it does appear in certain locations. The majority of the columns in the temple of Taharqa at Kawa in Upper Nubia were of this type, and the palmiform column is also found in temples of the Graeco-Roman Period.

• *Lotiform* columns usually have ribbed shafts to represent the plants' stems with a capital representing the closed (bud) or open lotus flower. Although open lotus capitals are evident in a number of ancient representations, few actual examples have been found and they seem to have been more commonly employed in domestic architecture. The simpler lotus-bud form saw widespread use in Old and Middle Kingdom temples and, despite a lessening of its popularity in New Kingdom times, saw use again in the temples of the Graeco-Roman Period.

• *Papyriform* columns with circular or ribbed shafts can represent singular or multistem papyrus plants. The single-stem form is first found in the Step Pyramid enclosure at Saqqara, though these examples are not free-standing but engaged. The single-stem form seems to have been used sporadically from this time on, and saw widespread use in New Kingdom temples with both wide bell-shaped capitals representing the opened umbel of the plant and a simpler closed or bud capital style. The multistem or bundle form

With the exception of some full-length pillars which display the image of the god Bes, the so-called Besiform or Beside columns are actually something of a misnomer. Where the image of the god Bes is placed on the abaci above the capitals of columns, such as those of the Roman birth house at Dendera, these images are technically part of the external temple decoration and not intrinsic to the basic column types above which they are placed.

Doors

As one passes deeper into the heart of an Egyptian temple it is necessary to move through doorways which both protected the sacred inner areas and also acted as liminal points – symbolic thresholds which were necessary elements in the enactment of ritual processions.

The door-leaves (*'awy*) which turned on pivots set into sockets in the threshold and lintel of the doorway (*seba*) were usually made of wood, and those of temples were frequently plated with metal and decorated with texts and inscriptions like their adjacent walls. While it is possible that some temple door-leaves were made entirely from cast metal, Egyptian descriptions of doors of 'metal' seem

(Above) An image of the king at the sides of doors within many temples symbolically cleanses all who enter.

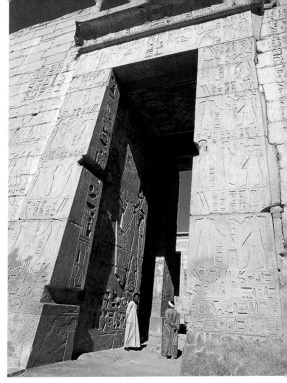

(Above) Channels in the thickness of the first pylon of the temple of Ramesses III at Medinet Habu held the massive doors which sealed the entrance.

first appears in the 5th dynasty and also became popular in the New Kingdom. Earlier examples from the 18th dynasty are often finely detailed, whereas from the 19th dynasty they tend to become more stylized. In the New Kingdom the shafts of most papyriform columns taper upwards from bases decorated with triangular patterns representing stylized stem sheaths.

- *Coniform* columns – fluted shafts bearing capitals apparently mimicking branches of conifer trees – appear in the Step Pyramid enclosure of Djoser but were apparently a short-lived form not found in later temples.

- *Tent-pole*-type columns were perhaps rarely used in stone. The wooden prototypes of this type of column were used to support light structures such as tents, shrines, kiosks or ships' cabins. While the design may possibly have been copied in brick architecture from very early times, the only surviving examples of the tent-pole column in stone are in the Festival Temple of Tuthmosis III at Karnak, though other columns of this type seem to be mentioned in texts.

- *Campaniform* or floral columns or pillars were of different types, having circular, ribbed or square shafts, but all with a capital in the form of an open flower. The Hall of Annals of Tuthmosis III at Karnak contains two famous campaniform pillars, one with the heraldic plant of Lower Egypt (the papyrus) and one with the Upper Egyptian heraldic plant (the lotus) positioned symbolically

on the northern and southern sides of the hall. Such columns were unusual, though stylized campaniform-type columns appear more frequently in temples of the Graeco-Roman Period.

- *Composite* columns were common in the Ptolemaic and Roman periods. The style probably derived from the campaniform column with capital decoration including floral designs derived from numerous real or invented plant forms, though these are often stylized and have lost many indications of their original floral motifs.

Other column and pillar types represented deities or their attributes:

- *Osiride* pillars originated in the Middle Kingdom and consisted of engaged statues of the king in the form of the god Osiris, usually on the pillars' front surfaces.

- *Hathoric* columns also originated in the Middle Kingdom and usually consisted of a shaft surmounted by a capital bearing the features of the cow-headed goddess. This type of column can be seen, for example, in the temple of Nefertari at Abu Simbel, though the hypostyle hall of the Ptolemaic temple at Dendera has the most famous examples in its twenty-four Hathoric columns surrounded on all four sides by the head of the goddess. Sistrum columns are also associated with Hathor, but represent in their shafts and capitals the handles and rattles of the sistrum – the principal attribute of the goddess.

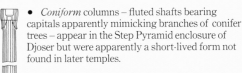

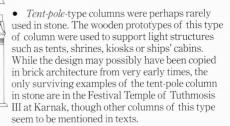

The small holes visible in the side of this doorway at the temple of Ramesses III at Medinet Habu were for metal pins which held hinge panels.

(Below) Steps lead down into a crypt in the temple of Hathor at Dendera.

(Below centre) Cross-section of the Opet Temple at Karnak, showing the crypts within walls and beneath floors.

(Below right) A stairway to the roof in the temple of Hathor, Dendera, with a relief showing gods in procession.

most likely to refer to plated doors, and actual cast metal was most probably used only in small doors such as those of shrines. Copper is the material most commonly specified in such cases, though doors are also described as being covered in bronze, electrum and gold.

Like other features of temple architecture doors were given names, such as that at Karnak Temple which was made by Tuthmosis III: '[The doorway] "Menkheperre, Amun-great-of-strength,whom-the-people-praise," its great door-leaf of cedar of Lebanon worked with bronze, the Great name upon it in electrum.' As noted above, doors also usually had symbolic significance. Like gateways, they represented thresholds as well as barriers and could signify transition in addition to protection. As important thresholds of other worlds or states, doors are commonly shown in representations of the shrines of gods, and the ritual act of opening these doors was symbolic of the opening of the 'doors' of heaven itself. The false doors found in many temples (p. 151) held this same significance as a threshold to the divine.

Subsidiary chambers, storerooms and crypts

Ranged around the central area of the temple's shrine were chambers where the statues of visiting deities would be placed – sometimes with connected suites of rooms for the visitor's use; storerooms for cultic equipment such as the clothing for the god's image, incense, etc; vesting chambers where the priests would prepare themselves for special ceremonies; and other rooms having to do with the daily course of temple ritual.

Many temples also had hidden crypts built into their walls and beneath their floors, especially in the inner part of the temple, and examples are known in temples ranging from the 18th dynasty to the Graeco-Roman Period. Although these crypts are sometimes fancifully believed to have been employed for the enactment of secret rites, the small size or difficulty of access of many of them indicate that they were mainly used for the giving of oracles by hidden priests, as secret storerooms for the safe-keeping of valuable items, or had some symbolic purpose.

Typical examples of hidden crypts may be found in the small temple of the hippopotamus goddess

Opet (p. 162) in the Karnak Temple complex. Despite its relatively small size, this structure has numerous crypts hidden within its walls as well as larger ones built beneath ground level which served as a symbolic 'tomb' for the god Amun (here associated with Osiris) and as repositories for the objects and materials necessary for the Festival of the 'Resurrection' of the god.

Stairs and roof areas

The roof areas of many gods' houses were incorporated into the overall temple structure through both architectural design and the enactment of ritual. In addition to the stairways built within pylon towers, most temples had stairways giving access to the roofs of the hypostyle and inner halls and chambers, and these roof areas were used not only for matters of practical building maintenance but also in the rituals of various temples. This is particularly well documented at Dendera, where we know that as part of the New Year's festival the image of Hathor was taken up one of the temple's staircases (which was itself decorated with figures of the king and the gods participating in this very procession) to the roof, where there was a special chapel in which the goddess awaited the year's first sunrise. In the same way at Edfu a statue of the falcon-god Horus was carried in its portable shrine, accompanied by ancestor gods – also depicted on the walls of the stairwell – to the roof of the temple for the same *khenem-aten* or 'uniting with the sun'. Many other temple processions involved the transfer of the god's image (often from subterranean crypts) up through the temple to the roof, and thus the effective space of the temple was expanded both downwards and upwards in an obvious symbolism embracing the god's activity in the underworld and heavens as well as on earth.

At the practical level, the roofs of many temples had drainage systems to vent rainwater, and the

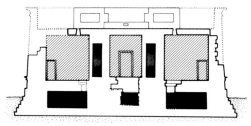

outpour spouts of these systems were often decorated with lion-headed gargoyles (the Hathor temple at Dendera has excellent examples of these) which fused functionality with the apotropaic nature of the lion. A number of later temples also appear to have been given wooden roofs which arched above the stone-built structures, though these wooden additions have long since disappeared.

The offering hall and altars

Altars were sometimes placed in the room preceding the sanctuary, and in such cases this room was used as an offering hall where the sacrifices to the god were made. In other cases, a small altar was placed in the inner sanctuary itself. Altars could take many forms, though the most common varieties were square offering blocks carved and decorated on their sides, or flat slabs resting on cylindrical bases.

In the more extensive temples, larger altars were often positioned in other courts and halls; and several types may be found in these areas, ranging from relatively low, table-like altars to taller, flat-topped altars and those of possible Syrian origin with raised corners. These larger altars sometimes had steps leading to their tops and could be significant structures of quite considerable size.

In all these offering areas the figure of the king is invariably shown standing, bowing or kneeling before the deity in the act of presenting the offerings. His is essentially the active role, and the god or goddess is correspondingly depicted in a static pose receiving the offerings and offices of the king. The reciprocal gifts of the deity to the king are, however, usually explicit in the texts accompanying the representations.

The barque chapel

The innermost parts of the Egyptian temple are often confusingly labelled sanctuaries, chapels, shrines, or other terms. In the present book the room which was the dwelling of the god is referred to as the sanctuary, with the small, often portable structure which held the god's image within that room being referred to as the shrine. One of the rooms often directly preceding the sanctuary was that in which the god's portable barque was housed: the 'barque chapel'.

(Left) A lion-headed waterspout on the rear wall of the temple of Hathor at Dendera.

(Below left) A reconstructed 'horned altar' of Asiatic type in the Great Temple of Amun at Karnak.

(Below) A view of the inner halls, sanctuary and naos in the temple of Horus at Edfu.

As in so many other parts of the Egyptian temple the practical and mythical aspects of the barque shrine were closely intertwined. Ancient Egypt relied on water transport for most journeys of any distance and so mythologically, just as the sun god was believed to traverse the celestial sea by boat, it was natural that the method of transportation of the gods was the barque. Almost every temple therefore had a barque 'shrine' which contained the portable barque used in transporting the image of the god in procession. Rather than an actual boat, the ceremonial barque was made only to be carried on the shoulders of the priests and would be loaded on to a real boat if transportation by water was necessary.

There were two arrangements for housing the ceremonial barque of the god, however. In some temples the barque shrine preceded the inner sanctuary of the god as a separate room or 'shrine', while in others the inner holy place itself contained a shrine housing the barque. In either case, the walls immediately surrounding the barque platform were often decorated with scenes showing the king, with censor, leading the barque as it is carried out of the shrine in procession.

The sanctuary and its shrine

'The shrines were enlarged, the favourites of all the gods,
every one in the shrine which he desired.'

– The Speos Artemidos Inscription of Hatsheput

The heart of every Egyptian temple was its most holy place, the sanctuary of the god which was regarded as the innermost chamber of the god's home. Situated at the rear of the temple, often at the furthest distance from its entrance and thus at its deepest core, the sanctuary invariably stood directly on the temple's main axis, though

subsidiary chapels of associated deities (such as other members of a triad) were often offset from the main sanctuary, sometimes in a symbolically oriented alignment.

Within the sanctuary, the god's shrine itself was often constructed of fine hard stone with bronze or gold-clad wooden doors, though occasionally in smaller temples the whole shrine might be of partially or wholly gilded wood. Usually, shrines took one of two forms. In what was apparently the more common design, the 'naos'-type shrine holding the god's image was closed in on all sides, with double doors facing towards the temple entrance. A second type of shrine – used in temples without separate barque shrines – was open ended, resembling a canopy-like structure in which the god's portable barque stood on a stand or plinth. In this type of shrine the god's image was kept within the cabin of the barque. Sometimes enclosed naos-type shrines were elevated on a raised podium accessed by steps, but this arrangement seems not to have occurred with open shrines – probably to facilitate movement of the god's portable barque.

Although there were only two basic types, the Egyptians nevertheless used numerous terms for their shrines (including the most commonly found *seh netjer*, *kari* and *khem*), no doubt to reflect certain differences in design or function, though often with considerable overlapping of usage. Because of the central importance of the shrine, these terms were also not infrequently used in extension to cover the innermost areas of the temple or even the temple as a whole. Individual shrines were given specific names, however, such as 'favourite of [the god]' or 'the holy shrine of [the god]' in their respective temples. As the most restricted area of the temple the sanctuary was usually accessible only to the king and to the highest echelons of the priesthood. Desecration of the sanctuary (as for instance by invading armies) was tantamount to the desecration of the temple as a whole and would require the rededication of the entire structure. This also meant that in the performance of the temple rituals the highest standards of purification were necessary for all who entered this area – which, for the Egyptians, was no less than a piece or 'place' of heaven on earth. It was here that the image of the god dwelt as the focal point of the whole cult.

The images of the gods were of different sizes, sometimes above, at, or below life-size depending on the material of their construction. The divine images were often of gold – the mythological 'flesh' of the gods – or in some cases (as with lunar gods) silver, sometimes with inset eyes of semiprecious stone and inlays of lapis lazuli, of which the hair of the gods was said to be composed. Even when not wholly made up of precious materials, as was often the case in larger statues mainly of stone or wood, the images were frequently gilded and inlaid in the finest manner.

A replica of the processional barque of Horus mounted on its carrying sled and displayed on a stand in the god's barque chapel at Edfu.

A drawing of a relief from the barque shrine of Amun at Karnak. The barque, supported by images of the king, is mounted at each end with a shield-like aegis bearing an image of the god. The god's statue was placed in the central cabin.

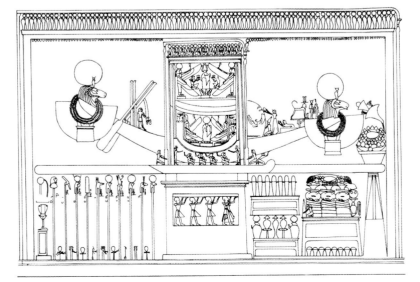

False doors

A number of New Kingdom and later temples have, within their structures, 'false doors' of the kind found in pyramid temples and private tombs from Old Kingdom times. The term 'false door' is itself something of a misnomer as, from the Egyptian perspective, these features were fully functional portals by which the spirit of the deceased might leave or enter the inner tomb to receive the offerings presented to them. In the developed New Kingdom mortuary temple it would seem that the false door, usually placed at the very back of the sanctuary, allowed the spirit of the king to enter the temple from his burial site which was, by this time, located elsewhere. In divine temples where the feature is found, the false door seems to have given special access for those without the temple to the deity within, often in conjunction with the so-called 'hearing' chapels or chapels of the 'hearing ear'.

Chapels of the 'hearing ear'

At the very rear of many temples, directly behind the sanctuary and in the outer walls of the temple structure, was located a chapel of the 'hearing ear'. These chapels were sometimes quite elaborate, but frequently consisted of little more than a niche with a statue of the temple's main god – or simply a pair of the carved ears of the god – to which common people could address their prayers. Such chapels were, in effect, 'back doors' to the temple to which those not purified or generally allowed might have some form of access – albeit indirect – to the inner sanctuary itself.

It is not known for certain when the practice of building these chapels or niches began, though they seem to occur in a number of New Kingdom

temples and to continue into the Graeco-Roman Period. At Karnak, a number of such chapels were built behind the Great Temple of Amun next to the city of Thebes. The earliest surviving was one built by Tuthmosis III and contains large alabaster statues of the king and Amun. A little closer to the city, Ramesses II built a complete small temple of 'the hearing ear' to fulfil the same function.

Although petitions of all kinds were brought to the gods through these chapels, they were, quite naturally, especially favoured by those in ill health. In the temple at Kom Ombo the chapel of the hearing ear takes the form of a niche which along with a cult statue and carvings of the god's ears also contained a pair of sacred eyes – both looking out at the petitioners and symbolizing the health and wholeness which many of them sought.

Often, small chambers or 'priest holes' were constructed within the temple behind such 'hearing ear' niches in order that priests might listen to the petitions of the people and perhaps, at times, deliver oracles on behalf of the god.

(Above left) The false door found in temples of the Old Kingdom pyramid complex – and in tombs, as in this example – is also present in many temples of the New Kingdom and later.

(Above) An intercessary chapel of the 'hearing ear' dedicated to the god Ptah in the entrance gateway of the temple of Ramesses III at Medinet Habu.

Other Temple Structures

Egyptian temples were seldom constructed as structures in isolation. Usually the core temple building was surrounded by a number of subsidiary structures which shared the sacred compound. Some of these ancillary structures – such as mammisis (see below) and sacred lakes – were directly related to the religious functioning of the cult, while others – such as storage magazines and administrative offices – were part of the support mechanisms of the divine estate. Nevertheless, there is evidence that even some of these latter structures were regarded as having religious associations which transcended their apparently mundane roles.

Sacred lakes

Most temples had a sacred lake within their compounds and many have been carefully excavated, showing that, at least from New Kingdom times, they were usually rectangular with straight or slightly incurved sides. Cut so as to access the level of the underlying ground water, the lakes were lined with stone and had a flight of steps leading down from the side of the lake adjacent to the temple proper. These steps were necessary in order to reach the level of the water which varied according to the time of year. Even where their outlines are clearly visible, the sacred lakes of most temples have become filled over time and cannot now be examined; but that at Karnak has been completely cleaned and reflooded to give a sense of the original appearance of this feature.

Normally termed *shi-netjer*, 'divine lake', but also given specific names, the purpose of the sacred lake was both functional and symbolic. Functionally, the lake provided a reservoir for the water used in offerings and rituals of purification, and it was there that the priests bathed at dawn before entering the temple to begin their service.

Symbolically the sacred lake played an important role in representing various aspects of the Egyptians' cosmogonic myths of origin. Because creation was believed to have occurred when the sun god emerged from the primeval waters at the beginning of time, the sacred lake represented in a tangible manner the same underlying forces of life and creation; and in this way creation was symbolically renewed each morning as the sun rose above the sacred waters. The sacred lake at Karnak also had a specific feature which allowed geese held in connected pens to emerge through a narrow tunnel on to the surface of the lake – symbolizing the role of the goose as a manifestation of Amun in original creation. Certain mystery rituals, such as those of the resurrection of Osiris at Sais, were also performed on the shores of the temple's sacred lake.

The sacred lake of the Great Temple of Amun at Karnak has an area of almost 9,250 sq. m (100,000 sq. ft). The water from such sacred lakes was used in ritual purifications and the priests bathed in them at dawn before entering the temple.

Sizes of Sacred Lakes of Selected Temples

[all measurements are approximate]

Karnak, Amun temple	120 × 77 m/395 × 253 ft
Tanis, Amun/Khonsu temple	60 × 50 m/197 × 164 ft
Sais, Neith temple	35 × 34 m/115 × 112 ft
Dendera, Hathor temple	33 × 28 m/109 × 86 ft
Armant, birth house	30 × 26 m/99 × 86 ft
el-Kab, Nekhbet temple	30 × 20 m/99 × 66 ft
Medinet Habu, Small Temple	20 × 18 m/66 × 59 ft
Karnak, Montu temple	18 × 16 m/59 × 53 ft
Medamud, Montu temple	17 × 15 m/56 × 49 ft
Tod, Montu temple	16 × 11.5 m/53 × 38 ft
Elephantine, Khnum temple	11 × 8 m/36 × 26 ft

Nilometers

Well-like gauges designed to measure the height of the river and to predict the annual flooding were probably constructed at points along the Nile from relatively early times. Important early nilometers were constructed at Aswan and Memphis and later ones at the second and fourth cataracts in Nubia. Nilometers can vary considerably in size and style. While some consisted of little more than a few measuring steps at the water's edge, the Nile gauge of Aswan belonging anciently to the temple of Satis consisted of 90 steps descending down the side of the island to the Nile.

Nilometers might be open or might have steps flanked by walls, sometimes covered with a roof.

The structures labelled nilometers on temple plans in some guidebooks are in fact ancient wells, and true nilometers can usually be recognized by their location relative to that of the course of the Nile in antiquity. Many later temples had their own nilometers even when they were in close proximity to those of other temples. On the island of Philae there are two such structures within a few hundred metres, one descending down the side of the cliff from the colonnade near the temple of Nectanebo I on the southwest corner of the island, the other further to the north near the Ptolemaic mammisi.

Mammisis

A mammisi or 'birth house' (a term coined by Champollion from Coptic Egyptian) is a special, independent structure located within the temple precincts in which the mysteries associated with the birth of a god's offspring (such as the child-god Harpocrates or Horus the Younger) were celebrated. Symbolically, these structures may be seen to be related to the birth rooms which were dedicated to the divine conception and birth of kings in some New Kingdom temples (p. 170). Though the focus on the birth of a god is clearly primary in mammisis, the divine relationship of the king to the gods is also frequently stressed.

Mammisis were present in all the major Graeco-Roman temples. Perhaps the best known and most complete is that of the Temple of Hathor at Dendera, which was dedicated to Ihy (the son of Hathor and Horus) by the Roman emperor Augustus and decorated during the reign of Trajan. A small temple in its own right, this mammisi provides graphic explanation in its decoration and texts of the purpose of these structures. There are also the remains of an earlier birth house at Dendera begun by Nectanebo I of the 30th dynasty. Other major birth houses may be found at Philae (celebrating the birth of Horus), Kom Ombo (Panebtawy), Edfu (Harsomptus) and Armant (Harpre).

The architectural style of the Ptolemaic and later mammisi is usually distinctive. An entrance or vestibule area opens into a somewhat shortened building, often within a surrounding peristyle with screen-like walls between the columns. Today, the forward areas of the birth house at Edfu are best preserved, while the rear section of that of Dendera is most complete. Both, however, provide a fine example of this type of building.

The inner walls of these structures are usually decorated with representations connected to their special purpose and are often inscribed with extensive hymns to the main members of the triad and the child deity. At Dendera, the whole range of events from the courtship of the parent deities through the birth and presentation of their child is depicted, including a particularly famous scene showing the formation of the child Ihy on the

(Far left) The Nilometer at Elephantine. Such structures were used to measure the height of the Nile's annual flood.

(Below) Ritual or possibly medical instruments depicted in a relief at the temple of Sobek and Haroeris at Kom Ombo may demonstrate the healing functions of some temples.

potter's wheel. In the birth houses at Edfu, Dendera and other sites a number of other deities were associated with the triads to whom the buildings were dedicated. Selected deities are frequently shown praising the young god, and apotropaic figures of the god Bes were often carved in relief on the abaci of the columns. In several birth houses the particular characteristics of Hathor are celebrated as goddess of music and intoxication in addition to her role as great mother goddess.

The house of life

The institution associated with the temples called *per ankh* or 'house of life' by the Egyptians seems to have fulfilled many functions. The exact relationship between the *per ankh* and the temple is not always clear, however, and it may be that some houses of life developed more of an independent identity than others.

Perhaps primarily the *per ankh* functioned as a scriptorium where the religious and mythical texts of the cult were written, copied, collated, edited and stored. These texts included not only the Egyptians' mythical and theological treatises and related documents, but also texts of recitations used in the performance of temple rituals and the master copies of new inscriptions which were to be carved on the temple walls or on obelisks or other features. Perhaps it was here, from the New Kingdom on, that the copies of the Book of the Dead often used in the Egyptian funerary assemblage were produced – sometimes for specific individuals and sometimes as templates later to be personalized by the inclusion of individuals' names.

Many of the texts preserved and copied in the house of life were considered sacred, as they dealt with divinely revealed matters – called by the Egyptians the *ba re* meaning the 'soul' or 'emanation' of Re. These sacred books were believed to be divinely inspired in virtually the same manner as the scriptures of the great monotheistic faiths of today. But there is some evidence to suggest that the house of life may have been divided into two areas, or in some cases abutted against a separate building

A detail from Papyrus Salt 825 depicting a per ankh – *the temple scriptorium and 'house of life'.*

where temple accounts, contracts, correspondence and other temple records were kept.

The house of life seems to have been much more than just a scriptorium and archive, however; it also appears to have functioned as a centre of priestly learning in many fields. While not necessarily a school as we might think of a modern educational institution, the subjects of writing, art, theology, ritual, magic, astronomy and medicine, among others, were certainly studied there. The large collections of books kept in the houses of life were famous throughout much of the ancient world, and in the 2nd century AD the medical writer Galen wrote that Greek physicians visited the library of the *per ankh* of Memphis to learn from its texts. Such libraries of the great temples were almost certainly the model upon which the famed Museion or Library of Alexandria was based, and the very idea of the university as it was later developed by Moslem and European societies, with its concentration of scholars and learned religious men, was to some extent the product of the ancient Egyptian tradition of the *per ankh*.

A final aspect of the *per ankh* is its role in relation to the court and to international diplomacy. Although the royal court employed numbers of scribes and scholars, it was unquestionably the *per ankh* that was regarded as the centre of learning in every sphere. It is no small boast that Ramesses IV made, therefore, in one of his inscriptions in the Wadi Hammamat, that he had studied all the texts of the *per ankh* in order to discover the secrets of the gods. Neither was this a purely religious statement, for it implies great learning in all aspects of knowledge. The priest Pa-ti-Ist who was selected to accompany Psammetichus (Psamtik) II in his expedition to Syria is said to have been told 'Look, you are a scribe of the House of Life, there is nothing on which you could be questioned to which you would not find an answer!'

Sanatoria

A number of the great temples probably had sanatoria within their compounds where the sick could be brought – primarily to seek healing from the gods but also, perhaps, to seek the wisdom of the priests and learned men of the temples. The remains of sanatoria in areas not originally built as such are, in fact, suspected in several temples – including the temple of Hatshepsut at Deir el-Bahri (p. 175) – but the only clear remains of a sanatorium built for this purpose survive at the Graeco-Roman Period temple at Dendera (p. 149).

Hathor was revered as a goddess of compassion, and her temple at Dendera developed a reputation for healing which meant that people perhaps travelled considerable distances to seek her help. Her sanatorium consisted of numerous chambers where the sick rested, awaiting the dreams that brought divine prescriptions for their recovery, and

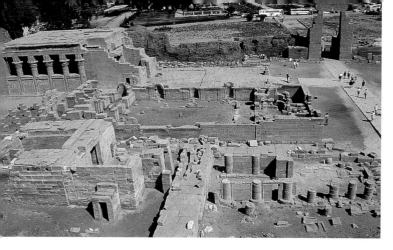

(Left) The remains of the sanatorium at the temple of Dendera are visible in the lower left; in the background is the Roman mammisi.

(Right) The sick awaited healing dreams in these cells at Dendera's sanatorium.

a central courtyard where priests poured water over statues inscribed with magical texts so that the healing power of the spells might pass into the water which was then used for drinking or bathing.

Kitchens, workshops and studios

The larger houses of the gods also often contained their own industries within the temple's perimeter walls. These supplied the practical needs of the cult and might include bakeries and breweries to produce the bread and beer which were among the staples of the Egyptian diet – and which were also offered in large quantities to the gods – as well as slaughterhouses, butchers' work areas, kitchens and various workshops which produced goods such as the fine linen garments worn by the priests.

There were also workshops and studios to provide and repair objects such as cult images and items of temple furniture used in the service of the cult, as well as areas for the preparation of food offerings, floral arrangements and other gifts for the gods.

Magazines, stores and granaries

Storage areas were also needed to hold supplies of items produced by the temple workforce as well as gifts, payments and offerings brought in from outside. Such magazines and granaries, which we might regard as purely mundane storage areas, were in the Egyptian mind integrated to some extent into the sacred realm of the divine estate. Granaries, for example, were often the sites of specific religious rituals. New Kingdom tomb scenes show offerings being made to the gods in these areas, and a relief on the granary of Amun at Karnak shows Hapy presenting offerings to the grain and harvest goddess Renenutet.

Likewise, a stone dais next to the magazines at the end of the portico along the façade of the Ramesseum on the Theban west bank and a similar dais in the court giving access to the magazines of Sethos I's mortuary temple at Abydos seem to include features with specific cultic functions tied to these areas. While our knowledge of the precise

situation is imperfect, it is clear that even the areas of storage found within temple compounds could be regarded as participating in the same religious sphere as the other temple features in the divine estate.

Beyond the temple walls

Beyond the sacred area which held the temple proper each house of the god had its own estates, often with their own related production and storage facilities. While most of the temple lands consisted of open farmland, there were also vineyards and gardens (Karnak alone had some 433 of the latter in the time of Ramesses III). Temple estates also included areas such as marshlands, quarries and mines, all of which were exploited for temple use and in the running of the temple economy.

Temple lands were sometimes at considerable distances from the environs of the temple itself, and in the New Kingdom we find the temple of Sethos I, for example, controlling large areas even south of the second cataract in Nubia. In totality, the Egyptian temple thus often represented no less than a slice of Egypt itself. The concept of microcosm is more than just a metaphor when applied to the Egyptian temple, for in many cases it functioned, as well as symbolically represented, a world within the world.

These large vaulted mud-brick magazines and other subsidiary structures are situated in the precinct of the Ramesseum, western Thebes.

Temple Symbolism

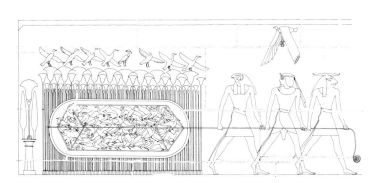

In this drawing of a relief from the temple of Khnum, Esna, the king, in the company of the gods, nets wildfowl in the marshes. The scene is symbolic of the king's role in controlling the forces of chaos.

In the world of giant metaphors which was the Egyptian temple, each element in the overall architectural programme played a role in symbolizing some aspect of the origins and function of the cosmos itself – a fact that has been touched upon repeatedly in this section and will now be addressed directly.

There is no single model by which we may understand the symbolic complexities of the Egyptian temple, for the ancient structures often represented many concepts that had evolved over time and in different locations and settings. In the developed temple, individual features might be designed and decorated to appeal to or to strengthen any one or more of those ideas. This is because Egypt's mythology was complex, many-faceted and replete with different, and even contradictory, ways of viewing the same facts – a situation which was nevertheless acceptable within the overall system of Egyptian religion.

From very early times, however, three great themes – original cosmic structure, ongoing cosmic function and cosmic regeneration – may be seen to be recurrent in Egyptian temple symbolism. Although separately developed, for the Egyptians these ideas were complementary, for the world's creation allowed its ongoing function and its regeneration – which was itself a form of continued creation. In the developed Egyptian temple these ideas are often all present, though some temples stress one aspect over the others.

Cosmic structure: original creation

At the beginning of time, according to a view which seems to have been ancient and widespread, a mound of earth rose from the ubiquitous primeval waters of existence. Eventually a great hawk or

falcon appeared which settled on a single reed growing on this island. As a sacred place, the area needed protection, and so a simple wall stood around the reed and the god who perched thereon. At its most basic level, this myth is reflected in the structure of the Egyptian temple from earliest times, with the original mound doubtless being the mythical prototype for the revetted mounds of sand found in the early temple sites of Hierankonpolis and elsewhere (p. 203).

A great many features of the later, developed temple reflect this same idea of the domain of the god as a created world in microcosm. The temple roof was the heaven of this model world, and as such was usually decorated with stars and flying birds. The floor, correspondingly, was regarded as the great marsh from which the primeval world arose; and the great columns of the pillared courts and halls were made to represent palm, lotus or papyrus plants, with their intricately worked capitals depicting the leaves or flowers of these species,

(Opposite above) Blue ceilings studded with gold stars symbolized the heavens in the microcosm which was the Egyptian temple.

(Left) Winged solar discs beneath the lintels of Ramesses III's monument at Medinet Habu trace the symbolic path of the sun along the temple's axis.

as much to reflect the nature of the original world as the original nature of the materials used to build such columns.

The lower sections of the temple walls were also often decorated with representations of marsh plants, and the entire effect was considerably heightened in temples where the outer courts and pillared hall were actually flooded – sometimes by design – in the annual inundation of the Nile. The 'Flood Stela' of Sobekhotep VIII which records such flooding at Karnak reveals that this could be seen as a divine sign in no way contrary to the nature and function of the temple. In the same way, as noted above, the girdle wall which surrounded the temple complex was often built with alternating concave and convex layers or foundation to represent the waves of the watery environment of the First Time.

In most Egyptian temples, the height of the various architectural elements gradually decreased towards the rear of the temple, while the floor level gradually rose towards the raised inner sanctuary. Symbolically, this was consistent with the lower, marsh-like environment surrounding the primeval earth mound that rose from the waters at the world's beginning. The elevated position of the temple's innermost area also symbolized the relation of the structure to *maat* – the underlying 'order' upon which the world rested – as the ramps and stairways leading up to the temple's entrance and its inner sections formed visual reminders of the ramps or plinths upon which statues of the gods were placed and which were made in the form of the hieroglyph ⊏ used to write the word *maat* itself.

Cosmic function: the solar cycle

Just as these elements of structural design seem to have symbolized the original creation of the world, other aspects of temple symbolism represented the ongoing functioning of the cosmos by reflecting the sun's diurnal cycle. The entrance pylons were built to mirror the form of the hieroglyph for *akhet*, 'horizon', on which the sun rose each day. The main

The akhet *or horizon hieroglyph is mirrored by the massive entrance pylon of the temple of Ramesses III at Medinet Habu and other Egyptian temples.*

Akhenaten's great solar temple at Amarna reversed standard temple symbolism in its progression from shadowed entrance to open temple core which was filled with hundreds of altars to the sun.

processional path of the temple thus replicated the course of the sun in its daily journey across the world, rising above the pylons in the east, moving through the columned halls and courts where its image appears under the lintels and architraves, and setting finally in the west, where the inner sanctuary was situated. The gradually decreasing height of the various elements of the standard temple plan towards the rear mimicked this movement, and in most cases the various areas became increasingly less well-lit until almost complete darkness was reached in the shrine itself.

Only in the Amarna Period, during the 18th dynasty, was this principle reversed when the heretic Akhenaten effectively turned the Egyptian temple programme inside out by designing the

Great Temple of the Aten at Amarna to progress from relative darkness into totally unshaded light. Unless something similar existed at Heliopolis, this radical shift from the normal temple plan did not survive Akhenaten himself and appears to have left little in the way of lasting influence. In some later New Kingdom structures – such as the Great Temple of Ramesses III at Medinet Habu – separate chapels are sometimes found with open courts dedicated to the sun-god Re or Re-Horakhty, but this is a far cry from the totally solarcentric revisions of the Amarna Age.

Other symbolic forms in the standard Egyptian temple plan also echoed the daily solar cycle. The pairs of obelisks placed on each side of the entrance pylons were certainly solar-symbolic and thus sometimes dedicated to the morning and evening manifestations of the sun god, but they may also have functioned to some degree as a form of the two mountains of the horizon upon which the pylons themselves were modelled. The papyriform columns found in many temples – closed in the outer courts and open in the inner halls – could be symbolic of the sun's journey as the furled umbels of the plant open with the daylight.

Carefully located texts and representations of the sun god delineate this solar journey in many temples, and the heraldic plants or other symbols of Lower and Upper Egypt which are often placed on the northern and southern walls of temples (p. 37) may have been primarily utilized to strengthen, clarify and enhance the east-to-west solar journey motif as much as to show the intersecting cardinal directions themselves.

Cosmic renewal: the temple as tomb

There is also a third, somewhat less obvious, aspect of temple symbolism. Unlike the previous features

(Left) The peristyle court and hypostyle hall of Luxor Temple present a veritable grove of papyrus bundle columns symbolic of the primeval marsh from which creation unfolded according to Egyptian mythology.

of cosmic structure and function which were incorporated into the overall design of the developed temple, the idea of regeneration or renewal effected by the temple as tomb was an important principle central to the meaning of many temples, but one often given more isolated expression within individual temple structures.

According to the Egyptian world view, the temple stood at the nexus of the three spheres of heaven, earth and the netherworld; and it thus served as a kind of portal by which gods and men might pass from one realm to the other. In the same way that the temple pylon functioned symbolically as an *akhet* or 'horizon' in terms of the solar cycle, so the whole temple functioned as a kind of temporal and spatial *akhet* (see box). Just as the physical horizon is the interface between heaven and earth – and in terms of the setting sun between today and tomorrow, the present and future, this world and the beyond – so the temple, of whatever type, was regarded as an *akhet* or interface between these spheres or realms and was often described as such.

Not only do many temple representations and texts make this clear, but the interface between temple and tomb was also reflected in certain architectural features. A number of temples have within their structures features such as 'false doors' of the kind found in pyramid temples and private tombs from Old Kingdom times (p. 71). Further, the inner sanctuaries of Graeco-Roman Period temples often appear to be nested like the shrines around royal coffins, and in all temples the image of the deity could be seen as a *ka*-statue (representing the life force), while the offerings of food and material goods made to the god resemble the offerings made to the dead. Pyramids were associated with temples by means of their mortuary cults, private tombs were sometimes made to resemble temples, and

The Egyptian Temple in Space and Time

The Egyptian temple functioned in both spatial and temporal dimensions. Spatially, the temple stood at a crucial point – the focal point or fulcrum between different worlds or spheres – between heaven and earth, human and divine, chaos and order. For the Egyptians most of these concepts were spatially related, just as the desert signified chaos and the fertile land of Egypt harmony and order. The temple's location, design, decoration and functions all mediated between these polarities and established harmony, security and balance where there would have been none of these things in its absence.

Temporally, the sanctuaries and shrines of the gods and kings also acted as a fulcrum which balanced the present and the past, the uncertain future and the ordered security and *maat* of original creation. Symbol and ritual together propelled the temple and thus the world through the continuum of time and created as much as they marked the passage of days, months, seasons and years.

Yet the Egyptian temple was not viewed as a perpetual motion machine – a *perpetuum mobile* – which would guarantee security and harmony forever. Just as Egyptian theology accepted the notion that the gods themselves could – and would – eventually die, and that the world would finally revert to the chaos from which it originally arose, so the temple was viewed theologically as a machine which was not immune from breakage and which, through ritual and mythology, symbol and festival, must be carefully guarded as it was operated, and strengthened as it was used.

temples were sometimes conceived as the tombs of gods or men or even contained such tombs (see p. 113, p. 148 and p. 193), so that the interrelationship between the rituals of life and death, this world and the next, were never distant in the minds and religious structures of the ancient Egyptians.

The symbolism inherent in the Egyptian temple was closely linked to the various temple activities – as in this Opet procession depicted in the first court of Luxor Temple – just as myth and ritual were inextricably intertwined in Egyptian religion.

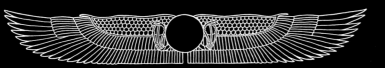

The Religious Functions of the Temple

'Hail to you … Lord of eternity, king of gods, of many names, of holy forms, of secret rites in temples!'

The Great Hymn to Osiris

Perhaps nowhere else and at no other time in the history of humankind have religious edifices functioned so perfectly both as symbolic models of the cosmos and as divine machines for its ritual support and renewal as in ancient Egypt. Designed with every detail as part of a carefully ordered symbolism, the Egyptian temple was indeed a working model of the universe. Served by the king himself and by the priests who were his surrogates, the Egyptian gods received the attentions of daily rituals and recurrent festivals which were aimed at the upholding of not only the world of the temple but also the larger world which it represented.

Perfectly positioned between the human and divine spheres, between this world and the next, between the ancient past and the distant future, the temple was, for the Egyptians, the great interface of reality and myth where all things came together. Thus the gods, kingship and a desire for the renewal of life – arguably the most important concerns of ancient Egyptian civilization – were all brought together in the functioning of Egypt's temples and the practice of their cults. Far from some slavish theocracy, the rituals which bound the gods and their human subjects were aimed at fulfilling the special needs of both.

Thus, although never a place of worship accessible to all in the sense of modern religious structures, the Egyptian temple nevertheless stood at the heart of all Egyptian life. In actual day-to-day practice, the vast numbers of priests and temple personnel who staffed the mansions of the gods were responsible not only for the temple's many religious rituals but also for many of the economic, educational, legal and other aspects of Egyptian society. Ultimately, the Egyptian temple was also the stage on which a transcendent cosmic play was performed: a play in which the king and the priestly echelons took leading parts, but in which even the people of Egypt themselves could play a collective role.

The king with deities from the temple of Kom Ombo.

IV BETWEEN HEAVEN AND EARTH

The Egyptian Gods and their Cults

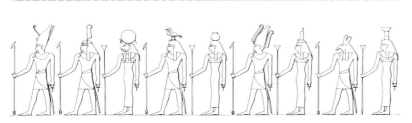

The Ennead of Heliopolis combined the solar god Re with the chthonic god Osiris and their associated deities. Egypt's gods were multiplied by the creation of artificial 'families' and the fusion of existing gods into new composite deities.

The great triads of Thebes: Amun, Mut and Khonsu (below); and of Memphis: Ptah, Sekhmet and Nefertem (bottom).

(Below right) Akhenaten's worship of the solar Aten had a profound impact on Egypt's religion and temples.

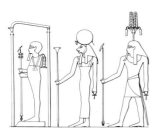

Although it was known throughout the ancient world for its seemingly countless gods – and could indeed boast hundreds of deities – the functional Egyptian pantheon was in many ways far narrower than it might ostensibly appear. The number of deities which inhabited the temples of ancient Egypt and which received the service of established cults was, in fact, surprisingly small.

Many supposedly separate deities were in reality the same god or goddess called by different names in different localities or represented in different manifestations. A distinction must also be made between the greater or cosmic deities who were the subject of the cosmogonic and cosmographic myths of ancient Egypt and who stood at the heart of the Egyptians' theologies, and the many minor household gods and demons which were the subject of popular religion and afterlife speculation. With very few exceptions, only the former group was represented in temple worship; and not all the cosmic deities themselves received veneration in any widespread manner. Of the group of gods which formed the Great 'Ennead' of Heliopolis, for example, none of the first six deities received the widespread dedication of cults, and of the Ogdoad of eight deities worshipped at Hermopolis only Amun received this same honour. One reason for this is perhaps because some deities were artificially created or assigned by priestly theologians in the construction of complex mythological systems. In any event, there may be no clear connection between a deity's cosmic or mythic role and the existence or non-existence of local cult centres.

More commonly, as time progressed, deities were organized into family triads of a 'father', 'mother' and 'son' in the cults of the major temples – as with Osiris, Isis and Horus at Abydos; Amun, Mut and Khonsu at Thebes; or Ptah, Sekhmet and Nefertem at Memphis. This principle effectively strengthened the position of some deities and meant that others, not included in important temple 'families', tended to be relegated to less influential status and to be less likely to receive cultic service.

Many gods and the oneness of the divine

Underlying the differences between the individual gods and their various manifestations Egyptian theology seems to have included the abstract notion of a kind of universal divinity. From the earliest times the Egyptian term for god, *netjer*, was represented in the written language by the flag flown at the entrance to primitive shrines – showing not only the close relationship between deity and temple but also that the term could be used to describe any and every god. The term 'god' is thus often used in Egyptian literature without any specification and in a general sense that cannot refer to one particular deity. Thus statements such as, 'It is not the will of man which comes to realization but the plan of god' (Wisdom of Ptahotep), which are found in at least the later periods of Egyptian history, represent a kind of universal divine power or oneness in which all the gods participated. This underlying unity may be clearly seen in the famous litany found in the Leiden Papyrus:

> 'All the gods are three:
> Amun, Re and Ptah, without their seconds
> His identity is hidden in Amun,
> His is the Sun as face, his body is Ptah.'

It is perhaps this attitude, rather than the monistic Atenism of the Amarna Period, which represents the closest the Egyptians came to monotheism – for from the traditional Egyptian perspective, Akhenaten's exclusive worship of the solar god would likely have been viewed as heretically limiting the universal divine rather than strengthening it, even apart from its obvious attack on the other established deities.

This movement towards the centrality or unity of the divine may also be seen in the process of syncretism. As time progressed, various Egyptian gods were often merged – a lesser deity usually being assimilated into a more well-known one. Thus there arose gods such as Montu-Re and Sobek-Re.

Sometimes there was a natural logic in the fusion of complementary opposites as in Atum-Khepri, the gods of evening and morning, and even the most important fusion of all, that of Amun-Re – the fusion of the Hidden One with the blazing sun god. Multiple gods could also become assimilated

(Below) Horus accompanied by falcon- and jackal-headed bearers in a relief from the god's temple at Edfu.

(Bottom) A Ptolemaic relief depicting Ptah (damaged), Isis and the tiny infant Harsomptus.

Deities of Some Principal Egyptian Cult Sites

Deity	Appearance, character or role	Relationship to other gods	Sacred animal object or attribute	Principal temple/s
Amun/ Amun-Re	Anthropomorphic New Kingdom king of gods	Husband of Mut Father of Khonsu	Ram Goose	Karnak Luxor
Aten	Solar disc		Sun disc	Thebes Akhetaten
Atum	Anthropomorphic The setting sun	Father of the Ennead	Lion, Ichneumon	Heliopolis
Bastet	Cat-headed woman		Cat	Bubastis
Hathor	Mother goddess		Cow, sistrum	Dendera
Horakhty	The morning sun		Falcon, sphinx	Heliopolis, Giza
Horus	Falcon, falcon-headed sky god/ Son of Osiris	Son of Osiris and Isis	Falcon	Hierakonpolis Behdet Edfu
Isis	Mother goddess	Wife of Osiris Mother of Horus	Throne	Philae Behbeit el-Hagar
Khepri	The rising sun		Scarab beetle	Heliopolis
Khonsu	Lunar god	Son of Amun and Mut	Moon	Karnak
Khnum	Creator, guardian of source of Nile		Ram	Elephantine Esna
Min	Mummiform god of fertility		Min fetish, lettuce	Coptos Akhmim
Mut	Vulture-headed goddess	Wife of Amun Mother of Khonsu	Vulture	Karnak
Neith	Warrior goddess	Mother of Re at Sais	Bow and crossed arrows, red crown	Sais
Nut	Sky goddess		Ceramic pot	Heliopolis
Osiris	Mummiform god of underworld	Husband of Isis Father of Horus	Crook and flail	Abydos Busiris
Ptah	Mummiform god of creation and craftsmen	Husband of Sekhmet Father of Nefertem	*Djed-was* sceptre Apis bull	Memphis
Re	Falcon-headed sun god	Father of Maat	Sun disc, falcon	Heliopolis
Sekhmet	Lion-headed goddess of desert, storm and pestilence	Wife of Ptah Mother of Nefertem	Lioness	Memphis Letopolis
Seth	Human or animal god of chaos	Brother of Osiris, adversary of Horus	Mythic hybrid	Ombos Tanis
Sobek	Crocodile god of water and fertility		Crocodile	The Fayum Kom Ombo
Thoth	Lunar god, patron of scribes		Ibis, baboon	Hermopolis Magna

Ramesses III presents gold and other precious gifts to Amun-Re. The gods regularly received huge offerings from the king.

The interrelation of cults

While some scholars see this process of syncretism as a movement towards monotheism, others feel the opposite was accomplished in the creation of ever more new gods. But however we judge this situation, it is clear that from the perspective of the Egyptian temple this process contributed to the fact that certain gods were able to attain functional alliances or fusions which strengthened their own positions and the power of their cults.

Another way that cults interacted and to some degree strengthened each other was through the visits that divine images would pay to other temples, and it is clear that interaction often occurred in this manner between cults of the same deity housed in different locations under different names or forms. Amun, Re and Osiris were gods with many such manifestations, and the Inundation of the Nile too was worshipped as a deity from one end of the country to the other. Rites and festivals of certain temples thus took cognizance of the god's forms in other areas and visits between two forms of the same god frequently occurred.

Deities unrelated except through mythology or popular belief also interacted. During the New

through the principle of association, the composite Ptah-Sokar-Osiris, for example, representing in one deity the related principles of creation, death and the afterlife.

A procession of deities related to fertility, including (right) the personification of the sea and marshes. This fine relief is from the mortuary temple of the pyramid of Sahure at Abusir.

Kingdom and later, for example, Amun-Re of Luxor would visit the 'tomb' of the primordial gods on the west bank of the Nile at Medinet Habu (p. 193) every ten days – each time that a new 'hour star' (a bright star whose rising marked the beginning of one of the hours of the night) rose heliacally according to the Egyptian's complex astronomical calendar. The frequency of these visits underscores the importance of the interactive relationship for the cult of Amun. In this sense even the royal mortuary temples interacted with major established cults in that they were dedicated as much to the assimilation of their patron kings with the deities Osiris, Re or Amun, etc, as they were to the deification of the kings as individuals.

Interaction between cults also extended beyond the religious to the economic and social spheres. Though these latter areas are more difficult to document, it seems that interaction was to the advantage of most temples, as smaller cults might profit from the prestige and power of larger ones and the larger cults could often accept their smaller neighbours as part of their own extended theological cosmos rather than as competitors.

Foreign Gods in Egyptian Temples

While some Egyptian deities were given epithets relating to foreign areas such as 'Hathor Mistress of Byblos', this practice often had nothing to do with the geographic origin of these deities, but rather associations made later in their histories. On the other hand, a number of deities of foreign origin were known to the Egyptians through trading, immigration of foreigners, or military activity, and some of these deities were eventually incorporated into the Egyptian pantheon. As might be expected, and as was the case with the later Greek and Roman acceptance of Egyptian gods, these deities were frequently identified with indigenous Egyptian gods and goddesses. The Syrian god Horan, for example, possessed a sanctuary close to the Sphinx at Giza with which he came to be directly associated.

Yet the non-Egyptian names, characteristics and iconographies of foreign deities are frequently preserved. Old Kingdom examples of this are the gods Dedwen and Ash, both of whom probably originated to the south of Egypt. Likewise, in New Kingdom times we find that the Western Asiatic gods Baal and Reshep and the goddesses Anat and Astarte were all assimilated into the Egyptian pantheon to a significant degree. The god Baal was frequently associated with the Egyptian god Seth, yet a temple was built to Baal as a distinct deity in the harbour district of Memphis; and the god Reshep also had a temple in that area. Temples to both Anat and Astarte are known to have been built at Tanis and perhaps elsewhere.

Later in Egyptian history an even wider range of foreign deities was represented in localized shrines, cultic niches and small temples (though many were simply worshipped by small groups of foreigners present in Egypt). For the Persian Period, for example, we have evidence of the worship of the Israelite Yahu (Yahweh) at Elephantine, and the Asiatic Banit, Bethel, (perhaps) Anat and Nabu at Syene and elsewhere. From the same time, decoration in the temple of Hibis catalogues a number of foreign deities revered at that location, including an unusual representation of the goddess Astarte depicted on horseback with bow and arrows.

Sometimes Egyptian deities were intentionally fused with those of foreign lands. Perhaps most successful of all Egypt's deities of this type was Serapis, the composite deity introduced during the reign of Ptolemy I. Based primarily on Osiris and Apis, but also embodying aspects of the Greek gods Zeus, Asklepios and Dionysos, the cult of Serapis was popular among Greeks and Egyptians alike, and spread from Alexandria through much of the Mediterranean world.

The Western Asiatic god Reshep (top) and the goddess Qadesh (above) both became established in Egyptian religion in New Kingdom times.

The Hellenistic composite deity Serapis combined Osiris and Apis with elements of various Greek gods in a complex fusion.

The Role of the King

'The king of Upper and Lower Egypt came. He made a great prostration before [the goddess], as every king has done. He made a great offering of every good thing ... as every beneficent king has done.'

– Inscription of Udjahorresne

Nowhere in the ancient world was the ideology of kingship more highly developed than in Egypt; and perhaps nowhere in human history was it more deeply intertwined with religious beliefs. As a veritable son of god the Egyptian pharaoh functioned as a bridge between perceived and believed reality – positioned between gods and mortals, he acted on behalf of the gods to his people and on behalf of the people to the gods themselves.

The service of the gods

The king's involvement in the service of the gods began with the very foundation of a new temple or the expansion of an existing structure in the 'stretching of the cord' ceremony (p. 38) whereby the site was oriented and the boundaries of the building delineated. Theoretically, from this point on everything which was done within the temple was done in the king's name and on his behalf. This included not only the building and decoration of the temple but also, once completed, its protection and upkeep, the perpetuation of its sacred status, and the regular sacrifices and offerings made for the care of the gods, as well as the special activities of the gods' festivals such as journeys to other temples or sacred locations.

(Below) A black granite statue of the pharaoh Amenemhet III wearing the wig, collar and leopard-skin of a setem *priest, from Mit Faris, Fayum.*

To what extent the king actually took part in these activities can only be surmised. Egyptian kings are known to have travelled in circuit to participate in the festivals of the most important cults, but while they did often personally visit the gods to offer to them and to officiate in important ceremonies, it is obvious that they could not have served all the gods all of the time in all of the temples. Thus, in addition to the recording of specific, actual, royal gifts to the gods (such as obelisks, statues and other monuments), the king's role is constantly depicted in the temple decoration in purely generic service. New Kingdom representations include scenes of the king in many aspects of the intimate service of the gods, ranging from offering food, drink, incense, clothing and other regular gifts, to leading the god's barque from its shrine in processional activities and participating in subsequent rituals.

The daily ritual

The primary ritual activities of the Egyptian temple – such as those which were aimed at the care and maintenance of the divine image – were performed frequently and with precise regularity by the king or, in practice, more usually by the priests.

Twice each day – in the morning and evening – the ritually purified king, or the high priest officiating on his behalf, would enter the inner sanctuary of the temple and break the seal on the door of the shrine containing the image of the god. Unveiling the image, the officiant would then prostrate himself before the god, and after intoning hymns of adoration he would circumambulate the shrine with elaborate censings and other activities such as the presentation of Maat (see below). The statue of the deity would then be brought forth and washed, its eyes lined with fresh kohl, anointed with fine oil and dressed in clean clothes and various insignia and items of jewelry.

Although various high priests claim that they alone performed these rituals or that they performed them with their own hands, it is likely that various attendants assisted. At Memphis, in the Old Kingdom, for example, the offices of 'robing priest' and 'keeper of the headdress adorning Ptah' were prerogatives of the high priest himself, though other high-ranking priests may have held practical responsibility for the god's wardrobe and treasures as they are known to have done elsewhere.

After the cleansing and revestment were completed, an elaborate meal was offered to the god, the

(Opposite) A relief showing the shrine of the cult image of Amun being opened by the king, from the temple of Sethos I at Abydos. Direct service of the image of the god was a royal prerogative exercised on at least certain occasions.

(Left) The jubilee 'race' was another royal ritual that affirmed the king's relationship with the gods through the fulfilment of his divinely sponsored role. This relief shows Djoser engaged in the ritual run, from the 'South Tomb' in his pyramid complex at Saqqara.

The King and the Temples in the Decree of Canopus

Although it is from the latest period in Egyptian history, the Canopus Decree – issued in 238 BC by a synod of priests in the reign of Ptolemy III – well shows the balance of interaction between the king and the temples, with the king's benefits to the gods and their temples being reciprocated by priestly support and deification for members of the royal family. The following points represent the main clauses of the decree:

I   Date.
II   Introduction.
III   Reasons for the decree. The royal couple are doing good deeds for the temples.
IV   Care of the royal couple for the divine animals. Return of statues of gods stolen by the Persians.
V   Protection of Egypt against foreign enemies and the maintenance of law.
VI   The mitigation of famine.
VII   Decision of the priests to increase the glory of the royal couple.
VIII   Appointment of priests of the 'beneficent gods' and arrangement of a fifth class of priests.
IX   Selection, rights and regulations of the new class of priests.
X   The festival for the 'beneficent gods' to be celebrated on the day of the heliacal rising of Sirius.
XI   Intercalation of a sixth epagomenal or leap day to prevent a displacement of the calendar year.
XII   At the demise of the princess Berenike the priests apply for her apotheosis and establish a cult for her.
XIII   The ceremony for the deified princess Berenike.
XIV   Setting up of a golden procession statue of the princess, with a special crown.
XV   Preparation of a second statue of the deified princess Berenike and its worship.
XVI   The living of the daughters of the priests. The 'bread of Berenike'.
XVII   The manner of publication of the decree.

'menu' of which is often to be found inscribed on the walls of the temple sanctuaries. Foods might include bread of different kinds, meat of oxen, cows and goats as well as wild animals such as antelopes and gazelle, and different types of birds such as ducks and geese. Vegetables, especially onions and leeks, and fruits such as dates, figs and pomegranates, were all presented in this meal, along with

A painted limestone relief depicting bearers of offerings brought at the pharaoh's behest, from the temple of Hatshepsut, Deir el-Bahri.

A kneeling 'nome' figure with
papyrus and water offerings
representing the produce of
the land, from the mortuary
temple of Ramesses II at
Abydos.

A kneeling 'nome' figure with
papyrus and water offerings
representing the produce of
the land, from the mortuary
temple of Ramesses II at
Abydos.

The king himself is shown
presenting a variety of
offerings in this relief of
Amenophis III in the barque
shrine at Luxor Temple. The
offerings are represented both
in literal depictions and in a
formulaic tabular version.

water, milk, wine and beer. Often the drink offerings
were presented in two matching jars symbolizing
the offerings of Upper and Lower Egypt.

All these foodstuffs were simply placed on the
altar before the god's shrine or in the hall of offerings immediately outside the sanctuary. The
practice of making burnt offerings is usually
thought to have appeared only relatively late in
Egyptian history and to have been of foreign origin
– although a burnt offering is made in the Middle
Kingdom story of the Shipwrecked Sailor, some of
the offering scenes from Amarna appear to depict
burnt offerings, and there are certainly instances of
this practice depicted in New Kingdom private

tombs. Normally, after the god had been given the
opportunity to take whatever nourishment or enjoyment he desired, the items sanctified as offerings
reverted to mundane status and were removed for
distribution among the priests and other temple
personnel. The offerings given to the deity were
nevertheless acknowledged by the announcement
that the deity had established ongoing life and stability for the king – and by extension, the people
and land as a whole.

In the evening the process was repeated: the god
once again received offerings and was then prepared for rest. The shrine was finally resealed and
the footprints of the retreating priest swept from
the floor in order to leave the sanctuary clean and
unmarked.

The presentation of Maat

Of the many offerings which the king is shown presenting to the gods, the most abstract yet important
was the 'presentation of Maat' in which the king
offered a small figure of that goddess as a symbol of
his maintenance of the order established by the
gods. In the New Kingdom, Maat was primarily
offered to Amun, Re and Ptah – the three great gods
of the imperial triad which ruled in that period –
stressing the great importance of the ritual.

As a deity, Maat represented truth, order,
balance, correctness, justice, cosmic harmony and
other qualities which precisely embodied the
responsibility of the king's role. In presenting Maat,
therefore, the king not only acknowledged his
responsibility in this area, but also effectively maintained Maat through the potency of the ritual itself.
There were also other ways in which the presentation of Maat symbolized the king's role. Maat was
the daughter of Re and thus the sister of the king
who was 'son of Re'; and the king could also be seen
to be acting in the role of the god Thoth, husband of
Maat, so that the ritual underscored the king's
special, divinely related status. As a result, he is
often shown in the company of the gods themselves
in representations of this important ritual.

The king's presentation of Maat can be viewed, in
fact, as the supreme offering into which all other
offerings were subsumed. This equivalence of the
presentation of the goddess with all other offerings
can be seen in the epithet of Maat as 'food of the
gods' and parallel statements which affirm that the
gods 'live on Maat'. Emily Teeter, who has studied
this ritual in great detail, has shown that representations and inscriptions of the king presenting
Maat are in fact essentially identical to those in
which the king presents food, wine or other forms of
sustenance to the gods – and in some cases, depictions of the presentation of wine jars are actually
labelled as the 'presentation of Maat'.

In fact, for the Egyptians, the metaphor went
even beyond food and drink and could include virtually anything. Erik Hornung has pointed out that in

(Left) The king presents a small figure of the goddess Maat, a key ritual in Egyptian monarchical ideology.

one version of the daily temple ritual the priest intoned 'Maat is present in all your dwellings so that you are furnished with Maat. The robe for your limbs is Maat. Maat is breath for your nose....' The ritual presentation of Maat therefore highlights the king's role in the service of the gods. Not only did the king's offerings supply the needs of the gods, but also from the Egyptian perspective through the offering of Maat he also renewed and strengthened the underlying fabric of the universe itself.

The king's cosmic role

The maintenance of order symbolized by the ritual presentation of Maat was also expressed in many aspects of temple iconography. Scenes of the king smiting enemies, hunting hippopotamus or netting wild birds in the marshes are thus not so much records of isolated activities of the king as they are virtual models of the suppression of elements symbolizing the forces of disharmony and disorder within the land of Egypt and in the cosmos at large.

In fact, activities such as these were sometimes planned and performed in a ritual manner. In the Ptolemaic temple of Edfu – and very probably in earlier structures on the same site – the destruction of the inimical god Seth was vividly portrayed in an annual ritual drama in which an actual, or more likely model, hippopotamus – symbol of Seth – was destroyed by harpoons (p. 206). Here the fulfilment of an action under ritual conditions is evident, though typically in the representations of the event the king is depicted in the company of the gods.

In other instances, it is clear that the king is acting on behalf of the gods in mythical or purely 'iconographic' actions that could only be accomplished by deities themselves – for the king is a servant of gods of whom he himself is at least partially a manifestation. The king is thus frequently shown holding up the ceilings above the god's shrines, which were decorated on their upper surfaces with the form of the sky hieroglyph to signify the king's symbolic upholding of the cosmos.

Religious and political interaction

Alongside, and functioning together with the mythic and ritual aspects of the king's religious role, there was, of course, a political reality – what Jan Assmann has called a theopolitical unity – which is not always clear to us. We do not know, for example, at what historical point the Egyptian king took over the role of highest priest of the various cults or if his office incorporated this from the beginning. We may surmise that the relationship between the religious and political spheres was bound by kings who saw that this was to their advantage in terms of strengthening their own position. But it must be remembered that the relationship between the king and the temples was a mutually profitable one which fulfilled the needs of both.

(Top) The king spears a hippopotamus, representing Seth and symbolically chaos and disorder, in a relief from the temple of Horus at Edfu.

(Above) A relief from the temple of Amun at Karnak includes diminutive representations of Ramesses II holding up the barque of the god and by extension supporting the cosmic framework itself.

Priests and Temple Personnel

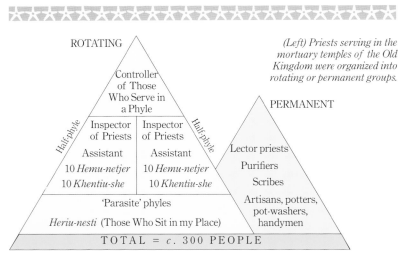

ROTATING			PERMANENT		
	Controller of Those Who Serve in a Phyle				
Half-phyle	Inspector of Priests	Inspector of Priests	*Half-phyle*		
	Assistant	Assistant	Lector priests		
	10 *Hemu-netjer*	10 *Hemu-netjer*	Purifiers		
	10 *Khentiu-she*	10 *Khentiu-she*	Scribes		
	'Parasite' phyles		Artisans, potters, pot-washers, handymen		
	Heriu-nesti (Those Who Sit in my Place)				
TOTAL = *c.* 300 PEOPLE					

(Left) Priests serving in the mortuary temples of the Old Kingdom were organized into rotating or permanent groups.

(Above right) A Sem *priest from the Book of the Dead of Ani.*

(Below) A statue of Ranefer, high priest of Ptah at Memphis in the 5th dynasty.

For a culture as formally religious as that of ancient Egypt it is surprising that no separate priestly class existed until New Kingdom times. In the Old and Middle Kingdoms many individuals employed in the state administrative structure served as priests for several months of the year, then returned to their normal secular duties.

Already in the Old Kingdom at the royal funerary temples, priests were organized into rotating shifts, though it is uncertain to what degree this was also the case in the divine cult temples. This practice continued throughout the Middle Kingdom; and even in the New Kingdom and later, when professional priesthood became widespread, most priests were organized into rotating phyles or companies.

Preparation and purity

Initiation for most priestly classes included ritual purifications and anointings and very likely the taking of vows of purity and obedience and even vows not to abuse the privileges of sacerdotal office. Jan Assmann has suggested that the 42 declarations of righteousness which are iterated in chapter 125 of the Book of the Dead as oaths spoken by the deceased before acceptance into the afterlife may have originated in such initiatory vows of priests.

For priests in active service strict standards of purity were maintained. These stipulations varied in different cults, but by New Kingdom and later times they usually required priests to shave their heads and bodies, pare their nails, perform multiple daily washings and lustrations (according to Herodotus, twice each day and twice each night), to

chew natron (a kind of salt) for inner purity, to be circumcised and to wear clean linen clothing (the wearing of other materials such as wool and leather was proscribed). Although priests were not celibate,

sexual intercourse rendered them unclean until purified. The eating of any ritually proscribed foods during the period of service was shunned, as was any other behaviour which might be taboo in the service of a specific deity.

It would seem that within a given cult, ritual standards of purification were the same for the different types of priest. Inscriptions at Kom Ombo specifically list all branches of the priesthood as being under the same purificatory requirements, and although a text from Oxyrhynchus specifies one particular priesthood to which it applies, it makes it clear that the same process of purification is to be applied to another grade of priest in the same temple.

Types of priest

From early times, the number of personnel employed in the temples varied according to the locality and the importance of the cult. Different types of priests were also in existence from relatively early times. The complex system of rotating phyles doubtless needed priestly administrators as well as servitors, and beginning in the 22nd dynasty, part-time priests assisted the full-time servants of the gods. Many temples were thus staffed mainly by 'hour-priests' who served set shifts within a period of service which was usually one month out of every four. Permanent priests were fewer in number, but it was they who controlled the key operations and functions of the

temple. While part-time priests lived in their own homes away from the temple, the full-time servants of the cult often lived close to, or actually within, the temple precincts. But priests of both types were paid by way of land allotments from the temple estates and by rations of the daily food offerings reverted from dedication to the gods.

Although many priestly titles and roles changed through time, certain generalizations may be made for much of Egyptian history. The priesthood of most temples consisted of two classes, the *hem-netjer* or 'god's servant' priests who were admitted to the temple sanctuary, and the lower *wab* or 'pure' (i.e. 'purification') priests whose roles often involved non-ritual tasks (state officials frequently held the nominal office of *wab* priest) and who were usually not permitted access to the sanctuary. Priests of *wab* rank could be elevated to the rank of *hem-netjer*, however, and in later times the term *wab* was often used generally of priests of both classes.

There were also several ranks of priestly specialists, though relatively few priests received training in these areas. The title *it-netjer* or 'god's father' was originally used of certain priests of even the highest rank, though in later times the term more usually signified a position between *hem-netjer* and *wab* priest. It was the duty of lector priests (*kheri-hebet*), who were distinguished by a sash worn across the chest, to recite the formulas to which the funerary and cult rituals were performed. This title too was a respected one and was claimed by inspectors, overseers and high priests. *Sem* priests, recognized by the leopard skin they wore along with the distinctive sidelock of youth adorning their heads, were originally associated with the rituals fulfilled by sons for their deceased fathers in early funerary cults. Already by the 3rd dynasty the title was applied to professional priests who performed this role in the Opening of the Mouth and other burial rites.

In Old Kingdom temples employing numerous priests, the priests were directed by an overseer (*imi-ra hemu-netjer*) who was assisted by an inspector (*sehedj hemu-netjer*) and sometimes also by a supervisor (*imi-khet hemu-netjer*). The overseer of priests appointed individuals to lower ranks when vacancies occurred, and the inspector of priests fulfilled a direct managerial role, being charged with the conduct of the temple's daily operations. As chief temple scribe the inspector also kept the temple accounts.

Over all these ranks the high priest presided. In the New Kingdom system, large temples also frequently employed a second, third or even fourth prophet or servant of the god who, like the first prophet himself, were all full-time members of the temple administration with specific responsibilities and, in some cases, with the power to officiate on behalf of the high priest when necessary.

(Centre below) Priests bearing the barque of Amun, from the Sanctuary of Philip Arrhidaeus, Karnak.

(Above) An iunmutef *priest, temple of Sethos I, Abydos.*

(Below) Statue of a priest with a model shrine, Ptolemaic Period, c. 200 BC.

Hereditary and Accrued Power

Although priestly offices largely became hereditary in later Egyptian history, the highest servants of the great temples of the New Kingdom attained power by various means, including, but by no means limited to, hereditary influence. The high priest of Amun Bekenchons who served under Ramesses II was the son of a 'second prophet of Amun' and held the posts of fourth, third and second prophet before attaining the high priesthood himself. Two of Bekenchons' own sons became mayors of Thebes, and he was succeeded by his younger brother Ramarai who had previously served as third and second prophet. Due perhaps to political influences, the high priestly office then passed to another family.

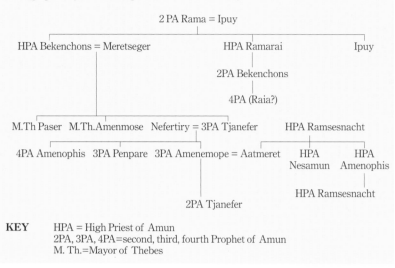

KEY   HPA = High Priest of Amun
2PA, 3PA, 4PA=second, third, fourth Prophet of Amun
M. Th.=Mayor of Thebes

High priests

The high priest of the temple was accorded the title *hem-netjer-tepy*, 'first servant of god'. Often he also bore special titles associated with his particular cult, as in the case of the high priests of the great religious centres of Re at Heliopolis (called 'Greatest of Seers'), Ptah at Memphis ('Greatest of Those Who Direct the Craftsmen'), with these special titles reflecting something of the nature of the deities with which they were associated. At Thebes, the high priest of Amun could be called 'Opener of the Gate of Heaven' – though this priest's title was usually just 'First God's Servant of Amun'.

High priests were frequently appointed by the king, but the highest priestly offices could pass from father to son and there was a tendency for them to become hereditary. In the 18th dynasty a number of trusted military officers were inducted into high-priestly offices, and it is possible that this was done to prevent those positions becoming hereditary and to help break the increasing power of the priesthood.

Other temple personnel

Because the temple functioned as a microcosm within Egyptian society, in addition to the priests a large number of administrative and productive personnel were necessary for the fulfilment of duties that ranged from the menial to the highly skilled. The many royal decrees made over time to exempt temple personnel from forced labour may be seen, in fact, as evidence of the sheer manpower required to run the temple estates as much as special treatment bestowed on the houses of the gods.

'Serfs' cultivated the temple lands and herdsmen tended temple-owned animals; fishermen, fowlers and beekeepers all worked within temple estates. Carpenters and builders were necessary for works of expansion and repair; bakers, brewers, butchers, weavers and other workers served within the greater temple complexes along with scribes of all types – including storage and archival clerks and other administrators. Large numbers of artists, sculptors, metalsmiths and other types of artisans prepared the smaller items of temple furniture and non-perishable items to be offered to the gods; and groups of musicians, singers and dancers supported the priesthood in the performance of the temple's rituals. All these classes of personnel worked within their respective niches in exchange for a portion of their produce or catches, or for a portion of the temple's income of offerings.

The combined numbers of priests and other temple personnel necessary for the functioning of

(Left) Music played an important role in many formal aspects of Egyptian life and religion, especially in temple and funerary contexts. This relief from Giza depicts various musicians and dancers.

(Right) A Hathor-headed 'naos' type sistrum made from faience, dating from the 26th dynasty. Sistra were rattle-like instruments used in ceremonies and were also made in other forms, such as the common 'hoop' style and in shapes depicting other deities, most notably Bes.

Egyptian temples utilized large numbers of servants and other non-priestly personnel, sometimes even soldiers (depicted here in a relief from the temple of Hatshepsut at Deir el-Bahri) and others, in the fulfilment of special projects.

few known examples of the masculine *hem-netjer* priests of goddesses such as Hathor, it has been argued that these women must have performed most of the same duties as their male colleagues. There is also limited but specific evidence from Old Kingdom times of a woman (a priestess of Hathor at Tihna) performing the same temple rituals as the male priests and receiving the same payment for her service as did her male (*wab* priest) counterparts. The exact functions performed by many temple women is not clear, however.

Female sacerdotal functions may also be seen in the less usual terms for priestesses: *wereshet*, 'watcher' of the god, and *hemet*, 'wife' of the god, although these terms do not seem to appear before the First Intermediate Period; it is also not until the Middle Kingdom that *wabet* (the feminine form of *wab*) priestesses of gods are found. The Middle Kingdom saw a gradual decline in the number of women involved in public life, however, and while priestesses of Hathor are still well attested at the close of the 11th dynasty, recent work has shown that they had all but disappeared from view 100 years later. The apparent gradual exclusion of women from the priesthood during this period has sometimes been thought to have been related to an increasing stress on purity and the resulting inability of women, because of childbirth and menstruation, to perform unbroken service, though it perhaps more likely simply reflects changing societal attitudes in general at this time.

In any event, by New Kingdom times priestly titles were certainly far less frequently given to women, and females associated with temples are on the whole referred to by the single title *shemayet*, usually translated 'chantress' (there were also male 'chanters'). Women may be found serving both male and female deities in this capacity; and although the role would appear to involve the use of instruments such as the rattle-like sistrum with which *shemayet*

(Below) Along with the sistrum the menat *necklace-rattle was the instrument most often associated with female temple personnel, as seen in this relief from the temple of Sethos I at Abydos.*

the divine estates thus often added up to a substantial percentage of the populace of major cult areas. It is known that in the time of Ramesses III, for example, the three largest cult centres in Egypt supported almost 100,000 male personnel between them. The breakdown recorded at that time gives a good idea of the importance of each of the cults. The 'Domain' of Amun centred at Karnak boasted 81,322 male personnel; the temple of Re at Heliopolis 12,963; and the temple of Ptah at Memphis 3,079 – in addition to the various 'chantresses' and other female personnel.

Female sacerdotal roles

The titles and roles of women in temple service were somewhat different from those of men and deserve special attention. In the Old Kingdom many women of well-to-do families held the title *hemet- netjer* 'god's (female) servant' or 'priestess', as 'priestess of Hathor' or less frequently, 'priestess of Neith' or some other goddess. Although women were usually the servants of female deities at this period, there are exceptions. Some (usually queens or princesses) are known to have served as priestesses of Thoth, Ptah and certain other gods as well as in the funerary cults of kings. All these women were *hemet-netjer* priestesses; and as there are

are frequently depicted, this does not necessarily mean that this was the only duty they performed or that all women with this title served thus. It is possible that some women described as *shemayet* held extended responsibility; but on the other hand, chantresses clearly did not perform the central offering ritual in the temple. It has been noted that in New Kingdom Thebes, nearly every woman of relatively high social status was described as 'chantress of Amun', and while this might be seen as a sign that the title could often have been somewhat nominal, the vastness of the cult of Amun with its ancillary cults of the god's family members undoubtedly did require great numbers of female personnel. Also, the title 'chantress of Amun' did not necessarily imply the direct service of that god in his own temple, and we find women serving, for example, as chantresses of Amun in the mortuary temples of New Kingdom kings.

Despite their relative rarity, certain religious titles applied to women in New Kingdom times seem to have been more than nominal. The wives and daughters of high priests were often actively involved in the service of the cult, with many wives of high priests performing the role of 'principal of the musical troupe' (*khener*) of a deity. Some New Kingdom temple scenes also show a class of male and female personnel called respectively *henuty* and *henutet* or 'servants'. While it is not clear what the exact functions of these servitors were, it would appear that their roles were practical ones not strictly differentiated by gender.

At times, women also held higher offices of priestly responsibility. At least two New Kingdom priestesses of the level of second prophet are known – one of Amun, one of Mut – and in the post-New Kingdom Period we know of at least two women with the rank of 'God's Wife and First Prophet of Amun'. Some at least of these women appear to have been formally educated, and one daughter of the 21st-dynasty Theban high priest Pinudjem II is known to have held the title 'worker on the scrolls of Amun-Re', ostensibly indicating actual involvement in the copying of sacred texts.

(Above) The Divine Consort of Amun, Karomama, c. 870 BC.

(Right) Hatshepsut, in male, kingly costume, before Amun-Re.

Wives of Kings and Gods

The role of the queen in temple ritual is somewhat anomalous, for some royal wives seem to have assimilated a number of the prerogatives of their husbands, although most did not; and most are never shown offering to the gods alone. But the specific title 'god's wife' which appeared in the Middle Kingdom certainly became an important epithet of certain New Kingdom queens. The title was bestowed on Ahmose Nefertari, wife of King Ahmose I, and for some time was handed down from one generation to the next, occasionally appearing to be used in preference to the otherwise superlative title 'king's great wife'.

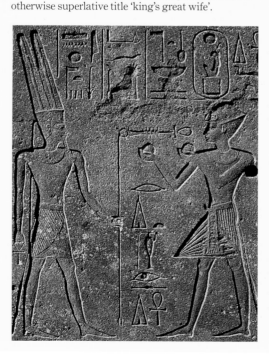

Reliefs of Hatshepsut from the Chapelle Rouge at Karnak and of Amenophis III in Luxor Temple show that the god's wife played an important role – apparently acting as the consort of the god – in certain temple rituals such as the annual Opet Festival of the god Amun. Interestingly, the title was held by Hatshepsut until she ruled as sole 'king', but seems to have been curtailed in usage after her reign, apparently never fully regaining its prestige. It is possible that Hatshepsut used the power of the office in establishing her own position and that the office was afterwards deliberately reduced in importance as a result, though this must remain speculative. In any event, from the time of Amenophis III to the end of the 18th dynasty there appears to have been no royal holder of this office.

Another female sacerdotal title which occurs in the New Kingdom is that of *duat netjer* or 'Divine Adoratrice'. This title was held by the daughter of the chief priest of Amun in Hatshepsut's time, and in the time of Ramesses VI was conferred upon the king's daughter along with that of 'God's Wife of Amun'. The position became a continuing one, but because the *duat netjer* was barred from marriage, each celibate adoratrice adopted a younger woman who would eventually accede to her own office. Something of the extent of the adoratrices' power may be seen not only in the political and economic influence which they apparently wielded in the Theban region, and perhaps beyond, but also in the iconography of their representations which included some scenes previously used only to depict kings. In addition the titles of the Divine Adoratrice were developed to imitate those of the Egyptian king. Like kings, these women utilized prenomens (for the adoratrice this was usually compounded with the name of Mut, divine consort of Amun) along with their own given names – both of which were written in cartouches.

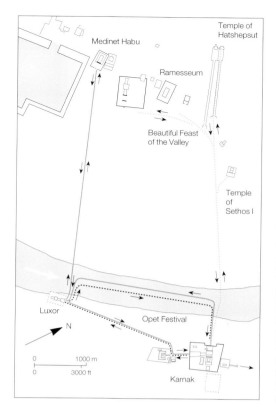

Herodotus thought it remarkable that while Greek gods were content to have a single festival held in their honour each year, 'The Egyptians hold a festival not once a year but they have frequent festivals'. As time progressed, the multiplicity of special days for the gods and other celebrations led to an almost constant succession of religious festivals, and it has been calculated, for example, that in Roman times the village of Soknopaiou Nesos in the Fayum celebrated festivals for more than 150 days each year. The general populace could hardly keep all these festivals, of course, and it is likely that many were of limited importance and celebrated only by the priests themselves.

Nevertheless a number of major festivals were celebrated on an annual basis (see box 'The Festival Calendar', p. 98), many lasting several days and some of the most important being held over several weeks. While certain festivals, such as those of Osiris, were celebrated throughout Egypt, many were peculiar to the worship of local or regional deities or national deities in specific locations. Details of a number of such festivals are known, especially those of the later Graeco-Roman temples of Edfu and Dendera and the New Kingdom temples of Thebes.

Some 60 festivals are known to have been celebrated annually at Thebes in the New Kingdom, some of which entailed ritual activities within the confines of the temple and others of which involved

the transportation of the god's image to other sites. The great god Amun left his temple twice each year for particularly special events – the Opet Festival (p. 171) and the 'Beautiful Feast of the Valley' – and these events appear to be fairly typical of the journeys made by the gods in visiting each other.

Travelling festivals

In festivals involving the transportation of the gods the image of the deity was usually placed in its shrine on a small portable barque which was then borne on the shoulders of priests to its destination or to the nearest quay, where it was loaded on to a real barque for movement by river. The Harris Papyrus describes the grandeur of one such barque of the gods during the reign of Ramesses III: measuring 67 m (220 ft) in length, it was constructed of the finest imported Lebanese cedar and was covered with gold and other precious materials fit for its purpose.

The festival known as *heb nefer en inet*, the 'Beautiful Feast of the Valley', involved travel by both land and water. It appears to have originated during the Middle Kingdom in the reign of Nebhepetre Mentuhotep, and from early New Kingdom times mortuary temples on the west bank of the Nile at Thebes were designed to accommodate the barque of Amun-Re during this event. The festival was celebrated during the second month of *shemu*, the 'harvest' season – which, during the New Kingdom, coincided with the beginning of summer.

In the course of the festival, Amun of Karnak, accompanied by the other members of the Theban triad, Mut and Khonsu, and a large retinue of attendants, processed to the west bank where they visited various gods whose shrines were located

(Left) The routes of the Opet Festival (on the east bank of the Nile) and the Beautiful Feast of the Valley (on the west bank), in New Kingdom Thebes. During such festivals images of particular gods travelled to meet other deities.

(Below) An artist's reconstruction of the great barge of Amun which transported the image of the god during various travelling festivals in the Theban area.

there and also the temples of deceased and deified kings. The festival was doubtless originally a remembrance of the dead, in which the living members of families visited the tombs of their deceased relatives. As the festival grew in importance it also seems to have taken on aspects of renewal and rejuvenation as well as other meanings for its human and divine participants.

The renewal of gods and men

'Travelling festivals', such as the 'Beautiful Feast of the Valley', as well as those celebrated within the gods' own temples were often aimed at renewal, as can be seen in the ancient descriptions we have of the 'Festival of the New Year' and the 'Festival of the Beautiful Meeting', as they were celebrated at Edfu and Dendera. At Dendera, on the night before the Egyptian New Year's Day, the statue of Hathor was carried up to a special kiosk on the temple roof. Here it was positioned to await the dawn when it was exposed to the rays of the rising sun in order to infuse it with new life.

Similarly, the 'Festival of the Beautiful Meeting' celebrated at Edfu began with the arrival of the cult statue of Hathor on the day of the New Moon in the third month of summer, and can be seen to have had the same essential purpose, albeit in a more sexually oriented ritual. There, after various ceremonies, the statue of the goddess was placed in the temple's birth house along with the statue of Horus of Edfu and the two deities spent the next nights together until the festival's conclusion at the full moon.

Festivals such as these, whose main intent appears to be one of fertility, rebirth or other life-giving or life-sustaining aspects, can clearly be seen to be renewal oriented; and while not all festivals had as their goal the idea of renewal, once established, many tended towards this meaning. Thus the festivals associated with divine and royal homage, such as the birthdays of the gods, and jubilees and other festivals held in honour of the king, or even great events such as military victories, could all take on the underlying idea of renewal through the repetitive celebration of their original themes.

(Left) The goddess Hathor, here depicted on the column capitals of the roof chapel at Dendera, was the focus of important festivals at the temples of Dendera and Edfu.

(Right) A divine scene showing the Nile's inundation and the resurrection of Osiris, from the temple of Philae – both symbolize rejuvenation.

The essentially rejuvenative nature of Egyptian festivals may also be seen in the symbolic nature of a number of their offerings. For example, flowers – for the Egyptians potent symbols of life and regeneration – were dedicated in great profusion on festival days. They were often placed in holders in the shape of the *ankh* or life sign or offered in large bouquets (the Egyptian word for 'bouquet' had the same consonantal structure as that for life). Flowers could be offered as symbols of life and renewal at any time, but a compilation of the floral offerings dedicated in a little under three years at the Great Temple of Amun at Karnak shows the incredible numbers involved – well over one million offerings each year – and the evident emphasis on this type of offering.

(Above left) A nome god bearing offerings: a detail of a temple relief of the 18th dynasty.

(Above) The festival calendar from Kom Ombo, reign of Ptolemy VI, c. 170 BC.

Floral Offerings at the Great Temple of Amun: total 1,057 days	
Fan bouquets	124
Tall bouquets	3,100
Scented bouquets	15,500
Bouquets	1,975,800
Flower bundles	1,975,800
Wreaths	60,450
Large Flowers	620
Strings of flowers	12,400
Flowers ('hands')	465,000
Flowers ('heaps')	110
Lotus ('hands')	144,720
Lotus bouquets	3,410
Small lotus ('hands')	110,000
Lettuce and flower bouquets	19,150
Total: 4,786,184 floral offerings	

The perpetuation of festivals

As is so often the case in many of the world's religions, some of the festivals celebrated in ancient Egyptian temples frequently continued beyond the life of the worship of the old gods. In certain cases they have even survived in their essential forms to the present day.

For example, the great festival day in honour of the rising of the Nile which was celebrated in the second month of the harvest season (in later Egyptian history, equivalent to 19 June) was important enough in the culture of the Egyptians and so embedded in their consciousness that it passed into

the calendar of Christian festivals as the feast day of St Michael. Furthermore, St Michael is the patron saint of the Nile and his feast day is still celebrated by the Coptic church on 19 June.

At Luxor a Christian basilica was built in the northeast corner of the first court of the temple which was in turn later replaced by a mosque dedicated to a locally venerated Moslem saint Abu el-Haggag. Even today, the portable barque of this saint is annually pulled through the temple and streets of Luxor in the re-enactment of a custom clearly harking back in its earliest form to Luxor's great Opet Festival of ancient times (p. 171).

The Festival Calendar

(Above and below left) Relief scenes of musicians and offerings of cattle in the Opet Festival, from the colonnade of Amenophis III in Luxor Temple.

The Egyptian calendar had three seasons: *akhet* (Inundation); *peret* (Growth); and *shemu* (Harvest), each divided into four 30-day months – theoretically approximating our mid-July to November, mid-November to March, and mid-March to July. In addition, five so-called epagomenal or additional days were dedicated to the 'birthdays' of certain deities in order to bring the year to a 365-day total. In reality, however, the seasons moved progressively forward – beginning a little earlier each year – due to the quarter-day discrepancy between the length of the Egyptian calendar year and the actual solar year.

Festivals of many types were scheduled throughout the year, with special provisions for each new moon as well as festivals tied to specific seasons. The dates and offerings of these recurrent festivals were carefully recorded and were inscribed on temple walls from Old Kingdom times. Such festival calendars appear in valley temples of pyramids and sun temples of the 5th dynasty and doubtless continued to be engraved in Middle Kingdom temples, although none has yet been recovered. More evidence survives from the New Kingdom, and examples of temple calendars may be found at Karnak, Abydos, Elephantine and at western Thebes in the Ramesseum and Medinet Habu. From the Graeco-Roman Period similar calendars are found in the temples of Dendera, Edfu, Esna and Kom Ombo.

According to these calendars, some of the major festivals of the Egyptian year were as follows (most festivals without locations were of regional or national character):

Akhet: Season of Inundation
First month: Opening of the Year; Wag Festival of Osiris; Festival of the 'Departure' of Osiris (Abydos); Festival of Thoth; Festival of Intoxication (a festival of Hathor)
Second month: Festival of Ptah South of his Wall (Memphis); Opet Festival (Thebes)
Third month: Festival of Hathor (Edfu and Dendera)
Fourth month: Festival of Sokar, Festival of Sekhmet

Peret: Season of Growth
First month: Festival of Nehebkau; Festival of the Coronation of the Sacred Falcon (Edfu); Festival of Min; Festival of the 'Departure' of Mut
Second month: Festival of Victory (Edfu); Great Brand Festival
Third month: Small Brand Festival; Festival of Amenophis
Fourth month: Festival of Renenutet

Shemu: Season of Harvest
First month: Festival of Khonsu; Festival of the 'Departure' of Min
Second month: Beautiful Feast of the Valley (Thebes)
Third month: Festival of the Beautiful Meeting (Edfu and Dendera)
Fourth month: Festival of Re-Horakhty; Festival of the Opening of the Year

Epagomenal Days
Festivals of Osiris, Horus, Seth, Isis and Nephthys (celebrated on five successive days)

The role of the common people in worship

In the earlier periods of Egyptian history, the boundary between the priesthood and the laity was blurred by the fact that temple service was conducted by individuals who, after their assigned rotation of duties, returned to secular work in their communities. Later, in New Kingdom times, when the priestly offices became professional and largely hereditary ones, the situation changed considerably, though Herodotus' assessment of the Egyptians – 'They are religious beyond measure … more than any other people' – seems to have applied not only to the great temples with their thronging priesthoods and burgeoning estates, but also to the piety of many of the common people themselves. Religious altars and shrines of minor household deities were often to be found in Egyptian homes, and many people placed votive offerings in the temples – ranging from simple beads and trinkets to finely carved and painted statues and stelae. Votive stelae were of different types, though many requested favours from the gods and sometimes gave thanks for their help when it seemed that a request to a god had been granted. The so-called 'hearing ears' of the temples (p. 71) and the colossal statues before their pylons (p. 59) were also readily accessible to the people as mediators of their prayers and requests to even the greatest of the gods.

Apart from these aspects of individual and personal religious activity, the common people also involved themselves, to the level that they were able, in the festival worship of the temples. They gathered to greet the processions of the gods directly outside the temple entrances and, in many cases, around the perimeters of their outer courts, as is evident from the Ptolemaic name for this area, 'the hall/court of the multitude', and the hieroglyphic signs representing the people of Egypt which were often inscribed on their walls and columns to indicate where the common people were allowed to stand.

With the exception of some apotropaic festivals (such as those of the epagomenal days which were regarded as being unlucky), textual evidence makes it clear that the Egyptian people eagerly anticipated festivals not only as a respite from labour but also as joyous events in their own right. Often the king would present awards and gifts on festival days, and the great number of offerings given to the temples at these times meant surpluses of fresh produce which, in some cases, were distributed among members of the community at large. But, beneath the general atmosphere of revelry inherent in many of their religious holidays, it seems clear that most Egyptians took their relationship with the temple seriously. One of the most poignant illustrations of this is seen in the countless shallow holes scraped into the outer walls of temples by devout individuals wishing to take away a small part of the sacred building – albeit only dust – for the purposes of healing and devotion: a practice which began in very ancient times and continued even long after the temples ceased to function.

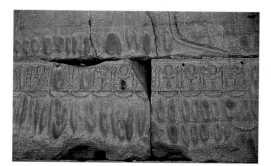

(Left) The grooves visible in this temple wall at Medinet Habu are the result of constant scraping by ordinary people who visited this sacred place – a practice which seems to have persisted beyond ancient times.

(Right) A statue of Sennefer and his family, dedicated by them at Karnak and dating from the reign of Amenophis III.

(Below) The rekhyt bird, seen here engraved on a column of a temple, indicated the areas where the ordinary people were allowed to stand.

A Journey up the Nile

*'Your monuments surpass those of all former kings. I commanded you to
make them, and I am satisfied with them.'*

Stela of Tuthmosis III

They are more religious than any other people', wrote
Herodotus of the Egyptians, and although we will never
know exactly how many temples, shrines and chapels were
built in Egypt over the 3,000 years of its ancient history,
the number must have been astonishingly high. A great many of the
deities of Egypt's massive pantheon had temples of their own; often
they owned several in different locations and, in some cases, even
multiple temples in the same area.

Although hundreds are known, perhaps as many temples have
vanished in the course of time as now remain. Certainly, many were
dismantled by the Egyptians themselves as new temples were built
on the sites of earlier structures; and others were lost over the
centuries as their stone was used in the building of churches, homes
and factories, and their mud-brick structures torn down and used as
fertilizer. Of those temples that remain or are recoverable at least in
plan, we find religious structures from the northern Delta to the
lowest areas of southern Nubia – and beyond the Nile in the desert
oases and outposts which dotted Egypt's ancient frontiers.

The following section of this book catalogues the riches of this
legacy, covering temples ranging from those of the almost unbeliev-
ably massive complex of Karnak and of other famous sites such as
Medinet Habu, Abu Simbel, Abydos, Edfu, Kom Ombo and Philae, to
much smaller and less well-known temples throughout the Two
Lands. The panoply of sites and shrines reveals much of the rich
history of Egypt and provides fascinating examples of the broad
range of structures and styles which are found in the sacred monuments of gods and kings. The most important examples of temple
development, the finest representational works, and the locations of
particular historical significance and interest are examined here.

Regardless of the actual accuracy of Herodotus' statement regarding the religious nature of the ancient Egyptians, they may well have
produced a greater number and greater range of monumental
religious structures than any other ancient culture. Indeed, perhaps in
no other place or time have the houses of the gods been so many, so
manifold, and – possibly – so magnificent.

The Sun Court of Amenophis III, Luxor Temple

From the Mediterranean to Memphis

LOWER EGYPT

Virtually half of Egypt, the Nile Delta covers an area of more than 15,000 sq. km (5,800 sq. miles) of fertile, irrigated land, and has long held the separate epithet of Lower Egypt to distinguish it from the narrow strip of the Nile Valley which is the rest of the country. While the Delta today holds two main branches of the Nile – the western Rosetta and eastern Damietta channels – there were in antiquity no fewer than seven such branches which deposited rich fertile silt over most of this low-lying region. Much of the Delta's early history thus lies buried under thousands of years of deposited earth and in the fluctuating swamps and lagoons which cover much of the area and is therefore extremely difficult to investigate.

Undoubtedly many cities and cult centres were built here from very early times, however, and from New Kingdom times the Delta came to dominate Egypt's economic and political life. This was due both to increasing land reclamation and resulting agricultural prosperity, and the fact that for reasons of realpolitik in the 19th dynasty the royal residence was moved to Pi-Ramesse in the Delta. Even after the decline of the New Kingdom, several Delta cities were centres of political power in the Third Intermediate and Late periods, and the region's proximity to the Mediterranean and Asia meant it played a central role in Ptolemaic and Roman times.

Alexandria

Rebuilt as a thriving Mediterranean city in the last two centuries, Alexandria was once the leading city of the ancient Hellenistic world. A cosmopolitan metropolis, the city contained temples dedicated to Greek as well as Egyptian deities, and distinctive Graeco-Egyptian gods such as the hybrid Serapis (Osiris/Zeus/Apis). The Serapeum, the most important temple of Serapis, was located in the native Egyptian quarter of Rakhotis. Evidently founded in the reign of Ptolemy III, much of the temple was constructed in the first centuries AD, though the famous granite column known as 'Pompey's Pillar',

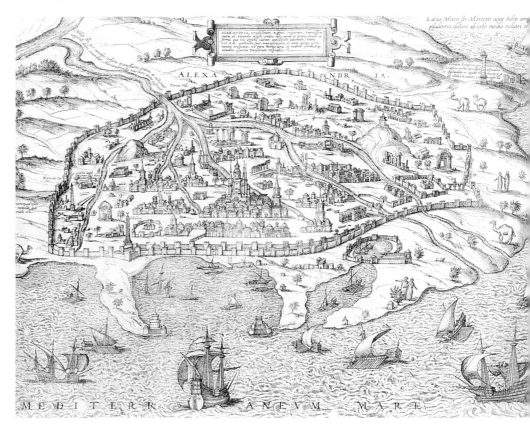

Alexandria, from Janssen's Atlas of 1617. During Ptolemaic and Roman times Alexandria was one of the leading cities of the world. With a population close to half a million by the middle of the first century BC, it was known as Alexandria ad Aegyptum – 'Alexandria next to Egypt' – almost a country in its own right.

A coin from the Alexandrian mint depicting the Serapeum, c. AD 2, which was rebuilt by the emperor Hadrian.

One of Alexandria's most famous and striking surviving monuments is the huge granite column known as 'Pompey's Pillar', although it was in fact erected by the emperor Diocletian in c. AD 297. The column stood in the city's Serapeum, the chief temple of the important Graeco-Roman god Serapis.

which is the most impressive remaining feature, dates to much later, around AD 297.

The column was built to commemorate the quelling of a riot in the reign of Diocletian, but, beginning in the Middle Ages, European visitors came to accept a story that the column once bore a globe containing the head of Caesar's rival Pompey and the monument has since retained its popular name. Today, little else remains. South of the column two red-granite sphinxes of probable Ptolemaic date still stand, with a damaged black-granite sphinx of the 18th dynasty; although a number of such sphinxes and other types of Egyptian statuary adorned the temple, its architectural style was doubtless more that of a Greek sanctuary than the classic Egyptian plan.

Abusir

Abusir lies about 48 km (30 miles) west of Alexandria and is the site of the ancient Taposiris Magna, an important city of the Ptolemaic Period. Although they have not been dated precisely, the remains of the unfinished and uninscribed temple at Abusir almost certainly date to this era. Interestingly, the enclosure walls of the temple were of limestone rather than the usual mud-brick, though mud-brick building techniques were employed in their construction. It is possible that the normal functions of the enclosure walls and interior structures were somewhat blurred in the structure, as the eastern wall is built in the form of the standard

(Right) Tell el-Fara'in, the site of ancient Buto, contains the remnants of the ancient temple enclosure that once honoured the Lower Egyptian goddess Wadjit. The site was thus the counterpart of el-Kab in the south – home of the Upper Egyptian vulture goddess Nekhbet.

(Below) A reconstruction of the walled temple complex of Behbeit el-Hagar, which is mostly in ruins today.

(Bottom) A plan of the Ptolemaic temple of Isis at Behbeit el-Hagar, one of the most important dedicated to the goddess in Egypt. It collapsed due to earthquake or quarrying, and today its blocks, decorated with finely carved reliefs, lie scattered at the site (right).

temple pylon gateway. The interior of the temple was heavily modified and utilized by Christians, and the present remains are those of a church and related buildings.

Tell el-Fara'in (Buto)

Situated a couple of kilometres to the north of the Damanhur highway in the north-central Delta, Tell el-Fara'in ('Mound of the Pharaohs') is the site of ancient Buto, home of the cobra-goddess Wadjit, the tutelary deity of Lower Egypt. As the southern counterpart of el-Kab or Nekheb, home of the vulture-goddess Nekhbet of Upper Egypt, Buto was an important symbolic site. Oddly, however, the importance of Buto in Egyptian history and ideology does not seem to be reflected in the area's ruins. There are three mounds, two of which contain habitation remains while in the third are the remnants of a temple enclosure. Apart from recent Egyptian finds of sculpture and an important stela of Tuthmosis III, relatively few small monuments have been found or traced to this site and little is known of the history of the temple.

Behbeit el-Hagar

About 8 km (5 miles) west of el-Mansura on the Damietta branch of the Nile, Behbeit el-Hagar is located close to Samannud (ancient Sebennytos), the home of the kings of the 30th dynasty. These

kings are known to have been especially devoted to Isis, and the temple of Behbeit el-Hagar was one of the most important Egyptian shrines of that goddess, functioning as a kind of Lower Egyptian twin to the temple of Isis at Philae.

The remains of the early Ptolemaic Period temple can still be seen within its enclosure, although the structure collapsed, perhaps even in antiquity, as a result of an earthquake or due to the quarrying of its stone. Although many Late Period monuments

Isis
sanctuary

○ ○ Columned hall
○ ○ ○
○ ○ ○
○ ○ ○

Façade

Samannud (Sebennytos)

The modern town of Samannud is located on the Damietta branch of the Nile, just east of the town of el-Mahalla el-Kubra, and is the site of the ancient Djebnetjer, called in Greek Sebennytos. According to Manetho, who was a native of the region, the town was the home of the kings of the 30th dynasty. Remains of the temple of the local god Onuris-Shu, the huntsman sky-god, lie within the large mound on the western side of the modern town, and the scattered granite blocks from the site are inscribed with the names of Nectanebo II, Alexander IV, Philip Arrhidaeus and Ptolemy II. None of the known inscriptions appears to predate the 30th dynasty.

A detail of sunk relief work on a block retrieved from Samannud, showing symbolic offerings being brought into the temple.

were built at least partially of hard stone, the fallen blocks of the temple reveal that this large structure was unusual if not unique in being built entirely of granite.

The carved reliefs of the wall decorations reveal finely executed work which well surpasses the quality of that found in the Ptolemaic temples of Upper Egypt, and one block from this temple was transported in Classical times to the chief Isis temple at Rome.

(Below) Very little remains today of the site of the ancient city of Sebennytos – modern Samannud – on the Damietta branch of the Nile. It was the home of the kings of the 30th dynasty.

banebdjedet, 'House of the Ram Lord of *djedet*', which may have served as a royal residence or capital in the 29th dynasty and was known in Greek times as Mendes. The cult of the ram god at this site was quite ancient and increased in importance as the ram (*ba*) of Mendes came to be associated with the soul (*ba*) of Osiris, Re and all the gods. Temples of other deities were no doubt also erected in the area. Parts of a Late Period temple enclosure of Amasis (later restored by Ptolemy II Philadelphus) are still visible, with a red-granite *naos* (one of an original four – perhaps relating to the first four divine generations: Re, Shu, Geb and Osiris – which were manifested in the ram god) almost 8 m (26 ft) high. However, little else has survived of this temple above ground level. Excavations have been conducted in the area by several North American teams including one led by Donald Redford of the University of Toronto. The remains of a number of New Kingdom monuments, including ones of Ramesses II, Merenptah and Ramesses III, suggest that there may also have been a Ramessid temple here, though such a structure has not been found; the monuments may have been relocated after the abandonment of the Ramessid site of Pi-Ramesse.

Sa el-Hagar (Sais)

The venerable city of Sais (Egyptian Zau) lies on the Rosetta branch of the Nile roughly midway between the modern city of Tanta and the village of Disuq to the north. Cult centre of the goddess Neith, Sais was an important religious centre from the Early Dynastic period and continued as a mythological destination of funerary rituals throughout the Old Kingdom. During the 26th dynasty Sais rose to become capital of the country, and many temples must have been constructed here in this period. On the evidence of Greek historians and artifacts

(Top) The monolithic granite naos of Amasis at Mendes marks the location of the earliest known temple at the site.

(Above) A black granite head of king Apries, who dedicated a shrine to Thoth at Hermopolis Parva.

(Right) Some of the few remaining blocks at the site of Sais, which has been decimated since ancient times.

el-Baqliya (Hermopolis Parva)

A few kilometres south of el-Mansura on the Damietta branch of the Nile, just outside the village of el-Baqliya, several low mounds reveal the site of the ancient 15th Lower Egyptian nome capital of Ba'h which was known in Graeco-Roman times as Hermopolis Parva. The area has been little excavated, but some remains have been identified. The basic outlines of the enclosure of a temple of the local god Thoth are visible on one mound, although there are few remains in the vicinity other than some scattered blocks and a large bell-shaped column capital which has given the mound its local name: Tell el-Naqus, 'Mound of the Bell'.

Another mound is the site of a quartzite shrine dedicated to Thoth by the 26th-dynasty king Apries, as well as a number of statues, blocks and parts of other monuments, most of which are late and none dated before the New Kingdom.

Tell el-Rub'a (Mendes)

A ruined site close to the modern village of el-Simbellawein in the northeast Delta represents the remains of the old nome capital Djedet or Per-

which evidently originated at the site, it is likely that cults of Osiris, Isis, Horus, Hathor, Amun and Atum were venerated here. The site has been decimated, however. Stone from the city's temples has been removed for building since the Middle Ages (the Egyptian Egyptologist Labib Habachi suggested that many blocks at Rosetta – including the Rosetta Stone – were from Sais) and mud-brick walls gradually removed for use as fertilizer. Although some remains of a massive enclosure (some 800 × 700 m, 2,624 × 2,296 ft) were visible at the end of the last century, virtually nothing remains today.

Naukratis

To the west of the Rosetta branch of the Nile, about 3 km (1.75 miles) southwest of the Cairo–Alexandria highway and some 80 km (50 miles) from Alexandria, lie the villages of el-Gi'eif, el-Nibeira and el-Niqrash, site of the ancient Greek trading

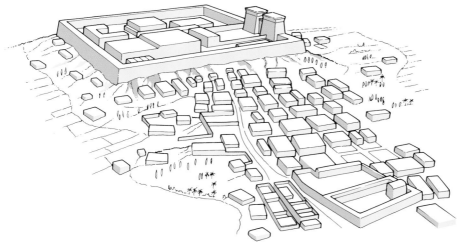

(Above) The sprawling site of ancient Naukratis is now largely swamped by ground water.

(Left) A reconstruction of Naukratis, a city which combined a thriving trading colony with numerous Egyptian and Graeco-Egyptian temples.

(Below left) A relief of a Greek soldier, from an Ionic column at Naukratis. Significant Greek presence at the site began by at least the 26th dynasty, and special concessions were made to its population in the reign of the 6th-century BC king Amasis.

centre of Naukratis. Here Greek traders first settled during the 26th dynasty, establishing a colony which was granted trade monopoly under Amasis in the 6th century BC. Naukratis boasted at least five temples of Greek deities – including Aphrodite, Hera and Apollo – and also an Egyptian temple dedicated to Amun, and probably sanctuaries of other Egyptian deities. The area seems to have been the site of the Egyptian Naju-keredj, 'The Establishment of Keredj', which might underlie the Greek name. Unfortunately, very little can be seen of the ruined monuments of Naukratis today. Parts of the site excavated successively by Flinders Petrie (1884–85), E.A. Gardner (1899) and D.G. Hogarth (1903) now lie under a lake of groundwater; and more recent surveys and excavations by W. Coulson and A. Leonard (1977–78, 1980–82) have concentrated on the 'Great Temenos' or temple enclosure wall to the south and other surrounding areas.

(Above) The remains of
the temple enclosure at Kom
el-Hisn – the site of ancient
Imu. The temple was
dedicated to Sekhmet-Hathor.

Kom el-Hisn

The mound of Kom el-Hisn, between Kom Abu Billo and Naukratis, represents all that is left of the ancient town of Imu, an important local administrative centre from New Kingdom times. Only the outline of a rectangular enclosure now remains of the temple of Sekhmet-Hathor, which has been identified by inscribed statues of Amenemhet III and Ramesses II found at this site.

Tell Far'un

Also called Tell Nabasha and Tell Bedawi, this site near the eastern Delta village of el-Huseiniya is the location of the ancient Egyptian city of Imet. At one time a nome capital, Imet was a seat of the cobra-goddess Wadjit, and the outlines of a temple enclosure (215 × 205 m, 705 × 673 ft) dedicated to the deity are still visible there, though little else has survived. The enclosure seems to have contained at least two temples, a larger structure (c. 65 × 30 m, 213 × 98 ft 6 in) built in the Ramessid era and a smaller Late Period temple (c. 30 × 15 m, 98 ft 6 in × 49 ft) to the northeast dated to the reign of Amasis (6th century BC). Both structures contained usurped monuments of Middle Kingdom date, suggesting their reuse from an earlier temple in the vicinity.

Qantir

The modern village of Qantir, about 9 km (5.5 miles) north of Faqus in the eastern Delta, marks the approximate site of the great Ramessid capital of Pi-Ramesse or Per-Ramesses ('House [or 'Domain'] of Ramesses'). Its exact whereabouts were long disputed and the first clues to the ancient city's location were found in decorated tiles, some with the names of Sethos I and Ramesses II, discovered in the area in the 1920s.

Recent German expeditions to Qantir, and those of the Austrian Archaeological Institute beginning in the 1970s under Manfred Bietak, have now established the location, stretching as far as Tell el-Dab'a to the south, as almost certainly that of Pi-Ramesse. Relatively little remains of the once-great capital, however. Because the branch of the Nile on which the city was located began to dry up during the 20th dynasty, virtually all the monuments were removed piece by piece by the kings of the 21st dynasty to their new capital at Tanis.

It would appear, however, that Pi-Ramesse's religious centres had included a great temple of Re along with temples of Amun, Ptah and Sutekh (or Seth), remains of the last having been identified in the southern part of the city. In addition to these great structures, the 'Domain of Ramesses' also contained smaller temples of Wadjit and Astarte, and doubtless many other minor shrines and chapels.

Tell el-Qirqafa

Near the village of el-Khata'na about 6 km (3.75 miles) north of Faqus in the eastern Delta, the site of Tell el-Qirqafa contains the remains of a granite entrance gate of a small pillared temple of Middle Kingdom date. The structure seems to have been built in the period between the reigns of Amenemhet I and Senwosret III.

(Left) Some of the reused temple blocks of Qantir now at Tanis, where they were taken by the kings of the 21st dynasty.

(Right) Czech excavations at the site of Tell el-Dab'a – the probable site of the Hyksos capital of Avaris.

(Below) The small temple of Ezbet Rushdi exhibits key elements of Middle Kingdom temple design. There were two phases of mud-brick construction, with elements of doorways and columns in stone.

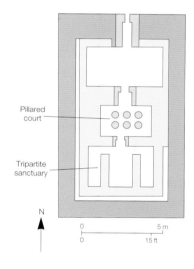

Pillared court

Tripartite sanctuary

N

0   5 m

0   15 ft

Ezbet Rushdi

Ezbet Rushdi el-Saghira, a little to the north of Tell el-Dab'a, is the site of a Middle Kingdom town with a temple that was apparently founded by Amenemhet I and expanded by Senwosret III. The structure was mainly of mud-brick with limited stone elements such as doorways and columns, but its plan reveals the common Middle Kingdom temple design, with a small pillared court before a tripartite sanctuary.

Tell el-Dab'a

Tell el-Dab'a, the probable site of the Hyksos capital of Avaris, lies just east of Tell el-Qirqafa near el-Khata'na. The site has a complex history, and New Kingdom building activity by Horemheb and the Ramessids included a large temple (c. 180 × 140 m, 590 × 459 ft) which was probably dedicated to the god Seth.

Tell el-Muqdam (Leontopolis)

Several large mounds located some 10 km (6.25 miles) southeast of the modern town of Mit Ghamr on the Damietta branch of the Nile represent the site of ancient Taremu (Leontopolis), perhaps the home of kings of the 23rd dynasty and a regional capital during the Ptolemaic Period.

A temple of the local lion-god Mihos (hence the Greek name Leontopolis, 'lion city') has been located in the eastern part of the site, but little remains of this structure and it has not been conclusively dated. The goddess Bastet, mother of Mihos, was probably also worshipped in the area.

Tell Basta (Bubastis)

On the southeastern side of modern Zagazig in the eastern Delta, Tell Basta is the mound of ancient Bast (classical Bubastis), a strategically located provincial capital and, during the 22nd to 23rd dynasties, capital of all Egypt. The city was the cult centre of the cat-goddess Bastet and her sons Mihos and Horhekenu. Herodotus (II, 5–60), who claimed to have visited the site in the 5th century BC, wrote that hundreds of thousands of pilgrims gathered there for the goddess' annual festival which he says was one of the greatest in Egypt. The remains of a number of temples are known at the site.

Tell Basta retains in its modern name the memory of the ancient temple of Bastet built at this site, some of the remains of which are seen here.

The temple of Bastet was excavated by Édouard Naville in 1887–89, but it has not been possible to reconstruct the structure's plan beyond its basic outline (200 × 300 m, 656 × 984 ft) and divisions: an entrance hall of Osorkon II (22nd dynasty), a festival hall and hypostyle of Osorkon III (23rd dynasty), and a sanctuary of Nectanebo II (30th dynasty). The Osorkon II gateway is an extraordinary structure, completely built of granite and decorated with scenes taken from the Sed festival reliefs of Amenophis III. Blocks of various periods, including some of 4th-dynasty date, were found to have been reused in the temple. According to Herodotus, the temple was already lower than the surrounding town in his day and partially surrounded by the branches of what was doubtless a sacred lake.

A number of smaller structures are ranged around the temple of Bastet. To the north stood a smaller, rectangular sanctuary of the lion-god Mihos which appears to postdate the larger structure and to have been dedicated by Osorkon III. To the west

was a *ka* temple of the 6th-dynasty king Pepi I, of which little more than the remains of two rows of pillars survive, and to the northwest stood a similar *ka* temple of his predecessor Teti. To the southeast, a temple of Atum was built by Osorkon I or II. There are also the remains of jubilee chapels of Amenemhet III (12th dynasty) and Amenophis III (18th dynasty) in the area, and a Roman temple of which may have been dedicated to Agathos Daimon, 'the protecting spirit'.

Saft el-Hinna

This village lies to the southeast of the modern city of Zagazig on the site of the ancient provincial capital of Per-Sopdu ('The House of Sopdu'). The city was named for the falcon deity Sopdu who came to be revered as a god of the eastern region, and remains of the brick-built enclosure walls (75 × 40 m, 246 × 131 ft) of the god's temple were found here by Édouard Naville in 1885. The site contains a Late Period granite *naos* of Sopdu built by Nectanebo I; few artifacts discovered here date before the time of Ramesses II.

Tell el-Retaba

About 14 km (8.75 miles) to the west of Tell el-Maskhuta, at Tell el-Retaba, is the site of a fortified military installation which guarded the Wadi Tumilat approach to the Delta in Ramessid times. The site contains the remains of a temple of Atum, who was venerated in this eastern region (see Tell el-Maskhuta below), dating to the Ramessid period.

Tell el-Maskhuta

This site, located strategically in the Wadi Tumilat about 15 km (9.25 miles) west of modern Ismailiya, represents the remains of the ancient city and nome capital of Tjeku. Excavations were conducted in the

(Top) The remains of pillars of the ka *temple of Pepi I at Bubastis.*

(Above) A Hathor column capital from Bubastis.

(Right) The plan of the main temple compound at Bubastis, with the smaller Mihos sanctuary to the north of the larger Bastet temple.

(Far right) A relief from Tell el-Retaba of Ramesses II, showing him in the act of slaying a Semitic enemy before Atum.

N

Mihos temple

Temple of Bastet

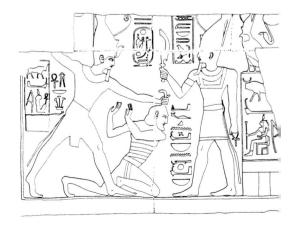

area in 1883 by Édouard Naville who uncovered a large enclosure (c. 210 × 210 m, 689 × 689 ft) with a badly damaged temple of Atum. He identified the site as the remains of the biblical city Pithom (*per Atum*: 'house of Atum') of the Exodus narrative. Recent excavations by J. S. Holladay of the University of Toronto have shown, however, that the site was founded in the reign of Necho (Nekau) II (610–595 BC) and was associated with the building of a canal which cut through the wadi to the northern tip of the Gulf of Suez. After centuries of decline the area experienced a revival under Ptolemy II who reopened the canal and installed a mortuary cult there to Arsinoe II around 270 BC.

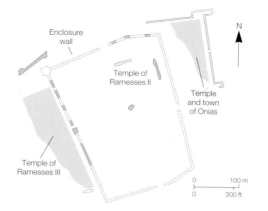

Tell el-Yahudiya, the 'Mound of the Jews' and site of ancient Leontopolis, holds a huge temple enclosure bounded by earth-built walls, little of which survive today.

Tell Atrib (Athribis)

Just a little to the northeast of the modern town of Benha on the Damietta branch of the Nile, Tell Atrib is the site of the ancient Hut-hery-ib – the Greek Athribis – a nome capital whose history stretches back to Old Kingdom times. Amenophis III constructed a temple here – the northernmost of his many great structures – but nothing of this building has survived. The remains of a number of temples have been located at this site, several dating to the Graeco-Roman Period, and one to the reign of the Late Period king Amasis (570–526 BC). These temple ruins are too fragmentary to allow any kind of full reconstruction, though most of the minor monuments found in the area can be dated from the 25th to 30th dynasties, and none are known to be earlier than the 12th dynasty.

Kom Abu Billo (Terenuthis)

The mound of Kom Abu Billo lies by the Rosetta branch of the Nile on the western edge of the Delta, near the route to the Wadi Natrun and the town of Tarrana, the classical Terenuthis. These names seem ultimately to be derived from that of the serpent goddess Renenutet or Termuthis, who clearly must have been an important deity of the area and was doubtless represented by a temple.

The earlier Egyptian name of the site may have been Per-Huthor-nbt-Mefket, 'The House of Hathor, Lady of Turquoise', however, and the temple found at this site by F. Ll. Griffith in 1887 was in fact dedicated to the goddess Hathor in her guise of 'Mistress of Mefket (Turquoise)'. Although Griffith was not able to determine the complete plan of the temple, it seems that the structure was begun by Ptolemy I (305–284 BC) – thus representing one of the few surviving monuments of that king – and completed by his successor Ptolemy II. Blocks from this temple were decorated with scenes of Ptolemy I and the goddess Hathor carved in extremely fine *bas* relief.

Tell el-Yahudiya (Leontopolis)

Some 20 km (12.5 miles) northeast of Cairo on the Ismailiya road is the site of ancient Nay-ta-hut, called in Greek Leontopolis. A huge earth-built enclosure wall (c. 515 × 490 m, 1,689 × 1,607 ft) dating to the late Middle Kingdom or Second Intermediate Period is usually thought to be of military origin, but could possibly be of a religious nature or perhaps saw use as both. Colossal statues of Ramesses II found in the northern part of the enclosure suggest the possibility of a temple of that monarch, and on the western side there was certainly a temple of Ramesses III. Outside the enclosure and to the northeast are the remains of the temple built by Onias, an exiled Jewish priest who was granted this favour by Ptolemy VI. The temple was closed by Vespasian in AD 71 following the rebellion of the Jews in Jerusalem.

Ausim (Letopolis)

About 13 km (8 miles) northwest of Cairo, this is the site of the ancient Egyptian town of Khem, known to the Greeks as Letopolis. As the capital of the second Lower Egyptian nome, both the area and its god Khenty-irty or Khenty-Khem, 'the Foremost One of Khem', are mentioned in texts dating back to the Old Kingdom. The deity was a form of the falcon-god Horus and doubtless had a temple in the area from early times, though the only monuments to have been found in the area are fragmentary ones bearing the names of the late kings Necho II, Psammetichus II, Hakoris and Nectanebo I of the 26th to 30th dynasties.

Heliopolis

Ancient Heliopolis, 'sun city' (Egyptian Iunu – the biblical 'On'), was situated in the area of Tell Hisn which lies on the northwestern outskirts of modern Cairo. Today, virtually nothing remains of what was once one of the most important cities of ancient

*A plan of the temple structure
at Heliopolis, based on an
ancient Egyptian plan.*

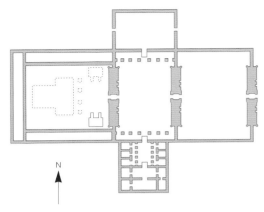

N

*The granite monolith of
Senwosret I at Heliopolis is
Egypt's oldest surviving
obelisk.*

Egypt – the third city after Thebes and Memphis – and the cult centre of the sun-god Re (along with the solar god Re-Horakhty, the primeval god Re-Atum and several associated deities). The form and size of the site's religious structures and even the main temple of the sun god are thus unknown, but it is possible that the solar temples of the 5th dynasty, of which we have evidence at Abu Ghurob and Abusir, were modelled at least to some extent on the solar temple of the Heliopolitan cult centre. If this is the case, then the sacred *benben* stone, the obelisk-like monolith which represented the primary symbol of sun-worship, was doubtless the central feature of the temple.

The remains of mud-brick walls in the area of Tell Hisn suggest a vast enclosure estimated at $1,100 \times 475$ m ($3,608 \times 1,558$ ft), and recent excavations have found signs of what may be a number of separate temples or parts of one great temple of New Kingdom date. Today, however, the only significant monument visible in the area is the red-granite obelisk of Senwosret I – the oldest surviving obelisk – which still stands in the area where Senwosret built a temple to the sun god. Although this temple has disappeared, we do know something of it from two ancient inscriptions. The first, found in the notes of a scribe written on a leather roll now in Berlin, records the decision of Senwosret to build a temple to Re-Horakhty in the third year of his reign – 1968 BC. The second is an actual plan of the temple inscribed on a thin sheet of stone (only fragments of which now exist) and which shows additions made to the temple by later kings along with the dimensions of the various parts and other information.

San el-Hagar (Tanis)

One of the most important Delta sites, San el-Hagar ('San of the stones') is the location of the ancient city of Dja'n (the biblical Zoan), called by the Greeks Tanis. This city was of particular importance in post-New Kingdom times, serving as the

burial site for the kings of the 21st and 22nd dynasties; a provincial capital in the Late Period; and a commercial capital of the Delta region until it was replaced by Naukratis and, eventually, by Alexandria. The site is located to the north of Faqus and Qantir in the eastern Delta and was excavated by Mariette (1860–80), Petrie (1883–86), Montet (1921–51) and others and is still undergoing study by French archaeologists.

The main temple precinct of Tanis lay within a massive mud-brick enclosure wall some 15 m (49 ft) thick and measuring almost 430×370 m ($1,410 \times 1,214$ ft). This great wall encompasses a number of independent structures as well as the remains of a separate, irregularly shaped inner enclosure. The complex is entered today from the west by way of the gate of Sheshonq III; and a processional avenue, originally decorated with over 15 obelisks of Ramesses II, leads from this entrance to the area of the Great Temple of Amun which stood at the enclosure's centre. The temple and its surrounding area are today a jumble of blocks, columns and mounds of rubble, but although few architectural features remain intact, the site has fortunately revealed much of its complex history.

While blocks of Old, Middle and New Kingdom structures are present, these all appear to be reused; and the earliest building on the site seems to have been the work of Psusennes I (whose foundation deposits were found beneath the sanctuary of the great Amun temple) and other rulers of the 21st and early 22nd dynasties. In the 30th dynasty Nectanebo I constructed a temple of Khonsu-Neferhotep on the northern side of the Amun temple

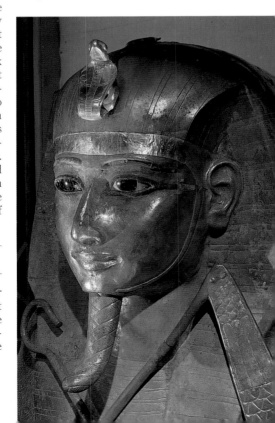

(built on a north–south axis) and utilized stone from earlier structures of Sheshonq V and Psammetichus I in the construction of a sacred lake to the east. A little further to the east, beyond the inner enclosure wall, are remains of a granite temple of Osorkon II containing Old Kingdom palmiform columns reused first by Ramesses II and again by Osorkon himself. Here also are the remains of a section of yet another enclosure wall and, to the southeast, the ruins of a temple dedicated to Horus of the eastern border region of Tcharu, built by Nectanebo II and completed by Ptolemy II.

Near the southwestern corner of the Amun Temple are the royal tombs of the 21st and 22nd dynasties (Psusennes I, Osorkon II, Takelot II, Amenemope, Sheshonq II, Sheshonq III) discovered by Pierre Montet in 1939. Apart from the burial of Tutankhamun, these temple tombs of Tanis remain the only royal Egyptian burials ever discovered relatively intact. Although the tombs appear to have had no superstructures and consisted only of underground mud-brick and stone chambers, they yielded a rich trove of royal burial treasures – including the hawk-headed silver coffin of Sheshonq II – now on display in the the Egyptian Museum, Cairo. The frequent reuse of earlier materials seen in the Tanite temples is also apparent in these Third Intermediate Period royal burials. Of the six royal interments, Psusennes' utilized the massive 19th-dynasty sarcophagus of Merenptah taken from the Valley of the Kings, Takelot II's appropriated a Middle Kingdom coffin, Amenemope's employed a sarcophagus lid made from a reused block of the Old Kingdom, and Sheshonq III's contained a sarcophagus made from an architrave of the 13th dynasty.

Outside the main compound, at its southern corner, is a smaller enclosure where Mut, Khonsu and the Asiatic goddess Astarte were worshipped. This temple was built by Siamun (21st dynasty) and Apries (26th dynasty) and restored by Ptolemy IV.

(Opposite below) The magnificent silver coffin of Psusennes I from San el-Hagar, the ancient Tanis, now in the Egyptian Museum, Cairo.

(Left) The site of San el-Hagar contains the temple complex of ancient Tanis, one of the largest and most impressive Delta sites and burial place of the kings of the 21st and 22nd dynasties.

(Below) The sprawling ruins of ancient Tanis are littered with the blocks and column stubs of many temples, some dating to as early as the Old Kingdom, though all the blocks predating the 21st dynasty appear to be reused.

Temple of Horus

Sacred lake

Temple of Nectanebo I

Great Temple of Amun

Inner enclosure wall

Royal tombs of 21st and 22nd dynasties

Monumental gate

N

0   100 m
0   300 ft

Temple of Mut, Khonsu and Astarte

From Memphis to Asyut

The region stretching from the Delta's base to Asyut in the south was the heartland of ancient Egypt for much of its history. Within the control of the great northern capital of Memphis, the area retained much of its unity – even in times of weakened centralized power. For the most part, the Nile Valley is broad in this region with a good deal of agricultural land which supported numerous cities and temples – as was also the case in the fertile depression of the Fayum which, at its height, was the most populous region of Egypt.

THE MEMPHITE REGION

On the border between the Delta and the Nile Valley, Lower and Upper Egypt, Memphis (Egyptian Mennefer) was the royal residence and capital of Egypt during the Early Dynastic period and Old Kingdom and a city of major importance throughout the rest of its history. Many great temples must have been constructed here, and the name of one of its sanctuaries – Hikuptah, 'The Temple of the *ka* of Ptah' – is thought to be the origin of the Greek word *Aigyptos* and our Egypt. Great as the city of Memphis was, it eventually declined and has long since disappeared under Nile-borne silt deposits. Only a few scant remains of one part of the sprawling site can be seen in the area of modern Mit Rahina.

While hardly anything of the ancient capital of Memphis and its temples has survived, the great burial grounds of the city proved to be more lasting and represent the greatest necropolises in the world. Along the high ground above the Nile's valley, successive dynasties of kings built their pyramid monuments – most with mortuary and valley temples (see below) – from Abu Roash in the north to Illahun at the entrance to the Fayum. Although most of these great complexes have been reduced to rubble over the millennia, the plans of many of their temples have been recovered and are of great interest for our understanding of temple development.

Mit Rahina (Memphis)

Ptah temple complex

About 15 km (9.25 miles) south of Cairo in the region of Mit Rahina are remains of the ancient city of Memphis. The enclosure of Ptah (probably the

The ruins of the ancient capital of Memphis today lie around the modern village of Mit Rahina. The southern enclosure of the temple of Ptah was one of the largest temple complexes of Egypt, but little remains and much is below the modern water table.

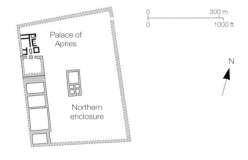

(Centre) The House of the Apis Bulls dates from the 26th dynasty and contains great calcite embalming beds over 5 m (16 ft 6 in) long.

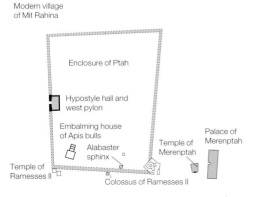

The Memphite Colossus of Ramesses II

Ramesses II's most famous colossi are the cliff-cut giants of his Great Temple at Abu Simbel (p. 223), and the great statue of the Ramesseum (p. 184), but even the more moderate-sized statues made for this king, such as the toppled colossus at Memphis, amaze by their awesome scale and the skill of their construction. The statue originally stood just outside the temple of Ptah.

The head of the toppled colossal statue of Ramesses II at Memphis. It once stood outside the temple of Ptah and is nearly 13 m (43 ft), from head to knees.

temple to the cult of Ramesses II in 'the domain of Ptah'), chief deity of the Memphite region, was one of the largest temple complexes in Egypt, but little remains within it except an embalming house for the Apis bull dating to the 26th dynasty. To its north, midpoint on the enclosure's western side, lie the remains of a hypostyle hall. This is the only area of the temple to have been systematically excavated (beginning with Flinders Petrie between 1908 and 1913), and the rest of the site is largely undisturbed due to the proximity of the modern village.

Temple of Hathor

Just outside the enclosure of Ptah at its southern corner in the area now called Kom el-Rabi'a are the scant remains of a small temple of Hathor built by Ramesses II.

Small temple of Ptah

A small temple of Ptah was built by Merenptah in the nearby area of Kom el-Qal'a, next to a palace of that king. As with its neighbouring structures, little of this building has survived, however.

(Below)The remains of the temple of Hathor, built by Ramesses II, outside the main temple enclosure at Memphis.

(Bottom) The small temple of Ptah built by Merenptah to the west of the main Ptah complex.

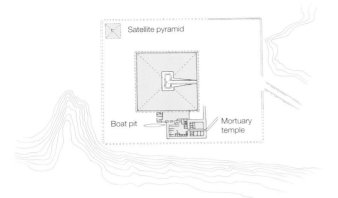

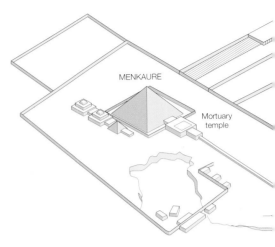

MENKAURE

Mortuary temple

The mortuary temple of Djedefre's pyramid complex at Abu Roash is unusual both in its position in relation to the pyramid and in its plan.

Abu Roash

Pyramid temples of Djedefre

Just west of Cairo, about 8 km (5 miles) north of Giza, Abu Roash is the northernmost site of the Memphite necropolis region and contains the pyramid of the 4th-dynasty king Djedefre (or Redjedef). Due to Djedefre's relatively short reign (2528–2520 BC), his pyramid complex was never completed, but something of its rather anomalous plan is clear. The mortuary temple stood to the east of the pyramid, but offset somewhat to the north. It was constructed with rough stone walls finished with mud-brick, and had various chambers or chapels around an open court. A deep recess in the masonry of the structure's rear wall is thought to have been prepared for a false door. The causeway, leading to the area in which the valley temple was planned, approaches the pyramid temple from the northeast rather than the east (as would be typical), though this orientation was determined by the region's terrain.

(Below) The remains of the mortuary temple of Djedefre at Abu Roash. It seems to have been rather hastily finished in mud-brick and rough stone, but the elements of the plan are still visible.

(Below right) A reconstruction of Khufu's mortuary temple, of which very little remains, shows its symmetrical and regular plan.

Pyramid temples of Khufu

Greatest and best known of all the pyramids, the Great Pyramid of Khufu (Cheops) has survived the ages since the 4th dynasty, yet nevertheless retains little evidence of its associated temples. The remains of the valley temple lie buried somewhere under the outskirts of Cairo, and little more than a rough area of basalt pavement shows the position of the mortuary temple against the pyramid's eastern side. It appears that this temple was square in shape with an inner sanctuary fronted by an open court with a pillared colonnade. Basalt (floor), granite (pillars) and limestone (walls) were used in its construction, though little more is known of its plan and appearance.

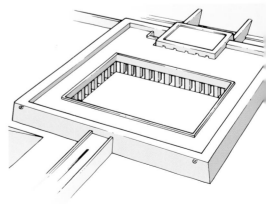

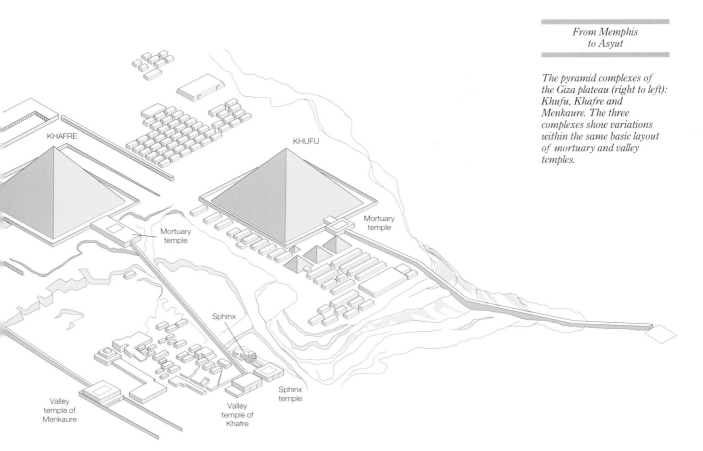

*The pyramid complexes of
the Giza plateau (right to left):
Khufu, Khafre and
Menkaure. The three
complexes show variations
within the same basic layout
of mortuary and valley
temples.*

Pyramid temples of Khafre

The second pyramid of Giza, that of Khufu's son
Khafre (Chephren), has survived in somewhat
better condition than its more famous predecessor,
and this is certainly true of its valley temple, which
stands next to the Great Sphinx and is substantially
preserved. This austere structure, while virtually
devoid of decoration, nevertheless impresses with
the clean lines and polished surfaces of its granite
pillars and calcite floors. Two doors (perhaps representing the two halves of Egypt or possibly the day
and night) open into a vestibule and a large, dimly
lit pillared hall which contained 23 seated statues of
the king (the central one, being wider, was possibly
counted twice in order symbolically to represent
every hour of the day). Above this area and the
storage chambers behind it, a roof-level court may
possibly have been incorporated into the architectural symbolism of the temple, providing a 'heaven'
in contrast to the chthonic depths of the darkened
chambers below. Certainly, the choice and arrangement of stone types and colours, and the numbers
of individual elements utilized in the architecture of
pyramid temples may indicate a conscious applica-
tion of cosmic symbolism, but its details must

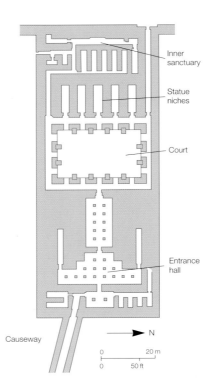

*Khafre's mortuary temple
was the most ambitious of
those on the Giza plateau in
both plan and decoration.
Each element of its plan is
significantly larger and more
complicated than those of its
neighbouring complexes,
though it includes the same
basic elements of entrance
hall, main court, five statue
niches and an inner
sanctuary, all of which would
become standard in later
mortuary temples.*

117

The interior of Khafre's valley temple, with its massive granite columns and lintels.

One of the masterpieces of ancient Egyptian sculpture: the statue of Khafre and the falcon god Horus.

The Old Kingdom Sphinx temple

This temple was apparently dedicated to the Great Sphinx before which it stands, but the absence of surviving contemporary inscriptions relating to the structure means that little is known of its history or specific purpose. The temple was probably constructed by the builders of Khafre's pyramid temples and the central court with its granite columns, each with a royal statue before it, is an almost exact copy of the court of Khafre's mortuary temple. As with Khafre's other temples, symbolic meaning has been seen in the numbers of columns (24 – perhaps one for each hour of the day and night), statues (10 or 12 – perhaps one for each hour of the day), and various chambers, but is just as unsure. Uniquely, the structure contains two sanctuaries – which may have had a significance associated possibly with the rising and setting sun – but the building is, as a whole, more symmetrically designed than any other temple of its period. Mark Lehner has shown that the temple may well have been solar oriented, however, and the Great Sphinx could, as Lehner suggests, have been visualized as an image of the king merging with the sun or perhaps presenting offerings in this temple. Nevertheless, this Sphinx temple was left unfinished by its builders, and it is possible that it was never dedicated to service in the age of its construction.

remain unsure. A number of statues were found in the temple, including that of Khafre on a throne, his head enfolded by the wings of the falconiform god Horus – one of the greatest works of Egyptian art.

The mortuary temple constructed close to the pyramid's eastern face is reduced almost to its foundations, but enough survives to understand its plan. It was distinctly larger than earlier pyramid temples and also more complex, containing all the basic elements of the developed form – entrance halls, main court, five niches and inner sanctuary – employed through succeeding generations. The forepart of the structure has many similarities to the plan of the valley temple, though the inner temple resembled the basic form of the earlier pyramid temple of Khufu. In Khafre's temple, huge limestone blocks were used to form the cores of the walls which were lined with smaller blocks of finer red granite, or in the case of some chambers, calcite. This temple also contained a number of statues of the king (including 12 seated statues nearly 4 m or 13 ft high) and the inner walls of its court may have been partially decorated with reliefs. As in the valley temple, symbolic meaning has often been seen in the number of chambers and their arrangement in this temple, but lack of textual verification means this must remain largely speculative.

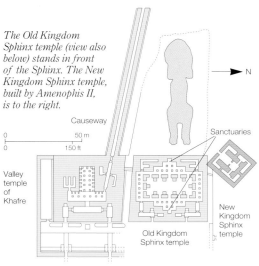

The Old Kingdom Sphinx temple (view also below) stands in front of the Sphinx. The New Kingdom Sphinx temple, built by Amenophis II, is to the right.

The New Kingdom Sphinx temple

On a rise a little to the northeast of the Great Sphinx, a New Kingdom temple was built when, at this much later time, the cult of the Sphinx is known to have become popular. The temple was constructed by Amenophis II in the first year of his reign (c. 1427 BC), and its cult was certainly activated; but the structure is now destroyed, with only fragmentary remains surviving.

Pyramid temples of Menkaure

The third of the great 4th-dynasty pyramids of Giza appears to have been left unfinished. Its valley temple was hastily completed in mud-brick and then rebuilt at a later date (some time in the 6th dynasty) after suffering substantial flood damage. The temple is now ruined, but its plan reveals an entrance area before an open court and a rear section with magazines and other chambers surrounding the sanctuary. A large amount of statuary was found in the temple, including the famous triads of the king with Hathor and various nome deities.

Like the valley temple, Menkaure's mortuary temple was begun with large limestone blocks, but completed in mud-brick, though the original intention was to face the walls with granite as in earlier temples. Constructed more along the lines of Khufu's mortuary temple, the structure was fairly square with an open court before an inner section of halls and smaller chambers. Evidence of statuary was also found here, including fragments of a larger-than-life statue of the king which may have stood in front of a false door at the rear of the temple – symbolizing the spirit of the king emerging from his pyramid tomb. The causeway connecting the two temples would have been roofed over, but was apparently never completed.

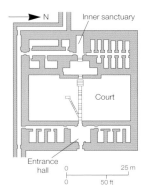

The relatively complex valley temple of Menkaure was begun in stone and finished in mud-brick.

Menkaure's valley temple contained a number of fine group statues of the king with the goddess Hathor (on the left below) and various nome deities.

The pyramids at Abusir (left to right): Neferirkare, Niuserre and Sahure. The sun temples of Userkaf and Niuserre are visible behind.

(Below) Niuserre's sun temple paralleled the standard pyramid complex in many ways, but in others was unique (see also p. 21).

(Below right) The court of Niuserre's sun temple contained a great calcite altar in the shape of four hetep *offering signs around the symbol of the sun.*

Abu Ghurob

Sun temple of Niuserre

The 5th dynasty saw the rise of special 'sun temples', built in addition to pyramid complexes and dedicated to the god Re. While the names of six of these structures are known, only two have been found. That of Niuserre at Abu Ghurob some 10 km (6 miles) southwest of Cairo is the best preserved and, although badly ruined, can be plausibly reconstructed. Based on the typical pyramid complex of the period, this sun temple was apparently first constructed in mud-brick and later rebuilt in stone. It consisted of a valley temple linked by a causeway to an upper temple area with a huge obelisk-like masonry structure – the *benben* – 36 m (118 ft) tall, which took the place of the pyramid and which served as a symbol of the sun god. The 'obelisk' itself stood on an enormous pedestal, 20 m (65 ft 6 in) high. In Niuserre's structure, the upper temple's entrance building opened to a large courtyard

flanked on its northern side by magazines and slaughterhouses, and with a great four-sided calcite altar – each side the shape of the *hetep* hieroglyph for offering – positioned before the obelisk.

The entrance vestibule and a corridor which ran around two sides of the complex were decorated with royal jubilee scenes (presumably stressing the king's relationship with the sun god), and a small, independent structure built against the obelisk's southern side, the so-called 'chamber of the seasons', was decorated with an array of painted reliefs depicting many vivid scenes from nature – the sun-god's 'realm'. Just outside the temple complex are the remains of a large brick-built model of a solar boat reminiscent of the boat pits and their buried vessels positioned around earlier pyramids. Already ancient by New Kingdom times, the temple was piously restored by Ramesses II, only to decay again as history progressed. The site was excavated by the German archaeologists Ludwig Borchardt and Heinrich Schäfer in 1898–1901.

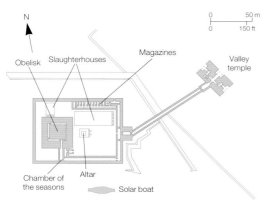

Sun temple of Userkaf

Halfway between Niuserre's sun temple and the pyramids of Abusir, the sun temple of Userkaf sits on a similar promontory on the desert's edge. Userkaf's is the earlier of the two known 5th-dynasty temples of this type; but the king's brief reign of seven years (2465–2458 BC) did not allow him to finish the structure or to decorate it, so that it was later completed by Niuserre.

As in the latter king's temple, a valley building is connected by means of a causeway to an upper temple area, but the plan of Userkaf's valley temple seems to have been somewhat anomalous, having a central court which fronted at least five ritual chapels. The valley temple was also curiously offset from its causeway; and, more importantly, both temple and causeway seem to have been oriented towards the general direction of Heliopolis, and perhaps, as Ronald Wells has suggested, towards stars that would have risen above the predawn horizon around 2400 BC. If the latter is true, it may indicate that Userkaf's valley temple functioned as a kind of astronomical clock for the sacrifices which were made at dawn.

Excavation and study completed by Herbert Ricke and Gerhard Haeny in the mid-1950s indicated multiple stages of building in the upper area of the sun temple proper. Initially the compound seems to have contained not an obelisk but a mast on a raised mound – similar to the sacred structure at Hierakonpolis. The name given to Userkaf's sun temple, Nekhen-Re or 'Stronghold of Re', may even refer, at one level, to the ancient Nekhen – the name of Hierakonpolis itself. The structure could thus have linked in its name, form and orientation the earliest temple worship of Egyptian tradition with the solar-oriented Heliopolitan cult of the Old Kingdom.

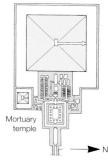

A schist head of Userkaf wearing the red crown; it was found in his sun temple.

Abusir

Pyramid temples of Sahure

The fourth pyramid field of the Memphite region (moving southwards from Abu Roash in the north), Abusir lies a little over 12 km (7.5 miles) south of Cairo and contains several important monuments. The modern name of the site is derived from the ancient Greek name Busiris, itself taken from the Egyptian Per-Wsir or 'House of Osiris' – a fitting name for a necropolis and one given to several sites in Egypt. The royal cemetery at Abusir was founded by the 5th-dynasty king Sahure who constructed his pyramid complex on a plateau a little to the south of the sun temple of his predecessor Userkaf. Several of the pyramids of the kings who followed Sahure in building at this site are aligned on a northeasterly axis – possibly a conscious orientation towards Heliopolis.

The 5th-dynasty pyramid complex of Sahure at Abusir is recognized as the conceptual predecessor of all subsequent Old Kingdom structures of this type. Although its valley temple was fairly simple in layout, with little more than a columned portico

(Above) The pyramids of Abusir today.

(Below) Sahure's pyramid complex, with its somewhat unusual valley temple.

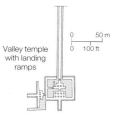

Mortuary temple

N

Valley temple with landing ramps

0   50 m
0   100 ft

The mortuary temple of Sahure provided the pattern for virtually all subsequent mortuary temples of the Old Kingdom.

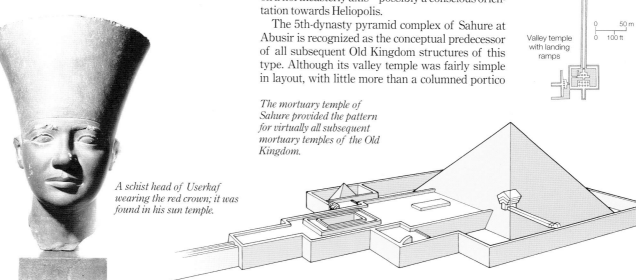

(Left) The pyramid of Sahure today is in a ruinous state. In front of it are the relatively extensive remains of the mortuary temple.

(Right) A reconstruction of Sahure's pyramid and mortuary temple, with its portico of graceful palm-frond columns.

(Below) The ruins of Sahure's mortuary temple still display much of the scale and complexity of this important monument.

preceding a 'T'-shaped hall, the mortuary temple built against the pyramid's east face was more complex than any which had gone before. At the top of the causeway a long narrow entrance hall opened into a corridor around a pillared court, which led in turn to a complex inner temple with various halls, magazines and statue niches for images of the king, and an 'offering hall' with a black granite statue of the king before a false door. Containing an estimated 10,000 sq. m (almost 108,000 sq. ft) of decoration (of which only one hundredth survives), the temple complex displayed representations of offering bearers and various scenes showing the king despatching enemies, fishing and fowling, and engaged in other activities signifying the protection of the temple and upholding of cosmic order.

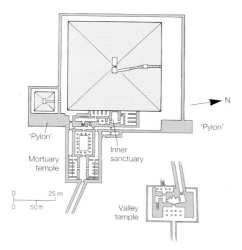

Pyramid temples of Niuserre

Just south of the pyramid of Sahure, Niuserre's valley temple (originally intended for Neferirkare – see below) consisted of a portico with papyrus-bundle columns and several chambers angled to meet the axis of the short section of pavement which connects to the causeway of Neferirkare which Niuserre usurped. The upper mortuary temple has most of the same elements as the influential temple of Sahure, but in a very different configuration, with much of the temple offset from the centre of the pyramid due to the presence of earlier mastaba tombs.

In the temple's decoration Niuserre is shown in the company of the gods in the manner which becomes standard in the inner sections of later temples. Of greatest importance for the subsequent development of temple form, however, were the massive masonry features at the end of the pyramid's court which seem to be the first precursors of the great pylons of later temples.

Pyramid temples of Neferirkare

Evidently planned to be quite close in layout to the structures of Sahure's pyramid complex, the temple

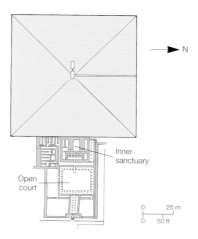

(Above left) Niuserre's mortuary and valley temples essentially continue the pattern established by Sahure, despite some differences in configuration.

(Above) Neferirkare's mortuary temple considerably widened the court before the inner temple area, but the inner chambers largely follow Sahure's plan.

(Left) The pyramid temple of Neferirkare was begun in stone but completed in mud-brick and wood, so little remains of its outer areas.

(Below left) The mortuary temple of Neferirkare at Abusir also contains the same essential elements as its immediate predecessors.

building of his brother Neferirkare was curtailed. The valley temple (later usurped by Niuserre) and causeway were unfinished at the time of the king's death, and while the inner sections of the mortuary temple were constructed in stone, the outer sections were completed in mud-brick with wooden columns in multiple-lotus-bud style. Fragmentary papyrus records (the earliest known texts written in the hieratic script on papyrus) found at the mortuary temple of Neferirkare provide detailed temple accounts, in addition to work rosters and lists of supplies. The texts describe regular deliveries (twice daily) of provisions from the king's sun temple to his pyramid, indicating that the temple at that site was supported by the nearby sun temple – perhaps because the latter was completed first and already had its support infrastructure in place.

Pyramid temple of Raneferef

The so-called 'Unfinished Pyramid' of this ephemeral ruler of the 5th dynasty is located at the southern end of the chain of pyramids at Abusir. Excavation of the pyramid by a Czech expedition in the 1970s determined that the complex was indeed unfinished, but that it was nevertheless made functional for the cult of the king. The excavators believe that a first stage of the mortuary temple was hastily completed between the king's death and his burial, and that only later were many of the other magazines and chambers added. Of special interest in the temple's earliest section is a hypostyle hall – one of the earliest found in any Egyptian temple – with four rows of five wooden columns of multiple-lotus-bud style. Other columns in this temple were of palm and papyrus style.

Saqqara

Some 14 km (8.75 miles) south of Cairo, Saqqara represents the oldest and largest of the pyramid fields of the Memphite region. One of the most important necropolises in Egypt, it is sometimes said to be named after the Egyptian chthonic and mortuary deity Sokar, though the modern name is more probably derived from that of a medieval Arab tribe of the area. The Saqqaran necropolis is a huge area stretching almost 6 km (3.75 miles) from north to south. The site also saw use over a vast span of time ranging from the Early Dynastic period to the Christian era. Central to the area is the great Step Pyramid complex of Djoser – the Horus Netjerykhet – but Saqqara also contains a number of other, lesser monuments which confirm developmental patterns in the history of the Egyptian temple.

Pyramid temple of Teti

The pyramid of Teti, founder of the 6th dynasty, is the northernmost known at Saqqara, and stands a few hundred metres northwest of Djoser's Step Pyramid complex (see below). The mortuary temple was pillaged for its stone and little remains, though the plan is clearly a continuation of the form followed by Djedkare-Isesi (p. 129) and Unas (p. 128) in which the entrance hall leads to an open court with both these elements being flanked by magazines arranged in a similar fashion. The inner temple area also contains the standard five statue niches and the sanctuary and its related chambers in a similar layout. There are a few archaizing features, however (such as the square granite pillars of the colonnaded court), showing that the Egyptian temple architects rarely forgot the more ancient models of their tradition. The valley temple – if it ever existed – has not been traced.

(Below) Raneferef's pyramid complex at Abusir: its unusual shape is due to the large southern annexe which provided the sacrificial animals for the ritual offerings in the temple itself. From papyri found at the site we know its name: the 'Sanctuary of the Knife'.

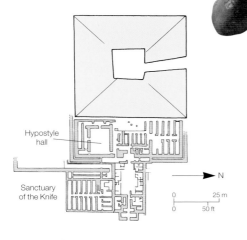

Hypostyle hall

N

Sanctuary of the Knife

0   25 m
0   50 ft

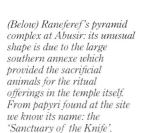

(Above) This limestone statue of Raneferef was found in the king's mortuary temple. The statue unites the king's image with that of the falconiform god of kingship, Horus, in an echo of the famous statue of Khafre.

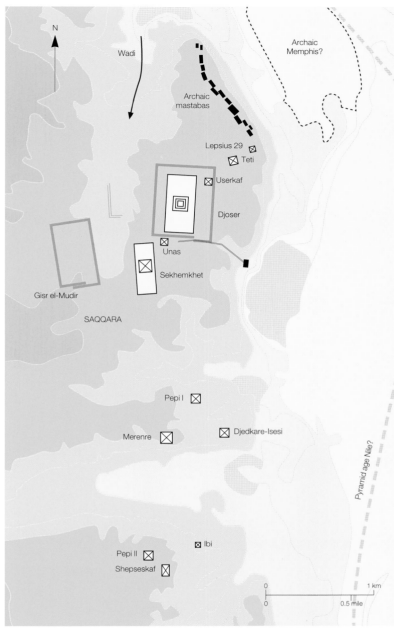

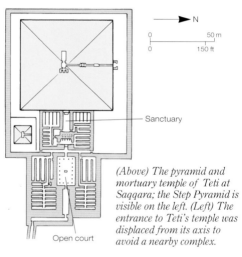

(Above) The pyramid and mortuary temple of Teti at Saqqara; the Step Pyramid is visible on the left. (Left) The entrance to Teti's temple was displaced from its axis to avoid a nearby complex.

Sanctuary

Open court

N

0   50 m

0   150 ft

(Right) The Saqqara pyramid field contains a number of ruined but important pyramid temples.

(Below) Much of the stone of Teti's mortuary temple was pillaged by stone robbers.

N

Wadi

Archaic Memphis?

Archaic mastabas

Lepsius 29 ⊠

⊠ Teti

⊠ Userkaf

Djoser

⊠ Unas

Sekhemkhet

Gisr el-Mudir

SAQQARA

Pepi I ⊠

Merenre ⊠

⊠ Djedkare-Isesi

⊠ Ibi

Pepi II ⊠

Shepseskaf ⊠

Pyramid age Nile?

0   1 km

0   0.5 mile

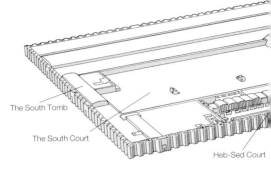

(Below) The funerary complex of Djoser at Saqqara was the first pyramid complex. It contained a number of temple and sanctuary-like structures, many of which were clearly for symbolic rather than actual use.

The South Tomb

The South Court

Heb-Sed Court

(Above) The pyramid of the 5th-dynasty king Userkaf rises above the sand hills of Saqqara – close to the great funerary complex of Djoser.

(Right) Atypically, the mortuary temple complex of Userkaf was constructed south of the king's pyramid.

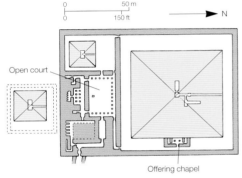

Open court

Offering chapel

Userkaf's mortuary temple, like others of its dynasty, contained particularly fine scenes in raised relief.

Pyramid temple of Userkaf

The first king of the 5th dynasty, Userkaf constructed his pyramid at the northeast corner of the great complex of Djoser. The most significant feature of this king's mortuary temple is that it was placed, unusually, to the south of the pyramid instead of on its eastern side. This may have been for some symbolic reason (possibly to ensure year-round exposure to the sun) or, perhaps more likely as the change is not continued, for some simple practical reason such as the possibility that a large moat which surrounded the pyramid complex of Djoser may have run along the eastern side of the area of Userkaf's pyramid, leaving only enough space for the small offering chapel which was constructed there. Whatever the reason for the relocation of the main mortuary temple, strangely, its orientation was also changed; and although the various architectural elements are standard, their arrangement is unique. Nevertheless, this anomalous structure does not seem to have included any new aspects which were of lasting influence. The head from a colossal statue of Userkaf was found in the temple debris.

Pyramid temples of Djoser

The 3rd-dynasty Step Pyramid of Djoser (Net-jerykhet) is not only Egypt's first pyramid and royal complex in stone but also represents one of Egypt's largest and most complex monuments. Although the vast compound contained many features which are not directly associated with the pyramid's temple structures – beyond the fact that the whole complex was aimed at the king's eternal rule – they should be mentioned here because of their influence on later stone architecture. It is here, for example (thanks to the work of the French Egyptologist, Jean-Philippe Lauer), that we find the first clear evidence of a portico, hypostyle hall, and colonnade as well as many smaller architectural features found throughout all later periods. Certainly no other monument in Egyptian history since the primitive

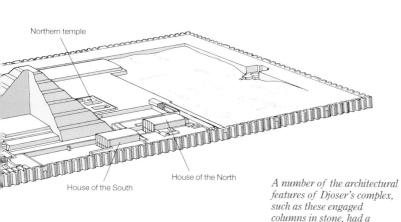

Northern temple

House of the North

House of the South

A number of the architectural features of Djoser's complex, such as these engaged columns in stone, had a lasting effect on successive Egyptian temple architecture.

shrine of Hierakonpolis (which provided a tradition in which Djoser's pyramid had its own roots – see p. 17) was so important in influencing future temple design and appearance. Space cannot be given here to all the individual features of the complex, but some are of particular interest in understanding temple development.

The Step Pyramid itself was built within an enclosure of some 15 ha (37 acres) bounded by a niched limestone wall 10.5 m (34 ft) high. The wall seems to have been surrounded by a great moat which together encompassed not only a mortuary temple and other features on the pyramid's northern side, but also scores of subterranean shafts and galleries and, to the south, the large open area known as the South Court which was adjoined by several complex suites of functional and dummy buildings. Those to the southwest of the pyramid were of special importance as they were associated with the celebration of the Sed festival – the king's royal jubilee of renewal celebrated during his reign and evidently intended to be continued in this mortuary complex throughout his afterlife.

The false chapels which surrounded the Heb-Sed Court are among the most famous structures within the compound, for those on the east were given the narrow elevation and curved roof of the canonical shrine of Lower Egypt (represented by the hieroglyph 𓉐), and most of those on the west were formed to reflect the shrine of Upper Egypt (𓉗). Both building types are merely stylized renderings of very ancient architectural types representing the shrines of the gods, but they nevertheless show the Egyptians' interest in maintaining the traditions of the earliest sacred buildings.

Beyond the Heb-Sed Court are the larger Houses of the North and South, so-named as they are believed to represent the archaic shrines of Upper and Lower Egypt at Hierakonpolis and Buto (p. 17 and p. 18) due to the heraldic floral images of the lily and papyrus carved on the capitals of their respective engaged columns. Like the Sed Chapels, these were dummy buildings, however, and thus of purely symbolic significance. It is thought that all these dummy buildings were at least partially covered with earth after their construction to symbolize their role in the underworld.

The mortuary temple built against the pyramid's northern face is also of interest as it is unlike later structures of its type in its orientation (in subsequent pyramids the structure would be moved to the east), in the layout of its individual elements (which here seem to follow the plan of an Early Dynastic brick temple found at Saqqara – also located on the north side of its associated tomb), and in the entrance corridor to the pyramid's

(Centre below) Dummy chapels within Djoser's complex are stone representations of much earlier wood and reed sanctuaries.

(Below) This statue of Djoser was found in his serdab *– a small shrine-like feature on the north side of the pyramid, adjacent to the northern temple.*

subterranean chambers which ran through the centre of the building. The entrance to this large rectangular structure was in its eastern wall. No actual doors seem to have been fitted to this portal, but, as in a number of other cases in Djoser's complex, a dummy door was carved into the stone of the wall adjoining the northern jamb. Little is left of this structure today, though the curtain walls which screened its entrance are relatively intact.

Pyramid temples of Unas

Unas, last king of the 5th dynasty, built his pyramid directly to the south of Djoser's great complex. The mortuary temple against its eastern face is almost identical in plan to that of Djedkare-Isesi (see below) with its entrance hall and columned hall flanked by magazines, and the inner temple with similarly arranged statue niches and sanctuary, etc; though the great pylon structures of that king's complex were substantially reduced. The valley temple of Unas is of fairly complex plan; and though it does not provide any important developments of its own, the surviving granite palm-frond columns show that a graceful style and high level of workmanship were applied to this building. More than a thousand years after Unas, Khaemwaset, the son of Ramesses II and high priest of Memphis, restored the complex – or its cult – in the course of dismantling Old Kingdom monuments in the area to build the so-called 'Ptah' Temple for the cult of Ramesses II at Mit Rahina.

(Right) The mortuary and valley temples of Unas – and the covered causeways which connected them – were all richly decorated. This relief fragment from Unas' mortuary temple shows the king being suckled by an unidentified goddess.

(Below and centre) The mortuary temple of Unas is transitional to the plan used in 6th-dynasty pyramid complexes.

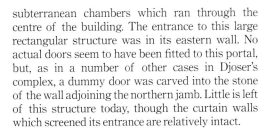

Sanctuary

Open court

Valley temple

N

0   50 m
0   150 ft

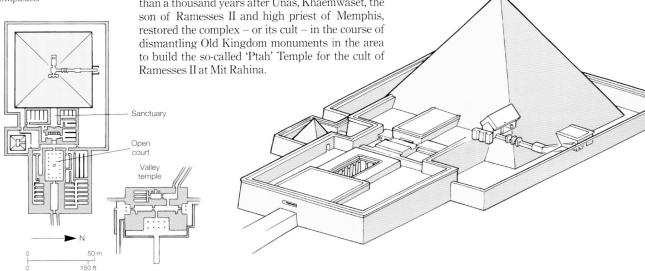

Granite palm-frond columns stand at the entrance to the ruins of Unas' valley temple. In the background is Djoser's Step Pyramid.

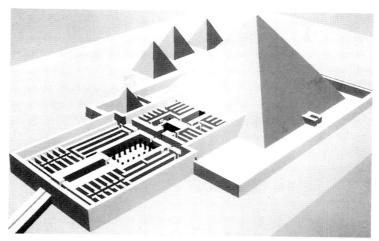

A cutaway reconstruction of the mortuary temple of Pepi I showing the various areas of the structure and revealing the high degree of regularity in the temple's design.

Pyramid temples of Pepi I

Like most pyramid complexes at Saqqara, that of the 6th-dynasty king Pepi I, built about 2 km (1.25 miles) south of the Step Pyramid, has suffered from extensive pillaging of its limestone; but careful work by the French mission has resulted in a good degree of understanding of its plan and features. The valley temple has not been excavated, but the mortuary temple was very similar to that of Pepi's predecessor Teti (p. 124). Magazines flank the narrow entrance hall and a porticoed court open to the sky, while the area of the inner temple contains the established statue niches directly before the sanctuary and other chambers of the temple's core. Statues of bound prisoners representing Egypt's enemies were found here, but their original location in the temple area is unknown.

Pyramid temples of Djedkare-Isesi

Towards the end of the 5th dynasty Djedkare-Isesi built his pyramid in a secluded position about 2 km (1.25 miles) south of Djoser's Step Pyramid. The valley temple of this complex remains buried, and while the mortuary temple is not completely cleared, the basic plan is clearly a continuation of the dynasty's previous structures. The causeway leads to a narrow entrance hall flanked by multiple

magazines (though, as usual, these are accessible only from the inner section of the temple), an open court is surrounded by a columned portico which leads in turn to a broad transverse hall followed by the inner temple with its five statue niches, offering hall or sanctuary and other rooms. Here the basic elements are more symmetrically arranged than in earlier structures, however, and the placement of

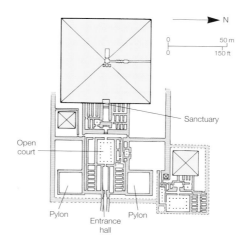

The mortuary temple of Djedkare-Isesi's pyramid complex contained massive proto-pylons on each side of its entrance, providing an important link in the development of this temple feature that became so prominent later.

The scattered remains of the mortuary temple of Djedkare-Isesi. Fragments of reliefs found suggest that it was richly decorated.

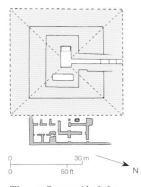

The small pyramid of the 8th-dynasty king Ibi had only a brick-built mortuary temple at the base of its eastern face.

the two massive masonry 'pylons' at the temple's entrance provides clear evidence of the further development of this important temple feature.

Pyramid temple of Ibi

The small, 8th-dynasty pyramid of Ibi, built 1.5 km (*c.* 1 mile) south of the pyramid of Pepi I, is very ruined. It did have a small mortuary temple against its east face (with an entrance at its north end), but this was only brick-built and apparently there was no causeway or valley temple.

Pyramid temples of Pepi II

The last king of the 6th dynasty constructed his pyramid complex 3 km (1.75 miles) south of the Step Pyramid close to the 4th-dynasty monument of Shepseskaf. Of standard size – yet relatively small considering the king's 94-year reign – the pyramid and its temples largely follow the layout and decoration of earlier structures and, while much has been destroyed, some notable, if fragmentary, features remain.

Although some areas of the complex were undecorated, it appears to have contained reliefs showing the king vanquishing the forces of disorder in human and animal form, as well as performing the ritual 'race' of the Sed festival, taking part in various religious festivals and being suckled by a goddess – ancient scenes which recur in temple decoration throughout most of Egypt's later history. Of architectural importance, the central one of the mortuary temple's five cult niches contained the base of a life-size royal statue which remains the only direct evidence we have that these ever-present chambers were in fact statue niches. The enlargement of the mortuary temple's eastern walls also continued the development of the pylon-like feature begun by Niuserre at Abusir.

Today, there are only scant remains of the valley temple of Pepi II.

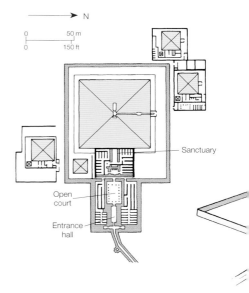

A carved block from the valley temple of Pepi II: while some of the relief decoration of Pepi's complex was of original design, much was copied from the earlier complex of Sahure.

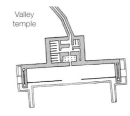

(Above) In plan the pyramid complex of Pepi II displays the culmination of the development of Old Kingdom mortuary and valley temple designs.

(Opposite) Khendjer's funerary pyramid complex incorporated a mortuary temple, but little is known about it.

Mastaba temple of Shepseskaf

The last ruler of the 4th dynasty, Shepseskaf chose to break with the tradition of four generations and planned his tomb not as a pyramid but as a giant mastaba – a rectangular 'bench'-like tomb structure – in the region of south Saqqara. The small mortuary temple on the eastern side of this monument was also quite different in layout from its predecessors, though the structure contained a false door and offering hall along with a number of magazines. The standard statue niches are absent and the greater part of the temple was taken up by a small inner and larger outer court. The valley temple is unexcavated.

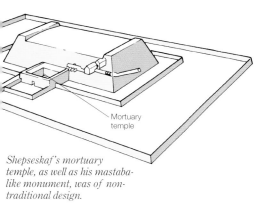

Shepseskaf's mortuary temple, as well as his mastaba-like monument, was of non-traditional design.

Pyramid temple of Khendjer

The pyramid of Khendjer at south Saqqara is the only pyramid known to have been completed in the 13th dynasty. A large mortuary temple was built against the pyramid's east face, but only parts of its pavement and some column and relief fragments remain.

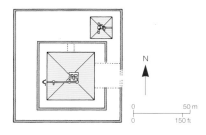

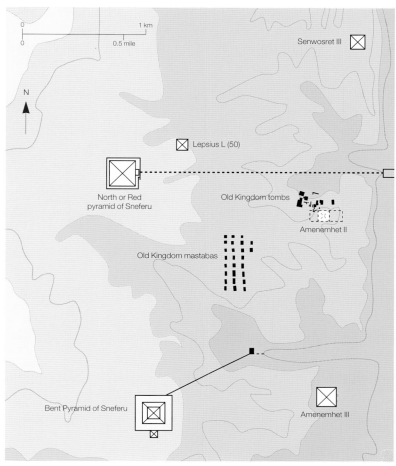

Dahshur

Some 20 km (12.5 miles) south of Cairo the area of Dahshur represents the second major pyramid field of the Memphite necropolis after Saqqara. A number of pyramid complexes were constructed there: the two largest being those of the 4th-dynasty monarch Sneferu – the Bent Pyramid and the North or Red Pyramid – which were followed by three somewhat smaller pyramids of the Middle Kingdom (Amenemhet II, Senwosret III and Amenemhet III) as well as other funerary structures.

Pyramid temples of Senwosret III

The northernmost of the pyramids of Dahshur, the 12th-dynasty monument of Senwosret III was expanded during the course of its construction. Although badly destroyed, we know that a small mortuary temple was originally built at the centre of its east face and a new, much larger temple constructed to the south when the complex was enlarged. Excavations conducted by the Metropolitan Museum of Art have determined that the earlier temple consisted of little more than an entrance

The area of Dahshur includes the remains of several important pyramids with their associated temples.

A red granite head of Senwosret III from Karnak.

chamber, magazines and offering hall with false door. Walls decorated in very high relief have panels containing the royal name and titles. The larger temple seems to have incorporated a fore-court with papyrus-bundle columns and various inner chambers. Built on a massive scale, this structure may have provided, as Dieter Arnold has suggested, the model for the great 'labyrinth' of Amenemhet III at Hawara. Numerous fragments of relief which have been recovered from this enormous temple – some depicting the king in a cloak worn for the Sed festival – may lead to at least a partial reconstruction of its outward appearance. Dieter Arnold, the excavator, believes that the south temple may foreshadow New Kingdom mortuary temple designs at Thebes.

Pyramid temples of Sneferu

The first 4th-dynasty ruler Sneferu (father of Khufu, builder of the Great Pyramid at Giza) constructed two pyramids at Dahshur. To the north is his 'North' or 'Red Pyramid', not built until the 30th year of Sneferu's reign. Its mortuary temple is somewhat small – nothing like as large as Khufu's at Giza – and seems to have been hastily completed.

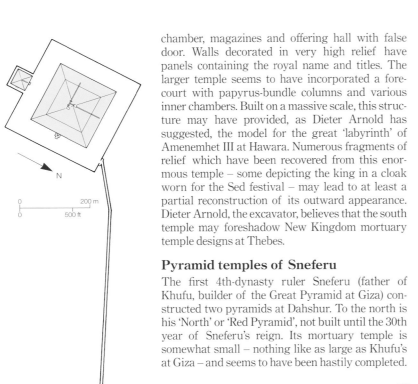

(Above) Sneferu depicted wearing a heb-sed *robe, from a stela discovered in the enclosure of the Bent Pyramid.*

(Left) The Bent Pyramid of Sneferu had only a small chapel on its eastern side but a fully developed valley temple.

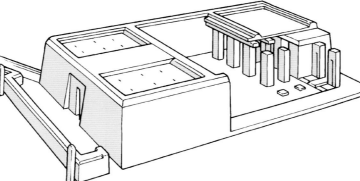

Valley temple

(Below) The mortuary temple of Sneferu's North Pyramid was destroyed to ground level.

The associated valley temple has never been excavated. The valley temple (not actually down in the valley) of Sneferu's earlier pyramid in this area, the so-called Bent Pyramid, is of particular interest in the history of temple development both as it represents the first instance of a 'valley'-type temple (though in this case located at the edge of a flood-plain rather than in the Nile Valley itself) and because it contains features of later mortuary temples such as the court, pillars and associated statues. Only a small chapel stood at the Bent Pyramid's eastern face. While Rainer Stadelmann has pointed out that this chapel was not part of the overall development of the mortuary temple because the Bent Pyramid was completed as a cenotaph rather than an actual tomb, it is also possible that the 'valley temple' was intended to fulfil functions which were later divided between the two areas of the complex.

Pyramid temple of Amenemhet II

The 'White Pyramid' of the 12th-dynasty ruler Amenemhet II was built in a long narrow enclosure to the east of Sneferu's pyramids in central Dahshur. The enclosure is oriented east to west and has two massive pylon-like structures at its entrance which presumably fronted a temple, but little else survives. A valley temple is not known for this complex.

Pyramid temples of Amenemhet III

A little more than a kilometre (0.5 mile) east of the Bent Pyramid in south Dahshur stands the 12th-dynasty 'Black Pyramid' of Amenemhet III. Despite the fact that this pyramid was not chosen for the king's tomb (another pyramid was built at Hawara), it was given temples of simplified design. The temple against the pyramid's eastern face is destroyed, but seems to have been little more than a court with papyrus-bundle columns and an offering hall. A number of houses believed to be the homes of priests were built along the northern side of the causeway leading to the valley temple, which consisted of an inner and outer court, the latter with thickened walls.

Mazghuna

The owners of the two small unfinished pyramids at Mazghuna, some 5 km (3 miles) southeast of the Bent Pyramid, are unknown, though Amenemhet IV or Sobekneferu of the very late 12th dynasty or a king of the 13th dynasty are all candidates. The northernmost of the two structures was only partially built. The southern monument is more complete, however. It included a small mud-brick chapel set into the eastern side of a type of wavy enclosure wall, perhaps crudely imitating in brick the idea of the recessed-niche walls of earlier periods but reminiscent of the undulating enclosure walls of later temples.

Lisht

Pyramid temple of Amenemhet I

Midway between Dahshur and Meidum, the area of Lisht has two pyramids, the first belonging to the 12th-dynasty king Amenemhet I. The much-destroyed mortuary temple of this structure was built on a terrace cut into a hill lower than the pyramid, showing that although the tomb followed the old Memphite pyramid pattern, its temple was influenced by Theban styles developed by Nebhepetre Mentuhotep in the previous dynasty (p. 180). Foundation deposits discovered in the temple included an ox skull, paint grinders and model vases. The valley temple lies below water level and has not been excavated.

(Above) Amenemhet I, from a decorated lintel in the king's mortuary temple at Lisht.

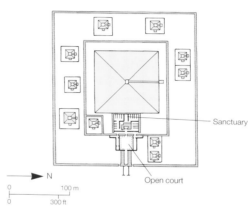

(Left) Senwosret I's pyramid at Lisht had a small chapel at its northern entrance as well as the main mortuary temple on its eastern side.

Pyramid temple of Senwosret I

The second 12th-dynasty pyramid at Lisht was built by Amenemhet I's son, Senwosret I, who returned to the more purely Memphite style of pyramid complex. The temple, built against the pyramid's east face, is now almost totally destroyed, but its apparent plan shows that it virtually recreated the typical mortuary temple of the 6th dynasty – with an entrance hall and open court (though here without flanking magazines) before the inner statue niche and sanctuary area – although the types of stone used were more economically chosen. The valley temple has never been found.

Meidum

In addition to his two pyramids at Dahshur, Sneferu also seems to have begun and later completed the pyramid at Meidum. Now a three-stepped tower, it is strangely denuded of its outer layers which were added in a later stage of construction. It was during this later work on the pyramid that a very small temple or chapel was constructed before its eastern face, though the structure seems not to have been

completed or at least not inscribed for its owner. The temple is so diminutive that it may not have been a true mortuary temple, but rather a commemorative chapel to the king. Here two stelae, 4.2 m (13 ft 9 in) tall, were placed in a small unroofed court. A long causeway led down to the valley, where mud-brick walls may be the remnants of a simple enclosure and landing place.

Hawara

Pyramid temple of Amenemhet III

In the latter part of the 12th dynasty Amenemhet III built his second pyramid (after his monument at Dahshur, p. 133) near the entrance to the Fayum in the general region chosen by his grandfather Senwosret II. The enclosure of this pyramid is the largest constructed in the Middle Kingdom and seems to follow that of Djoser (p. 126) in basic plan – running north to south with the entrance at the southeast. Between the entrance and the pyramid the great enclosure contained a mortuary temple of such size and complexity that it surpassed all others. It was probably this structure that was known throughout the Classical world as the 'Labyrinth', recalling the legendary Labyrinth beneath the palace of King Minos in Crete. Herodotus mentioned it and Strabo described it in some detail (*Geographica*, Book XVII, I, 37), so that we know it was one of the greatest tourist attractions of Egypt in the Graeco-Roman Period. The Classical authors are in disagreement, however, on many of the details of this labyrinthine structure. While all seem to attest the presence of multiple

courts, they do not concur as to their number. Herodotus also speaks of 'rooms' and 'galleries' as well as subterranean crypts – the latter being confirmed in the writings of Pliny the Elder.

In addition to the regular features of the mortuary temple, the structure seems to have contained a vast array of individual chapels dedicated to each of the many nome gods of Egypt. Sadly, however, through the ages the complex was quarried for its stone. Little remained when the site was excavated by Petrie in 1888–89, and this massive structure is now reduced to little more than scattered stone chippings. Petrie did find evidence of two great granite shrines which must have weighed between 8 and 13 tons each and which had contained statues of the king. As these were located near the back of the temple, on its central axis, Mark Lehner has suggested that they may have fulfilled a parallel role to the five statue niches in the rear centre of the mortuary temples of Old Kingdom pyramids. While unique in many of its aspects Amenemhet's Labyrinth may thus have represented an impressive elaboration of the established temple plan rather than a purely anomalous monument.

Illahun

Pyramid temples of Senwosret II

Some 3 km (1.75 miles) from the modern village of Illahun at the entrance to the Fayum, Senwosret II built his 'Shining Pyramid' of limestone and mud-brick. Constructed within a roughly square enclosure which seems to have been encircled with rows of trees – perhaps symbolic of the grove

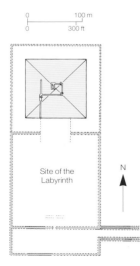

The great enclosure to the south of Amenemhet III's pyramid at Hawara was the site of the immense temple complex known throughout much of the ancient world as the 'Labyrinth'.

0   100 m
0   300 ft

Site of the
Labyrinth   N

*The crocodile god Sobek –
here depicted in his temple at
Kom Ombo – was the chief
deity of the Fayum region,
where a near obsession with
this god paralleled the huge
numbers of crocodiles which
existed in the area.*

associated with the burial mound of Osiris if not the vegetation surrounding the primeval mound of creation – the pyramid appears to have been completed, but the plan of its mortuary temple is unknown. Although the location of the monument's valley temple is known, it is destroyed – probably quarried for stone in Ramessid times.

THE FAYUM

Situated 70 km (43.5 miles) southwest of the base of the Delta, the Fayum is a large, fertile depression of over 4,500 sq. km (48,439 sq. miles) connected to the Nile by a small arm, the Bahr Youssef ('River of Joseph'), which leaves the main river near modern-day Assuit. Much smaller now than in ancient times, the lake of the Fayum, Birket Qarun, is the remnant of the famed Lake Moeris or Mer-wer, 'the great lake' – the Coptic name of which, Peiom, is the origin of the region's modern Arabic name. Inhabited from early times, by the New Kingdom the population density of this area is believed to have been higher than that of the whole Nile Valley, and the region was of great importance in the Graeco-Roman Period. A number of temples of different periods are located in the Fayum, and the great number of crocodiles in the area made it a natural centre of worship for various crocodile gods, particularly the widely venerated Sobek or Suchos.

The region of the Fayum, connected to the Nile Valley by a branch of the river, developed into an agricultural region of primary importance, becoming a virtual national breadbasket in the Graeco-Roman Period. Not surprisingly, many temples were located in the numerous towns and cities of the Fayum.

Kom Aushim

The first village of the Fayum on the desert road 79 km (49 miles) from Cairo is Kom Aushim, 'The Lord's Town', the site of ancient Graeco-Roman Karanis, which is famed for its papyrus finds. The site contains two temples of the Ptolemaic Period. The undecorated limestone temple of the crocodile gods called Pnepheros and Petesuchos is in many aspects constructed according to traditional Egyptian temple design, with a quay fronting a processional way which leads in turn to the temple entrance. The second room of the inner temple has a niche which once contained a mummified crocodile sacred to the temple's patron deities, and within the sanctuary a hidden chamber beneath the altar was probably used by priests for the giving of oracular pronouncements.

The remains of the second, lesser, temple which is situated a little to the north date to the 1st century AD; there are indications that the structure was abandoned in the 3rd century.

Qasr es-Saghah

A small (some 9 × 21 m, 29 ft 6 in × 69 ft) unfinished and uninscribed temple is located at the foot of Gebel Katrani, some 25 km (15.5 miles) to the west of Kom Aushim. The exact date of this structure is unknown, but based on its plan and other features in the area it would appear to have been founded no later than the Middle Kingdom. The seven small shrines and the offering room are reminiscent in their plan of the Middle Kingdom temples of Hierakonpolis and Medinet Madi.

Dimai

The remains of the Graeco-Roman town of Soknopaiou Nesos or 'Crocodile-God Island' – though due to the reduction of the Fayum lake the area was no longer an island even in Ptolemaic times – lie 27 km (16.75 miles) to the west of Kom Aushim and some 10 km (6.25 miles) south of Qasr es-Saghah. The site contains a fairly large but ruined temple of Soknopaios (a form of Sobek) dating to the Ptolemaic Period, with a broad processional way running from the nearby ancient town to the temple enclosure.

Qasr Qarun

Near the western edge of Lake Qarun, Qasr Qarun marks the location of the ancient Dionysias and

The temple of Sobek-Re at Qasr Qarun: this small temple was mainly brick built and although its core has survived, most of the outlying structures have been destroyed through time.

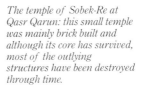

contains two temples. The larger, two-storey structure dates to the Late Period and has been restored by the Egyptian Antiquities Service. The smaller temple of Sobek-Re is of Roman date and is constructed mainly of mud-brick with Ionic-style columns within.

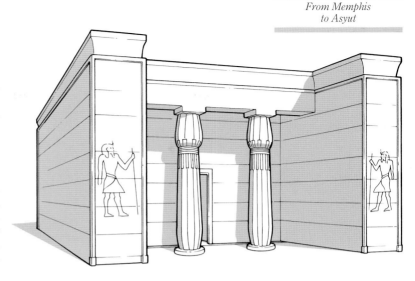

Batn Ihrit

The site of ancient Theadelphia lies about 8 km (5 miles) south of the Fayum lake and contains the ruins of a Ptolemaic temple of the crocodile-god Pnepheros. Several objects found in this temple are now displayed in the Egyptian Museum in Cairo. They include a wooden door dedicated by a citizen of Alexandria in 137 BC, as well as frescoes from the temple walls and the portable shrine on which the god – perhaps in the form of a living crocodile – was borne in processions.

Medinet el-Fayum

East of Batn Ihrit are the ruins of ancient Crocodilopolis (later Arsinoe) which was called Shedyet by the Egyptians and which was a major centre of the cult of the crocodile-god Sobek. The site contains the ruins of a Middle Kingdom temple of the god which was expanded by Ramesses II and, at the northern end of the site, a small Ptolemaic Period temple.

Medinet Madi

Medinet Madi (Narmouthis), 30 km (18.5 miles) southwest of Medinet el-Fayum, contains a small, well-preserved temple dedicated to Sobek, Horus and the cobra goddess Renenutet. Established by the 12th-dynasty king Amenemhet III and his

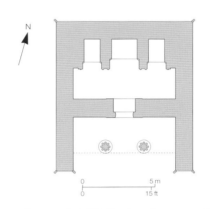

A reconstruction of the Middle Kingdom temple at Medinet Madi, fronted by a small twin-columned portico. The temple (left) contained three shrines dedicated to Sobek, Horus and the cobra goddess Renenutet.

son Amenemhet IV, the temple was restored in the 19th dynasty and expanded, front and back, in Graeco-Roman times. The walls of the temple are carved with texts and various scenes, and an important Greek inscription from the structure is now in the Alexandria Museum.

Kom Medinet Ghurab

Some 3 km (1.75 miles) to the southwest of Illahun, by the Bahr Youssef's entrance to the Fayum, there are the remains of two temples associated with a pharaonic town site. The larger of the temples is known to have been built by Tuthmosis III of the 18th dynasty, but little is known of the other.

Tell Umm el-Breigat

The site of the ancient town of Tebtunis at the southern edge of the Fayum holds the ruins of a small Ptolemaic temple.

MIDDLE EGYPT

Although not always clearly defined, the area of Middle Egypt was essentially that between Memphis and the region of the city of Asyut – which served as a boundary between the southern and northern administrative regions for much of Egyptian history. The temple remains of this area are mainly not well preserved, but there are important temple sites such as el-Ashmunein – the ancient Hermopolis – cult centre of the god Thoth, and el-Amarna – the site of Akhenaten's capital with its anomalous temples to his one god, the Aten.

Ihnasya el-Medina (Herakleopolis Magna)

(Below) The reconstructed entrance façade of the temple of the ram god Herishef at Herakleopolis Magna.

About 15 km (9.25 miles) west of the modern town of Beni Suef, Ihnasya el-Medina preserves in its name that of the ancient city of Henen-nesut. It was a nome capital and a centre of worship of the ram-headed god Herishef or Harsaphes, who was associated with the Greek Herakles for whom the city was given the Classical name Herakleopolis Magna. The remains of the temple of Herishef lie to the west of the modern village and were excavated by Édouard Naville (1891–92) and Flinders Petrie (1904), and more recently by the Spanish archaeologist José López.

The compound contained a sacred lake known to be quite ancient. The layout of the temple itself is not always clear and it is uncertain when exactly the structure was founded, though it was enlarged in New Kingdom times, especially by Ramesses II, and continued in use to the Late Period.

Southeast of the Herishef temple, at Kom el-'Aqarib, another smaller sanctuary was also built by Ramesses II.

el-Hiba

Some 32 km (20 miles) south of Beni Suef, this site – which was a royal residence in the Third Intermediate Period – contains an almost completely destroyed temple of the founder of the 22nd dynasty, Sheshonq I, of which little is known.

Tihna el-Gebel

A few kilometres north of the modern city of el-Minya, on the east bank of the Nile, is the site of ancient Akoris, which has fragmentary remains of three small temples of the Graeco-Roman Period.

Remains of the Graeco-Roman temple at Tihna el-Gebel, the ancient Akoris.

Beni Hasan

A little more than 20 km (12.5 miles) south of el-Minya are the remains of the Middle Kingdom provincial capital of Beni Hasan, with its famous tombs. Just to the south of this site is the Speos Artemidos, an unusual rock temple built by the New Kingdom queen-pharaoh Hatshepsut for the local lion-goddess Pakhet.

The temple is unfinished, as may be seen by the rough nature of the Hathor-headed columns of the façade, but an extensive dedicatory text containing a famous denunciation of the Hyksos (foreign rulers preceding the New Kingdom) was completed above the temple's entrance. The pillared hall of the temple is decorated with painted scenes depicting Hatshepsut and various deities. The cartouche names in this hall, however, are those of Sethos I who usurped the monument without completing it. The inner room is unfinished, but contains a rock-carved image of the goddess Pakhet in a niche cut into its back wall.

el-Sheikh 'Ibada (Antinoopolis)

About 10 km (6.25 miles) to the north of Mallawi, on the east bank, el-Sheikh 'Ibada is the site of the ancient Antinoopolis which was founded in AD 130 by the emperor Hadrian to commemorate his friend and lover Antinous who had drowned in the Nile here. The largest ancient monument of the site is the temple of Ramesses II which was dedicated to the gods of Hermopolis (el-Ashmunein) across the Nile, and of Heliopolis.

el-Ashmunein (Hermopolis)

Just a few kilometres northwest of Mallawi is the area of the nome capital known to the Egyptians as Khmun or 'eight-town', named for the eight primeval deities of Egyptian mythology. It was called Hermopolis, 'City of Hermes' by the Greeks (Hermes was equated with the Egyptian god Thoth), as it was the main cult centre and an important pilgrimage site in the religion of the god of healing, wisdom and scribal arts, honoured in the quartzite baboon colossi of Amenophis III found at this site. A number of temples stood in the central, sacred area of the city which was enclosed in the 30th dynasty by massive mud-brick walls. The largest structure within the enclosure, the main temple to Thoth, may have been quite ancient, but was substantially rebuilt by Nectanebo I in the 30th dynasty and received other additions in the time of Alexander the

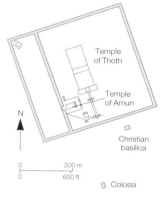

(Top) Standing columns and lintels at Hermopolis, as drawn by Vivant Denon and published in his Voyages *in 1802.*

(Above) A plan of the large enclosure area at el-Ashmunein – ancient Hermopolis – which contained several temples.

(Left) Columns of a temple of Ramesses II dedicated to the gods of Hermopolis and Heliopolis at the site which in Classical times was called Antinoopolis, after Antinous, the favourite of the Roman emperor Hadrian.

Great and Philip Arrhidaeus. Unfortunately, the magnificent portico was demolished in the 1820s for building stone, and although the general outline of the structure can be made out, the remains of this temple have now been flooded by the rising water table.

To the southwest of the Thoth temple are the remains of a small limestone sanctuary of Amun which was begun by Merenptah and evidently completed by Sethos II. Although the entrance pylon and hypostyle hall of this building are relatively well preserved, the rear part of the structure is destroyed. Also to the south was an earlier pylon of Ramesses II. In the core of this, the German excavator Gunther Roeder discovered, between 1929 and 1939, more than 1,500 blocks from the dismantled temples of Akhenaten at el-Amarna, a few kilometres to the southeast. A little to the south, parts of the façade and entrance passage to a Middle Kingdom temple of Amenemhet II survive, but are unfortunately badly damaged and surrounded by ground water.

Outside the area of the temple enclosure the site has the remains of a Roman Period Christian basilica which was built from blocks taken from an earlier Ptolemaic temple. The structure retains most of its granite columns and is the only building of its kind to have survived to this degree anywhere in Egypt. A couple of hundred metres further to the south, two seated colossi of Ramesses II stand before the completely ruined remains of a temple which has not been clearly dated, as well as those of a small temple dating to the time of the emperor Nero.

One of two colossal statues (over 4.5 m, 14 ft 9 in high) of the god Thoth as a baboon at Hermopolis – the god's chief cult centre. The statues date to the time of Amenophis III.

el-Amarna

Built on virgin ground roughly between the old capitals of Memphis and Thebes, some 10 km (6.25 miles) south of modern Mallawi, el-Amarna was the ancient Akhetaten or 'Horizon of the Aten', the short-lived capital and cult centre of the heretic pharaoh Akhenaten (1353–1333 BC) for much of his reign. Because of its physical location and the absence of modern buildings in the area, it is one of the few ancient Egyptian towns which it has proved possible to excavate, and the site has been investigated by a succession of archaeologists including Petrie, Bouriant, Barsanti, Borchardt, Woolley, Frankfort and Pendlebury. More recently, since 1977, various areas of the site have been excavated and studied by Barry Kemp for the Egypt Exploration Society. In addition to two temples proper, two other complexes of more doubtful cultic nature have also been discovered at el-Amarna.

The Great Temple

The largest single structure and certainly one of the most important buildings of el-Amarna was the Per-Aten-em-Akhetaten, 'The House of the Sun Disc

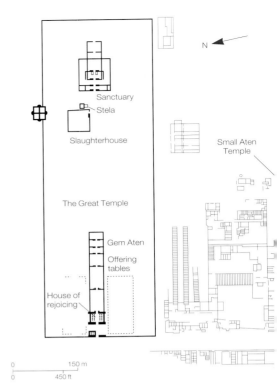

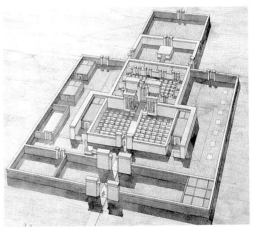

in Akhetaten' or the 'Great Temple' as it is called. The enormous enclosure – 760 m long and 290 m wide (2493 × 951 ft) – stood at the northern edge of the 'central city' which was the official heart of Akhetaten.

Unlike orthodox Egyptian temples in almost every way, the reconstructed plan of this great enclosure appears relatively empty due to its largely open-air design (p. 25), yet it contained a number of discrete temple structures. Within the entrance was a narrow hypostyle hall, the 'house of rejoicing', which opened to the Gem-aten, 'The sun disc is found', a series of six diminishing courts that were flanked by a forest of open air altars (365 on each side, one for each day of the solar year). At the

(Above) A relief fragment originally from Amarna, with depictions of altars loaded with offerings in a temple court.

(Left) Plan of the Great Temple and city centre of Akhenaten's short-lived capital at el-Amarna.

(Below left) A reconstruction of the sanctuary of the Great Temple complex with some of the hundreds of offering tables which filled the temple.

Small Aten temple

To the south and adjacent to the king's house in central Amarna stood the Hut-aten or 'Mansion of the Sun Disc', often referred to as the 'Small Aten temple', as its dimensions were considerably less than those of the Great Temple – approximately 127 × 200 m (416 ft 6 in × 656 ft). It has long been thought that this structure served as a kind of private chapel for the royal family, but there is no evidence for this, and it is perhaps more likely, given its name, that it was built as a mortuary temple for the king – it does also appear to have been aligned with his tomb. Best preserved of the Amarna temples, the Hut-aten has a partially surviving mud-brick entrance pylon with vertical flagpole channels, though the interior of the structure, with columned courts and stone sanctuary, has disappeared. Recently, however, Kemp has directed the laying in of new stone blocks to preserve the original plan of the temple, and to provide bases upon which surviving sections of columns have been set up.

River temple

A complex discovered in 1922 on the southern side of Amarna near the village of el-Hagg Qandil and close to the river included what has been termed the 'river temple', though the original function of this structure is in doubt. Built on a layer of sand, the site seems to show a stratified building sequence with recent work placing it after the Amarna Period.

Maru temple

Located in the southern area of Akhetaten, between the modern villages of el-Hawata and el-Amariya, the scant remains of an unusual complex were excavated by Leonard Woolley in 1921 and identified by him as the surviving features of a *maru* or 'viewing' temple in which members of the Amarna royal family might be rejuvenated by the sun's rays. The complex consisted of gardens, walkways and pools in addition to various chambers and open-air kiosks – some of which had been constructed of very fine materials including calcite, sandstone and granite inlaid with faience and coloured stones. While undoubtedly cultic, the real purpose of this temple – if it may be called such – is not known, and the site no longer exists.

eastern end of the enclosure stood the focal Hut-benben, a round-topped stela on a raised dais, with its associated slaughterhouse and various cult chambers. Set in the northern side of the enclosure wall was a large altar – the so-called 'Hall of Foreign Tribute'. To the south and outside the compound proper stood buildings housing the various offices and storerooms associated with the temple.

Suffering the brunt of thorough destruction after the close of the Amarna Period, the Great Temple now retains little to even hint at the impressive complex it must once have been. Some at least of the decorated blocks which were taken from the site have been recovered in excavations at Hermopolis (el-Ashmunein), and allow a partial reconstruction of the types of decoration chosen by Akhenaten for this temple. There were scenes depicting the king and members of the royal family offering to the sun disc and engaged in various other activities, as well as depictions of royal apartments, cult chambers and storehouses – not unlike scenes from Akhenaten's earlier temples at Thebes. And despite the often cheap and hurried construction methods utilized in the construction of the buildings themselves, the Amarna scenes were usually carved on limestone facing blocks in a style more developed and refined than that of any of the king's earlier sandstone temples.

Recently re-erected column sections set up on new bases at the site of the Small Aten temple at Amarna. New stone blocks have also been set down to mark the original plan of the temple.

From Asyut to Thebes

NORTHERN UPPER EGYPT

This region, between Asyut and Thebes, was the cradle of Egypt's earliest dynasties and continued to be important heartland for much of the country's ancient history. Abydos, Dendera and Qift (Koptos) were all significant religious centres at various times, and literally dozens of temples were built in these sites and at others in the area. Important deities in the region included Osiris, Min, Isis, Horus and Hathor; and at Abydos, the greatest religious centre of the area, a number of monarchs were also elevated to divine status in mortuary cenotaphs.

Asyut

Asyut is the site of the ancient Egyptian city of Zawty, a nome capital which rose to importance due to its strategic location at a point where the Nile Valley is particularly narrow. Several temples are mentioned in ancient texts relating to the area of Asyut – especially that of the local wolf-god Wepwawet. None of these temples has survived, however, or has yet been disclosed in excavations in the area.

Qaw el-Kebir (Antaiopolis)

About 40 km (25 miles) south of Asyut, Qaw el-Kebir is the site of ancient Tjebu (the Graeco-Roman Antaiopolis) where there was a Ptolemaic Period temple believed to have been dedicated by Ptolemy IV and enlarged and restored by Ptolemy VI and the emperor Marcus Aurelius. Sadly, this temple was destroyed in the first half of the 19th century, swept away by high floods, but an old view survives in the *Description de l'Égypte*.

Wannina (Athribis)

Across the Nile from Akhmim, and a few kilometres south of modern Sohag, Wannina is the site of a small temple of the goddess Triphis or Repyt, whose Egyptian name, Hut-Repyt, is the origin of the town's Greek name Athribis. The temple was built in the reign of Ptolemy XV and south of it was an earlier sanctuary of Ptolemy IX. Limestone blocks from these temples were quarried for use in the building of the 'white monastery' a little to the west of Sohag.

Akhmim

The ancient Egyptian nome-capital of Ipu, later Khent-menu, became the Greek Khemmis and eventually the modern Akhmim. It is located on the east bank of the Nile across the river from modern Sohag. The ancient town has almost completely disappeared, and its temples were dismantled for building stone by local villagers. Surviving traces indicate that one temple was constructed in the 18th dynasty by Tuthmosis III and expanded or restored by several later rulers, while another was built in Roman times. Somewhat to the north of the area there is a small rock-cut temple of Min, the god of fertility, believed to have been made by Tuthmosis III but which received some decoration in the reign of Ay (reliefs of the king and his wife before local gods) and was restored in the time of Ptolemy II a thousand years later. The god Min was equated by the Greeks with Pan, leading to the Greek name of the site: Panopolis.

The Ptolemaic temple of Antaiopolis (Qaw el-Kebir), as it appeared in the late 18th century, from the Description de l'Égypte. *The temple was destroyed in the first half of the 19th century by disastrous floods.*

(Opposite) The ancient site of Abydos contains many temple enclosures. By the Middle Kingdom Abydos was the most important cult centre of Osiris and a number of Egyptian kings built their cenotaphs here.

Abydos

A little past the midway point between the modern cities of Asyut and Luxor, the ancient city of Abydos (Egyptian Abedju) dates from the very beginnings of the Dynastic Period, with evidence of habitation extending back well into prehistoric times. The site was a cult centre of the canine necropolis god Khentiamentiu, 'Foremost of the Westerners' (i.e., ruler of the dead), whose temple evidently existed here from very early times. During the 5th and 6th dynasties Khentiamentiu became assimilated with the important Lower Egyptian god Osiris, and by Middle Kingdom times the site was the most important religious centre of the ruler of the dead. Because of its association with the afterlife, many Egyptian kings constructed cenotaphs at Abydos, including the great New Kingdom cenotaph temple of Sethos I.

Osiris temple

Apart from the ancient, outlying royal structures of Abydos which seem to figure in the earliest development of temple forms, the northernmost of the central Abydene monuments is the oldest. A little more than 1 km (0.6 mile) to the northwest of the Sethos I temple in the area called Kom el-Sultan is the site of an ancient temple of the god Khentiamentiu and, from the 12th dynasty on, of Osiris. Artifacts found at the site show activity ranging from the beginning of the 1st dynasty to the Graeco-Roman Period. They include a fragment of a vase of the 1st-dynasty king Aha as well as small figures of men and animals of the same period. Most kings of the Old Kingdom are attested here, as are a number of rulers of the Middle and New Kingdoms including the 18th-dynasty monarchs Amenophis I, Tuthmosis III and Amenophis III, who all undertook rebuilding here. But the temple itself was built almost entirely of brick – with only

(Below) A general view of the Osiris temple at Kom el-Sultan, Abydos. Finds at the site range in date from the 1st dynasty to the Graeco-Roman Period.

(Bottom) These pillars on the eastern side of the Osiris temple are among the few features made of stone in this temple.

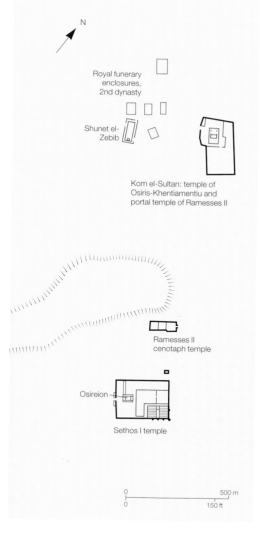

Royal funerary enclosures, 2nd dynasty

Shunet el-Zebib

Kom el-Sultan: temple of Osiris-Khentiamentiu and portal temple of Ramesses II

Ramesses II cenotaph temple

Osireion

Sethos I temple

```
0          500 m
0       150 ft
```

The Festival of Osiris at Abydos

Cups, bowls, flasks and other pottery offering vessels still litter the desert as they were left by pilgrims on the mound at Abydos, which is therefore known as Umm el-Qaab, the 'Mother of Pots'. This sacred site was venerated as the area of the burial of Osiris throughout much of Egyptian history.

Though the ancient Osiris temple is ruined and almost obliterated, it represents the heart of the cult of the god at Abydos, and the site of one of Egypt's more important local temple events. Each year in the annual festival of Osiris, the cult-statue of the god in its portable barque was carried on the shoulders of priests from the god's temple to his supposed tomb on the mound known as Umm el-Qaab ('Mother of Pots' – a name taken from the countless votive offerings left by pilgrims in this area). From at least the 12th dynasty, the god's tomb was in fact the ancient tomb of the 1st-dynasty king Djer. The procession seems to have consisted of two phases – the first public and the second secret to the priests. The god first processed from his temple complex through the small portal temple (see below) and through the cemeteries on the temple's western side. This was the public section of the ritual, accessible to all, and many people dedicated stelae to the god in this area to celebrate the festival and to pray for continued participation in it in the afterlife. Following this first stage, the procession swung out into the desert where the mysteries of the divine rites were performed.

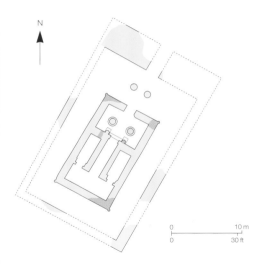

(Above right) The recently discovered temple of Tuthmosis III at Abydos.

a few elements such as doorways constructed of stone – so that very little survives today. The large mud-brick ramparts which surround the area date to the 30th dynasty.

Portal temple of Ramesses II

Just outside the mud-brick walls of the Osiris temple, on the enclosure's southwest side, are the remains of a limestone structure built by Ramesses II. The site was excavated by Flinders Petrie who thought that the remains represented a kind of 'portal' temple marking the entrance to the cemetery outside the Osiris enclosure. However, the plan is different from that of any known Egyptian temple and, as Petrie noted, its layout might be the result of the structure's function as the terminus of a processional route.

Temple of Tuthmosis III

A previously unknown temple was discovered in 1996 by the Pennsylvania-Yale-Institute of Fine Arts expedition just southwest of the Osiris temple enclosure. The excavations revealed the remains of a small limestone temple (some 9 × 15 m, 29 ft 6 in × 49 ft) with a twin-columned entrance before a transverse inner chamber which doubled back into two shrines at its ends. The unusual configuration of the temple was doubtless related to the special needs of a symbolic alignment, though what that was is not yet clear. The temple was fronted by a forecourt with two large sacred trees and a mud-brick pylon some 2.5 m (8 ft) thick. Remains of two colossal Osiride statues of Tuthmosis flanked the entrance to the inner temple and the structure also incorporates several other architectural features reminiscent of the entrance to the king's Festival Temple at Karnak. The high quality evident in the building and decoration of this newly found temple is comparable to the finest produced for the king at Thebes – perhaps revealing an equal level of concern with temples at sites such as this as was lavished on those of the most important cities.

Ramesses II cenotaph temple

About one-third of a kilometre to the northwest of the temple of Sethos I (see below), Ramesses II built himself a smaller limestone temple which, while not completely preserved, retains the details of its plan and many of its brightly painted reliefs on walls which still stand to a height of 2 m (6 ft 6 in) or more. Although it served essentially the same purpose as that of Sethos' cenotaph, the design of Ramesses' temple is more standard and is patterned after contemporary royal mortuary temples at Thebes. A granite portal leads into a peristyle court behind the pylons, surrounded by Osiride pillars. This court ends in a portico with two chapels at each end – representing, in balanced fashion, on the left the deified Sethos and the royal ancestors, and

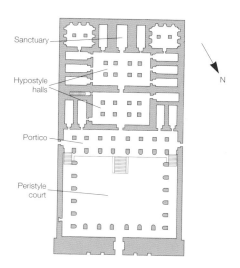

Sanctuary

Hypostyle
halls

Portico

Peristyle
court

N

on the right the Ennead (group of nine gods) and
Ramesses II. The portico is followed by two interior
hypostyles around which are arranged the chapels
of various other deities, with the chapels of the
gods of Thebes (on the left) and Abydos (on the
right) each having their own suites. The unusual
columned inner rooms of each of these suites are
ringed with highly decorated statue niches, including one with an interesting humanoid *djed* pillar. At
the centre of the rear wall is the sanctuary, composed of fine limestone blocks set on sandstone
bases, which contains a grey granite statue group
of Ramesses, together with his father Sethos, Amun
and two goddesses.

Because it has lost its roof, this temple allows the
visitor an especially clear view of its decoration, on
much of which the colour has survived well despite
its modern exposure to the elements. Classic scenes
of offering processions line the inner walls along
the sides of the court; and on the north and west
sides of the temple's outer walls are reliefs showing
a version of the Battle of Kadesh (*c.* 1285 BC, fought
by Ramesses against the Hittites). Although not as

*(Above left) The cenotaph
temple of Ramesses II at
Abydos parallels the king's
actual mortuary temple in
western Thebes.*

*(Above) A statue niche in
Ramesses II's cenotaph temple
contains an unusual scene of
the king before Osiris and a
humanoid* djed *pillar.*

*(Left) Hittite and Egyptian
chariotry are vividly depicted
in scenes from the Battle of
Kadesh on the outer walls of
Ramesses' cenotaph temple.*

Factfile

Monument
Temple of Sethos I
Various chapels
The 'Osireion'
Location
Central Abydos
Dates of construction
19th dynasty, reigns of
Sethos I and Ramesses II
Dedication
Main temple: Amun,
Sethos I
Chapels: Theban, Abydene,
Memphite deities
'Osireion': Osiris-Sethos I
Studies and reports
Mariette, A., *Abydos*, 2 vols.
(Paris, 1869–80)
Calverly, A.M. et al., *The
Temple of King Sethos I
at Abydos*, 4 vols. (London
and Chicago, 1933–38)

complete as the parallel versions in Luxor Temple (p. 168), the Ramesseum (p. 185) or Abu Simbel (p. 228), these reliefs nevertheless surpass the others in the quality of their production (among the finest of Ramesses' reign), made possible by the fine limestone used in this temple. A separate, T-shaped chapel near the northwest corner of the temple was added to the complex at a later date.

Sethos I temple

Begun by Sethos I and completed by his son, Ramesses II, this temple – the 'Memnonium' of the Greeks – was built of fine white limestone and is one of the most impressive religious structures in Egypt. The temple is approached through its ruined outer courts (the first with massive tanks for the priests' ablutions), with rows of mud-brick storage magazines grouped around a stone entrance hall visible to the left. This area of the temple's outer pylons and courts and the first hypostyle hall were completed and somewhat hastily decorated by Ramesses II, who is shown in part of the decoration worshipping the temple's major triad of Osiris, Isis and Sethos I. The wall of the portico leading to the first hypostyle hall was originally pierced by seven doorways which opened to the same number of processional paths leading, between clustered columns, to the seven chapels at the rear of the temple. Most of the doorways were filled in, however, when Ramesses added the outer sections of the temple – revealing, perhaps, an abbreviation

of the temple's original plan. The second hypostyle hall, which thus serves as a vestibule for the chapels beyond, contains 36 lotus-bud columns carefully aligned to give access to the multiple sanctuaries. The columns are of somewhat squat dimensions typical of a number of 19th-dynasty structures, but the raised reliefs carved in this part of the temple in Sethos' own reign are of superb quality – ranking with the finest produced in any Egyptian temple. Ritual scenes of many types are depicted – including representations of Sethos before various gods, performing sacrifices and presenting the image of Maat (p. 88). The quality of the carving extends from the carefully modelled figures to even the smallest details of minor items and hieroglyphs.

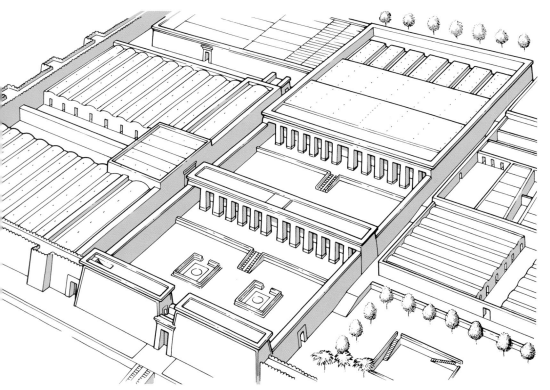

(Left) A reconstruction of the impressive temple of Sethos I at Abydos, surrounded by ancillary buildings.

(Right) Plan of the temple of Sethos I at Abydos. Uniquely, the temple had seven chapels, dedicated to (from left to right): Sethos I; Re-Horakhty; Amun; Osiris; Isis; and Horus. The chapel of Osiris led to a suite of rooms occupying the space behind all seven chapels. Behind the temple itself was the Osireion, on the same axis as the main temple.

The decoration produced for Ramesses II, while mostly of somewhat inferior sunken relief, includes some unusual scenes such as the lively representation of the young king lassooing a bull with his father, Sethos, which is depicted in a passage of the temple's south wing.

The seven chapels which uniquely form the focus of the main temple were dedicated (from south to north) to the deified Sethos I, Ptah, Re-Horakhty, Amun, Osiris, Isis and Horus, and each is decorated with representations of the rituals associated with various festivals. Six of these sanctuaries contain false doors (p. 71) on their rear walls, but that of Osiris was given a real door leading to a suite of rooms dedicated to him in the space lying behind

The first hypostyle hall of the Sethos I temple at Abydos: the columns were carefully positioned to allow processional access to the multiple chapels which lay within the temple's core.

the whole row of chapels. The first and largest room of this suite is a columned hall decorated with various scenes of the king offering to Osiris. On its north side are three chapels dedicated to Horus, Sethos and Isis (in which the king is doubtless assimilated with Osiris), behind which is a secret crypt wherein the temple's chief treasures were probably stored. At the south end of the Osiris suite is a smaller pillared hall also with three chapels, but now in more damaged condition.

The southern wing of the temple's unusual L-shaped plan contains cult chapels of the Memphite gods Ptah-Sokar and Nefertem – Osiris' northern counterparts – as well as a hall where the barques of the temple's gods were kept, and various service

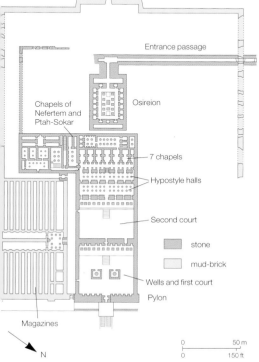

Entrance passage

Chapels of Nefertem and Ptah-Sokar

Osireion

7 chapels

Hypostyle halls

Second court

| | stone |
| | mud-brick |

Wells and first court

Pylon

Magazines

N

0 ____ 50 m
0 ____ 150 ft

The young Ramesses II lassoos a bull with his father Sethos I, in an unusual scene depicted in relief on a wall of the south wing of the Sethos I temple.

(Above left) The passageway leading from the Sethos I temple to the Osireion.

(Above right) Megalithic granite blocks form the structural core of the Osireion, the symbolic tomb of the god Osiris which adjoins the temple of Sethos I.

chambers and magazines. Of particular interest is the narrow hallway which connects the second hypostyle hall with this wing. On its inner wall, opposite the fine relief of Sethos and his son – the young Ramesses II – lassooing a bull, is one of the few surviving Egyptian king lists. The list begins with Menes, the traditional founder of Egypt, and ends with Sethos, but is selectively edited to delete such undesirable individuals as the kings of the Amarna Period. The list would seem to be associated with the royal cult of ancestors, but the reason for its placement in this narrow passage is not entirely clear. A doorway in the passage leads to another hallway with flights of steps leading due west to the temple's cenotaph.

Behind the temple proper, and carefully aligned on the temple's axis, is the unusual structure known as the 'Osireion', a cenotaph constructed by Sethos, and decorated mainly by his grandson Merenptah, in the form of a royal tomb (p. 36). In fact, the main temple stands as a mortuary temple before its tomb in relationship to this structure. A long passage, decorated with scenes and texts from the funerary Book of Gates, turns sharply at its end and leads into an enormous hall. Similar in appearance to the massively pillared chambers of the royal tombs in the Valley of the Kings, the large (some 30 × 20 m, 98 ft 3 in × 67 ft 6 in) granite-built hall has an anachronistic look but one which strangely fits its symbolic purpose. At the centre of this structure a kind of pseudo-sarcophagus and canopic chest (chest for the royal viscera) stood on an island surrounded by ground water symbolizing the primeval waters of creation. The secondary, transverse rooms positioned at each end of this hall were decorated with astronomical and funerary texts and representations including a depiction of the sky-goddess Nut. The structure thus reflects, in both its overall plan and decoration, many elements of the New Kingdom royal tomb – which tied it firmly into its role of cenotaph.

Temple of Senwosret III

Scant remains of this temple stand at the edge of the desert some 2 km (1.25 miles) to the southeast of the Sethos temple. The ruins of the cenotaph of this king (unless, as Dieter Arnold believes, they represent his actual burial place), now sanded over, lie to the west near the base of the escarpment.

Temple of Ahmose

Little remains of the terraced temple of Ahmose a kilometre southeast of the Senwosret cenotaph and some 4.75 km (3 miles) from central Abydos, though fragments of its reliefs have been found there.

Hiw

The ancient nome capital of Hut-sekhem or simply Hut (Coptic Hou), modern Hiw, is located on the Nile's west bank where the river turns back to a northward course after its distinctive loop in the Theban region. The site is known to date to at least the time of Senwosret I, but no temples of pharaonic date have been discovered here – although several are mentioned in ancient texts such as Papyrus Harris I from the reign of Ramesses III. The local deity Bat, who was worshipped in the form of a human-headed, bovine-eared goddess (later assimilated with Hathor), doubtless had a sanctuary here. Remains of two temples of the Graeco-Roman Period still exist, however. The first was built by Ptolemy VI, and the later under the Roman emperors Nerva and Hadrian. In the Graeco-Roman Period Hiw was known as Diospolis Mikra or Diospolis Parva.

Dendera

Dendera is one of the most important temple sites of Egypt and provides examples of a particularly rich variety of later temple features. The area in which the temple is located is that of ancient Iunet or Tantere (Greek Tentyris), a provincial capital and important religious site during several periods of Egyptian history. Early texts refer to a temple at Dendera which was rebuilt in Old Kingdom times, and several New Kingdom monarchs, including Tuthmosis III, Amenophis III, and Ramesses II and III are known to have embellished the structure. The temple of Hathor which stands at the site today dates to the Graeco-Roman Period, however, and is one of the best-preserved temples of this period in Egypt, surviving despite the destruction of the temples of Hathor's consort Horus and their child Ihy or Harsomptus which originally stood close by.

Like most Egyptian temples, Dendera is oriented towards the Nile, but because the Nile bends here, the structure actually faces north, rather than east–west as would normally be the case. The temple area is fronted by several Roman period kiosks and a propylon gateway, built during the reigns of Domitian and Trajan, which was set into the massive mud-brick walls which surround the enclosure. Although the site lacks a colonnade and the two pylons which ought to precede the inner temple, an unfinished inner enclosure wall of stone surrounds a courtyard with side entrances which open before the large hypostyle hall added in the 1st century AD by the emperor Tiberius. Unlike those of earlier temples, the façade of this hypostyle is constructed as a low screen with intercolumnar walls exposing the hall's ceiling and the Hathor-featured sistrum-capitals of its 24 columns. Each column bears a four-sided capital carved with the face of the cow-eared goddess, though every one of the faces was vandalized in antiquity. The ceiling of the hall retains much of its original colour, however,

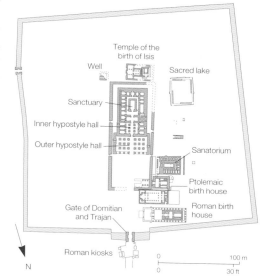

and is decorated as a complex and carefully aligned symbolic chart of the heavens, including signs of the zodiac (introduced by the Romans) and images of the sky-goddess Nut who swallows the sun disc each evening in order to give birth to it at dawn.

The great hall leads to a smaller, inner six-column hypostyle called the 'hall of appearances', as it was here that the statue of the goddess 'appeared' from her sanctuary for religious ceremonies and processions. Scenes on the walls of this hall depict the king participating in the foundation ceremonies for the construction of the temple, and on either side doors open into three chambers which were used as preparation areas for various aspects of the daily ritual. An opening through the outer eastern wall allowed offering goods to be brought into this area, and a parallel passage from one of the western chambers led to a well.

The temple's inner core was constructed by several later Ptolemaic kings – the uninscribed cartouches of its walls reflecting the often uncertain

Factfile

Monument
Temple of Hathor
Chapels, birth houses
Isis temple
Location
Dendera near modern Qena
Date of Construction
Graeco-Roman Period
Dedication
Main temple: Hathor
Chapels: Osiris, various deities
Temple of Isis: Isis
Studies and reports
Mariette, A., *Denderah*, 4 vols. (Paris, 1870–73)
Chassinat, E. and F. Daumas, *Le temple de Dendara*, I- (Cairo, 1934–)
Daumas, F., *Dendara et le temple d'Hathor* (Cairo, 1969)

(Above left) A number of significant structures, of various dates, lie around the main Hathor temple at Dendera.

The façade of the hypostyle of the temple of Hathor at Dendera is unique in its proportions and its engaged sistraform columns.

(Left) A relief showing a massive image of a menat necklace behind a seated figure of Hathor, from the temple of the goddess at Dendera. The menat, used in rituals, consists of a detailed pectoral, here with decorations in the form of sistra, attached by chains to a counterweight which hung down the wearer's back.

(Right) The celebrated 'zodiac' of Dendera depicts astrological figures and symbols in a fusion of Egyptian and foreign ideas. The original was removed by Napoleon's Expedition and is now in the Louvre.

nature of their reigns. The area includes an offering hall, in which sacrifices were dedicated, and a 'hall of the ennead' where statues of other deities assembled with Hathor before processions began, as well as the sanctuary of the goddess herself. Although empty, decorations on the sanctuary walls suggest it once contained a stone shrine for the statue of Hathor as well as her portable barque (and possibly during 'visiting festivals' the barque of her consort, Horus of Edfu). Around the central sanctuary are eleven chapels of the other deities who associated with Hathor at this site, including ones for Hathor's chief attributes, the sacred sistrum and the *menat* necklace. A niche in the wall of the chapel directly behind the main sanctuary is sunk into the temple wall at the point where a shrine of the 'hearing ear' is located on its outside surface – allowing the goddess to 'hear' the prayers directed to her.

A number of crypts where temple treasures were stored (p. 68) are located in the walls and beneath the floors of the chambers in the rear part of the temple. The most important object kept in these crypts was a statue of the *ba* of Hathor which was taken from its hiding place to the roof of the temple in the important New Year's festival celebrated at this site (p. 98). A staircase to the west of the offering hall (with the ascending figures of the king and various priests with the shrine of the goddess carved on its right-hand wall) gave access to the roof of the temple and a chapel, where the goddess stayed overnight before beholding the rising sun in a symbolic union with the solar disc. The stairs to the east of the roof (with corresponding scenes of descending figures) were used for the procession's return. The roof of the inner temple also has two parallel sets of rooms on its eastern and western sides which functioned as chapels dedicated to the death and resurrection of Osiris, and also contain representations of the goddess Nut and various

chthonic deities. One of these chapels contained a zodiac (now in the Louvre and replaced by a copy). The roof of the hypostyle was reached by another flight of steps with various gods carved along its wall, and this highest area of the temple was used in antiquity by pious pilgrims who awaited signs and miracles from the goddess there. Gaming boards carved into the stone blocks helped these faithful pass the time during their vigils.

At the very rear of the temple, beneath the apotropaic lion-headed waterspouts which drained

(Right) The Hathoric or sistraform columns which are a hallmark of the temple of Dendera were badly damaged by early Christians so that most of the faces of the goddess have been obliterated.

rainwater from the roof, the exterior wall has scenes showing the massive figures of Cleopatra VII and her son by Julius Caesar, Caesarion, who became the great queen's co-regent as Ptolemy XV. At the centre of the wall, directly behind the sanctuary, is the large false door with a gigantic emblem of Hathor – diminished over the centuries by pilgrims who scraped at it to obtain a little of the sacred stone at the point where they could come closest to Hathor herself.

Beyond the stone enclosure wall are the ruins of various outlying buildings of the complex. Moving towards the main temple from the gate and on its western side are the remains of the Roman period birth house (p. 73) built by Augustus shortly after Egypt was added to the Roman Empire. Its scenes depicting Augustus' later successor Trajan offering to Hathor are among the finest to be found in Egypt. The structure was dedicated to the goddess and her child Ihy, and its birth theme is reflected in the figures of the god Bes (a patron of childbirth) carved on the abaci above the column capitals.

Directly south of this mammisi are the remains of a Christian basilica of the 5th century AD, and an earlier birth house of the 30th dynasty and Ptolemaic Period. The latter structure was split by the building of the Roman enclosure wall which required the building of the later birth house. Next are the remains of a mud-brick sanatorium, the only one of its type known from Egyptian temples (p. 74), where visitors could bathe in the sacred

From Asyut to Thebes

Images of the protective god Bes – often associated with childbirth – surmounted the columns of the Roman birth house at Dendera.

waters or spend the night in order to have a healing dream of the goddess.

To the west of the sanatorium, a small 11th-dynasty chapel of Nebhepetre Mentuhotep once stood, which seems to have been dedicated to the cult of the king rather than that of the goddess Hathor, and as such was probably ancillary to the main Middle Kingdom temple. The chapel was moved in modern times, however, and has been re-erected in the Egyptian Museum in Cairo. Further to the south, at the temple's southwest corner, lies the compound's sacred lake which provided water for the priests' ablutions. With flights of stairs descending from each corner, this stone-lined ceremonial basin is the best preserved of its type in any Egyptian temple. Immediately to the south of Hathor's temple is the Iseum, the temple of the birth of Isis. The plan of this building was uniquely split, with the main part of the structure and its hypostyle hall facing east, but the sanctuary rotated to face north towards the main temple of Hathor. Within the rear wall of the sanctuary a statue of Osiris (now destroyed) was supported by the arms of Isis and Nephthys.

Qift (Koptos)

This is the site of ancient Gebtu (Greek Koptos, Coptic Kebto or Keft), a provincial capital which was located near the entrance to the Wadi Hammamat and served as an important settlement on the route to the Wadi's quarries and the Red Sea beyond. The main deity of the area was Min, regarded as god of the eastern deserts, and in later times Isis and Horus who were also venerated there. Remains of three temples exist at the site.

To the north, the temple of Min and Isis was built under Ptolemy II, with later additions from the

A detail of a relief from the Middle Kingdom chapel of Mentuhotep incorporated into the temple complex at Dendera.

times of Ptolemy IV, Ptolemy VIII and the Roman emperors Caligula and Nero, though it was never fully decorated. Blocks from a gateway almost certainly of this temple and discovered on its north side have recently been reassembled in the Boston Museum of Fine Arts. The temple was evidently built on the site of an earlier religious structure, the remains of a Late Period (reign of Amasis) shrine of Osiris having been located in one of the inner courts. A little to the south, the middle temple was also built under Ptolemy II with additions in the time of Caligula, Claudius and Trajan, but the site has revealed many earlier features including a gate of Tuthmosis III, and various blocks of Senwosret I; and it was here that stelae dating to the 6th and 7th dynasties were found with the famous 'Koptos Decrees' detailing royal provisions made for the temple and its personnel.

In the southern part of the enclosure, the temple of Geb appears to be less ancient, with elements dating from the Late Period on. The entrance was constructed by Nectanebo II with later additions, and the present inner shrine built in the reign of Cleopatra VII and Ptolemy XV. This temple was evidently a popular oracle, and the small crypt where a priest would sit at the rear of the shrine can still be seen. A little to the northeast of Qift at el-Qal'a, a small temple (c. 24 × 16 m, 78 ft 9 in × 52 ft 6 in) was dedicated to Min, Isis and Horus by the emperor Claudius.

Qus (Apollinopolis Parva)

Ancient Gesa (modern Qus, Greek Apollinopolis Parva), just south of Qift was similarly located near the entrance to the Wadi Hammamat. A temple of Haroeris and Heqet was built at the site in Ptolemaic times, but the two ruined pylons are virtually all that remain of this structure.

Tukh (Ombos)

Just across the Nile from modern Qus lies Tukh, the ancient town of Nubt (the Greek Ombos), the history of which reaches back to the Predynastic period. Relatively little has been found here, however, and although the site contains the remains of a temple dedicated to the god Seth, this appears to date only to New Kingdom times, with construction accomplished by Tuthmosis I and III, Amenophis II and several Ramessid kings. One remarkable object found here is the massive *was* sceptre dedicated by Amenophis III – the largest faience object known – which was discovered by Petrie and is now in the Victoria and Albert Museum in London.

Shenhur

About 6 km (3.75 miles) south of Qus in the village of Shenhur is the site of a small Roman temple. Although little now remains of this temple, it was visited by several 19th-century scholars, including C.R. Lepsius (1845), who copied a number of its inscriptions. The temple was of an interesting 'T'-shaped layout consisting of a sanctuary surrounded by several small chambers and fronted by two transverse halls. To this temple a larger transverse hypostyle was added in the form of a 16-columned hall at right angles to the temple's main axis. Completed under the reigns of several emperors, the temple seems to have been begun in the time of Augustus and completed perhaps in the reign of Nero.

A detail of a relief from the walls of the Ptolemaic temple at Qus, near the entrance to the Wadi Hammamat. Unfortunately, little now survives of this temple beyond the ruined pylons.

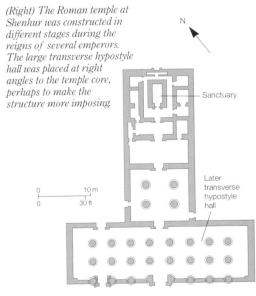

(Right) The Roman temple at Shenhur was constructed in different stages during the reigns of several emperors. The large transverse hypostyle hall was placed at right angles to the temple core, perhaps to make the structure more imposing.

N

Sanctuary

0   10 m
0   30 ft

Later transverse hypostyle hall

Columns of different types filled the peristyle court and outer hypostyle hall of Ptolemy VII in the temple of Montu at Medamud, a little to the north of Thebes.

(Below centre) The Graeco-Roman temple complex at Medamud contained the outer temple of Montu, Rattawy and Harpocrates, and – immediately to the rear of this structure – a second temple dedicated to the sacred bull of Montu, which probably included rooms for the living animal as well as other features such as an oracle of the Montu bull.

Medamud

Medamud (ancient Madu) lies about 8 km (5 miles) northeast of Luxor and was a centre of worship of the falcon-headed god Montu who was an important deity in the early history of the area. A Montu temple of Middle Kingdom date (and perhaps earlier) is known to have existed here (p. 22), but was destroyed at some point. Still surviving are the ruins of a temple of the Graeco-Roman Period dedicated to Montu, Rattawy and Harpocrates, which may have been built on the same site.

The temple, which is surrounded by an enclosure wall with a portal built by Tiberius, is unusual in that its façade consists of a triple portal formed by three kiosks of Ptolemy XII. Behind this entry is a large courtyard, which was embellished by Antoninus Pius, leading to a conventional hypostyle hall of Ptolemy VIII. Today, a few columns of the peristyle court are virtually all that survive intact. To the rear of the main temple was a smaller sanctuary of the sacred bull of Montu, of which little more survives than some small sections of exterior wall. Still visible on one of these is a relief of the king worshipping the sacred bull at the point where oracles were delivered.

Inscriptions show that both these and the outer walls of the main temple received decoration in the time of the emperors Domitian and Trajan. The temple enclosure contained a sacred lake, and a small Ptolemaic chapel once stood at its southwest corner, while a processional way ran from the main temple entrance to a quay which stood on a canal linking this temple to that of Montu in the precinct of Karnak.

(Below) A carved block with a figure wearing the elaborate atef crown, from Medamud. Many of the carved reliefs of this temple were desecrated by early Christians who chiselled out the faces of kings and deities alike.

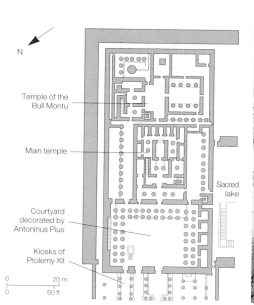

N

Temple of the Bull Montu

Main temple

Courtyard decorated by Antoninus Pius

Kiosks of Ptolemy XII

Sacred lake

0   20 m
0   60 ft

Karnak and Luxor

'In Egyptian Thebes the heaps of precious ingots gleam, the hundred-gated Thebes.'

Homer, *Iliad*, Book 9

Luxor and Karnak, visible in the foreground, together constituted the core temple areas of the ancient capital of Thebes. Across the Nile, western Thebes also contained the temples of a number of Middle and New Kingdom monarchs – the two areas together made the single greatest concentration of temples of any site in Egypt.

One of the greatest cities of the ancient world, Thebes grew in importance during the Middle Kingdom and was the political capital of Egypt during much of its New Kingdom period of glory; it was then a religious capital for centuries thereafter. References to Thebes – as a legendary if not fabulous place – occur in Classical literature from Homer and continue throughout medieval literature long after the city's true location and identity had been forgotten. It was not until the 18th century that the temples of Karnak and Luxor were recognized as those of ancient *Waset*: Thebes; but today they and the many other temples of the Theban area represent the largest and greatest concentration of temples in Egypt and possibly anywhere.

Although badly ruined, no site in Egypt is more impressive than Karnak. The largest temple complex ever built by man, it represents the combined achievement of generations of ancient builders and covers a truly massive area. Approximately 3 km (1.75 miles) north of the modern city of Luxor, Karnak requires half a day just to walk around its many precincts and years to come to know it well.

The modern name of this great complex, covering over 100 ha (247 acres), is taken from the nearby village of el-Karnak, but its ancient name was *Ipetisut*, 'The Most Select of Places', and it represented not only the seat of the great god Amun-Re but also contained or adjoined many chapels and temples dedicated to different deities. There are three main compounds. The main precinct, that of Amun, along with its subsidiary temples, lies in the centre; directly to the south is the precinct of Amun's consort Mut; and to the north is the precinct of Montu, the original falcon god of the Theban area who was displaced by Amun. The small temple of Khonsu, third member of Karnak's great triad (Amun, Mut and Khonsu), stands within the main Amun precinct, along with some 20 other temples and chapels.

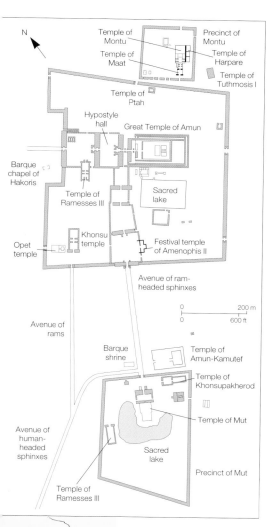

Temple of
Montu

Temple of
Maat

Precinct of
Montu

Temple of
Harpare

Temple of
Tuthmosis I

Temple of
Ptah

Hypostyle
hall

Great Temple of Amun

Barque
chapel of
Hakoris

Temple of
Ramesses III

Sacred
lake

Khonsu
temple

Opet
temple

Festival temple
of Amenophis II

Avenue of ram-
headed sphinxes

0   200 m
0   600 ft

Avenue of
rams

Barque
shrine

Temple of
Amun-Kamutef

Temple of
Khonsupakherod

Temple of Mut

Avenue of
human-
headed
sphinxes

Sacred
lake

Precinct of Mut

Temple of
Ramesses III

Great Temple of Amun

Built along two axes (east–west and north–south), this sprawling mass of ruined temple must be carefully studied in order to understand its original plan and subsequent growth. The original core of the temple was located near the centre of the east–west axis on a mound which was doubtless an ancient sacred site. From there the temple spread outwards, both towards the Nile in normal temple expansion and also on its other axis towards the outlying Mut temple to the south.

The modern entrance on the west is by way of the quay built by Ramesses II which gave access to the temple from a canal linked to the Nile in ancient times. To the right stands a small barque chapel of Hakoris (393–380 BC) used as a resting station on the gods' processional journeys to and from the river. A short processional avenue of cryosphinxes – their rams' heads symbolizing the god Amun and each holding a statue of the king between its lion's paws – runs from the quay to the temple's first pylon. This huge entrance structure – originally some 40 m (131 ft) high – is actually unfinished, as may be seen by the unequal height of its upper surface, the uncut blocks which project from its undecorated surfaces, and the remains of the mud-brick construction ramp still present on its inner side. The structure may have been built as late as the 30th dynasty by Nectanebo I who raised the *temenos* walls to which the pylon is attached, but this is uncertain and it is possible that an earlier pylon may have stood on this same spot. High on the thickness of the gate an inscription left by Napoleon's Expedition is still visible.

The first court encloses an area originally outside the temple proper and so contains a number of cryosphinxes displaced from their positions along

Factfile

Monument
Great Temple of Amun with numerous contiguous chapels and associated temples
Location
Karnak, Thebes (East Bank)
Dates of construction
18th dynasty (probably on the site of an earlier temple) to the Graeco-Roman Period
Dedication
Main temple: Amun-Re
Subsidiary temples: Khonsu, Ptah, etc.
Excavation reports
Legrain, G., *Les temples de Karnak* (Paris, 1929) Centre Franco-égyptien d'étude des temples de Karnak, *Cahiers de Karnak*, 6 vols. (1943–82)
Wall decoration
See the various volumes of the Epigraphic Survey, *Reliefs and Inscriptions at Karnak* (Chicago, 1936–), etc.

(Above) Karnak contains not only the Great Temple of Amun, but also the temples of Mut and Khonsu, the other members of the Theban triad, and many other deities. The precinct of Mut stands a little to the south and that of the god Montu lies just outside the northern wall of Amun's complex.

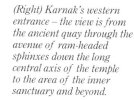

(Right) Karnak's western entrance – the view is from the ancient quay through the avenue of ram-headed sphinxes down the long central axis of the temple to the area of the inner sanctuary and beyond.

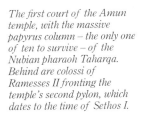

the processional route as well as several once-isolated buildings. To the left is the granite and sandstone triple barque chapel of Sethos II with three chambers for the barques of Mut (left), Amun (centre) and Khonsu (right). Niches within the structure's walls once held royal statues positioned in watchful attendance on the resting gods. Opposite the triple shrine is a small sphinx with the familiar features of Tutankhamun.

In the centre of the court are the remains of the gigantic kiosk of Taharqa – later usurped by Psammetichus II and restored under the Ptolemies. Originally consisting of ten huge papyrus columns linked by a low screening wall and open at its eastern and western ends, the building now retains only one great column and a large altar-like block of calcite. Although the function of this building is often presumed to be simply that of a barque shrine, the fact that it was open to the sky suggests that it may in fact have had a special purpose in one of the ritual activities associated with the temple – possibly a type of 'uniting with the sun' ceremony as was practised in later times at Dendera and elsewhere.

To the right is the entrance to the small temple of Ramesses III. In reality it was an elaborate barque shrine designed as a miniature version of that king's mortuary temple at Medinet Habu (p. 193). The structure's first court is thus lined with Osiride statues of the king, and the walls are decorated with various festival scenes and texts. Beyond is a portico and small hypostyle hall and the darkened area of the barque shrines for the members of Karnak's triad. Next to this temple, on its eastern side, is the so-called 'Bubastite Portal' which gives access to the famous scenes of Sheshonq I – the Shishak of biblical fame (1 Kings 14: 25–26) – smiting captives on the south face of the main temple's side wall. The portal on the court's opposite, northern, side leads to an open-air museum where a number of small monuments have been reconstructed from dismantled blocks found within

(Left) Osiride statues of Ramesses III line the court of that king's barque shrine, which takes the form of a small, mortuary-style monument incorporated into the Amun temple's outermost court.

(Right) Karnak's Great Hypostyle Hall – one of the most impressive buildings of the ancient world – contains 134 columns of open or bundled papyrus form. The massive post and lintel hall was illuminated by high clerestory windows, as seen here near the hall's centre.

the temple's walls and pylons. These structures include the beautiful and nearly complete limestone barque chapel of Senwosret I, shrines of Amenophis I and II, and Hatshepsut's only recently reconstructed red quartzite 'Chapelle Rouge'.

The second pylon was fronted by two striding colossi of Ramesses II, of which only the feet of one remain. In front of these is a third, standing statue of the king – with the diminutive figure of the princess Bent'anta standing between his feet – which was later usurped by both Ramesses VI (20th dynasty) and the priest 'king' Pinudjem I (21st dynasty). The pylon itself was begun in the time of Horemheb but not completed till the reign of Sethos I, and from its core many sandstone *talatat* blocks of an earlier temple of Akhenaten have been removed.

The second pylon opens into the Great Hypostyle Hall, the most impressive part of the whole Karnak complex. A veritable forest in stone, the hall was filled with 134 papyrus columns, the centre 12 being larger (some 21 m or 69 ft tall) and with open capitals, the remaining 122 along the sides smaller (some 15 m or 49 ft tall), with closed capitals. Even when standing at their bases it is difficult to grasp the true size of these columns, for a crowd of 50 people could easily stand together on the capitals of the largest. Originally these great columns supported a roof with small clerestory windows – a few of which survive – which would have provided purposely muted illumination for the primeval papyrus swamp which the hall represented. In ancient times the spaces between the columns thronged with statues of gods and kings, a few of which have been placed here in recent times. Against the southern pylon wall is a low alabaster block decorated with Egypt's enemies, the 'nine bows', which served as a

The inscribed 'Son of Re' names of Sethos I beneath the Great Hypostyle Hall's lintels still retain much of their original paint. The inscriptions declare the king 'Beloved of Amun-Re'.

A detail of a relief showing the sacred barque procession, in the Great Hypostyle Hall, Great Temple of Amun. The barque of Amun-Re is borne aloft by falcon- and jackal-headed figures and by the king, whose prerogative it was to escort the god to and from his temple.

barque rest during processions. Although the hall was initiated by Amenophis III, the decoration was begun by Sethos I and completed by Ramesses II, whose more hurried and less subtle sunk reliefs can easily be differentiated from the earlier, raised reliefs in the northern half of the hall. The interior decorations show scenes from the daily ritual as well as processional scenes and mythical topics such as the kings interacting with various gods. The exterior walls of the hall are covered by reliefs celebrating the military exploits of Sethos and Ramesses in Syria and Palestine, including Ramesses' battle at Kadesh (p. 228).

The third pylon was begun by Amenophis III, though its entrance porch is part of the Ramessid construction of the hall. A great number of reused blocks were found within this pylon – from which most of the monuments of the 'open-air museum' have been reconstructed. Behind this pylon, four obelisks were erected by Tuthmosis I and III at the entrance to the original, inner temple, though only one of those of the former king remains. The space between the third and fourth pylons is also the area where the temple's second axis branches off to the south.

The Standing Obelisk of Hatshepsut at Karnak

Of the four obelisks erected by Hatshepsut at Karnak, two have disappeared entirely, and of the two which were placed between the fourth and fifth pylons only the northern monument (the tallest standing obelisk in Egypt) still remains in place.

The inscriptions on this obelisk make clear the queen's reasons for donating the monuments and also stress the fact that each obelisk was made from a single piece of granite and gilded with great amounts of the finest gold. Each face of the monument begins with names and titles of the queen and continues with specific details of the donation. Of these, the inscriptions of the western and eastern faces are of particular interest, as they show the obelisks were dedicated to the god Amun in memory of Hatshepsut's father, Tuthmosis I – though this and other aspects of the inscription may reflect a legitimizing attempt on the part of the queen. The queen is referred to alternately as both son and daughter of the god. Words in square brackets are explanatory additions to the inscription:

Continuing to the east on the main axis, the fourth and fifth pylons were constructed by Tuthmosis I, and together with the narrow, once-pillared area between them constitute the oldest part of the temple still remaining. This inner temple area received several later additions, however, including the two rose-granite obelisks of Hatshepsut (see also p. 58), one of which still stands on the northern side; the other lies shattered to the south.

Little remains of the sixth pylon, built by Tuthmosis III, though the walls still retain the lists of conquered peoples of the south (southern wall) and the north (northern wall). The pylon precedes a court with two magnificent granite pillars bearing the floral emblems of Upper and Lower Egypt on the respective northern and southern sides (p. 37). The court, which also holds on its north side two large statues of Amun and Amaunet dedicated by Tutankhamun, leads to a granite barque shrine. This structure was built by Alexander the Great's successor, Philip Arrhidaeus, and appears to have replaced an earlier shrine of Tuthmosis III. It is divided into two halves: an outer where offerings were made to the god; and the inner, which still contains the pedestal upon which the god's barque reposed. The inner walls are decorated with depictions of offering rites, with Amun appearing in both his usual anthropomorphic guise and also in his alternative ithyphallic form. The outer walls show various festival scenes, some still retaining much of their original brightly coloured paint. The sand-

Western face

Horus, Mighty of ka's; Two Ladies, Flourishing in Years; Golden Horus, Divine of Diadems; King of Upper and Lower Egypt, Lord of the Two Lands, Maatkare [Truth is the ka of Re].

She made as her monument to her father Amun, Lord of the thrones of the Two Lands, the erecting to him two great obelisks at the august gateway [the temple pylon called] Amun, great of majesty. [Their upper surfaces] made with fine gold, they illuminate the Two Lands like the sun disc. Never was the like made since the beginning of the world. Made for him by the Son of Re, Hatshepsut Khnenemet Amun, Given life, like Re, eternally.

Eastern face

Horus, Mighty of ka's; King of Upper and Lower Egypt, Maatkare, beloved of Amun-Re.

Her majesty recorded the name of her father upon this enduring monument. Because favour was shown to the king of Upper and Lower Egypt, Akheperkare [Tuthmosis I], by the majesty of this god [Amun] these two great obelisks were erected by her majesty for the first time. For it was spoken by the lord of the gods 'Your father, the king of Upper and Lower Egypt, Akheperkare, gave orders to erect obelisks, [so] your majesty shall multiply monuments and live forever.'

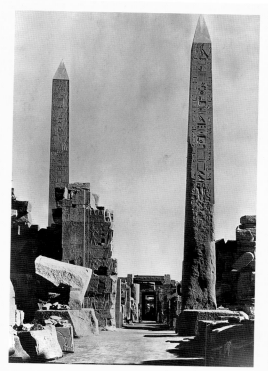

Factfile

Monument
Obelisk of Hatshepsut
Location
Great Temple of Amun, Karnak, between fourth and fifth pylons
Material
Red granite
Height
29.5 m (96 ft 9 in)
Weight
323 tons
Dedication
Amun-Re and Tuthmosis I

The obelisks of Tuthmosis I (right) and Hatshepsut (left), the latter being the larger. In both cases these represent only one of an original pair.

stone chambers surrounding the granite shrine were built by Hatshepsut, though the walls closest to the structure were added by Tuthmosis III and decorated by him with the 'annals' of his military campaigns and dedications to the temple – including a scene in which the king presents his two obelisks.

Behind these broken walls is the so-called 'central court', an open area upon which the very earliest temple at this site probably once stood and which became the heart of the later temple – the sanctuary with the image of the god. This building was plundered for its stone in antiquity, however, and the area now contains little of note other than the large calcite or 'alabaster' slab on which a shrine once stood. Beyond the central court is the relatively complete Festival Temple of Tuthmosis III, one of Karnak's more interesting and unusual features. Tuthmosis built this small complex as a kind of memorial to himself and his ancestral cult (his mortuary temple is on the west bank just north of the Ramesseum) and called it the 'Most Splendid of Monuments'. The entrance, originally flanked by two statues of the king in festival dress, is at the building's southwest corner, and leads into an antechamber with magazines and other rooms on the right, and on the left the temple's great columned hall. The roof of this hall is supported around its perimeter by square pillars, but in the central section by curiously shaped columns imitating ancient tent poles (rather than tent 'pegs' as many books call them). Although this tent-pole

architecture may recall ancient religious booths, it is perhaps more likely that it symbolizes the military tents so familiar to this great warrior pharaoh. In the Christian era the hall was reused as a church, and haloed icons may still be seen near the tops of several columns. Other chambers in the building include a 'chamber of the ancestors' and suites of rooms dedicated to the chthonic god Sokar, to the sun god in his morning manifestation, and to Amun. The chapel of Amun contains a massive

The Festival Temple of Tuthmosis III, called 'Most Splendid of Monuments', stands at the rear of the Amun temple complex. This structure has several features that are unique among Egyptian temples.

(Above) The central columns of the Tuthmosis III temple resemble the tent poles of temporary structures such as military tents.

(Above right) Osiride and striding royal statues in the first court of Karnak's southern axis. It was in this area that the great cachette of statues was discovered in 1902.

quartzite pedestal which once supported the shrine of the god, and the vestibule of this 'inclusive temple' is the famous 'Botanical Room' with its representations of exotic flora and fauna encountered on Tuthmosis' foreign campaigns.

The rear walls of Tuthmosis' complex are largely broken down, and it is possible to exit there and to examine the niche shrines (p. 71) built against the temple's back, to which the inhabitants of ancient Thebes brought their petitions for transfer to the great gods within Amun's domain. On either side of the shrines are the bases of two obelisks – long since destroyed – which Hatshepsut set up at the rear of the temple; and a little further to the east, past a reconstructed 'horned' altar of late date are the remains of a small 'temple of the hearing ear'

built for the same purpose as the niche shrines by Ramesses II. This structure also once contained a single obelisk on the central axis (probably the so-called 'Lateran Obelisk' in Rome), unusual in that it stood alone on the central axis of the temple. This temple stretched almost to the rear gate of the Karnak complex, an imposing portal nearly 20 m (65 ft 6 in) tall constructed by Nectanebo I. This is the termination of Karnak's main east–west axis, but to the north, inside the crumbling remains of the mud-brick wall, may be seen the remains of a small 22nd-dynasty temple of Osorkon IV dedicated to Osiris Hekadjet, 'Ruler of Eternity', and several other small shrines.

Turning to the south the visitor may walk back towards the sacred lake which, filled by ground water, supplied the water for the priests' ablutions and other temple needs. There the excavated remains of the priests' homes now lie beneath the seating erected for the sound and light show at the lake's eastern end. The lake's rough-hewn stone edging is punctuated on the southern side by the opening of a stone tunnel through which the domesticated geese of Amun were released into the lake from the fowl-yards a little further to the south. At the lake's northwest corner is the chapel of Taharqa, a rather strange building, the underground chambers of which contain descriptions of the sun-god's nightly journey through the earth and his rebirth each day as a scarab beetle. This seems to explain the significance of the large scarab sculpture which was brought from the west bank mortuary temple of Amenophis III and placed here.

Beyond the pyramidion of Hatshepsut's second obelisk which also lies at the lake's northwest corner is the first court of Karnak's north–south axis. Although the pylon (the seventh) of this court was constructed by Tuthmosis III, the side walls are the work of Ramesses II's son Merenptah. It was here, at the south end of the court, that the great Karnak Cachette containing some 20,000 statues and stelae was discovered at the beginning of the century (p. 64). Although most of the wooden statues had been destroyed by ground water, and many of the bronze ones were also damaged, hundreds of stone figures survived in good condition.

The remaining pylons on this axis are currently undergoing restoration by combined Franco-Egyptian teams. The eighth pylon was built by Hatshepsut and the ninth and tenth by Horemheb, who made considerable use of stone quarried from the temples of Akhenaten (p. 243).

Incorporated into the southern wall of the court between these last two pylons is a small Sed-festival or jubilee temple of Amenophis II, recently reconstructed by American Egyptologist Charles Van Siclen III. The temple's central hall contains some finely carved reliefs which retain much of their original colour, though the figures of the god Amun were desecrated by Akhenaten's agents and repaired by Sethos I. Van Siclen believes that the structure once stood in the area before the eighth pylon and has shown that it was apparently removed, stone by stone, by Horemheb and rebuilt at its present location when the king extended the Great Temple of Amun's south wing and added the ninth pylon.

The tenth pylon served as the southern entrance to the precinct of Amun and led, through its gate, past two limestone colossi (doubtless of Horemheb) to the sphinx-lined processional way which connected with the precinct of Mut. Within the Amun precinct's walls, however, lie a number of other smaller temples.

Khonsu temple

In the southwest corner of the precinct of Amun the Khonsu temple, dedicated to the lunar deity who was the son of Amun and Mut, provides an excellent example of a small but quite complete New Kingdom temple. Begun by Ramesses III, the structure was finished and decorated by a number of later rulers, including some of the Libyan generals who ruled as virtual kings of Upper Egypt at the close of the New Kingdom. The entrance pylon was thus decorated by Pinudjem I who is shown before the gods and whose inscriptions come very close to representing him as a king. The forecourt and hypostyle hall were likewise decorated by the earlier general Herihor, who appears along with Ramesses XI in the columned hall but who usurps

(Below left) Decorated pillars of the jubilee temple of Amenophis II, which was built on Karnak's southern axis.

(Below) This propylon gateway of the Khonsu temple opens to the avenue of rams linking the temple with the Mut complex and Luxor to the south.

the king's position (presumably at his death) in the later court. The inner part of the temple was decorated in Ramessid times but also received some Ptolemaic period relief work and was renewed in some areas by the Romans. At the back of the temple is the barque shrine of the god, with a carved pedestal at the rear. Stairs lead from the southeast corner of this part of Khonsu's house to the roof, with its sun chapel, and provide an excellent panorama of Karnak captured in a well-known drawing by the 19th-century artist David Roberts. The frequent appearance of blocks with unmatching and inverted decoration (including an upside-down chariot above the top of the stairs) here and in other parts of the temple shows the extent to which stone from earlier buildings was used in this temple. The temple's propylon gate in the enclosure wall, known as the Bab el-'Amara, was built by Ptolemy III and opens to its own avenue of rams leading southward to the Mut precinct and Luxor.

Opet temple

Behind the Khonsu temple is the small Graeco-Roman Period sanctuary of the hippopotamus goddess Opet, who was venerated as a helper of women in childbirth. The rather strangely laid-out temple was chiefly built by Ptolemy VIII and decorated by several later rulers including the emperor Augustus. Despite the proximity of the Bab el-'Amara gate, the Opet temple had its own gateway through the Amun precinct's western *temenos* wall, suggesting a level of importance and interaction with other cults. Entrance into the temple is by way of a door in the back wall which opens into the sanctuary and then the outer offering hall. The reliefs throughout the temple's interior, though

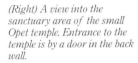

(Right) A view into the sanctuary area of the small Opet temple. Entrance to the temple is by a door in the back wall.

(Below) The temple dedicated to the hippopotamus goddess, Opet, and the entrance pylon to the Khonsu temple, near the southwestern corner of the Karnak complex.

smoke-blackened, are quite well preserved. Although the structure was nominally dedicated to Opet, it was actually a monument in the service of Amun, and particularly of the mythic resurrection cycle which he had assimilated from the god Osiris. The temple has several crypts hidden within its walls as well as larger ones built beneath ground level which served as a 'tomb' for Amun-Osiris and as repositories for the items used in the Festival of the Resurrection of the god.

Temple of Ptah

On the northern perimeter of Amun's great complex, just inside the gate leading to the Montu precinct, is a small temple of the Memphite creator-god Ptah. Like the great Amun temple, the structure is oriented west to east. Its inner core was constructed by Tuthmosis III, and this area was expanded and restored by the Nubian king Shabaka and several Ptolemaic and Roman rulers. Interestingly, the Ptolemies who conducted restoration work did not replace the earlier royal cartouches with their own but actually replaced damaged and missing sections with the names of the original builders. The temple consists of five gateways of different dates and with depictions of kingly figures wearing the red and white crowns of Upper and Lower Egypt on their respective northern and southern jambs. The gateways lead to a small columned hall with flower-capitalled columns fronting three chapels, two of which are dedicated to Ptah and the third (on the southern side) to Hathor. A headless statue of Ptah stands in the central chapel, but the southern chapel now contains a statue not of Hathor but of Ptah's 'consort', the lion-headed Sekhmet. This over life-sized, intrusive, black-granite statue is illuminated by light from a small hole in the roof, giving some idea of the atmosphere of the darkened ancient sanctuaries.

Precinct of Montu

North of the Amun complex lies the precinct of Montu, smallest of Karnak's three walled compounds. The square-shaped enclosure contains the ruined temple of Montu, the old falcon god of the Theban area, as well as a sacred lake and several smaller chapels to various deities. The Montu temple itself was built by Amenophis III, but several other kings, including Taharqa, carried out modifications to its plan. The temple is oriented on a north–south axis and is fronted by its own quay and a propylon gate (locally called the Bab el-'Abd) built by Ptolemy III and IV. Beyond the propylon rows of human-headed sphinxes run to the north along a processional entryway. Parallel to the Montu temple and built against its eastern side is a small temple of Montu's son, Harpare. And directly behind Montu's shrine is a simple temple of Maat, oriented in the opposite direction on the same axis and consisting mainly of a court fronting a small pillared hall. Outside the compound, on the east, are the ruins of a small temple of Tuthmosis I, and on the west, an even smaller chapel of Osiris.

Precinct of Mut

South of the Great Temple of Amun and linked to it by a massive causeway of ram-headed sphinxes is the precinct of Amun's consort, Mut. Mostly destroyed, the compound contains the remains of the temple of Mut itself, a sacred lake – the *isheru* – which curves around it on three sides, and several smaller temples. The Mut temple was mainly built by Amenophis III, though it received later additions at the behest of Taharqa, Nectanebo I and other kings. A large pylon opened to a narrow court before a second pylon and the temple's inner areas, though the ruined condition of the structure precludes detailed knowledge of its original form and decoration. The temple is perhaps most famous for the black-granite statues of the goddess Sekhmet which Amenophis had placed there – it is estimated that over 700 of these statues originally adorned the temple precincts.

(Above) A statue of the lion goddess Sekhmet, in the south chapel of the temple of Ptah, Karnak. The statue stands in the darkened sanctuary, lit only by a narrow slit of light, giving visitors a sense of the shadowy interior of the innermost part of the Egyptian temple.

(Left) A view towards the sanctuary of the temple of Ptah. On both sides of the successive gateways figures of the king (wearing the red crown on the northern side and the white crown on the southern) declare purification on those who enter.

On the western edge of the sacred lake Ramesses III built a small temple which still retains some of the military scenes on its outer walls, along with two headless colossi of the king before its entrance. Of the other shrines and chapels built within the compound only that of Khonsupakherod ('Khonsu the Child') is of significant size. Largely built from reused blocks from New Kingdom structures, the temple retains some of its decoration, including a number of birth and circumcision scenes. The propylon gateway set into the *temenos* wall to the north was constructed by Ptolemy II and III. Two other structures stood just outside this entrance to the compound: to the east, a temple of Amun-Kamutef ('Amun Bull of his Mother'), and to the west, a small barque shrine dating to the reigns of Tuthmosis III and Hatshepsut. Little more than the foundations of these structures remain, however. The precinct of Mut is undergoing continued study and excavation by the Brooklyn Museum and the Detroit Institute of Arts.

Akhenaten temple

A little to the east of the Nectanebo gate, outside the precinct of Amun enclosure wall, are the remains of the Gem-pa-aten, the temple built by Amenophis IV for his new religion during the first five years of his reign, before changing his name to Akhenaten and moving his capital to the area of el-Amarna (p. 140). The temple's existence was first suggested in 1926 by Henri Chevrier, who found a number of its small *talatat* building blocks and colossal statues of Akhenaten. Since 1966, the site has been investigated by the Akhenaten Temple Project of the University of Toronto under the direction of Donald Redford. The project began by photographing and systematically studying the blocks already in storerooms. Since then it has completed over 20 seasons of excavation and research at the site.

This investigation has revealed much of the Aten temple, but the area is quite large (*c.* 130 × 200 m, 426 ft 6 in × 656 ft) and a full ground plan has not yet been established because much of the central and eastern parts of the complex lie beneath modern houses. The temple was doubtless oriented towards the east, and there is only one small (4 m, 13 ft) gateway in the west wall opening to the remains of an approach leading to where the 18th-dynasty palace is believed to have been. The temple itself seems to have consisted primarily of an open court, around which ran a colonnade of square sandstone pillars more than 7 m (23 ft) high. On the south side, against each pillar, a colossal statue of Akhenaten depicted the king in the somewhat grotesque style characteristic of his early reign and wearing, alternately, the royal double crown and the twin-feather headdress of the god Shu. Statue fragments of life-sized figures of the king and queen were found at regular intervals along the line of the western colonnade and a large number of granite offering

tables were also found, perhaps intended to stand before the statues and colossi. The *talatat* blocks of the Gem-pa-aten which have been recovered depict the Sed jubilee which Amenophis IV celebrated in the second or third year of his reign, along with religious sacrifices, musicians, dancers, foreigners and, most importantly, the royal family. In fact, Nefertiti – the king's chief queen – figures very prominently in the decorative programme, and is actually depicted on more blocks than Akhenaten, making offerings alone or with her daughters.

All building in the area ceased when Akhenaten moved to el-Amarna, and was only briefly resumed under Tutankhamun and Ay (judging by a few *talatat* blocks bearing their figures and names), and the temple was ultimately destroyed during the reign of Horemheb, when its mud-brick sections were burned and the stone structures dismantled. Many of the 36,000 or more *talatat* blocks which formed the Gem-pa-aten were found reused in the ninth, second, and possibly the third and tenth pylons, as well as the hypostyle hall of the Great Temple of Amun.

It is known that Amenophis IV constructed other structures in the Theban area – notably the so-called Hut-benben, Rud-menu and Teni-menu,

(Right) Excavated figures of Amenophis IV/Akhenaten, positioned against the southern piers of the court of the Temple of Aten in East Karnak. Most were broken at the time of the temple's destruction.

(Opposite) A colossal sandstone figure from Karnak's Aten temple. This figure, which holds a crook and sceptre like others from the temple, is somewhat androgynous in form and has been interpreted in various ways. The figures all seem to parallel Osiride statues found in royal mortuary temples.

though the precise nature and location of these buildings is not known. Judging by its name, the Hut-benben or 'Mansion of the Benben' may have contained something like the pyramidion used in the solar worship of Heliopolis (p. 111), though the greater part of what has been reconstructed of this temple from its recovered blocks consists only of a number of pillars, each about 9.5 m (31 ft) high, showing Nefertiti with one of her daughters, offering to the Aten.

A talatat *block from one of Amenophis IV/Akhenaten's temples with a representation of Nefertiti. Thousands of such blocks were reused in the construction of later pylons and other religious structures at Karnak when Akhenaten's temples were systematically dismantled after his death.*

Temple C

About 75 m (246 ft) to the east of the southeast corner of the Amun complex are the remains of a small temple of Ptolemaic date. The complex is known to have consisted of a mud-brick *temenos* wall, in the eastern half of which lies a small sandstone structure known only as 'Temple C'. It was here that Champollion discovered the 'Bentresh Stela', now in the Louvre, which purports to record events relating to a princess of the time of Ramesses II. Recent excavations under the direction of Donald Redford have shown that the temple was fronted by a peristyle with four columns within an inner *temenos* wall which was linked by a short processional way to the outer gate. Various chambers including what may be the remains of a sanatorium were also found on the temple's southern side. The excavations indicate that the temple core was constructed or refurbished in the 3rd century BC within the area of an earlier religious structure. The present forecourt appears to have been added in the 2nd or 1st century BC, and the temple apparently saw continued use into Roman times.

The façade of the small structure known as Temple C, East Karnak, as reconstructed by Donald Redford; this temple appears to have been in use in Ptolemaic and Roman times.

Factfile

Monument
Temple of Amun
Various chapels
Location
Luxor, Thebes (East Bank)
Dates of construction
18th dynasty (probably on
the site of an earlier temple)
to Graeco-Roman Period
Dedication
Main temple: Amun of
Luxor
Chapels: Mut, Khonsu
Excavation reports
See Bibliography under
Gayet, etc.
Wall decoration
Epigraphic Survey, *Reliefs
and Inscriptions
at Luxor Temple*, Volume
1– (Chicago, 1991–)

*Luxor Temple from the south,
showing the pylons of
Ramesses II in the
background, the colonnade
completed by Tutankhamun,
the peristyle sun court of
Amenophis II and, in the
foreground, the inner core
of the temple, which was
built and rebuilt over
hundreds of years.*

Luxor

Luxor Temple

Luxor Temple, the southernmost of the monuments of the Theban east bank, was located in the heart of ancient Thebes and, like Karnak, was dedicated to the god Amun or Amun-Re. A special manifestation of the god was worshipped here, however. Like the Amun of Karnak he is depicted in two principal forms – as the blue-painted sky god and the black-painted ithyphallic fertility god – but maintained a kind of separate identity and was 'visited' by the Amun of Karnak each year (see box, p. 171). The temple was called the Southern Opet or 'Place of Seclusion' and its god Amenemope 'Amun of the Opet'.

3,000 years of growth in 'The Place of Seclusion'

Luxor Temple provides a fascinating case study in the growth and expansion of Egyptian temples (see plan p. 48). While it may have been built on the site of even earlier temple structures, the history of the present structure nevertheless embraces over 3,000 years of growth.

It is known that Hatshepsut built extensively in Luxor Temple, but much of her work was eventually replaced. The core area of Luxor Temple as it stands today was constructed by Amenophis III, the 18th-dynasty's great 'sun king'. He built in two stages: in the first stage he constructed and decorated a multi-roomed complex on a raised platform that today is the southernmost part of the temple. Later in his reign the king added an open peristyle sun court to the north and also laid the foundations for a large colonnade to the north of that.

Work was interrupted, however, during the reign of Amenophis' son Akhenaten who strove to diminish or destroy the power of Amun's temples. The colonnade was thus not completed and decorated until the time of Akhenaten's eventual successor Tutankhamun, who officially restored the worship of Amun in Thebes.

For almost half a century the temple remained in this form until it was expanded again by Ramesses II. This prolific builder constructed a huge pillared court and pylon on a new axis which swung to the east in order to align itself with Amun's main temple at Karnak – to which Luxor Temple was joined by a long processional way. The triple shrine constructed to hold the barques of Amun, Mut and Khonsu when they visited Luxor was also built by Ramesses at this time, on the location of an earlier way station (built by Hatshepsut), when the king enclosed this southern part of the processional way in his great court.

Although no further expansions were made on this scale in the following centuries, the Late Period king Shabaka seems to have constructed a large pillared kiosk before Ramesses' pylon, and some 300 years later Nectanebo I added a broad courtyard in the same open area before the pylon and embellished the temple's processional avenue to Karnak with hundreds of human-headed sphinxes.

The continuing importance of Luxor is also seen in the complete renewal of the central barque shrine in the name of Alexander the Great shortly after the Macedonian's conquest of Egypt. Likewise, the cult of emperor worship was established in the temple, with certain architectural features being added or modified, when Egypt became an imperial province of Rome in the 1st century BC. Later still, in the 4th to 6th centuries AD, the whole temple was incorporated into a Roman *castrum* or fortified military encampment, the massive stone-paved avenues and pillared streets of which can still be seen today.

After the conversion of Rome to Christianity and in the Byzantine Period, several Christian churches were built in and around the temple precincts. In the 6th century one of these churches was built within the Ramessid court, and on top of this same build-

ing, in the 13th century, the Mosque of Abu el-Haggag was constructed. This mosque still remains in use today and effectively brings the history of Luxor Temple as a sacred precinct from its beginnings, some time before 1500 BC, to the present day – a history of well over 3,000 years of change, development and growth.

(Above left) The diminutive but graceful figure of Nefertari stands at the foot of a colossal statue of her husband, Ramesses II, in Luxor's first court.

(Above) The entrance to the inner temple at Luxor was sealed, flanked by Corinthian columns and made the focus of cult for the Roman troops stationed at Luxor.

Remains of the Roman castrum, *or military complex, are still visible to the west of Luxor's inner peristyle court.*

Monuments and artwork

Compact in plan, Luxor Temple may be explored in little more than an hour; but the complexity and richness of this structure warrant many times that. The temple's artwork includes some of the finest relief carving in Egypt and is often very well preserved because much of the temple was buried for many centuries. The present entrance is through the pylon of Ramesses II, once fronted by six colossi of the king (two seated and four standing) and two obelisks. One of the obelisks and two of the statues were transported to Paris in the last century, but those that remain provide impressive examples of these monuments.

The outer walls of the pylons were decorated in the time of Ramesses with a depiction of the Battle of Kadesh (1285 BC), and the reliefs of the inner walls of the gateway were added by the Nubian king Shabaka in the 25th dynasty. Beyond the pylons, the temple's large peristyle court is surrounded by two rows of papyrus-bud columns and contains, on the left, the Abu el-Haggag mosque, and on the right, the tripartite barque shrine built by Ramesses for use by the visiting deities Amun, Mut and Khonsu of Karnak. The statues between the ambulatory's columns were usurped or carved at the behest of Ramesses II; those of the southwest corner are particularly well preserved.

The imposing processional colonnade of Amenophis III, with its massive papyrus capital columns,

*The so-called papyrus-bud
columns of the eastern
colonnade constructed by
Ramesses II around his great
court: colossal statues bearing
the king's name stand between
the columns in the areas
where the people were allowed
to congregate during religious
processions.*

each in excess of 19 m (62 ft 3 in) tall, once fronted
that king's temple and was the architectural prototype for the Great Hypostyle Hall of Karnak. Its
walls were decorated by Tutankhamun and preserve scenes of the great Opet Festival (p. 171)
celebrated here. The west wall depicts the southward
procession from Karnak and the (better-preserved)
east wall depicts the return sequence.

*(Right) The great papyrus-
bundle columns of Luxor's
hypostyle hall frame the
processional way towards the
temple's inner sanctuaries –
beyond the later niche
dedicated to the cult of the
legions stationed here in
Roman times.*

*(Far left) A view along the
sphinx-lined causeway of
Nectanebo I towards the
entrance pylons of Luxor
Temple. Hundreds of these
human-headed statues lined
the processional route between
Luxor and Karnak.*

*(Left) The triple barque shrine
built by Ramesses II for the
visiting deities, Amun, Mut
and Khonsu of Karnak,
directly behind the west pylon
within the king's peristyle
court at Luxor.*

(Left) Alexander the Great depicted as pharaoh, standing before Amun, on the walls of Luxor Temple's innermost sanctuary. This barque shrine, constructed within the sanctuary of Amenophis III, was made in Alexander's name and decorated for him.

(Below) The 'birth room' of Amenophis III: on the walls were depicted scenes showing the king's divine conception and birth – an aspect of royal propaganda which may possibly reflect a 'sacred marriage' performed by the king and his queen, the 'god's wife', during the Opet Festival.

Beyond the colonnade is the Great Sun Court of Amenophis' temple which received decoration from the time of Amenophis himself to that of Alexander. The side walls retain some of their original colouring, and it was here that a spectacular cache of statuary (p. 64) was unearthed in 1989. At its southern end the court now blends almost imperceptibly into the hypostyle hall consisting of four rows of papyrus columns whose roof no longer survives. The hypostyle leads to a smaller eight-columned hall or portico which originally opened into the inner temple, but which was transformed by the Roman legion stationed at Luxor into a chapel dedicated to the imperial cult. The hall is flanked by chapels for Mut and Khonsu and leads to an offering hall and sanctuary in the form of a large barque shrine. In Amenophis' temple this was originally a large, square room (the bases of its columns are still visible in the floor), but the present shrine was erected within this space by Alexander the Great who is depicted on the shrine's walls, dressed as a pharaoh and presenting offerings to the ithyphallic Amun.

Directly behind the barque shrine are the innermost chambers of Amenophis' temple, including, in the central location, the original sanctuary or 'holy of holies', containing the base of the block which once supported the god's image. The surrounding rooms form the suite of private or intimately secluded chambers which gave the temple its name of Opet or 'harem'. Separated from the main temple, this area formed a kind of temple within the temple, apparently with special mythic significance relating to the particular nature of the Amun of Luxor. The various chambers are ranged around an unusual small hall with 12 pillars – possibly symbolizing the hours of the day since depictions of the sun-god's day and evening barques appear on the room's opposing east and west walls. These innermost parts of the temple stood on a low mound which was held to be the original site of creation – the mound which rose from the primeval waters (p. 76) – so that the roles of the chief gods Amun and Re and the concepts of creation and cyclic solar renewal were here particularly intertwined.

To the east of the barque shrine is the 'birth room', so-called because of its decorative sequence. On the west wall is depicted the divine conception and birth of Amenophis III, along with his subsequent presentation to the gods and nurturing, as well as the determination of the future king's reign. It is possible that the scenes depicted here in fact reflect a ritual 'divine marriage' that was celebrated between the king and the 'god's wife' – the queen – during the Opet Festival, but in any event, they affirm the overall theme of renewed royal and divine vitality celebrated in the festival. The mound on which this area of the temple stood was also held to be the very site of the birth of Amun so that the theme of birth was clearly one shared by temple and festival alike.

The outer surfaces of the eastern walls of the inner temple area can be seen to contain many blocks apparently randomly decorated with unrelated images. This 'out-of-the-way' area represents a 'practice wall' where the ancient masons and sculptors learned the skills of temple decoration. The carved practice representations were then plastered over, only to be revealed again in the course of centuries as the underlying stone became exposed.

The Opet Festival

A scene of a procession of the Opet Festival, from Luxor's colonnaded hall.

The barque of Amun leaving Karnak, as depicted on the sanctuary of Philip Arrhidaeus in Karnak's Amun temple.

Once each year, in the festival called 'The Beautiful Feast of Opet', the great god Amun-Re of Karnak visited the sanctuary of Luxor – some 2 km (1.25 miles) to the south – for what was doubtless the most important festival of the Theban area. There, in the 'inner chambers' or 'Opet of the South', the god visited the Amun who resided in Luxor Temple along with the other members of the Theban triad – Mut and Khonsu.

Celebrated in the second month of the inundation season of Akhet, the Opet Festival was linked to the Nile's flood season and its symbolic fertility, and although not documented before the 18th dynasty, this festival attained great importance in New Kingdom times. It is known to have lasted some eleven days during the reign of Tuthmosis III and to have grown to almost a month in duration by the time of Ramesses III.

Representations and texts carved on the walls of the colonnade and elsewhere at Luxor Temple detail the processions to and from the Luxor sanctuary and allow the festivities to be reconstructed to a large degree (p. 95), though certain changes took place in the observance of the festival over time and not all details are clear. Early in the New Kingdom, in the reign of Hatshepsut, we know that Amun's image was transported by land to the southern temple in the god's portable barque carried on the shoulders of *wab* priests. The return journey, however, was made by river, with the god's ceremonial barque being escorted by the barge of the king himself. Later in the New Kingdom, and certainly by the time of Tutankhamun, both journeys – south and north – were sometimes made by river, and the members of the Theban triad, Amun, Mut and Khonsu, were transported in their own barge which was towed southwards – upstream – by boats under sail and by gangs of men who strained at ropes as they proceeded along the bank of the Nile. The representations from this time show the procession accompanied by various dignitaries and by groups of musicians, dancers and singers.

On arrival at Luxor the god was greeted by princes and other dignitaries bearing gifts and sacrifices, and the route from the river to the temple was lined with offering booths and welcoming temple personnel – including troupes of acrobatic dancers who performed for the gods' enjoyment. The procession came to a halt at a triple shrine built by Hatshepsut which originally stood outside the temple proper. Once rested, the statues of the deities were moved from this point to shrines within the temple, and the various ritual ceremonies of the great festival were begun. The religious rites of this particular festival are imperfectly understood, but may have included rituals intended to celebrate a sacred marriage which intimated the divine parentage of the ruling monarch. The celebration also functioned as a renewal of the king's role and power as it encompassed the ritual repetition of the coronation rites, with the king receiving the various crowns as he knelt before the image of the god. The god's rejuvenation of the king was also reciprocated in special offerings presented by the king throughout the celebration of the Opet, so that the event may be seen as a festival of renewal of both god and king, and as a reassertion of the ties that bound the gods and their subjects in the Egyptian view of the cosmos.

Western Thebes

Western Thebes holds the remains of some 36 temples in varying degrees of preservation and dating from Archaic times to the Graeco-Roman Period, though most were built in the 18th to 20th dynasties.

Both the east and west banks of the Nile in the area of modern-day Luxor represent the site of ancient Thebes. While the early New Kingdom city focused on the east bank, Amenophis III built his great palace at Malqata on the west bank, and by the 19th dynasty western Thebes had become central to the administration of this part of Egypt. The temples

of the area are generally aligned east–west according to the local orientation of the Nile, and although the oft-repeated statement that the temples on the east bank of the Nile are 'divine' temples and those of the west bank are 'mortuary' temples is inaccurate, in western Thebes the division appears to be apt. Here, almost all the temples which line the edge of the Nile's western flood plain are of the cults of kings. The few exceptions, such as the early temples of Thoth Hill, are not so obvious and rarely seen by the casual visitor.

Thoth Hill

Temple of Horus

High on the southern spur of the great plateau which forms the backdrop to western Thebes, the 11th-dynasty pharaoh Sankhkare Mentuhotep constructed a remote temple. (This king's and his father's mortuary temples lie to the south in the bay of Deir el-Bahri.) The remains of this structure were virtually unknown until the beginning of the 20th century, when they were found by George Sweinfurth in 1904 and examined by Flinders Petrie in 1909. Petrie's assessment that the temple represented a Sed-festival chapel was incorrect, for the site has recently been excavated by a Hungarian expedition led by Gyözö Vörös for Eotvos Lorand University (1995–98), which found that although there is a columned Sed-festival building in the area, the temple itself was, in fact, a small temple of Horus. This brick structure was built on an artificial terrace and consisted of an entrance pylon and walls surrounding a free-standing inner sanctuary with the three rooms typical of its period. Foundation deposits and fragments of the foundation text and dedicatory inscriptions from the limestone door

*The site of Thoth Hill in
western Thebes holds two
temples: a Middle Kingdom
temple of Sankhkare
Mentuhotep and a much
earlier, Archaic Period
sanctuary beneath the
11th-dynasty structure.*

jambs of the temple were found, along with parts of
a lintel with hieratic graffiti indicating that it might
have already fallen as the result of an earthquake
by the end of the 11th dynasty. Of particular interest, the excavators believe that the temple was
carefully oriented towards the point of the heliacal
rising of the star Sirius – which was worshipped as
the god Horus to whom the temple was dedicated
(see p. 37).

The Archaic temple

The Hungarian excavation on Thoth Hill revealed a
previously unknown temple beneath the Middle
Kingdom structure of Sankhkare Mentuhotep – the
oldest known temple in the Theban region. This
small Archaic temple was similar in plan to the
building which replaced it, though it evidently had
only a single chambered sanctuary. The earlier
temple was also slightly offset in its axial orientation (by just over 2 degrees towards the south), to
the point at which the heliacal rising of Sirius
would have occurred around 3000 BC.

Dra Abu el-Naga

Temple of Sethos I

Located just south of the hill of Dra Abu el-Naga, at
the northern end of the line of temples constructed
throughout the New Kingdom, the temple of Sethos
I was one of the major monuments of the area.
Today the pylons and courts of this temple are

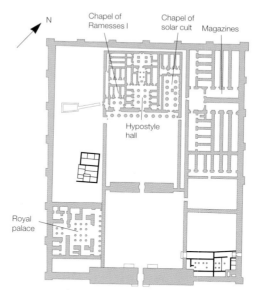

*The mortuary temple of
Sethos I is one of the less-
visited monuments in western
Thebes but has several
interesting features and
contains some fine examples
of the excellent raised relief
carving of Sethos' reign.*

largely destroyed, making it seem much less significant than it once was. Nevertheless, what remains of
this temple is not unimpressive. Begun by Sethos
and completed by his son Ramesses II, the sand-
stone-built temple was called 'Glorious Sethos in the
West of Thebes'.

A row of sphinxes connected the pyloned
entrance with the inner temple, where a portico at
the rear of the second court leads into a central
hypostyle which was completed during the co-

regency of Sethos and his son Ramesses II; but the raised relief decoration – at least in this section of the temple – is of the same high quality for which Sethos' monuments are renowned.

To the sides of this hall are chapels dedicated to the cults of the Theban triad and the Osirian deities, as well as to Sethos. To the south of the hypostyle, with its own entrance from the portico, is a chapel dedicated to Sethos' father, Ramesses I – whose reign was too short to allow the building of a mortuary temple – with a wonderfully preserved false door at the rear of its sanctuary. On the northern side of the hypostyle, again with its own entrance, is a chapel of the solar cult with a pillared court and central altar. The god Amun, with whom Sethos is here identified, is central to the cult of the temple, however. At the rear of the temple are barque shrines of Mut, Amun and Khonsu, with the innermost sanctuary, with its false door for the use of the king, being directly behind the barque shrine of Amun. On the south side of the sanctuary were chapels associated with the royal cult.

The outer complex has been excavated by the German Archaeological Institute, whose work has added considerably to our knowledge of the temple. Rows of magazines ranged around a columned hall were constructed along the northern side of the site, and the complex also contained a royal palace which was built on the south side of the first court, just inside the entrance pylon. This is the earliest known example of a royal palace within a New Kingdom temple and, although the building seems to have been largely ritual in nature, it was copied in many succeeding temples. The pylons themselves, doubtless added after Sethos' death, were largely constructed of unbaked brick which has not withstood the periodic flooding which has occurred in the area.

The mortuary temple of Sethos marked the first west bank stop of the important 'Beautiful Feast of the Valley' (p. 95) which was commemorated annually in Thebes, and the temple apparently continued to fulfil this function until Roman times. During the Christian era, however, part of the northern courtyard was transformed into a Coptic church, and, as was the case with many west bank temples, numerous houses were built within its precincts from its ample supply of easily available stone. Today, the temple is rarely visited compared with the more famous west bank monuments, but the site is well worth the time taken to examine it.

Temple of Nebwenenef

Nebwenenef was a high priest of Onuris and Hathor at Dendera who gained appointment to the position of first prophet of Amun in the first year of Ramesses II. One of the few private individuals to be granted a mortuary temple at Thebes, Nebwenenef's small facility was built beneath the slope of Dra Abu el-Naga close by the temple of Sethos which Ramesses completed. Two broken colossi of Ramesses II were found lying at the entrance to the court, but the temple is now destroyed.

Temple of Amenophis I and Ahmose Nefertari

While some uncertainty remains as to the exact location of the tomb of this early New Kingdom ruler, the site of the small mortuary temple dedicated to him and his queen is known to be at the edge of the floodplain just to the south of Dra Abu el-Naga – possibly making him the first Egyptian king to situate his mortuary temple in an area other than that of his tomb, or at least the first in the New Kingdom. Various blocks showing Sed festival scenes have been recovered from the site, along with assorted statue and stelae fragments, but virtually nothing now remains of this temple.

Deir el-Bahri

Lying directly across the Nile from the Great Temple of Amun at Karnak, the great rock amphitheatre of Deir el-Bahri provides a natural focal point of the west bank terrain and an inviting site for the temples of any rulers ambitious enough to attempt to incorporate the high cliffs of the Theban massif into the architectural programme of their own monuments. The first Egyptian monarch to achieve this was the Middle Kingdom ruler Nebhepetre Mentuhotep, whose temple became a template for similar, later structures both here and elsewhere. But the crowning achievement of Deir el-Bahri is, of course, the mortuary temple of Hatshepsut which now commands the whole area and which remains even in its ruinous state one of the great monuments of Egypt.

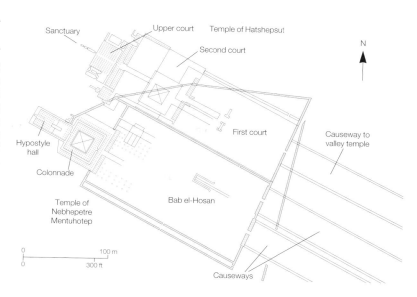

(Above) Plan of the major temples of Deir el-Bahri: that of Hatshepsut (top) is the largest, followed by the temple of Nebhepetre Mentuhotep (bottom). The small temple of Tuthmosis III was sandwiched between and behind the earlier structures.

Aerial view of the great bay of Deir el-Bahri, showing the temples of Hatshepsut, Tuthmosis III and Nebhepetre Mentuhotep at the base of the high cliffs which form the dramatic backdrop to this anciently sacred area. Behind are the eastern and western branches of the Valley of the Kings.

175

Factfile

Monument
Mortuary temple of
Hatshepsut
Various chapels
Location
Deir el-Bahri, Thebes (west
bank)
Date of construction
18th dynasty
Dedication
Main Temple: Amun,
Hatshepsut
Chapels: Hathor, Anubis,
Parents of Hatshepsut
Excavation reports
Naville, E., *The Temple of
Deir el Bahari*. EEF, 12–14,
16, 19, 27, 29. vols. 1–7
(London, 1894–1908)
Winlock, H. E., *Excavations
at Deir el-Bahri,
1911–1931* (New York, 1942)
Wall decoration
See Further Reading under
Pawlicki and Wysocki

*Hatshepsut's temple consists
of broad, rising terraces and
courts leading to an inner
temple area built against and
into the cliff face itself. The
painted limestone head of
Hatshepsut (right) came from
an Osiride column on the
upper portico of the temple.*

Temple of Hatshepsut

'A palace of the god, wrought with gold and silver,
it illuminated the faces [of the people] with its brightness.'

– Tomb inscription of Hatshepsut's official, Djehuty

Called by the Egyptians Djeser-djeseru, 'sacred of sacreds', Hatshepsut's terraced and rock-cut temple at Deir el-Bahri is one of the most impressive monuments of western Thebes. Situated directly against the rock face of Deir el-Bahri's great rock bay, the temple not only echoed the lines of the surrounding cliffs in its design but fused so effectively with them that it seems a natural extension of its setting. The temple was little more than a ruin when it was excavated by Édouard Naville (1891), and later by Herbert Winlock and Émile Baraize, but the work of the Polish–Egyptian mission, which has laboured at the site since 1961 (currently directed by Franciszek Pawlicki), has led to a great deal of successful reconstruction.

It is known that the construction of this temple took 15 years, and modern studies have shown that it underwent a number of substantial modifications in that time. In the completed structure, the approach to the temple was along a sphinx-lined causeway, some 37 m (121 ft) wide, which led up from the valley to pylons which are now gone. Designed in multiple levels, the temple itself consisted of three broad courts separated by colonnades, linked by ascending ramps and bounded by dressed limestone walls. Hatshepsut recorded that she built her temple as 'a garden for my father Amun', and the first court once held exotic trees and shrubs brought from the land of Punt (perhaps southern Sudan or Eritrea). Its portico was decorated on its northern side with scenes of the marshes of Lower (northern) Egypt and on the south with the quarrying and transportation of the queen's great obelisks in Upper (southern) Egypt. The portico of the second court was carved on its southern side with relief scenes of the famous expedition sent by Hatshepsut to distant Punt, and on the north, the renowned and finely executed 'birth' scenes showing the queen's divine inception (and hence regnal legitimacy), which probably served as a model for the later scene of this type in Luxor Temple.

(Left and below) Hatshepsut's expedition to the land of Punt is famously depicted in the 'Punt Portico' of her temple. Here, the king and queen of Punt receive the Egyptian expedition, set within a drawing of the wall scene in which the block appeared. The exact location of Punt is still unknown, though it was evidently an area somewhere along the eastern coast of Africa, perhaps modern Somalia, southern Sudan or Eritrea.

(Below left) A relief from the temple of Hatshepsut shows soldiers parading in honour of the goddess.

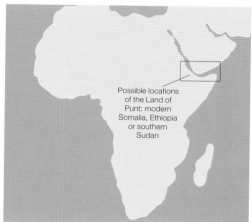

Possible locations
of the Land of
Punt: modern
Somalia, Ethiopia
or southern
Sudan

The area of Deir el-Bahri was long sacred to the goddess Hathor, and at the southern end of the second colonnade is a complete Hathor chapel, originally with its own entrance. The chapel contains a vestibule with characteristic Hathor-headed pillars, a 12-columned hypostyle hall and inner rooms decorated with various scenes of Hatshepsut and Hathor, and a hidden representation of the queen's favourite Senenmut. At the northern end of the same colonnade is a somewhat smaller chapel of Anubis, again with a 12-columned hall and inner rooms.

The upper terrace had an entrance portico decorated with Osiride statues of the queen before each pillar, though most of these have been destroyed. The portico opened to a columned court flanked on the left with a chapel dedicated to the royal cult (here Hatshepsut and Tuthmosis I) and

Elaborate Hathoric or sistraform columns stand within the Chapel of Hathor at the southwestern corner of Hatshepsut's temple.

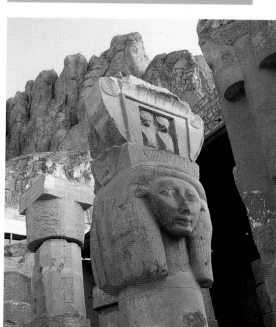

on the right by a chapel (with its own open court and altar) of the solar cult. A small ancillary chapel attached to this solar court is now believed to have been dedicated to the parents of Hatshepsut. At the very back of the central court the innermost part of the temple is cut into the cliff face. Eighteen cult niches – nine on each side – flank the rock sanctuary of Amun which was the focus of the whole complex and which received the sacred barque of the god during the annual celebration of the 'Beautiful Feast of the Valley' (p. 95).

During the Ptolemaic era the sanctuary of Amun was renewed and expanded to include the cults of two great architects: Amenophis son of Hapu – the skilled overseer of works for Amenophis III; and Imhotep – the builder of Djoser's Step Pyramid. These individuals were also associated with wisdom and medicine, and the upper court may in fact have been used as a sanatorium (p. 74) and frequented by the sick at this time. Later yet, in the 7th century AD, the temple area became the site of a Coptic monastery, the 'Monastery of the North', from which the modern Arabic name of the site – Deir el-Bahri – is derived.

Sadly, because of her unorthodox reign and the tensions between Hatshepsut and her erstwhile ward, Tuthmosis III, the temple suffered much destruction and mutilation. Hatshepsut's name and many of her representations were hacked away in the reaction which inevitably followed her rule as pharaoh. During the Amarna Period many of the images of Amun were also destroyed at the behest of Akhenaten, and even further attrition occurred in the 19th dynasty when the Osiride statues of Hatshepsut were destroyed. The early Copts too, in their zeal to do away with the old pagan images, defaced many representations of the gods, so that little of the temple's artwork was left undamaged. Restoration carried out at the temple over a good many years has successfully reconstructed many of the scenes, however, and the Polish–Egyptian team working in the temple has recently been able to restore the wall of the upper terrace with more than 70 recovered carved blocks. The newly repaired registers depict the procession of the sacred barque of Amun; and the Egyptian antiquities officials plan to open this long-closed area to the public.

A valley temple of Hatshepsut's monument – similar in type to those found in earlier pyramid complexes – originally stood at the foot of the long causeway which stretched from the cliff temple to the edge of the flood plain. The structure was destroyed in antiquity, but its foundation deposits were discovered by Howard Carter, and blocks from the walls of this temple (now in the Metropolitan Museum of Art in New York) were found with the name of the structure's architect, Puimre, written in hieratic on their undersides.

Deir el-Bahri and the Location of Key Temple Elements

Temples of different periods tended to group certain key elements of their structural layouts in different ways. Old Kingdom pyramid temples, for example, frequently grouped their entrance halls, open courts, statue niches and sanctuaries in expected patterns. In the New Kingdom mortuary temple, beginning mainly with Hatshepsut's monument at Deir el-Bahri, a clear pattern also emerges – not only of the layout of basic temple elements, but also of specific chapels dedicated to different deities or individuals. In this New Kingdom configuration, a solar court with its own altar is often placed on the right side of the temple, a chapel or suite of chapels for Amun is usually located at the temple's centre rear, and chapels of the deceased king are usually positioned on the left, as are chapels dedicated to the royal ancestors, or Osiris.

The plan and decoration of the inner areas of Hatshepsut's temple follow a specific pattern which is recognizable in other royal mortuary temples of the New Kingdom. The pattern is first observed at Deir el-Bahri and may have originated there.

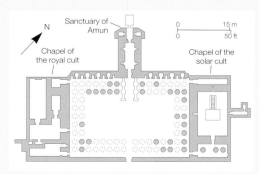

N
Sanctuary of Amun
Chapel of the royal cult
Chapel of the solar cult
0   15 m
0   50 ft

This basic trichotomy of 1) king/ancestors/Osiris; 2) Amun; 3) Re/Re-Horakhty is essential to the full New Kingdom theology of divine kingship and parallels patterns found in royal tomb decoration of the period. The paradigm is clearly established at Deir

*A view from the Theban cliffs
of the remains of the small
temple of Tuthmosis III which
was built behind and between
the larger temples of
Hatshepsut and Nebhepetre
Mentuhotep. Hatshepsut's
Chapel of Hathor is visible
at the top right.*

Temple of Tuthmosis III

Only discovered in 1961 in the course of restoration and cleaning work between the monuments of Hatshepsut and Mentuhotep, the temple of Tuthmosis III was found perched on the rising rock of the Deir el-Bahri cliffs. Built towards the end of the king's reign, the structure was dedicated to the god Amun

*The upper terraces of
Hatshepsut's temple, with
some of the remaining
colossal Osiride statues of the
queen engaged to the pillars
of the uppermost portico.*

and was probably intended to receive the barque of the god during the 'Beautiful Feast of the Valley' and thus functionally to replace the temple of Hatshepsut.

As with Hatshepsut's temple, this structure also held a chapel of Hathor and was of similar design, with a series of ramps and terraces. The temple appears to have been abandoned by the end of the 20th dynasty, however – probably as the result of a landslide which may have seriously damaged it. It was then heavily quarried for its stone, and later the site was used as a cemetery for the adjacent Coptic monastery. Some magnificently carved and painted blocks (two of which are on display in the Luxor Museum) have been recovered from the site by the Polish–Egyptian mission, directed by Jadwiga Lipinska, which has continued to study and to restore the temple where possible.

*Tuthmosis III wearing the
atef crown, on a splendid
relief carved block from the
king's temple at Deir el-Bahri,
now in the Luxor Museum.*

-Bahri and then appears in subsequent New
ingdom mortuary temples of sufficient size to
clude all the necessary structural elements as may
e seen by comparing, for example, the mortuary
mples of Sethos I (p. 173) and Ramesses III (p. 193).

*(Right) The mortuary temple
of Nebhepetre Mentuhotep
at the southern side of the bay
of Deir el-Bahri. The forest of
column bases surrounding the
central superstructure on the
upper level of this temple is
still clearly visible, as is the
ramp leading up from the
lower court and the entrance
to the king's tomb. The
superstructure was once
thought to be pyramidal, but
may instead have been flat
(see illus. p. 22).*

Temple of Nebhepetre Mentuhotep

Nebhepetre Mentuhotep (listed as Mentuhotep I or II), first ruler of the 11th dynasty which reunited Egypt at the beginning of the Middle Kingdom, reigned for some 50 years, during which he was able to plan and construct a major mortuary monument: Akh Sut Nebhepetre, 'Splendid are the places of Nebhepetre'. The temple was the first to be built in the great bay of Deir el-Bahri, just south of the *saff* (row) tombs of Mentuhotep's ancestors. Why the king chose the specific location within the bay for his temple, rather than the higher and seemingly better area later chosen by Hatshepsut is not known, though symbolic issues of positioning and alignment may have affected the decision. The temple was discovered by Lord Dufferin during his travels to Egypt (1859–69) and was excavated by Édouard Naville and C. Currely (1903–07) and Herbert Winlock (1920–31). It has undergone more recent study by the German Archaeological Institute and the Polish–Egyptian mission.

Though smaller and not as well preserved as its famous neighbour, Mentuhotep's temple is of great interest. The temple was entirely novel in its multi-level construction and in its plan and, unlike the later mortuary temples of Thebes, it also functioned as a tomb. A processional causeway led up from a small valley temple to a great, tree-lined court beneath which a deep shaft was cut. Discovered by Howard Carter in 1900 when his horse stumbled into its rubble-filled entrance, this sloping shaft led to unfinished rooms believed to have origi-

nally been intended as the king's tomb. The shaft was converted into an Osirian cenotaph, however (in which Carter found a linen-wrapped statue of the king, now in the Egyptian Museum in Cairo), when the temple was set further back against the cliff. The sides of the ramp leading to the upper terrace were colonnaded and the upper terrace itself was given a colonnade on three sides. Here, a forest of octagonal columns surrounded a large square-built structure that for many years was interpreted as the base of a pyramid, but which has more recently been seen as a low mastaba-like building representing the 'divine booth' or funerary chapel, or even symbolizing the mound of creation. The enclosure also contained six chapels and shaft tombs for Mentuhotep's wives and family members. In the 18th dynasty the rock on its northern side was cut back to hold the small painted chapel of Hathor, with a statue of the cow goddess which was moved to the Egyptian Museum in Cairo.

The inner part of the temple consists of a columned courtyard, beneath which was the entrance to the king's tomb cut into the rock and thus foreshadowing the later royal tombs of the Valley of the Kings at the other side of the same mountain. At the level of the terrace, the hypostyle hall – the most extensive yet built – contained at its end the sanctuary of the royal cult, with a statue of the king in a niche carved into the rock face, though much of this area of the temple is now destroyed. Likewise destroyed is the valley temple of the complex which was probably levelled by Ramesses IV, who began a temple on its site.

*This portrait of Nebhepetre
Mentuhotep in the embrace
of deities is from the king's
tomb-temple at Deir el-Bahri
and is now in the British
Museum, London.*

Colonnaded temple of Ramesses IV

Ramesses IV constructed this temple at the entrance to the bay of Deir el-Bahri just to the north of Hatshepsut's valley temple. Carter, Spiegelberg and others have examined the site, but little more than its foundation deposits along with a few inscribed sandstone wall blocks and some minor items have been recovered. The structure is completely destroyed.

Ramessid temple

Just to the south of the area of the previous structure, Ramesses IV appears to have begun a large mortuary temple which he soon decided to build a little further to the south. The structure may have received additional work by Ramesses V and VI, but seems to have remained unfinished. Foundation deposits of Ramesses IV were found here, along with many re-used blocks from a range of earlier temples (including those of Tuthmosis II, Amenophis II, Hatshepsut, Ramesses II, Merenptah, and Ramesses III). As with the other structures built in this area, the temple is now destroyed.

Temple of Tuthmosis III

A little to the south of the entrance to Deir el-Bahri, beneath the hill of Gurna, Tuthmosis III constructed his mortuary temple. Apparently this

Understanding the temple of Mentuhotep is not an easy task, especially as less than 5 percent of its reliefs survive. Much of the decoration applied to the structure appears to be that of the standard pyramid temple – hunting in the marshes, agricultural scenes, the king trampling enemies, etc; but the Osiride religion which grew in strength in this period reveals its influence in the temple's decoration, statuary and design – especially if the central feature is seen as a mound or funerary booth set within an Osiride 'grove'. In any event, Mentuhotep's tomb-temple certainly forms a transition between the classic pyramid complex of the Old Kingdom and the mortuary temple and tomb of the New Kingdom.

Temple of Sankhkare Mentuhotep

Sankhkare Mentuhotep carried out a number of building works – including the construction of several temples (see, for example, his temple on Thoth Hill, p. 172) – in his 12-year reign. However, his own mortuary temple was initiated but never completed. The structure was begun at the southern end of the Deir el-Bahri bay, behind the hill of Gurna, only a few hundred metres from the temple of his father. Little is left there beyond the remains of a causeway which ends at the temple platform, and a sloping passage cut back into the rock face. This leads to a corbel-roofed chamber constructed from red quartzite blocks. Hieratic graffiti scratched in this area appear to have been written by priests of the king's mortuary cult and indicate that, despite the incomplete monument, the king's burial was nevertheless accomplished.

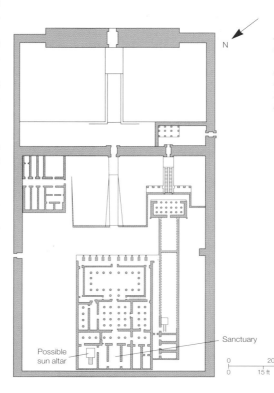

N

Possible sun altar

Sanctuary

0   20 m
0   15 ft

A restored plan of the temple of Tuthmosis III at Gurna. Unlike his temple at Deir el-Bahri, which was a temple dedicated to Amun, the king's temple at Gurna functioned as a mortuary monument.

temple was begun in the early years of the king's reign, while he still fell under the regency of Hatshepsut, and before he constructed his memorial-related temple within the Amun temple complex at Karnak. The west bank temple was called Henkhet-Ankh or 'Offering-Life', and although excavated in the early part of the 20th century little was found, and a later reinvestigation did not add much to our knowledge of the temple. The enclosure walls of the compound were partly cut from the rock of the area and partly built of brick. The temple itself apparently contained a number of Osiride columns and a chapel of Hathor. A false door dedicated in the king's name was set in the rear wall of the sanctuary, and this room was of particular interest as it had a vaulted ceiling decorated with the hours of the day and night – a feature closely paralleled by the decoration found in a number of the royal tombs of the Valley of the Kings. It has been suggested that the temple may also have had a court with an altar to the sun god.

Temple of Siptah

Towards the end of the 19th dynasty Merenptah Siptah began a small monument between the temple of Tuthmosis III and the Ramesseum. The site was excavated by Petrie who examined the remains of all the minor temples in this area, but little was recovered of this structure beyond the foundation deposits of the king and the chancellor Bay.

Temple of Amenophis II

Just to the north of the site on which the Ramesseum was later built, Amenophis II constructed a temple with a court bordered on all four sides by a columned portico. The structure was plundered for its stone at an early date, but does not seem to have been large considering the king's reign of at least 26 years. The temple's foundation plaques were found by Petrie.

Chapel of the White Queen

West of the above site, just outside the walls of the Ramesseum, Petrie excavated the remains of a small structure, the chapel of the 'White Queen'. The structure's name derives from the pale limestone bust found there of Merit-Amun, daughter and royal wife of Ramesses II, depicted in her role as 'Sistrum-player of Mut' and 'Dancer of Horus'.

Ramesseum

> 'The Ramesseum....most noble and pure in Thebes as far as great monuments are concerned'.
>
> Jean-François Champollion, 1829

Ramesses the Great began his mortuary temple in the second year of his reign, and it was not to be completed until some 20 years later. The 'House of millions of years of User-Maat-Re Setepenre [the throne name of Ramesses] that unites with Thebes-

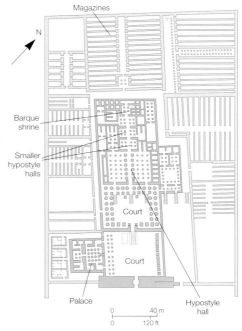

the-city in the domain of Amun' was ambitiously planned even by Ramesses' standards; and although ruined and robbed, the temple remains one of the great monuments of Egypt. Diodorus Siculus referred to it as the 'tomb' of Ozymandias (derived from User-Maat-Re), and Strabo gave it the name the Memnonium, and it was widely known until

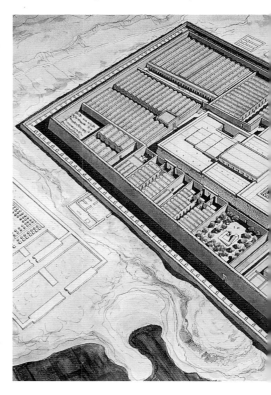

Factfile

Monument
Mortuary temple of Ramesses II
Contiguous chapel: Tuya and Nefertari
Location
Gurna, Thebes (west bank)
Dates of construction
19th dynasty: years 2–22 of the reign of Ramesses II
Dedication
Main temple: Ramesses II, the god Amun.
Temple of Tuya and Nefertari: the king's mother and his chief wife
Studies and reports
The journal *Memnonia: Bulletin édité par l'Association pour la Sauvegarde du Ramesseum*, ed. Christian Leblanc (Cairo, 1991–) is devoted to studies of this monument. Volume 2 (1991) contains extensive bibliographies of works on the Ramesseum.

time forgot it. Also called the Memnonium by
Napoleon's Expedition, the temple complex – for it
originally consisted of two temples and a palace as
well as many administrative buildings – was first
called 'The Ramesseum' by Champollion, who
regarded it as perhaps the greatest of all the
storeyed monuments of Thebes.

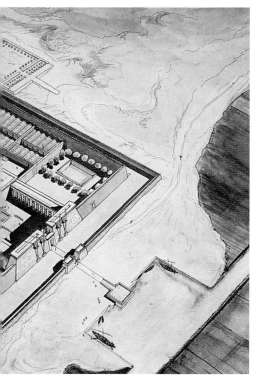

We are fortunate to know much of the Ramesseum's history. It was constructed for Ramesses by
two architect-foremen, Penre of Coptos and Amen-
emone of Abydos, and built with a number of
original features. The temple's pylons, for example,
constructed up to this time of mud-brick, were here
first built of stone; its great colossus, 'Ozymandias'
(p. 184), was the largest free-standing statue ever
made in Egypt. No effort was spared to make this
the most splendid of all Ramesses' many monuments. Unfortunately, like so many of the mortuary
complexes of western Thebes, the life of the temple
was not to be long. By the 22nd dynasty the
complex was already in use as a necropolis for
members of the Theban clergy, and several
princesses and Divine Adoratrices (p. 93) were
buried there. From the 29th dynasty onwards the
Ramesseum was subject to much destruction
through the dismantling of its walls, pillars and
other features, with many blocks being used in the
late additions to Medinet Habu (p. 193). In the 1st
century AD the remaining core of the temple was
transformed into a Christian church, when many of
the reliefs were hammered and numerous graffiti
were painted or engraved upon its walls. For centuries thereafter the Ramesseum remained a
cluttered, broken and puzzling – if romantic – ruin,
as impressive for the incredible destruction
wrought upon it as for its surviving features.

Since its rediscovery in the modern era, the
Ramesseum has attracted much attention. After the
explorations of Napoleon's Expedition and of
Champollion, the site was studied by Carl Richard
Lepsius in 1844, then by Flinders Petrie and James
Quibell in 1899, and between 1900 and 1908 Howard

'Ozymandias, King of Kings' – The Greatest Colossus of All

The head and shoulders of the shattered hulk of the largest colossus ever constructed in Egypt lie where they fell against the walls of the Ramesseum's second court. The inspiration for Shelley's romantic poem 'Ozymandias', this great statue was probably the first of a planned pair but was never to be matched.

Factfile

Monument
Fallen colossus of Ramesses II
Location
Originally in the first court (now in first and second courts) of the Ramesseum, Thebes (west bank)
Material
Cyenitic limestone
Height
Originally over 20 m (66 ft)
Weight
Originally over 1,000 tons
Dedication
The deified Ramesses II
Name of Statue
'Ramesses, the Sun of Foreign Sovereigns'

This mighty statue of the seated Ramesses II, which now lies toppled and fragmented in the temple's second court, originally stood over six storeys high – one ear alone is just over a metre (3 ft 6 in) long – and must have weighed in excess of 1,000 tons. The titanic figure was one of the largest works of sculpture ever achieved in human history and is the inspiration for Shelley's haunting poem 'Ozymandias' (1817) – the Grecianized form of part of Ramesses' throne name: User-Maat-Re 'Powerful is the Truth of Re':

> I met a traveller from an antique land
> Who said: Two vast and trunkless legs of stone
> Stand in the desert … Near them, on the sand,
> Half sunk, a shattered visage lies, whose frown,
> And wrinkled lip, and sneer of cold command
> Tell that its sculptor well those passions read
> Which yet survive, stamped on these lifeless things,
> The hand that mocked them, and the heart that fed.
> And on the pedestal these words appear:
> 'My name is Ozymandias, King of Kings:
> Look on my works, ye Mighty, and despair!'
> Nothing beside remains. Round the decay
> Of that colossal wreck, boundless and bare,
> The lone and level sands stretch far away.

In actuality, the legs of this great colossus do not remain intact, though the base – without Shelley's fanciful inscription – is still to be seen in the Ramesseum's first court. The only original inscriptions surviving on the huge head and torso are the cartouches of the king – yet the size of the statue and the name of Ramesses alone are suggestive of the might which Shelley characterizes. The cruel and mocking nature of Shelley's Ozymandias is a literary embellishment of the poet, however, as such titanic manifestations of the spirit of the Egyptian god-kings were anciently viewed as benign sources of support and protection, and a number of votive stelae have been found showing individuals adoring the colossi 'who listen to their prayers' (see p. 59). The name of the statue was 'Ramesses, the Sun of Foreign Sovereigns', referring to the ubiquitous power and benevolence of the god-king.

The monolithic block of limestone from which this gargantuan statue was carved was cut from the quarries of Aswan – some 400 km (about 250 miles) to the south of Thebes. The work of moving and transporting the huge block must have been immense and certainly equalled that involved in the transportation of the greatest obelisks.

Although there is only evidence for the remains of this one colossal statue having been set up on the south side of the entrance into the Ramesseum's second court, an indication that a second and equally large colossus was planned for the northern side of the entrance – according to the normal temple plan – is seen in the position of the mighty colossus and the existence of a second pair of smaller colossi set up on either side of the entrance into the temple's third court. As it is, the scale of this huge statue was never matched again.

Carter and Émile Baraize carried out work here. In recent decades the Ramesseum has been the subject of intensive ongoing study by French and Egyptian research groups, and we now have a better understanding of this monument than most of the temples in the area.

The main temple

The temple's great entrance pylon, decorated with scenes from the Battle of Kadesh (1285 BC), collapsed due to the continuing flooding of the temple forecourts and the resulting erosion of its foundations, and now lies crumbling at the front of the first court. Originally the court was lined by pillars on its northern side, and on the south a columned portico stood before the doors of the temple's palace. It was at the rear of this court that the truly colossal seated figure of the king (see box) was set up and flanked by a statue of his mother, the queen Tuya. From here stairs led up to the second court.

The second pylon is also badly destroyed, and the remains of its southern wall are partially covered by the shattered remnants of the toppled colossus.

On the remaining northern wall the Battle of Kadesh is again celebrated, along with scenes from the festival of Min. The current visitors' entrance is on the north side of this second court, which was originally bounded by a portico on three sides, with Osiride statues of the king against the pillars of its eastern and western sides. Here too, colossi were set

Intricately decorated and inscribed capitals crown the papyriform columns of the Ramesseum's hypostyle hall.

A portico with Osiride pillars forms the entrance into the Ramesseum's hypostyle hall. Before the entrance is the colossal black granite head of one of the two statues of the king which once stood here.

Ramesses II sits before the sacred ished tree upon which his names and regnal years are inscribed by the gods in a mythical ritual of the eternal continuation of the king's reign.

A vast maze-like array of magazines and administrative buildings surrounded the temple on three sides. Of little interest to the robbers of stone, many of the outlying structures of the temple complex have survived better than the temple itself, as stone was usually only used for doorjambs and thresholds in this kind of building. The temple stores were housed in magazines, some larger with roofs of wood and others smaller with vaulted brick roofs. Holes spaced about every 6 m (20 ft) in some of the roofs of these magazines were to allow grain to be poured into them. A well stood outside the second court to the west of the royal palace, and a sacred lake probably existed within the complex but has not yet been found.

Temple of Tuya and Nefertari

Although the small 'contiguous temple' which adjoined the main temple on its northern side may have stood on the site of an earlier chapel, in its finished form it appears to have been dedicated to Ramesses' mother Tuya and to his great wife Nefertari. The temple was demolished by the pharaoh Hakoris in the Late Period, but the basic plan of the structure, with an apparent bipartite design reflecting its dual dedication, is known.

Temple of Tuthmosis IV

Tuthmosis IV's mortuary temple was built just a little to the southwest of the site of the Ramesseum. Two pylons fronted narrow courts and a portico with one row of pillars and one of columns before a hypostyle court. This led in turn to a transverse hall and the inner sanctuary and its associated rooms.

The particular interest of this temple lies in the fact that the structure seems to have served as a model for the temples built by Tuthmosis' successor – Amenophis III – such as that king's mortuary temple and also the core area of Luxor Temple itself.

up, though only the black granite head of one remains; the upper part of the other, known as the 'Younger Memnon', was removed with great difficulty by Belzoni in 1816 and is now in the British Museum. This was the first royal colossus to be seen in England, where it revolutionized European appreciation of Egyptian art.

The temple's hypostyle hall was supported by 48 elegant papyrus columns and, like the hypostyle of the Great Temple of Amun at Karnak, it was lighted only by high clerestory windows and designed to mimic the marshes of primeval creation. The eastern wall shows military scenes such as the king and his sons attacking the Hittite fortress of Dapur, while the western wall displays various scenes of Ramesses before the gods. Behind the hypostyle hall is the so-called 'astronomical room' or 'hall of the barques', decorated with scenes from the 'Beautiful Feast of the Valley', and an astronomical ceiling showing the constellations and decans, or divisions of the night sky.

This small hypostyle is followed by another – the 'hall of the litanies', with ritual offering scenes involving the solar (Re-Horakhty) and the chthonic (Ptah) aspects of cultic service. Behind this was yet another eight-columned room, a four-columned hall in which the god's personal barque was kept, and the sanctuary. Though this and the rest of the main temple is destroyed, it seems that the sanctuary of Amun was probably flanked by chapels of the royal cult on the left and the solar cult on the right.

Unusually, the plan of the Ramesseum can be seen to be a parallelogram rather than a true rectangle as would be expected. This was perhaps a result of orienting the temple along the lines of a small pre-existing chapel of Ramesses' mother Tuya while angling the pylons in order to achieve a desired orientation with Luxor Temple on the Nile's east bank.

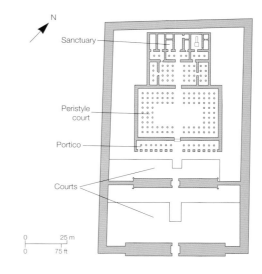

*The remains of the Late
Period Temple of Khonsuirdis
with the Ramesseum visible in
the distance. This mud brick
temple directly to the north of
the Temple of Tausert is
largely destroyed, though a
single section of standing wall
is a noticeable landmark.*

Temple of Wadjmose

A small temple between the Ramesseum and the
temple of Tuthmosis IV was built for the 18th-
dynasty individual Wadjmose (Wezmose), a son
of Tuthmosis I, unless – as Stephen Quirke has
suggested – the structure actually represents the
temple of Tuthmosis himself. A number of blocks,
stelae and statue fragments were found here – many
from the time of Tuthmosis III – but very little can
be ascertained of the history of this temple.

Temple of Tawosret

Directly north of the Temple of Merneptah lie the
ruins of the memorial temple of Queen Tawosret,
the final ruler of the 19th dynasty. The site was
briefly examined by Petrie in 1896, but excavations
by the University of Arizona have shown that the
temple was much further developed than Petrie
believed and then destroyed by a later ruler.

Temple of Merenptah

The destroyed mortuary temple of Ramesses II's
son Merenptah evidently followed, albeit in a much
reduced way, the plan of his father's great mortuary temple, the Ramesseum. Like Ramesses'
monument, the forecourt was colonnaded at its
sides, with a palace adjoining the southern wall,
and the second court held Osiride pillars at least on
its inner side. A 12-columned hypostyle hall was
followed by a single 8-columned hall and the inner
sanctuary and related chapels – including a court
with a large sun altar. Magazines and other mud-
brick buildings were ranged along the sides of the
temple, and a small sacred lake stood to the south
within an extension of the compound. Built with
many reused blocks of Amenophis III, the temple
and its compound are just over half the size of the
Ramesseum, showing the degree of compression
present in the plan of the later monument.

*The scattered blocks and
foundation stones of the
mortuary temple of
Wadjmose lie between
that of Merneptah and
the Ramesseum.*

*(Left) The plan of the
mortuary temple of
Tuthmosis IV may have
influenced the design of the
great temples of the king's
successor, Amenophis III.*

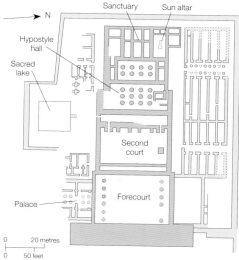

*(Right) In plan, Merenptah's
mortuary temple is similar
to the Ramesseum, though
on a much smaller scale.*

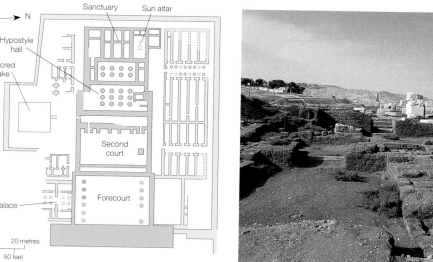

Merenptah's temple was excavated by Petrie and it was here, in 1896, that the archaeologist discovered the celebrated 'Israel Stela' in the first court. This stela, which is now in the Egyptian Museum in Cairo, was originally made for Amenophis III and was recarved on its other side with a text describing Merenptah's victories over the Libyans and other foreign peoples – including the earliest known historical reference to Israel. It was Petrie's excavations that revealed that the temple mostly consisted of reused stone blocks and columns from the nearby mortuary temple of Amenophis III.

Temple of Amenophis III

Kom el-Hetan, a few hundred metres to the north of Medinet Habu and almost directly across the Nile from Luxor Temple, is the site of Amenophis III's mortuary temple. In its day this was the greatest temple built on the Theban west bank. Unfortunately, virtually nothing remains of this once great edifice beyond the two immense 'Colossi of Memnon' which stood before its entrance. These great sandstone statues of Amenophis III flanked by small figures of his mother and his wife Tiye are nearly 18 m (59 ft) high and were famous in antiquity not only for their size but, following an earthquake in 27 BC, for the bell-like tone which was emitted by the expanding stone of the northern figure at sunrise. Greek travellers thus equated the figure with Memnon, the son of Aurora, the

goddess of the dawn, but repairs to the statue in the reign of the Roman emperor Septimius Severus silenced the sound forever. The stone for the Colossi is believed to have been quarried at Gebel Ahmar, near modern Cairo.

Behind these behemoths were two great courts with other colossal seated statues – perhaps, as Betsy Bryan has suggested, the largest sculptural programme in history. Eventually also a long processional way similar to that built by the king in Luxor Temple stretched from the innermost pylons to a large peristyle solar court. A huge quartzite stela which has been re-erected here was probably one of a pair set up at the entrance to the court, describing Amenophis' building accomplishments. Many of the column bases of the solar court are also still in place, though overgrown, along with fragments of colossal standing statues of the king which once stood in this part of the temple. Some of the colossi bases at this site have important lists of foreign place names, for instance there is one with those of distant regions, including the Aegean.

A small, separate limestone temple to Ptah-Sokar-Osiris stood in the northern part of the huge compound with its own gateway flanked by two quartzite standing statues of the king. The complex was so thoroughly raided of its stone that little more is known of the other features of this great temple, however.

The temple's location on the flood plain was interesting and apparently unique. The ground level of

(Right) Marking the site of Amenophis III's massive temple, the 'Colossi of Memnon' alone remain to indicate the original scale of this huge monument.

(Below) The great mortuary temple of Amenophis III was one of the largest and most magnificent of all the religious structures created in Egypt. Ironically, only the most salient features of its plan are known.

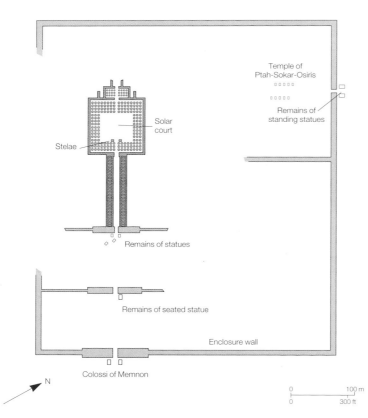

Temple of
Amenophis I

Hathor
chapel of
Sethos I

Ptolemaic
temple

N

0   50 m
0   150 ft

the temple was low and the structure was purposely built so that the annual inundation of the Nile flooded its outer courts and halls, perhaps leaving only the inner sanctuary area – which stood on a low knoll – above water level. The whole temple thus symbolized, as the waters retreated, the emergence of the world from the primeval waters of creation.

Deir el-Medina

The small hollow in the foothills to the northwest of Amenophis III's temple was the area where the community of workmen who constructed the royal tombs in the Valley of the Kings had their village. On the north side of this village several temples were built, the largest of which was begun by Amenophis III and almost completely rebuilt and expanded in later times – long after the village had been deserted by its population of tomb makers.

Temple of Amenophis I

The temple of the cult of Amenophis I stands on the terrace above the Ptolemaic temple enclosure (see below) at its northern corner. The original structure was a small one, and many of the walls surrounding it are later accretions.

Hathor chapel of Sethos I

On the northern side of the Ptolemaic temple is the site where Sethos I built a temple for the workmen

of the village. Considerably larger than the earlier structure of Amenophis I, it consists of a series of elements before a tripartite sanctuary.

Ptolemaic temple of Hathor

This compound embraces the site of several earlier temple structures, and the remaining Ptolemaic temple itself is fronted by a staircase of Ramesses II. The temple, which was built and decorated in the

(Above) The temple complex area of Deir el-Medina contains the remains of a number of discrete temples dating from the reign of Amenophis I to Ptolemaic times.

(Right) The imposing entrance gate and mud-brick wall of the Ptolemaic temple of Hathor lie close to the tomb-builders' village at Deir el-Medina.

3rd century BC by Ptolemy IV and several later Ptolemies, is in almost perfect condition. A columned hall opens into a narrow vestibule before three sanctuaries, the central one dedicated to Hathor, the eastern one (on the right) dedicated to Amun-Re-Osiris and the western one to Amun-Sokar-Osiris – the latter sanctuary having an Osiride judgment scene more commonly found in tombs than in divine temples. Here, as in the temple of Hatshepsut at Deir el-Bahri, chapels were also dedicated to both Imhotep and Amenophis son of Hapu – the quintessential builders of Egyptian tradition. A stairway leads from the left side of the vestibule to the temple's roof. The remains of several small votive chapels stand around the enclosure's north wall. The temple shows the continued sanctity of this sacred site long after its associated dwellings were deserted. Eventually the complex was transformed into a Coptic monastery from which the site's present name, Deir el-Medina – meaning 'Monastery of the Town' – is derived.

Temple of Amun

Across the valley from the Ptolemaic temple enclosure are the remains of a temple to Amun and the other members of the Theban triad (Mut and Khonsu) which was built by Ramesses II.

Nag Kom Lolah

The village of Nag Kom Lolah sprawls around Medinet Habu, and its surroundings cover the area between the temple of Amenophis III in the north to the Malqata palace site in the south. Apart from the great temple of Ramesses III, a number of smaller mortuary temples were built in this area, including those of Ay and Horemheb and, although no longer existing, that of Tutankhamun.

Temple of Ramesses IV

This temple was built on a site just across the modern road from the temple of Amenophis III – directly behind the present Office of the Antiquities Inspectorate. The structure was small and virtually nothing of it survives.

North Temple

A small, destroyed temple built partially on the same site as the Ramesses IV temple is known simply as the 'North Temple'. Although diminutive in size, the structure contained all the elements of the developed temple form with a tripartite sanctuary. The temple is closely paralleled by a similar structure a little to the south.

Temple of Amenophis son of Hapu

Amenophis son of Hapu was a high court official of Amenophis III who constructed the king's great mortuary temple as well as several other of his monuments, including the massive temple of Soleb in Lower Nubia. He was honoured above all other servants of the king by the gift of a mortuary temple which was built just behind and a little to the west of that of the king.

Minuscule by comparison with the giant temple of the king, the temple was nevertheless of splendid design and just as large in area as that of Tuthmosis III at Gurna. Behind the entrance pylon a large court contained a tree-encircled basin and a portico before a second pylon and court. The inner temple contained many chambers, and the whole structure was laid out with almost perfect symmetry. The fame of the son of Hapu continued to grow after his death, and a 21st-dynasty copy of the decree endowing his temple indicates that his cult still flourished after some 300 years. He was deified for his wisdom and, as we have seen, chapels dedicated to his worship were set up in the temple of Hatshepsut at Deir el-Bahri (p. 178) and the Ptolemaic temple of Hathor at Deir el-Medina (p. 190).

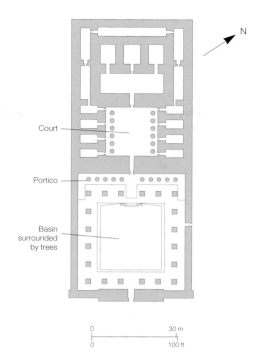

Western Thebes

Court

Portico

Basin surrounded by trees

0   30 m
0   100 ft

The temple of Amenophis son of Hapu (plan left) was the largest of the Theban temples of non-royal individuals. Of impressive design, it was as large as some of the royal mortuary temples of later periods and dwarfed the temple of Tuthmosis II just next to it (below).

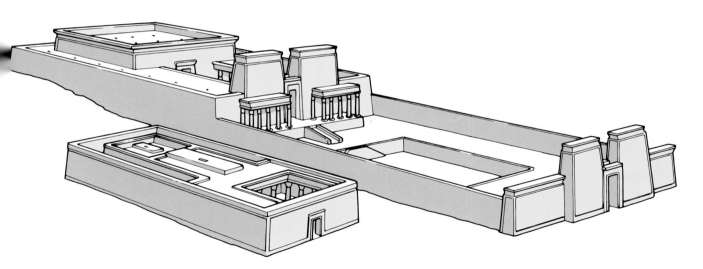

Temple of Tuthmosis II

Located just north of the later temple of Medinet Habu, only traces have been recovered of the outline of this small temple. It was not more than a couple of dozen metres long and was dwarfed by the monument of the sage Amenophis son of Hapu that was built beside it. Called 'Shespet-ankh', 'Chapel of Life', the temple was completed by the king's son, Tuthmosis III.

South Temple

A few metres to the south of the Tuthmosis II temple, this structure is similar to the 'North Temple' already mentioned – except for the sanctuary area where the chambers are laterally arranged. Although its basic plan is known, like the 'North Temple' nothing of this structure now survives.

Reconstruction of the impressive 18th-dynasty temple of Amenophis son of Hapu and the smaller temple of Tuthmosis II. Unusually, the rear section of the larger structure was built on sloping ground.

Column-bases in the temple of Ay and Horemheb a little to the north of Medinet Habu. Begun by Ay, the temple was completed and usurped by his successor Horemheb.

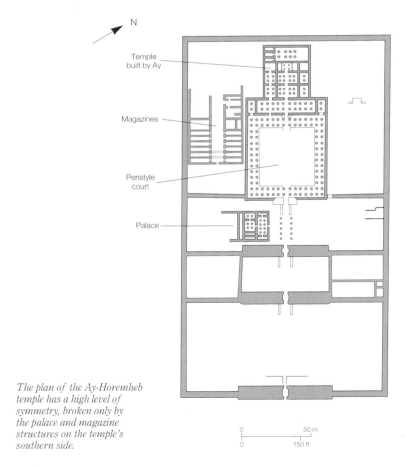

N

Temple built by Ay

Magazines

Peristyle court

Palace

The plan of the Ay-Horemheb temple has a high level of symmetry, broken only by the palace and magazine structures on the temple's southern side.

0   50 m
0   150 ft

Temple of Ay and Horemheb

Tutankhamun's successor Ay built his mortuary temple at the southern end of the line of royal cult temples which fronted the west Theban hills. But Ay's monument was soon taken over and reused by his successor Horemheb. The inner temple was thus constructed by Ay, and the outer areas were added by Horemheb, who also erased the name of his predecessor from the temple, replacing it with his own. The completed structure features three pyloned courts with a small palace in the third, a large peristyle court, and a series of pillared halls and chambers before the sanctuary. Constructed on sloping ground 8 m (26 ft 3 in) higher at the rear, the temple core was built of sandstone with the surrounding areas of brick.

Temple of Tutankhamun

Although a mortuary temple of Tutankhamun has not been discovered, a high priest of the king's funerary cult, named Userhat, is attested on a fragment of a stela in New York's Metropolitan Museum of Art, and an *ushabti* (funerary figurine) of a *wab* priest of the king named Pairy is in the British Museum.

The young king's mortuary temple was probably built in the vicinity of Medinet Habu and near or beneath the present ruins of the temple of Ay and Horemheb – where two reused colossal quartzite statues of Tutankhamun were found. Tutankhamun's temple was almost certainly demolished during the reign of Horemheb.

Medinet Habu

One of the most impressive temples in Egypt, Medinet Habu is both a temple complex and a complex of temples, for the great estate encompasses the main temple of Ramesses III and several smaller structures from earlier and later periods. The main temple itself is the best preserved of all the mortuary temples of Thebes – containing more than 7,000 sq. m (75,350 sq. ft) of decorated surfaces across its walls and providing an excellent example of the developed New Kingdom temple form and plan. The temple is aligned approximately southeast to northwest, but conventionally the southeast side facing the Nile is described as east.

The modern name of the site, Medinet Habu or 'City of Habu', is often said to have originated from the temple of Amenophis son of Hapu, which stood a few hundred metres to the north; but this seems unlikely historically and the actual meaning of the name is unsure. Anciently the site was called Djamet by the Egyptians, and according to popular belief its holy ground was the place where the Ogdoad, the first primeval gods, were buried. As such it was a particularly sacred site long before the construction of Ramesses' temple and remained so long after that great institution fell into disuse. During New Kingdom times, each year at the Ten Day festival the god Amun of Luxor – where the Ogdoad were supposed to have been born – crossed

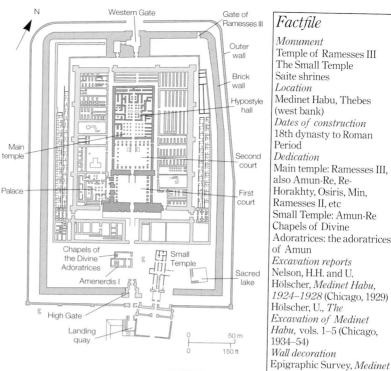

Factfile

Monument
Temple of Ramesses III
The Small Temple
Saite shrines
Location
Medinet Habu, Thebes (west bank)
Dates of construction
18th dynasty to Roman Period
Dedication
Main temple: Ramesses III, also Amun-Re, Re-Horakhty, Osiris, Min, Ramesses II, etc
Small Temple: Amun-Re
Chapels of Divine Adoratrices: the adoratrices of Amun
Excavation reports
Nelson, H.H. and U. Hölscher, *Medinet Habu, 1924–1928* (Chicago, 1929)
Hölscher, U., *The Excavation of Medinet Habu*, vols. 1–5 (Chicago, 1934–54)
Wall decoration
Epigraphic Survey, *Medinet Habu*, vols. 1–8 (Chicago, 1930–70)

Plan (top) of the temple complex at Medinet Habu, and reconstruction drawing (left) showing the main temple of Ramesses III with the later form of the Small Temple added to the right of the temple entrance. Some features of intermediate periods, such as the Later Period chapels of the Divine Adoratrices, are not shown.

The main temple of Ramesses III from the southwest: just to the left of the temple are the remains of the large, two-storey palace complex which adjoined Ramesses' monument.

over from his temple to re-enact the funerary services for these primeval deities in order to renew them and thus creation itself.

During the reign of Ramesses III and even after the king's cult had declined, Medinet Habu functioned as the administrative centre of western Thebes. It was here, for example, that the workmen who constructed the royal tombs in the Valley of the Kings came to demand payment when they went on strike; and it was in the great fortified complex that many of the area's inhabitants took refuge when Upper Egypt was engulfed in civil war after the close of the 20th dynasty and in other times of trouble. Eventually the great walls of the complex were breached in a sustained attack, and later, during the Christian era, the whole area was covered by the Coptic town of Djeme and even the great temple itself was filled with dwellings and one of its courts used as a church. Nevertheless, the administrative and defensive values of the site far outlived the cult of Ramesses' monument, and it was able to avoid many of the predations to which other temples inevitably fell victim.

The High Gate

In ancient times Medinet Habu was fronted by an impressive landing quay at which the boats that came to the site via the canals which linked the temple to the Nile could moor. This quay stood before the main, eastern entrance to the complex – a large gateway of distinctive design modelled after a western Asiatic *migdol* or fortress. Fronted by guard houses, the sides of this gateway are decorated with images of the king trampling the enemies of Egypt, and sculpted figures of the monarch standing atop the heads of captives project from the walls. A large relief representation of the god Ptah at this point also served an interme-

diary function, having the power to transmit the prayers of those unable to enter the temple to the great god Amun within.

The upper rooms of the gate house are of particular interest as they functioned as a kind of royal retreat or harem, and are replete with representations of the king relaxing with young women. It was probably here that the assassination attempt directed against Ramesses III by one of his minor queens was carried out; and although the plot was discovered and the perpetrators brought to justice, the king died during the course of the trial and it is not known whether this was the result of natural causes, or of the effects of the attempt on his life.

Chapels of the Divine Adoratrices

Inside and to the left of the gateway are the remains of several mortuary chapels constructed during the 25th and 26th dynasties for the Divine Adoratrices of Amun who ruled Upper Egypt at that time, at least nominally, on behalf of the king. The first

chapel, that of Amenerdis, is the best preserved and consists of a forecourt with offering table and an inner and mortuary chapel, beneath which the adoratrice was buried in a hidden crypt. The relief carvings in this monument are well executed and,

Saite chapels of the Divine Adoratrices of Amun within the Medinet Habu complex.

(Right) The Divine Adoratrice Amenerdis I, her names in cartouches before her, depicted on the walls of her burial chapel – the best preserved of the Saite chapels within the Medinet Habu complex.

(Left) Modelled on a Near Eastern migdol or fortified gateway, the impressive eastern entrance to Ramesses III's monument is the probable site of the assassination attempt made against him.

for the most part, in fairly good condition. On the lintels above the entrances to these chapels may still be seen the 'Appeal to the Living' which encouraged passers-by and visitors to pronounce the offering formula – the ancient prayer for afterlife sustenance – for the spirits of these Divine Adoratrices.

The Small Temple

The Small Temple of Medinet Habu was begun in the 18th dynasty under Hatshepsut and Tuthmosis III and continued to expand through Roman times. Eventually it was the only functioning temple within the great religious complex.

To the right of the entrance stands the so-called 'Small Temple' which was founded in the 18th dynasty and repeatedly expanded and usurped under later dynasties. Although the core of this monument was begun by Hatshepsut and Tuthmosis III, the queen's name was replaced by those of her predecessors, Tuthmosis I and II. The structure was incorporated into Ramesses' temple complex and its entrance later replaced by a pylon of the Nubian king Shabaka and then usurped by his nephew Taharqa. A small fronting gateway was built during the 26th dynasty and usurped during the 29th by Nectanebo I. During the Ptolemaic Period the inner colonnade was developed, along with a stone-faced pylon (containing many reused blocks from the Ramesseum) and a large gateway.

Finally, in the Roman Period, a columned portico and court were begun but left unfinished by Antoninus Pius. This structure outgrew the encircling walls of the larger temple and in was later the only part of the massive complex still to function.

To the north of the Small Temple are the sacred lake, and the so-called 'Nilometer'– actually a well constructed by Nectanebo I with a passage leading down to the groundwater level.

The main temple

Called 'The Temple of User-Maat-Re Meriamun [the throne name of Ramesses III] United with Eternity in the Possession of Amun in Western Thebes', this great monument is uniquely impressive. The massive outer pylons are perhaps the most imposing of any temple in Egypt and are decorated with colossal images of the king destroying captured enemies before the gods. On the northern pylon the king wears the red crown of Lower (northern) Egypt and, on the southern tower the dual crown incorporating the white crown of the south, thus marking a theme of orientational dualism which appears quite frequently in the temple's decoration.

The temple's outer walls also depict historically important battle and victory scenes, showing Ramesses and his army triumphing against the Libyans and Sea Peoples who attacked Egypt during the king's reign. These themes are continued within the temple's first court with scenes of soldiers counting hands and phalli of the enemy dead, showing the grisly realities of war. This court was flanked on the northern side by large engaged statues of the divine king as Osiris and, on the south, a columned portico with the 'window of appearances' in which the king stood or sat during formal ceremonies and festivities.

The large Osiride statues of the second court were ruthlessly destroyed in the early Christian era by the Copts, who converted the area into a Christian church, though many of the original relief scenes that were painted over at this time have in fact survived in fairly good condition. These scenes depict various rituals connected with the ithyphallic fertility god Min and, on the rear wall of the portico, a procession of the king's numerous sons and daughters.

The hypostyle halls and areas beyond are largely destroyed, but a number of side rooms still stand dedicated to various gods (including the deified Ramesses II whose mortuary temple Ramesses III copied in many aspects) and to the needs of temple administration. The chambers contain several well-preserved scenes; of particular interest are ones in

The massive entrance pylon of Ramesses III's temple has lost a number of its upper courses of masonry, but remains one of the most imposing structures of this type in Egypt.

(Left) Faience tiles depict Libyan, Nubian and Syrian captives, from the royal palace at Medinet Habu.

(Below) The second court of the main temple at Medinet Habu: the engaged statues of the king as Osiris were hacked away by early Christians when the court was converted into a Christian church.

On this lintel from the solar chapel of the main temple at Medinet Habu the king kneels in worship of the sun god, accompanied by symbolic apes whose daybreak howling was interpreted by the Egyptians as worship of the rising sun.

Ramesses III receives eternal renewals of his reign from the great god Amun in the presence of the god's son Ptah and consort Mut – the three members of the Theban triad.

the treasury on the southern side (Ramesses with Thoth weighing gold before Amun-Re), in the internal temple of Re-Horakhty on the north (the king and baboons worshipping the solar barque and the king offering before the *ka* and *ba* of Re), and in the suite or internal temple of Osiris on the southwest (including Thoth and Iunmutef before the deified king and the temple personified as a goddess).

The shrines of the three members of the Theban triad, Amun, Mut and Khonsu, at the rear of the temple are backed by a large false door through which the spirit of the king might enter and leave his monument, as well as a number of concealed rooms which were probably used to store the temple's most important treasures – as opposed to those kept openly in the treasury.

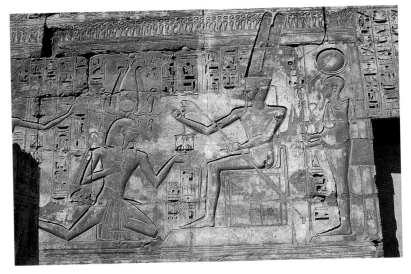

The royal palace

The main temple is surrounded by the remains of many buildings: houses, magazines and storerooms, workshops, barracks, offices, etc; but the most important of these ancillary structures is the royal palace on the monument's southern side. Today, only the lowest courses and some repaired features of this palace can be seen, but the originally two-storey building was of considerable size and contained a number of rooms of different purposes. The palace seems, in fact, to have possibly functioned as both an actual dwelling for Ramesses when he visited the temple to officiate in its ceremonies, and also as a kind of spiritual abode for the king in the afterlife. Thus, like the temple itself, the palace contains a false door for the coming and going of the king's spirit. The structure was directly connected to the temple's first court by means of doorways and also by means of the 'window of appearances'.

Excavation, study and recording

Archaeological exploration of Medinet Habu began in 1859 with successive campaigns being directed by Auguste Mariette (1859–63), George Daressy (1888–99), Theodore Davis (1912), and finally, between 1926 and 1932, by the German archaeologist Uvo Hölscher on behalf of the Oriental Institute of the University of Chicago. These discovered much of the previously unknown history of the monument. The continued recording and study by the Oriental Institute at the site has also led to the

Ramesses' struggles with the Sea Peoples are depicted on the walls of his temple, with scenes including the great naval battle (below) and some of the Sea Peoples taken prisoner (below left).

The Sea Peoples were a loose confederation of migrant peoples who seem to have originated in the Aegean, Asia Minor and other areas of the eastern Mediterranean and who almost overthrew Egypt twice in the course of their mass movements. They first attacked in the 19th dynasty, in the fifth year of Merenptah, when they allied with the Libyans and swept into the Egyptian Delta. Fortunately for Egypt Merenptah's forces retaliated with crushing force, killing over 6,000 of the invaders and routing the rest.

But the Sea Peoples were far from finished. Some 33 years later, in the eighth year of Ramesses III, they again attacked Egypt; and scenes of the battles of this second war were carved on to the north wall of the main temple at Medinet Habu, showing that Ramesses deployed his forces to counter an attack which came both by land and sea. Once again Egyptian military might prevailed, and Ramesses' navy defeated the enemy's ships off the Delta coast while his army overthrew their land-based forces. The peoples of the enemy host are listed on Ramesses' mortuary temple and included the Denen (the Danaoi of the *Iliad*?), Peleset (Philistines), Shekelesh (possibly the Sicels), Sherden, Tjekel, Teresh and Weshwesh.

In addition to the scenes carved at Medinet Habu, Ramesses' victories against the Sea Peoples were also celebrated in the Great Harris Papyrus (now in the British Museum) which at one time was part of the temple's official archives. The papyrus was made in order to list the many benefactions the king had made to various temples throughout Egypt, and after listing these gifts to the gods the document concludes with a section which provides much historical evidence for the Sea Peoples' attacks on Egypt.

complete epigraphic and architectural documentation of Ramesses' great temple – one of the few temples in Egypt so extensively recorded.

Deir el-Shelwit

Temple of Isis

Site of a small Roman temple to Isis on the west bank of the Nile just over 3 km (2 miles) south of Medinet Habu. The entrance gate was decorated for Galba, Otho and Vespasian, and the core structure (consisting of the façade and sanctuary with three adjacent chambers and stairs to the roof) under Hadrian and Antoninus Pius.

Malqata

Temple of Amun

Amenophis III built a massive palace city on the Theban west bank in the area now called Malqata, a few hundred metres southwest of Medinet Habu. The complex of buildings included a large temple of Amun which was constructed north of the central palace area on higher ground than the king's mortuary temple (p. 188). Beyond its nominal dedication to Amun, the temple is also known to have incorporated a sanctuary of Re, but little now remains of the site beyond the ubiquitous fragments and sherds for which the area is known.

Foundations of the temple of Amun built by Amenophis III northeast of his Malqata palace in the now-desolate area to the west of Medinet Habu.

From Thebes to Aswan

SOUTHERN UPPER EGYPT

Southern Upper Egypt – the region between Thebes and Aswan – was the most southerly area of Egypt proper, before Nubia and the regions of the south. Here the Nile Valley narrows considerably between encroaching cliffs, and the rocky outcroppings of the region provided much of the stone used to build Egypt's temples. Sandstone predominates here so that many of the temples of this area have fared well, unlike limestone-built monuments in other regions whose stone was taken to be burnt for lime. The region has a long history and was not only the home of Montu, the early god of the Theban region, and of other deities for whom a number of important temples of the Ptolemaic and Roman Periods were built, but also the location of the most ancient sites of Nekheb and Nekhen (el-Kab and Kom el-Ahmar), perhaps the earliest of all Egypt's temple sites.

Armant

The site of ancient Iuny (Graeco-Roman Hermonthis) lies on the west bank of the Nile about 15 km (9.5 miles) south of Luxor. In ancient times the location was one of the most important cult centres of the falcon-headed war-god Montu, whose influence spread throughout the whole Theban region. A temple to Montu existed at the site from at least the 11th dynasty, with continued growth in Middle and New Kingdom times. It was largely destroyed at some point in the Late Period, however, and only the remains of the pylon of Tuthmosis III survive from this structure. A later temple seems to have been begun in the 30th dynasty (Nectanebo II); and a birth house with a lake was built at this site by Cleopatra VII and her son Caesarion. Building also continued here in the Roman period. Unfortunately, in the 19th century the Pasha Muhammad Ali razed whole temples both here and at Elephantine in order to build sugar refining factories, and hardly anything now remains of the temples of this site.

Tod

Tod, the site of ancient Djerty (Graeco-Roman Tuphium), a little over 20 km (12.5 miles) south of Luxor and on the east bank, is known to have had a small mud-brick temple in the 5th dynasty and also had a local cult of the god Montu from Middle Kingdom times. Major building activity in association with this cult was completed by the first two Mentuhoteps and Senwosret I, though their temples are now mostly destroyed. There was also, as early as the reign of Userkaf in the 5th dynasty, a small chapel here; blocks from this and later structures built here may be seen in the small open magazine at the site. In 1936 the French archaeologist F. Bisson de la Roque discovered a rich hoard – the so-called 'Tod treasure' of gold, silver and lapis lazuli objects in four bronze chests beneath the floor of the Middle Kingdom temple. Many of these items were of foreign manufacture and reveal much of direct or indirect trade with areas as distant as Mesopotamia and the Aegean.

(Below) Only broken remains survive of the temples of Armant, which were systematically quarried for building stone in the 19th century.

(Right) The Ptolemaic temple of Tod. It was at this site, in the ruined Middle Kingdom temple, that the rich cache known as the 'Tod treasure' was discovered.

The surviving monuments of Tod are of New Kingdom and later date. A partially preserved barque shrine of Montu built by Tuthmosis III and restored by Amenophis II, Sethos I, Amenmesse, and Ramesses III and IV stands before a small temple constructed in the Ptolemaic and Roman periods. This, the main temple still standing at Tod, was begun by Ptolemy VIII and consists of a columned court and hall with various chambers, including a hidden treasury room above the chapel on the south side of the hall. The temple was built in front of and connecting with Senwosret I's earlier structure – only the front wall of which now survives, though this has good examples of later usurpation and reworkings. A Roman kiosk was located near the Ptolemaic temple.

Gebelein

Located some 28 km (17.5 miles) south of Luxor on the Nile's west bank, Gebelein is ancient Yenerty, 'two hills' – reflecting the local topography and explaining the the modern Arabic name. The area was called Aphroditopolis and Pathyris by the Greeks (the latter name from Per-Hathor or 'Domain of Hathor'), and an ancient temple of this goddess stood here, on the eastern hill. This temple seems to have existed as early as the 3rd dynasty and to have still functioned in the Graeco-Roman Period, though it was later destroyed for its limestone. Numerous demotic and Greek papyri were found at the site, giving a detailed insight into daily life at Gebelein in Ptolemaic times.

Esna

Esna is built in the area of ancient Latopolis and is the first site of a major surviving temple south (55 km, 34 miles) of Luxor. Its Egyptian name was

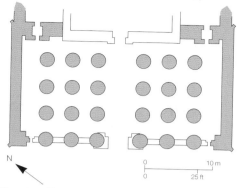

Iunyt or Ta-senet (from which the Coptic Sne and Arabic Isna). The temple, which now stands in the middle of the modern town, some 9 m (29 ft 6 in) below the level of the surrounding buildings, dates to Ptolemaic and Roman times and is one of the latest constructed in Egypt. It was dedicated to Khnum and several other deities, the most prominent being Neith and Heka (whose name means 'magic'). Only the hypostyle hall has survived, but this is well preserved. The back wall is the oldest part of the building, being the façade of the old Ptolemaic temple, with reliefs of Ptolemy VI and VIII. To this the Romans added the present structure which has decoration dating all the way to the 3rd century AD. The roof of the hall is supported by tall columns with composite floral capitals of varied design, and the façade of this hypostyle is in the form of an intercolumnar screen wall similar to those of the temples of Dendera (p. 149) and Edfu (p. 204), which this structure probably resembled in its original complete state.

The decoration and inscriptions of Esna temple are often well executed, and some are of particular interest. The scene depicting the king netting wild-fowl (representing inimical spirits) on the north wall continues ancient Egyptian themes, but other

Factfile

Monument
Temple of Khnum
Location
Esna, south of Luxor
Dates of construction
Graeco-Roman Period
Dedication
Khnum with Neith, Heka and various other deities in minor roles
Reports
Downes, D., *The Excavations at Esna 1905–1906* (Warminster, 1974)
Sauneron, S., *Esna*, I– (Cairo, 1959–1967)

(Above left) The hypostyle hall of the Graeco-Roman temple of Esna was built outward from an earlier Ptolemaic temple.

(Below) The façade of the temple of Khnum at Esna, showing the side doors which were the normal entrances for the priests.

representations – such as that on a column at the rear of the hall to the right showing the king offering a laurel wreath to the gods – are of decidedly late character. Some of this temple's texts are also of interest – including a full coverage of the sacred calendar (p. 98) and a pair of cryptographic hymns to Khnum, one written almost entirely with hieroglyphs of rams and the other written with crocodiles. These are inside the front corners of the hall, next to the small doors which were used by the priests to enter and exit the temple. The whole structure is extremely regular in design, its symmetry being broken only by a small engaged chamber – perhaps a robing room for the priests – on the southern side of the entrance, a feature also found at Edfu. The temple was originally linked by a ceremonial way to the Nile, where its ancient quay (with cartouches of Marcus Aurelius) may still be seen.

el-Kab

Some 32 km (20 miles) south of Esna, el-Kab, or Nekheb as it was anciently known, is one of Egypt's most historic sites. Together with Nekhen (Kom el-Ahmar) on the opposite bank of the Nile, this was an important area of Predynastic settlement. El-

Kab was the home of the vulture-goddess Nekhbet, 'She of Nekhen', who became the tutelary goddess of Upper Egypt, paralleling the cobra-goddess Wadjit of Lower Egypt. It is likely that a simple temple structure was present at el-Kab from the Early Dynastic period; and rulers of the Middle Kingdom certainly built here, though the present remains are mainly of temples of New Kingdom and post-New Kingdom eras.

The central temple within the massive brick-walled enclosure of el-Kab (*c.* 550 × 550 m, 1,800 × 1,800 ft) actually contains a number of structures built against and into each other and is difficult to understand without a plan. The construction of the older of the two remaining structures, the temple of

The main temple complex at el-Kab contains many different structures.

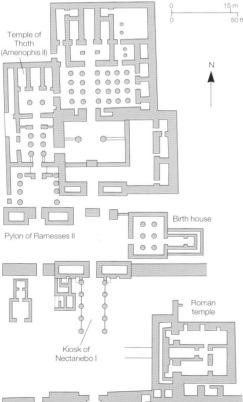

Temple of Nekhbet

Temple of Thoth (Amenophis II)

0   15 m
0   50 ft

N

Pylon of Ramesses II

Birth house

Roman temple

Kiosk of Nectanebo I

(Above right) The temple of Thoth at el-Kab, begun in the 18th dynasty.

(Below) A detail of a relief from the chapel of Tuthmosis III.

Thoth, began in the 18th dynasty with Amenophis II and other rulers, the outer pylon area being mainly completed by Ramesses II. To the east of this structure and contiguous with it is the temple of Nekhbet, which was also built in many stages, the greater part of the building being completed in the 29th and 30th dynasties of the Late Period. Many reused blocks of Middle and New Kingdom date can be seen within the ruins of both temples, however. In the temple area are also the remains of a birth house and a small temple of Roman date, along with a number of other, subsidiary structures and a sacred lake.

About 750 m (2,460 ft) to the north of the temple compound, between the river and the hills, are the remains of a small chapel of Tuthmosis III, and in the wadi to the east of the town are those of a Ptolemaic temple and a small chapel of Amenophis III dedicated to Hathor and Nekhbet. The first of these wadi temples was built by Ptolemies VIII–X, perhaps on the site of an earlier temple. It has two columned halls and a sanctuary carved into the cliff face. The small temple of Amenophis is further out – about 4 km (2.5 miles) from the modern road – and is really a way station for the barque of Nekhbet when she visited this area of her domain. The chapel has painted scenes (restored in the Ptolemaic era) showing the king enthroned with his father, Tuthmosis IV.

Kom el-Ahmar (Hierakonpolis)

Across the river from el-Kab and about 1 km (0.5 mile) southwest of the modern village of el-Muissat on the west bank of the Nile is Kom el-Ahmar, the 'Red Mound'. This is one of Egypt's most important sites: ancient Nekhen. Along with Nekheb (el-Kab), Nekhen represented Upper Egypt in parallel with the twin towns Pe and Dep (Tell el-Fara'in – Buto –

in the Delta) of Lower Egypt. The town's Greek name was Hierakonpolis, 'city of the falcon', as this was the site of the worship of an extremely ancient falcon god, Nekheny, 'The Nekhenite', whose worship and cult seem to go back to the very roots of Egyptian religion.

The archaeological story of Hierakonpolis must begin with the town enclosure of Kom el-Ahmar which contains a temple compound partially excavated by James Quibell and F.W. Green in 1897–99. These excavations found that the temple complex encircled a mound of clean sand, revetted with stones, upon which some Egyptologists think an Early Dynastic shrine may have stood – though this may or may not be the case. Certainly, a temple of mud-brick was later built on the site of the early mound, though perhaps not until Middle Kingdom times, with further building occurring south of the mound in the New Kingdom (a stone temple of Tuthmosis III) and later. The part of the temple built on the mound and apparently dating to the Middle Kingdom contained a five-chambered sanctuary. Beneath the floor of the central chamber was buried a divine image – the famous falcon's head surmounted by two twin feathers, all of gold, which is now in the Egyptian Museum in Cairo and which doubtless represented the primary deity of the site.

Evidence of early cult activity was also found in the so-called 'Main Deposit', a cache of items located between two walls of an Old Kingdom temple complex on the east side of the great mound. This deposit included a number of ceremonial objects of the Protodynastic period including the great Narmer Palette and Scorpion Macehead – two of the most famous artifacts to have survived from this early period. While the precise date of this deposit remains unknown, several of its items – including the Narmer Palette itself – show the importance of the falcon deity worshipped here right from the beginning of the Dynastic period.

(Above left) The Ptolemaic temple to the east of el-Kab.

(Above) The golden head and plumes of the image of a sacred falcon discovered in the Middle/New Kingdom sanctuary at Hierakonpolis.

The Protodynastic Narmer Palette (reverse) from the 'Main Deposit' at Hierakonpolis. The falcon restraining a 'marshland' enemy of the king is doubtless some form of the ancient deity of the site of 'Nekhen'.

But of greatest importance for the history of temple development are the remains that have come to light in recent years in the area of Predynastic settlement at the edge of the desert to the west of Quibell and Green's temple site. Beginning in 1985, in excavations begun by the American archaeologist Michael Hoffman, Egypt's earliest known temple began to emerge from the barren desert floor (p. 17). This temple was constructed of wood with reed-matting panels of the type of architecture later imitated in Djoser's Step Pyramid complex. The core of the temple consisted of a large, sloping roofed sanctuary of three rooms, fronted by an entrance with four huge wooden pillars at least 12 m (over 39 ft) high – which must almost certainly have been imported from a great distance even at this early time. This impressive structure stood before a court with a mound upon which stood only a single pole – no doubt surmounted by a fetish or symbol of the falcon god worshipped here.

The layout of this earliest known complex casts some doubt on whether a shrine was originally built upon the mound of Quibell and Green's temple, although one was certainly added later – perhaps to an already long sacred site – especially as archaeological evidence at other sites (such as that of earliest Medamud, p. 22) suggests that the format of a mound with a separate temple structure may have been widespread. If this was the case, then the positioning of the 'mortuary temple' before the pyramid in the Old Kingdom pyramid complex may be a reflection of this most ancient pattern. Certainly,

many questions remain as to the nature and dates of Hierakonpolis' earliest monuments – the brick-built structure known as 'The Fort' a little way into the desert may also figure in the early development of Egyptian religious structures; but in any event it seems clear that the area of Kom el-Ahmar was of the greatest importance in the earliest stages of the evolution of the Egyptian temple.

Wadi Mia

On the north side of the outskirts of Edfu, the road to Marsa Alam on the Red Sea coast follows the ancient route to the gold mining district of Barramiya. Some 50 km (31 miles) from Edfu on this road is a small rock-cut temple of Sethos I. It was built to commemorate his digging of wells in the area and the subsequent reopening of the old road which had become impassable for lack of water.

Edfu

The site of ancient Djeba (Coptic Etbo, Arabic Edfu) was the traditional location of the mythological battle between the gods Horus and Seth; and its sandstone Ptolemaic temple, dedicated to Horus, is the most complete and best preserved of all the temples of Egypt. Built on the site of a New Kingdom temple which was oriented east to west, the Ptolemaic structure follows instead a

The Ptolemaic temple of Horus at Edfu seen from the south. The twin pylon towers of this temple were decorated with scenes of Ptolemy XII smiting enemies in almost exact mirror images of each other.

south–north axis and thus left the remains of the old (and apparently much smaller) temple's entrance pylon standing at a 90-degree angle to its own entrance. Due to an unusually high number of building inscriptions preserved here, we know many of the details of the newer temple's history. It was evidently begun by Ptolemy III in 237 BC and completed 180 years later in 57 BC. The inner part of the structure, with its decoration, was finished in 207 BC, though political unrest in Upper Egypt (especially in the time of Ptolemies IV and V) meant that the dedication of the temple did not occur until 142 BC and some final work was not accomplished till 140 BC. In the following decades the hypostyle hall was built (completed in 122 BC); and the outermost elements – the peristyle court and entrance pylons – were then added and finally completed in 57 BC, in the reign of Ptolemy XII Auletes, the father of the last Cleopatra.

Unusually, the twin towers of the great entrance pylon of the temple were planned as perfect mirror images of each other, both in their construction and in the rather curiously rendered scenes carved on their surfaces. Two statues of Horus as a falcon flank the entrance gate, and behind the pylon, at the base of the walls on either side of the entrance, are scenes depicting the 'Feast of the Beautiful Meeting' in which Horus of Edfu was united with Hathor of Dendera. The peristyle court is now paved in the manner of its original surface, and the columns of the surrounding colonnade are carefully arranged with paired capitals of varied forms.

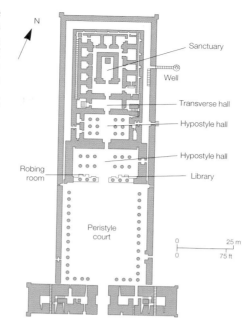

Gates at the court's inner corners lead to the long passage-like ambulatory – really a narrow inner court – which lies between the inner temple and its surrounding enclosure wall. The walls are here decorated with scenes and inscriptions of various types including a mythical foundation text and, of particular interest, the text of the 'dramatic' ritual in which Horus defeats his enemy Seth.

Factfile

Monument
Temple of Horus
Birth house
Location
Edfu, between Luxor and Aswan
Dates of construction
Ptolemaic Period, 237–57 BC
Dedication
Main temple: Horus
Various other deities in minor chapels
Reports
de Rochemonteix, M. and E. Chassinat, *Le temple d'Edfou*, 14 vols (Paris, 1892; Cairo, 1918–)
Michalowski, K. et al. *Tell Edfou*, 4 vols. (Cairo, 1937–50)

Plan of the temple of Horus at Edfu which has chapels for a number of deities arranged around the central barque sanctuary.

The colonnades of Edfu's peristyle court are constructed with 32 paired columns of various types.

The Edfu Drama

A scene from the ritual drama depicting the triumph of Horus over the god Seth in the form of a hippopotamus, from the outer ambulatory of the Ptolemaic temple of Horus at Edfu.

The mythological triumph of Horus over his arch-enemy Seth – who contested his rightful position on the throne of Egypt – was celebrated at Edfu in the form of a religious 'drama' which was acted out each year in the 'Festival of Victory'. This play, which was summarized in texts and vignettes on the walls of the temple ambulatory, casts Seth in the form of a hippopotamus (often an inimical creature for the Egyptians). Seth is systematically destroyed by Horus, who uses ten harpoons, each piercing a different part of the creature's anatomy. The first harpoon pierces the animal's snout – the area usually deleted in the subduing of dangerous images – and the succeeding barbs are thrust into the rest of the animal from front to back.

The vignettes of the Edfu inscriptions show the Seth hippopotamus as a diminutive, rather pitiful creature; but this is necessary according to the canonical approach of the Egyptian artists who refrained from ascribing power through stature to the play's antagonist. In the performance of the ritual a model hippopotamus would have been despatched by the king or priest representing Horus. In the final part of the Edfu ritual a hippopotamus cake was solemnly cut up and eaten to signify the total annihilation of Seth.

Before the façade of the hypostyle hall stands the famous statue of Horus as a giant falcon wearing the double crown of Egypt, a statue embodying the majesty of the ancient god as well as his fusion with the institution of kingship. The façade itself, with its intercolumnar screen wall and engaged columns, is not unlike that of Dendera, and the interior parts of the temple show a progressively increasing simi-

larity with that temple. The first hypostyle hall has two small engaged chambers on its south wall, one a library and the other a robing room similar to that at Esna. The hall contains 12 impressive columns and although the ceiling they support has no decoration, the side walls have traditional scenes including several showing the foundation ceremony of the temple. The second, smaller hypostyle which

(Left) A colossal black granite statue of Horus as a falcon – wearing the double crown of Egyptian kingship – stands in the court before the entrance to Edfu's first hypostyle hall.

(Right) A scene from the peristyle court at Edfu. In addition to scenes of the temple's tutelary deity Horus, much of the decoration of Edfu depicts the great goddess Hathor, here the consort of Horus, who is featured in both the main temple and in the temple's birth house.

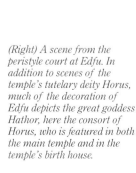

lies beyond also has 12 columns, though oriented in a room deeper than it is wide. The eastern side has an exit leading out to the temple's well and a chamber for storing liquid offerings, while a door on the western side accessed a chamber for solid offerings. Another door led to the 'laboratory' where incense was prepared.

Beyond the two hypostyles is a transverse offering hall and vestibule and the sanctuary itself, which still contains a granite *naos*-type shrine of Nectanebo II – the oldest element in the temple and one clearly saved from an earlier temple on the site to provide continuity to the newer structure. The main sanctuary is surrounded by a number of chapels including those of Min, Osiris, Khonsu, Hathor and Re, as well as a 'chamber of linen' and a 'chamber of the throne of the gods'. The chapel at the very rear of the sanctuary contains a modern reproduction of the god's barque (p. 70) which gives a good idea of its size and general appearance, if not of its precious materials. To the east of the sanctuary entrance a door opens to the small court which led in turn to the stairway used to reach the temple roof in the New Year's festival which was celebrated here in a manner similar to that of the ritual of Dendera (p. 149). As there, the figures of priests and standard bearers line the stairwell walls, but only that on the west side of the temple (originally the descending stair) can now be accessed. The roof of this temple lacks many of the features still found at Dendera, though some of these may have originally existed here also. Instead of cult chapels the only remaining structures are magazines, several with hidden chambers within or beside them.

To the south of the temple of Horus, just outside the portal of the processional way, is the mammisi. Like the Roman period mammisi of Dendera – which was modelled after this building – this birth house was built at right angles to the main temple, and the two structures follow the same general plan. Here, however, more of the forward part of the structure is preserved. A little more of the colonnade, for example, is intact, its intercolumnar screens decorated with the rather curious mixture of pharaonic and classical motifs sometimes found in these late structures. The birth room itself was surrounded by an ambulatory of columns linked by low walls – strangely, cut down in antiquity to about half their height – but which preserve in places their original colouring, especially on the south side of the building. Many of the motifs found here are the same as those decorating the mammisi of Dendera: the figures of the dwarf-god Bes on the abaci of the columns; and on the lintels, the representation of the infant Harsomptus (offspring of Horus and Hathor) worshipped by pairs of deities. The birth room contains various offering and ritual scenes of the king (Ptolemy VIII) and the gods, and in the upper registers of the north and south walls birth scenes and scenes of Harsomptus being nursed by various goddesses. At the centre of the south wall the god Thoth establishes the reign of the king who is followed by his mother, wife and son in the kind of legitimizing scene often associated with birth rooms. Elsewhere the 'Feast of the Beautiful Meeting' in which Horus and Hathor were united is subtly evoked in scenes of the barques of the two deities.

(Above left) The birth house at Edfu was the model for the somewhat later mammisi of Dendera.

(Above) A scene from the birth house showing the young Harsomptus nursed by Hathor in the marshes.

The great naos-*type shrine of Nectanebo II in the sanctuary of Edfu stands some 4 m (13 ft) high and is constructed from a single block of grey granite.*

(Above) The Great Speos or rock-cut sanctuary of Horemheb at Gebel el-Silsila north of Aswan. The temple was dedicated to seven deities, including the deified Horemheb himself.

(Left) Several of the seven deities to which the Speos of Gebel el-Silsila is dedicated appear on the pillars of its entrance portico.

Gebel el-Silsila

This site is located about 65 km (40.5 miles) north of Aswan. The area was famous in antiquity for its sandstone quarries, utilized in temple construction from New Kingdom times until the Graeco-Roman Period. On the west bank of the Nile at this location is the 18th-dynasty Great Speos (rock-cut temple) of Horemheb, dedicated in the name of that king to seven deities. The temple may have been cut in a disused quarry and has several entrance bays in the façade. Five portals, of various widths, open into a long transverse hall at the centre of which a doorway leads to the axial sanctuary. In the niche at the back of this inner sanctum, the seven deities to whom the chapel was dedicated – including Amun, the local crocodile-god Sobek and Horemheb himself – are represented by seven seated statues.

Three small rock-cut chapels which functioned as minor cenotaphs were also made to the south of the Great Speos of Horemheb by the Ramessid kings Sethos I, Ramesses II and Merenptah. The first was split in two at some point by an earthquake which also destroyed the quay in front of the shrines.

Kom Ombo

Situated between Aswan and Edfu, Kom Ombo is the ancient city of Pa-Sebek, 'the Domain of Sobek', the crocodile god worshipped since Predynastic times, and part of the Upper Egyptian region which was the realm of the old falcon-god Horus. A temple seems to have been built here in the New Kingdom, perhaps on the site of an even earlier structure, but the area did not rise to prominence until Ptolemaic times – to which period almost all the surviving monuments date. The temple, which is dedicated equally to Sobek and to Haroeris (Harwer) or 'Horus the Elder' and their associated deities, stands on a plateau cut by two long dry streams which isolate the site and provide the most spectacular setting of any of Egypt's river temples. Part of the temple's forecourt has, in fact, been eroded by the river, but modern control of the water has checked the threat of further damage and much of the temple remains.

The temple is oriented east to west according to the 'local north' determined by the river, and today the temple is entered through the remains of the Ptolemaic portal at the southwest of the precinct. The surviving part of the temple is flanked on the left by the scant remains of a birth house (situated, as elsewhere, at right angles to the main temple) and at the right by the remains of a gate of Ptolemy XII 'Auletes' the 'flute player'.

On the eastern side of the temple there is a small independent chapel of Hathor, and on the west the remains of a particularly deep well and a small pond where crocodiles, sacred to Sobek, are believed to have been raised. A number of the mummified creatures are stored, along with their clay coffins, in the Hathor chapel.

The temple itself was begun by Ptolemy VI – at least he is the earliest ruler named in it – but most of the decoration was not completed until the time of Ptolemy XII Auletes, and the outermost areas were not built until Roman times. The structure was made of the local sandstone by troops stationed here (Kom Ombo was a training ground for African elephants used by the army); and although the layout of the temple is similar to that of Dendera or Edfu, its somewhat smaller design often displays a pleasing architectural elegance based on the careful planning of its architects. The whole temple reflects its dual ownership, and even the Roman forecourt was 'divided' into equal shares for Sobek (east side) and Haroeris. An altar base is situated in the court's centre with small basins – to receive libations – sunk into the ground at each side for the respective gods. The relief carvings on some of the surviving

Factfile

Monument
Joint temple of Sobek and Haroeris
Chapel of Hathor
Birth house
Location
Kom Ombo, north of Aswan
Dates of construction
Graeco-Roman Period
Dedication
Main temple: the crocodile-god Sobek and Haroeris – 'Horus the Elder'
Reports
de Morgan, J., *et al.*, *Kom Ombos*, 2 vols. (Vienna, 1909)

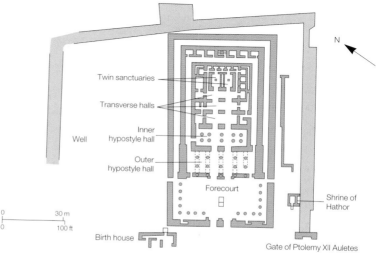

Twin sanctuaries
Transverse halls
Inner hypostyle hall
Well
Outer hypostyle hall
Forecourt
Shrine of Hathor
Birth house
Gate of Ptolemy XII Auletes

0   30 m
0   100 ft

N

Kom Ombo's hypostyle hall and inner chambers are symmetrically divided between the temple's two deities.

(Above) The temple of Sobek and Haroeris at Kom Ombo, with its irregularly shaped compound.

(Left) A view towards one of Kom Ombo's twin sanctuaries. Though atypically arranged, the inner halls of the temple of Sobek and Haroeris provide an excellent example of temple architecture.

(Right) Although the temple at Kom Ombo was begun during the Ptolemaic period, most of its decoration was completed in the 1st century BC. The temple also contains several texts of historical interest, including one in Greek recording the contribution of troops to the cult on behalf of Ptolemy VI and Cleopatra II.

columns of the colonnade are well preserved and many maintain their original colouring.

The façade of the hypostyle, with its intercolumnar screen walls and small side doors for use by the priests, is typical of its period, though the capitals of the columns within are often wrought with ingenious compound forms. As would be expected, the decoration of the hall and remaining parts of the temple is divided between the two gods, with scenes of Sobek on the east and Haroeris on the west. A second hypostyle repeats the design on a smaller scale and again allows two separate processional paths towards the inner sanctuaries behind three narrow transverse halls or vestibules.

The twin sanctuaries, like much of the temple's interior, are broken down but still contain the pedestals which supported the sacred barques of the two gods. The reduced condition of the chambers reveals the secret chamber beneath them which was used by priests to overhear petitions or deliver oracles on behalf of the deities. In fact, much of the inner part of the temple is honeycombed with crypts and hidden passages, and many of these can be explored by visitors to the temple. As at Dendera and Edfu, the sanctuary rooms are surrounded by smaller cult chapels, but unlike the other two sites, a small, internal hallway runs around the perimeter of the inner temple, between it and the outer wall of the building. The back wall of this area has six small rooms – three on either side of a stairwell leading to the roof – with varying degrees of decoration. The outer ambulatory which encircles this area, as at Edfu, is decorated with Roman period scenes of varying quality, but contains, towards the left end of the rear wall, the famous and controversial scene in which the king presents a group of ritual and/or surgical instruments. Some of these implements were certainly used in the practice of the cult, but others may be medically related (p. 73); and it is known that pilgrims came to Haroeris, the Healer, to be treated for their infirmities. They apparently waited on the god in the temple's hallways where game boards were scratched into the stones of the floors.

Most striking of the features of the rear part of the temple, however, is the false door (see p. 71) at the centre of the back wall of the sanctuary area, which is here modified and expanded in form to include a central niche flanked by hearing ears and seeing eyes and the figures of the two gods: Sobek, on the left, with a lion-headed sceptre or baton, and Haroeris, on the right, with a strange human-legged knife. Between the two gods a double hymn extols them; and above the niche, along with the figure of Maat who holds up the sky, the figures of the four winds are represented by a lion, a falcon, a bull and a many-headed serpent – oddly echoing the later Christian use of the ancient images of lion, eagle, bull and man as symbols of the four Gospel writers. The outer surfaces of the temple-encircling walls are decorated with colossal relief figures, predictably divided in the subjects of their representations between the realms of the two gods.

Elephantine

The island of Elephantine sits midstream in the Nile, just above the first cataract, by modern Aswan. Anciently the capital of the 1st Upper Egyptian nome, the site was a true border between Egypt and the areas to the south and represented a point of primary strategic and commercial importance. But the region was also an area of considerable religious importance for the deities associated with the Nile and with the desert regions.

The main town and temple area of Elephantine was located at the southern end of the island, and excavations by German archaeological teams have found that this area was inhabited almost continuously from the Early Dynastic period. Many temples doubtless stood here over the millennia, and the existence of several is known, though none of these structures remains intact today. Some have vanished in only recent times, and a small temple of Amenophis III was virtually intact as late as 1820, as was a structure of Tuthmosis III.

The main temple site of which anything can be seen is that of the temple of Khnum, ram-headed lord of Elephantine, which was oriented east to west from the direction of the Roman-era quay near the southeast corner of the island. The surviving pavement of the front section of this structure was actually added in late antiquity and built around the earlier columns of Ramesses II. Today only fragmentary examples of these survive, along with

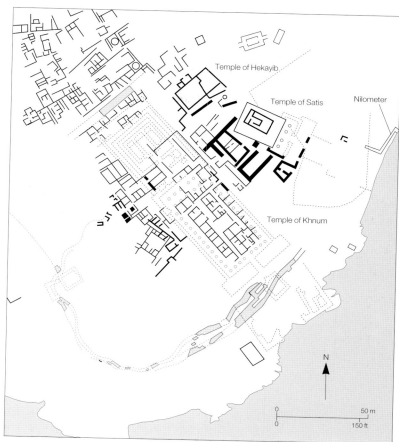

(Above) The site of Elephantine was of strategic military and commercial importance in ancient times and contained a good many temples of various periods. Today, however, little remains of these structures.

(Left) A decorated block at Elephantine depicts royal offerings before the major triad of the area, Khnum, Satis and Anukis.

211

The gateway of the temple of Khnum on Elephantine is one of the few remaining elements of this complex to have survived intact.

beneath the 18th-dynasty floor was found the remains of a structure of the 12th dynasty and another of the 11th dynasty. An Old Kingdom temple dating to the 6th dynasty then emerged. Beneath all these ancient structures the level of an even earlier shrine of the Early Dynastic period was eventually reached.

This structure represents one of the earliest temples to be found in Egypt and consisted of a small sanctuary area utilizing a natural niche in the surrounding rock and expanding from there through several small rooms from which many small votive objects were recovered. These artifacts do not make clear what deity or deities were worshipped here at this early period, but by the time of the 11th-dynasty structure the three principal deities of the area, Khnum, Satis and Anuket, are all attested.

Behind the Satis temple site is that of a small Middle Kingdom chapel of Hekayib, the deified governor of the region, and near the southern tip of the island is a small Ptolemaic chapel which has been reconstructed from blocks built into the Roman temple of Kalabsha and only revealed when that structure was dismantled for relocation in the 20th century. The chapel is of historical interest as it received decoration of the Nubian 'pharaoh' Arkamani who ruled that region in the 3rd century BC. On the outer walls Caesar Augustus is depicted, showing that the Romans completed the decoration of the chapel before deciding to dismantle it.

some altars, several of which are inscribed in Greek. The inner part of the temple is marked by a granite gateway which represents the only standing element of substance (most of the limestone of the walls having been burnt for lime), and the area beyond this is one of tangled remains with few recognizable features other than a large granite shrine begun in the 30th dynasty by Nectanebo II but never fully completed.

A little to the north, behind the Antiquities Museum, is the site of the temple of Satis, consort of Khnum. The New Kingdom temple of Tuthmosis III has undergone reconstruction by the German Archaeological Institute in recent years, and this small site is of particular importance. Due to restrictions in the topography of the site, the ancient builders sealed, under multiple floors, previous temples built on the same spot. First,

Aswan

The city of Aswan is located on the east bank of the Nile opposite Elephantine and was an important trade and quarrying area which developed somewhat later than Elephantine itself. It shared the

The New Kingdom temple of Satis, consort of Khnum, has recently undergone reconstruction on Elephantine.

island's strategic and commercial location, however, and the modern name, Aswan, seems to be derived from the ancient Egyptian word *swenet*, 'trade'.

Several temple sites are located here. Not far from the river, near the southern edge of the city, is a small Ptolemaic temple to Isis built by Ptolemy III and Ptolemy IV. The temple is sunk now, like that of Esna, well below the level of the modern habitations, but it is quite well preserved and has several interesting features. There are lion-headed waterspouts on the south side of the building (those of the other sides were not completed); and the rear wall of the central chapel carries scenes in which one of the Ptolemaic kings offers to Khnum, Satis and Anukis on the left and Osiris, Isis and Horus on the right, a combination of deities found in other temples of this area. Close to this temple is the site of a small Roman temple now destroyed.

Philae

The island of Philae, famous for centuries for its rich heritage of temples, now lies submerged beneath the waters of Lake Nasser to the south of Aswan. Thankfully, however, when the Aswan High Dam was built in the 1960s the island's temples were dismantled and then reconstructed on the higher terrain of nearby Agilkia Island, which was prepared and landscaped to look like the original Philae.

The ancient Egyptians saw in their name for Philae an etymology with the meaning 'island of the time [of Re]' – i.e., creation; but the island's history is a fairly late one. The earliest evidence of religious structures goes back only to the time of Taharqa (25th dynasty), and it was not till the Graeco-Roman Period that Philae rose to importance. Philae was, however, the cult centre *par*

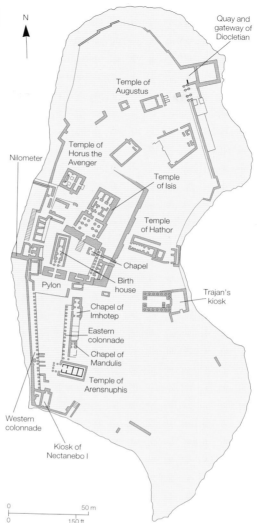

Factfile

Monument
Temple of Isis with many other structures
Location
New Philae island south of Aswan
Date of construction
Graeco-Roman Period
Dedication
Main temple: Isis
Reports
Lyons, H.G., *A Report on the Island and Temples of Philae* (London, 1897)
Junker, H. and E. Winter, *Philä*, I– (Vienna, 1958–)
Vassilika, E., *Ptolemaic Philae* (Leuven, 1989)

The temples on the island of Philae were dismantled and relocated on nearby Agilkia Island at the time of the construction of the Aswan High Dam.

David Roberts' romantic watercolour view of the island of Philae as it appeared in 1838.

*The western colonnade,
Philae: the preservation of
many of the temple structures
of Philae is exceptionally good
as relatively little stone has
been removed for use
elsewhere.*

*The first pylon of the temple
of Isis at Philae, with the gate
of Ptolemy II at the right and
the rear wall of the east
colonnade to the left.*

structure is the kiosk of Nectanebo I, the oldest
structure still standing here. To the north, the processional way leads to the main temple of Isis. The
western half of the colonnade is the more complete
and is pierced with windows originally looking out
toward the island of Biga; a nilometer (p. 73)
descends the cliff from here.

The eastern side of the colonnade, which was
never completed, reaches only to the destroyed
temple just opposite. This was the temple of the
rather obscure Nubian god Arensnuphis who was
venerated here as the companion of Isis. Other
structures also stand behind the eastern colonnade,
notably the ruined chapel of Mandulis, another
Nubian deity, at the southern end and the better-preserved chapel of Imhotep (the deified chief
architect of Djoser) to the north.

The entrance to the main temple is fronted by the
pylon of Ptolemy XII which is decorated with the
canonical scenes of the king despatching enemies
and which contains both a main (earlier) portal and
a subsidiary gate in the west tower leading into
the birth house of Ptolemy VI and later rulers.
The mammisi (birth house) is similar in plan and
decoration to those of Dendera and Edfu, but here
shares roughly the same axis as the main temple.
Its most notable scenes are those of Isis nursing
the infant Horus in the marshes, carved on the
outside of the back wall, and the triumphant Horus
on the inner side of the same wall. A decorated
colonnade with elegantly carved columns (as is the
case with most of the columns of this temple) runs
along the eastern side of the forecourt and fronts a
number of chambers including a 'library' dedicated
to Thoth. A Roman chapel stands in the court's
northeast corner before the second pylon which was
built on a natural outcrop of rock and stands at an
angle to the outer entrance. The second pylon opens
to the hypostyle hall of the main temple, the first
part of which is left open so that it forms, in effect, a
combined peristyle and hypostyle.

Beyond are the chambers of the inner temple –
standard, if somewhat anomalously arranged – and
the sanctuary, which still contains the pedestal, dedicated by Ptolemy III and his wife Berenike, of the
barque of Isis (although the granite shrines were
removed to European museums in the 19th
century). As in other temples of the Graeco-Roman
Period, the roof holds an Osiris room and other
chambers, though here they are sunk well below the
level of the roof at each of its four corners. The
Osiris room has its own vestibule with scenes of the
gods bewailing the dead Osiris, and the inner room
contains scenes relating to the collection of the
god's scattered limbs.

A number of subsidiary pharaonic structures
were built to the west of the Isis temple. A gateway
of the emperor Hadrian, which stands before a
stairway leading down to the river, contains several
interesting scenes relating to the death and ultimate

excellence of Isis who was revered throughout much
of the Roman world; and the site survived as a last
outpost of the old pagan religion well into the
present era, not being officially closed till the reign
of Justinian in AD 550.

The monuments of Philae are numerous. Beginning at the ancient quay where boats now land at
the southwestern corner of the island, the first

apotheosis of Osiris, including one of Isis who watches while a crocodile bears the body of her husband to an area representing the mound of Biga which rose from the Nile opposite this gateway. A little to the north are the ruins of the temple of Horus the Avenger (Harendotes), and yet further north are the remains of other structures, including a temple of Augustus and the quay and gateway of Diocletian.

To the east of the Isis temple stand the somewhat more substantial remains of a temple of Hathor, built by Ptolemies VI and VII, which preserves a number of scenes, including one of the king rejoicing before the goddess, along with figures of Bes, and an ape which plays a guitar-like instrument.

Just to the south is perhaps the most famous of Philae's monuments, the kiosk of Trajan, nicknamed 'pharaoh's bed'. While the roof of this structure – presumably of wood – has long since disappeared, it is still imposing. Fourteen columns, connected by screen walls, support the great architraves overspanning this building, which once served as the formal entrance to the island.

Biga

Just to the south of the new Philae and a little to the west of the original island is the island of Biga. By the start of the Graeco-Roman Period this site had come to be viewed as both the tomb of Osiris and the source of the Nile, which was believed to issue from a cavern deep beneath the island. A special sanctuary was built there in ancient times, but the area was proscribed to people and thus became known in Greek as the Abaton – the 'forbidden place'. Although originally of greater religious importance than the nearby island of Philae, Biga thus remained outside the normal developmental cycle of temple building and growth and it was Philae which developed instead. The remains of the small temple are on the eastern side of the island, opposite the location of the original Philae.

A view of the interior of the Roman entrance kiosk built by Trajan and known as 'pharaoh's bed' – one of Philae's best-known monuments.

The temple of Biga, near Philae, painted here by David Roberts in 1838, was partly converted into a Christian church.

From Aswan to Gebel Barkal

NUBIA

Nubia, the land south of the first cataract of the Nile, was a key area of strategic and economic importance to the ancient Egyptians. Not only was Nubia a buffer zone which protected Egypt's southern frontier, but it was also a gateway through which many trade goods reached Egypt from Africa. In antiquity control of the region fluctuated between the Egyptians, who regarded it as a province of Egypt, and the indigenous peoples of the region who regarded it as their own. In the Old Kingdom the Egyptian presence was transitory, but in the Middle Kingdom Egypt's control extended to the second cataract; and during New Kingdom times the effective area of Egyptian control was pushed to the fourth cataract and beyond. Interestingly, the realization in New Kingdom times that the Nubians of the region of Kerma and Gebel Barkal worshipped a deity in ram form led to the Egyptian acceptance of this Nubian god as a form of Amun. After this time, Nubians were included in key Egyptian religious events such as the Opet Festival and were largely accepted as co-religionists by the Egyptians. Many Egyptian temples were built in Nubia, and while most of these exhibit traditionally Egyptian architectural designs and decorative programmes, a number honour deities not usually seen in other areas of Egypt, and some incorporate even more exotic elements of this region. Due to the construction of the Aswan High Dam in the 1960s many of the temples of Nubia were threatened by the rising waters of the newly formed Lake Nasser. Through a massive internationally co-ordinated program of dismantling and relocation, many temples were moved to higher elevations beyond the reach of the water and some others were transferred to foreign countries as gifts to the governments who collaborated on this project.

Dabod

About 10 km (6.25 miles) south of the Aswan High Dam (on the west bank), Dabod was the site of a small temple of Amun built by the Meroitic king Adikhalamani in the first half of the 3rd century BC. Several Ptolemaic kings (Ptolemy VI, VIII and XII) enlarged the structure and rededicated it to the goddess Isis, and the temple received final decoration in the time of Augustus and Tiberius. Dismantled in the 1960s, it was presented to the people of Spain and reconstructed in Madrid.

Qertassi

Located on the west bank about 30 km (18.75 miles) south of the High Dam, the Roman kiosk of Qertassi was moved in 1960 to the site of New Kalabsha. Although incomplete and for the most part uninscribed, the four internal composite columns and two Hathoric entrance columns of this small structure give it an extremely graceful appearance.

Tafa

At Tafa, a few kilometres south of Qertassi and also on the west bank of the Nile, there were two Roman period temples. The northernmost, undecorated temple was dismantled and given to the Netherlands' Rijksmuseum of Leiden in 1960, while the other temple at this site was destroyed in the late 19th century.

The Roman kiosk of Qertassi, moved in 1960 to the area of New Kalabsha.

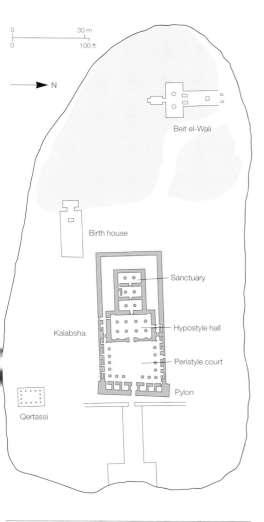

Scale: 0–30 m / 0–100 ft

N

Beit el-Wali

Birth house

Sanctuary

Kalabsha

Hypostyle hall

Peristyle court

Pylon

Qertassi

(Left) The temples of Kalabsha, Qertassi and Beit el-Wali were relocated to the island of New Kalabsha a little to the south of the Aswan High Dam to escape flooding after the dam was built. The first two structures date to Roman times, while the rock-cut temple of Beit el-Wali was constructed by Ramesses II.

Nubian monuments carved into the sandstone hillside. Originally fronted with a brick-built pylon, the rock-cut temple was dedicated to Amun and other gods and consists of an entrance hall decorated to celebrate Ramesses' victories over various enemies; a broad columned hall with two proto-Doric style columns; and the sanctuary, with statues of Isis, Horus, Khnum, Satis and Anukis – deities of the region of Aswan and Lower Nubia. Although the sanctuary's statues were mutilated during the Early Christian era, the brightly painted reliefs in the inner parts of the temple are well preserved.

(Above) Ramesses II presents offerings in this wall relief from the inner part of the temple at Beit el-Wali.

(Below left) The temple of Beit el-Wali was entirely cut into the rock of a cliff face.

Kalabsha

Originally located some 50 km (31 miles) south of the present High Dam at Aswan, the temple of Kalabsha, ancient Talmis, was dismantled in 1962–63 and its 13,000 blocks moved to a higher site just south of the new dam (New Kalabsha). The largest free-standing temple of Lower Nubia, the structure was built in the reign of the last Ptolemies and

(Below) The quay and entrance pylon of the temple of Kalabsha, which has been reconstructed at its new site just south of the Aswan High Dam.

Beit el-Wali

About 50 km (31 miles) south of the Aswan Dam, not far from the temple of Kalabsha (see below – and now moved close to that temple's new site, outside Aswan), stood another of Ramesses II's

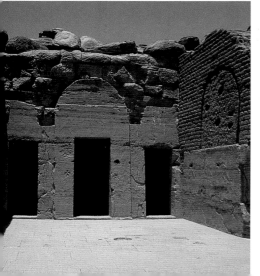

Augustus (though a temple may have stood on its site as early as New Kingdom times) and dedicated to the Nubian god Horus-Mandulis and to Isis and Osiris. Although never completed, Kalabsha is regarded as one of the finest examples of Egyptian architecture in Nubia. The temple was constructed entirely of sandstone and its interior skilfully decorated considering the difficulty of accomplishing fine work in this stone. It also contains several later inscriptions of historical interest, including one of the local king Silko which describes, in untutored Greek, his victory over nomadic tribes who threatened the area in the 5th century AD. The granite gate of the temple, which was found during the dismantling operations, was moved to the Ägyptisches Museum in Berlin. This led to the pylon (which, oddly, was turned at somewhat of an angle from the rest of the structure), a peristyle court and then a hypostyle followed by three inner, twin-columned rooms – the innermost of which functioned as the sanctuary, later used as a Christian church. As in many temples of the Ptolemaic Period, gates at the sides of the hypostyle opened to an enclosed space which surrounded the inner part of the structure. Beyond this area, the temple precinct also enclosed a small birth house and an independent chapel which seems to have been constructed by Ptolemy IX.

Dendur

Originally standing on the left bank of the Nile a little less than 20 km (12.5 miles) south of Kalabsha and some 77 km (about 48 miles) south of Aswan, in 1963 the temple of Dendur was dismantled and given by the Egyptian government to the United States in recognition of its part in helping to save the monuments of Nubia threatened by the rising waters of the High Dam. It now stands, reconstructed, in the Metropolitan Museum of Art in New York. The temple was originally built by Augustus in honour of two brothers, Peteese and Pihor, who were elevated to divine status in the area of Dendur, though the reason for their deification is unclear. The temple is small and simple in plan: a pylon fronts a small court with a columned pronaos, inner hall and sanctuary. The main building measures only about 13.5×7 m (44 ft 3 in $\times$ 23 ft), though

it is a fine example of its type. Its decoration shows the king (Augustus) before various gods, including the two deified brothers, along with the solar god Mandulis, Satis of Elephantine, and Arensnuphis, the 'companion' of Isis – deities honoured in a number of Nubian temples.

Gerf Hussein

On the west bank of the Nile (but now covered by Lake Nasser) a few kilometres south of the site of Dendur, Gerf Hussein contained a temple of Ramesses II which was partly free-standing and partly cut into the rock face at the rear of the structure. Its basic plan was, in fact, very similar to that of Abu Simbel, on a smaller scale. The temple was dedicated to the gods Ptah, Ptah-Tenen, Hathor and the deified Ramesses himself and, like Abu Simbel, contained seated statues of these deities in the cult niche at the back of the sanctuary.

el-Dakka

Originally about 100 km (62 miles) south of the Aswan High Dam, the temple of Thoth at Dakka (Egyptian Pselqet, Greek Pselchis) was moved to the site of el-Sebua a little more than 40 km (25 miles) upstream between 1962 and 1968. It was begun by the Meroitic king Arkamani about 220 BC, and construction continued in the reigns of several kings including Ptolemy IV, Ptolemy VIII and the emperors Augustus and Tiberius.

The well-decorated temple has two sanctuaries, an earlier one of Arkamani and a second added by Augustus. When the temple was moved, it was found to contain a number of reused blocks from an earlier structure dedicated to Horus of Baki (Quban) by Hatshepsut and Tuthmosis III.

(Above) The forecourt of the temple of Ramesses II at Gerf Hussein. The colossal statue of the king is carved in the rather heavy, powerful style sometimes employed in Nubian art. The entire temple is now submerged.

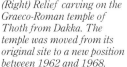

(Right) Relief carving on the Graeco-Roman temple of Thoth from Dakka. The temple was moved from its original site to a new position between 1962 and 1968.

Quban

This site (Egyptian Baki, Greek Contra Pselchis) stood on the east bank just across the Nile from el-Dakka. During the New Kingdom it was one of the more important Egyptian centres in Nubia, and several temples were built there. The area is now covered by Lake Nasser.

el-Sebua

El-Sebua is about 140 km (85 miles) south of the new Aswan Dam on the west bank of the Nile. Two Egyptian temples were built here in the New Kingdom: a temple of Ramesses II which was moved to a new site several kilometres to the north-west, and an earlier temple of Amenophis III which was left in its original location and is now covered by Lake Nasser. Both temples were partly free-standing and partly cut into the surrounding rock. The temple of Amenophis was dedicated first to a Nubian form of the god Horus and later to Amun. Damaged in the Amarna Period, it was restored by Ramesses II. Ramesses' own temple was dedicated to Amun-Re and Re-Horakhty and consisted of a sphinx-lined approach leading to a series of three pylons with colossi of the king (only one of which now remains) fronting the remaining pylon of stone. The court within also has ten statues of Ramesses, depicted in the heavy, rather rounded style often used in this area, engaged to its pillars. Within the rock a 12-pillared hall stands before a transverse vestibule and the sanctuary chambers. The entrance to the central niche was decorated to show Ramesses worshipping the gods within (probably Amun-Re, Re-Horakhty and Ramesses himself), but was changed by the ancient Christians, who converted the temple to a church, to show him offering to St Peter instead.

The temple of Amun and Re-Horakhty at el-Sebua (plan right) is fronted by two courts with a number of human-headed sphinxes. One of an original four colossi of the temple's builder, Ramesses II, still stands before the inner pylon.

N

Sanctuary

Transverse vestibule

Rock-cut section

12-pillared hall

Court with engaged statues of king

Pylon

Pylon

Pylon

0   15 m
0   50 ft

Amada

About 180 km (112 miles) south of the High Dam and dedicated to the important New Kingdom gods Amun-Re and Re-Horakhty, the temple at Amada was built by Tuthmosis III and Amenophis II, with the hypostyle hall added by Tuthmosis IV. Sethos I, Ramesses II and several other 19th-dynasty kings also made small additions or restorations to the temple. Due to the rising waters caused by the

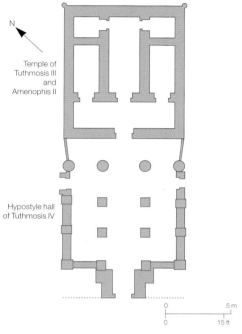

N

Temple of
Tuthmosis III
and
Amenophis II

Hypostyle hall
of Tuthmosis IV

0   5 m
0   15 ft

building of the Aswan Dam, the temple was moved between 1964 and 1975 to a new, higher position some 2.5 km (1.5 miles) from its original site. Despite the predations of the Atenists during the 18th dynasty, the temple retains much of its painted relief work. It also contains several important historical texts. One, carved on a stela on the rear wall of the sanctuary in the third year of Amenophis II, describes an Egyptian military campaign into Asia. The other – carved on a stela on the northern side of the entrance doorway – describes a Libyan invasion of Egypt in the fourth year of Merenptah. Graffiti of the 19th dynasty inscribed in this temple include scenes of the viceroy of Nubia, Messuy, which appear to show the royal uraeus added to the viceroy's brow.

(Above left) The small temple of Amun-Re and Re-Horakhty at Amada was built during the 18th dynasty and contains a number of important historical inscriptions.

(Above) A relief of Amun in the Amada temple: the god's name was excised from the structure by Atenists and only restored later in the 19th dynasty.

el-Derr

A few kilometres to the west of Amada (though on the Nile's east bank due to the reversing of the river's course at this point), Ramesses II built a rock-

(Above) The first pillared hall, with remains of engaged Osiride statues along the bases of the pillars, of the temple of Ramesses II at el-Derr. In many ways the temple resembles the king's larger monument at Abu Simbel.

(Left) Decorated pillars in the temple of el-Derr. Cleaned and restored in recent years, the temple's relief decoration is unusually bright, with vivid colours accentuating the familiar scenes of the king with various deities.

cut temple similar to that of Abu Simbel, though without seated colossi at its entrance. There are two pillared halls: the first is transverse and has three rows of four columns – the third row with engaged statues of Osiris. The second hall follows the axis of the temple and leads to three chapels, the central one containing cult statues of the four gods worshipped here: Ptah, Amun-Re, Ramesses II and Re-Horakhty. Some of the temple's decoration was lost due to its use as a church by early Christians, but a number of scenes remain, including one of a procession of the king's children, and the paint is often vividly preserved. The temple was dismantled in 1964 and moved to a new site close to the temple of Amada.

el-Lessiya

Just under 20 km (12.5 miles) upstream from el-Derr, and on the same side of the Nile, el-Lessiya was the site of a small rock-cut chapel of Tuthmosis III which was moved in the salvage operations of the 1960s and now stands reconstructed in the Museo Egizio in Turin, Italy. Although only a single-room structure, the chapel is interesting in its decoration which includes scenes of the king before the Nubian god Dedwen and the deified Senwosret III. A niche in the rear wall of the chapel originally contained statues of Tuthmosis with Horus of Miam (Aniba) and Satis of Elephantine; but these were damaged in the Amarna Period and subsequently renewed by Ramesses II to represent Amun, Horus of Aniba and himself.

Aniba

Across the Nile from Qasr Ibrim and only a little downstream from that site (about 230 km – 143 miles – south of Aswan), Aniba held a temple of Horus of Miam (Aniba), though this is now destroyed. The temple may have been founded as early as Middle Kingdom times (Senwosret I), though the remaining evidence comes mainly from the 18th dynasty, from the reigns of Hatshepsut (?), Tuthmosis III, Amenophis II and III and Ramesses II and X.

Qasr Ibrim

A few kilometres upstream from el-Lessiya (about 235 km – 146 miles – south of Aswan), and again on the same side of the Nile, Qasr Ibrim (the Greek Primis and Latin Prima) served as a fortress site in pharaonic and Roman times and held at least one temple of New Kingdom date – though the names of the ruler who built it and the deity to whom it was dedicated have not survived. This small stone temple was apparently restored (in mud-brick) by Taharqa, and the structure was later converted to use as a church in early Christian times.

Abu Simbel

The Great Temple

The rock-cut temple of Ramesses II on the west bank of the Nile at Abu Simbel is the greatest of the seven rock-cut temples which the king constructed in Nubia and the most impressive of all the Egyptian monuments in the area. The temple was not seen by Europeans until the 19th century, when it was discovered by J.-L. Burckhardt in 1813 and penetrated by Giovanni Belzoni in 1817. Today, as a result of the international effort which moved the huge, cliff-cut temple and the Small Temple (p. 227) to higher ground during the construction of the Aswan High Dam in the 1960s, the monument is one of the most famous in Egypt.

Sanctuary
Transverse vestibule
Small pillared hall
Magazines
Magazines
Large pillared hall
Colossi
Colossi
Chapel of Thoth
Sun-chapel

N
20 m
50 ft

Factfile

Monument
Great Temple: rock-cut temple of Ramesses II
Small Temple: rock-cut temple of Nefertari-Hathor
Location
Abu Simbel, Lower Nubia
Date of construction
19th dynasty
Dedication
Great Temple: Ramesses II, Amun, Ptah, Re-Horakhty
Small Temple: Nefertari-Hathor
Reports and studies
MacQuitty, W., *Abu Simbel* (London, 1965)
Desroches-Noblecourt, C. and C. Kuentz, *Le petit temple d'Abou Simbel*, 2 vols. (Cairo, 1968)
Säve-Söderbergh, T. (ed.), *Temples and Tombs of Ancient Nubia* (London and New York, 1987)

Plan of the rock-cut Great Temple of Ramesses II at Abu Simbel. To the left of the main temple entrance is the separate chapel dedicated to Thoth, and to the right, the remains of a covered court dedicated to the worship of the sun.

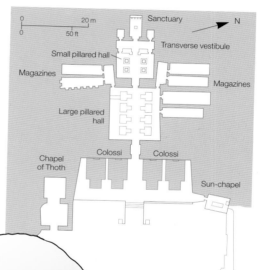

Cutaway elevation of the Great Temple: behind the rock-cut façade the temple's inner chambers stretch some 60 m (200 ft) to the inner sanctuary.

223

The colossal seated figures of Ramesses II which flank the entrance to his temple at Abu Simbel are some 21 m (69 ft) high and are among the largest made in Egypt. Their location in Egypt's southern borderland may well have carried a message of national might to her neighbours to the south.

The temple was evidently begun fairly early in Ramesses' long reign – it was commissioned sometime after the king's fifth regnal year but was not completed until his 35th year. During this time the conception of the monument's purpose may have changed to some degree, and the cult images in the temple's innermost shrine were recarved to include a representation of Ramesses himself, along with the three great state gods of late New Kingdom Egypt, Re-Horakhty of Heliopolis, Ptah of Memphis, and Amun-Re of Thebes. At its completion, the temple was called simply Hut Ramesses Meryamun, 'The temple of Ramesses, Beloved of Amun'.

The forecourt which fronted the temple contained two tanks for the ablutions of the priests, which flanked the stairs leading up to the entrance terrace. On the northern side of this terrace stood a small sun-chapel and on the south a chapel of Thoth. The massive façade of the main temple is dominated, of course, by the four seated colossi of Ramesses which, at some 21 m (69 ft), are among the tallest made in Egypt. Beneath these giant sculptures are the carved figures of bound Negro (on the south) and Asiatic (on the north) captives – symbolic of Egypt's borderland enemies. Next to the giant figures of the king, members of Ramesses' family – including images of his great royal wife Nefertari and mother Muttuya, as well as several children – stand at his feet. The figure of Re (worshipped by flanking images of Ramesses) above the entrance not only spells out the king's throne name

in rebus form, User-Maat-Re (see p. 226), but also stresses the solar nature of the outer temple. A stela at the southern end of the external terrace records one of Ramesses' diplomatic triumphs, his marriage to a daughter of the Hittite king Hattusilis III.

Within the temple a series of chambers becomes increasingly smaller as the floors of the rooms rise noticeably – following the basic convention of temple design in a somewhat foreshortened manner. The first hall is nevertheless cut on an imposing scale and contains eight large Osiride

The four colossal seated figures of Ramesses were carved wearing the double crown of Egyptian kingship as well as the nemes headdress, in the style most frequently used for colossi of the king.

The pillared hall within the Great Temple with the colossal engaged statues of the king as Osiris on the inner faces of the pillars. This hall introduces a chthonic theme to the temple's decoration, which is fused with the solar aspects of its entrance.

Abu Simbel's Great Temple: The Fusion of Light and Darkness

(Right) The frieze of sun-worshipping baboons which was carved above the temple's façade.

(Below) Above the temple's entrance is a statue of the sun-god Re holding signs for power (user) and truth (maat), thus forming a rebus of Ramesses' throne name.

In many ways a fusion of 'divine' and mortuary temples (p. 25), the Great Temple of Abu Simbel was constructed to face eastwards so that the sun's rays illuminated the structure's façade each sunrise. First the sunlight lit the row of baboons (symbolic greeters of the sun god) carved along the top of the cliff-face façade, then as the sun rose its rays illuminated the four colossal faces of the king and the central niche statue of Re which formed a rebus of Ramesses' throne name. Finally, the solar rays entered the temple itself. The temple's axis was aligned in such a way that twice each year, in February and October, the sun's rays penetrated some 60 m (200 ft) through its inner halls to the very depths of the rock-cut monument where they illuminated the statues of the deified Ramesses and his companion gods – though the statue of the chthonic deity Ptah remains in partial shadow.

In the sanctuary at the heart of Abu Simbel are statues of four gods: Ptah, Amun, the deified Ramesses and Re. Ptah, left, remains in partial darkness when the sun's rays penetrate the sanctuary.

statues of the king engaged to the pillars which support its roof. The walls are decorated in relief with scenes showing the king in battle (including the great Battle of Kadesh (p. 228), on the north wall, and Syrian, Libyan and Nubian wars on the south wall), and presenting prisoners to the gods. The wall carvings retain some of their original colour. A series of magazines radiates off from this first hall; behind it the smaller, second pillared hall with ritual offering scenes stands before a transverse vestibule and the sanctuary which is flanked by special storerooms for cultic objects. The sanctuary contains a small altar and, in its rear niche (left to right) are the four statues of Ptah, Amun-Re, the deified Ramesses and Re-Horakhty. While the horizontal rays of the rising sun did illuminate these statues twice each year (and still do through the careful orientation of the relocated temple), the specific dates of these occurrences are not as important as is often thought, as the phenomenon would occur with any south-facing structure of this type at some point or points of the year. Nevertheless, the occurrence itself was important as it achieved the symbolic fusion of solar and chthonic forces celebrated in this great temple.

The Small Temple

To the north of the main temple a smaller, yet still impressive, temple was built in honour of Ramesses' great wife, Nefertari, and the goddess Hathor, the deity most closely associated with queenship in ancient Egypt. As with Ramesses' own temple, the cliff face was cut back to resemble the sloping walls of a pylon and colossal standing figures (about 10 m or 33 ft high) of Ramesses and Nefertari – four of the king and two of the queen – were cut, along with diminutive figures of the royal family. Inside, Nefertari's temple is both smaller and simpler in plan, with a single pillared hall – here with carved Hathor images on the sides facing the centre of the hypostyle; a vestibule with ancillary rooms at either end; and the sanctuary. Although the sanctuary itself was completed, two spaces were left on its side walls for doors to rooms which were never cut. The inner chamber contains a

number of images interrelating the royal couple and the gods. On the rear wall, in high relief, Hathor is depicted as a cow emerging from the 'western mountain' with the king standing beneath her chin. On the left wall Nefertari is seen worshipping before Mut and Hathor, and on the right Ramesses

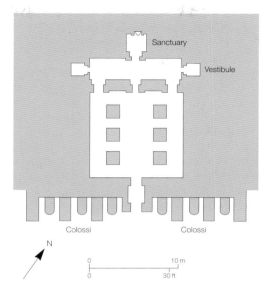

(Left) Although smaller than the temple of Ramesses II, the temple dedicated to Nefertari and Hathor contains most of the same basic elements.

(Below) The façade of the Small Temple contains six colossal standing statues of the king and queen, each flanked by smaller figures of the royal children.

The Battle of Kadesh

Ramesses II at Kadesh: although depicted here as a seemingly invulnerable leader, the king came close to suffering defeat and possible capture in this crucial battle. This drawing of the Abu Simbel relief is by I. Rosellini.

worships before images of his deified self and his wife. The importance granted to Nefertari here and throughout the temple is immense, and the queen is repeatedly shown as participating in the divine rituals on an equal footing with the king.

Abahuda

A small rock-cut temple of Horemheb dedicated to Amun and Thoth stood at this site on the east bank of the Nile, across from Abu Simbel. The temple consisted of a four-columned hall with two side chapels and a sanctuary with scenes of the king before the gods. It was converted into a church in early Christian times when a number of Coptic graffiti and representations were added to the walls. Blocks from the structure are now being installed in the new Nubian Museum at Aswan.

Faras

Plan of the largely destroyed temple of Tutankhamun at Faras, now covered by the waters of Lake Nasser.

This site, originally on the west bank of the Nile between Abu Simbel and the Wadi Halfa – but under Lake Nasser since 1964 – had a destroyed temple of Tutankhamun and an early New Kingdom rock-cut chapel of Hathor of Ibshek (pre-sumably the Egyptian name of the site). Although its origins are not precisely dated, this chapel is known to have been enlarged in the reigns of Tutankhamun and Ramesses II. The hundreds of

228

In the summer of the fourth year of his reign, Ramesses the Great conducted a successful military campaign in the Syrian Levant by which he cemented his control of the region – establishing it as an effective buffer zone between Egypt and the growing might of the Hittite empire. By the following spring it was evident that the Hittites would soon wrest these gains from him, and in April of that year the king set out to meet the Hittite threat directly. For this expedition Ramesses fielded an army of some 20,000 men – one of the largest forces ever seen up to that time in Egypt or across the whole of the Near East. The host was divided into four divisions of about 5,000 men – each with infantry and chariotry, and each named for one of Egypt's major gods: Amun, Re, Ptah and Seth. Marching along the coast of Canaan and then moving inland towards the Bekaa Valley, within a month of their departure the army reached the Orontes River less than 16 km (10 miles) from Kadesh. Here, a pair of captured spies asserted that the main Hittite army was still 190 km (120 miles) to the north, near Aleppo, so Ramesses led his Amun division, followed by that of Re, across the Orontes and established a camp just outside Kadesh. It was then that the main Hittite army – actually hidden just behind Kadesh – attacked. The enemy forces were even more numerous than those of Egypt – consisting of two huge groups of 18,000 and 19,000 men and an additional 2,500 chariots.

In the resulting panic the Egyptians were almost routed, but Ramesses personally led a charge against the enemy with the troops he could muster. Fortunately, Ramesses' elite guard which had travelled a separate route to Kadesh appeared and entered the battle at just this moment and the Hittites, finding themselves caught between two flanks, retreated. Fighting continued throughout the following day, but the battle ended in a stalemate with both sides almost having met defeat.

When the two armies separated, both Ramesses and the Hittite king Muwatallis were able to claim victory for their respective sides, and eventually a lasting peace based on a hard-won mutual respect was established. In Egypt, detailed accounts of the great battle were inscribed in prose, poetry and narrative representations on the walls of many of the temples which Ramesses constructed throughout the land. These have survived at Abydos, Karnak, the Ramesseum (two accounts), Luxor (three accounts), and in Nubia at Abu Simbel and at el-Derr. It is no coincidence that Ramesses chose to celebrate the battle in Nubia as well as in his mortuary temples and the great temples of Thebes. The Battle of Kadesh was Ramesses' greatest military accomplishment – victory or not – and its representation was fitting for the great rock-cut temple which portrayed Ramesses as the god-protector of Egypt on the frontier between the Two Lands and the wild and restive areas to the south.

reused Tuthmosid blocks found at this site were probably removed from the temple at Buhen next to the second cataract.

Aksha (Serra West)

Aksha, on the west bank of the Nile some 25 km (15.5 miles) north of the Wadi Halfa, had a temple and various chapels of Ramesses II in which the king was depicted with Amun and Re and before his own deified form. Beginning in 1961 the temple was removed to Khartoum.

Buhen

The site of the famous fortress of Middle Kingdom times which guarded the second cataract of the Nile, Buhen lay on the west side of the river and was an important frontier outpost. The town contained a temple of Isis and Min built by Amenophis II (probably on the site of an earlier temple of Ahmose) and a temple of Horus of Buhen (one of the four Horuses of Nubia) built by Hatshepsut and Tuthmosis III, with later additions by Taharqa. The temples were recorded by Randall-MacIver and Leonard Woolley in 1909–10 and by

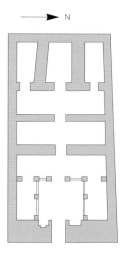

N

R. Caminos in 1960–61. Both temples were removed to Khartoum in 1962–63.

Mirgissa

Located in the region of the second cataract, on the west bank of the Nile some 15 km (9.25 miles) south of Wadi Halfa, Mirgissa contained a small New

The temple of the fortified outpost of Buhen in Lower Nubia: the small but relatively intact temples of this site were dismantled and moved to Khartoum in the 1960s.

*Plan of the small New
Kingdom temple of Hathor
at Mirgissa. The temple is
now covered by Lake Nasser.*

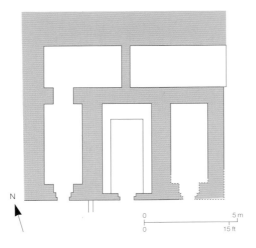

Kingdom temple of Hathor, perhaps replacing an earlier Middle Kingdom structure. The site is now covered by Lake Nasser.

Uronarti

This small island (the Arabic Geziret el-Melek) just north of Semna contained a mud-brick temple of Tuthmosis III (but possibly established in Middle Kingdom times) dedicated to the Theban war god Montu and the Nubian god Dedwen.

Kumma (Semna East)

A New Kingdom temple of Khnum dating to the reigns of Tuthmosis II, III and Amenophis II was built at this Middle Kingdom fortress site. The temple was removed to Khartoum before the site was flooded after the construction of the New Aswan Dam.

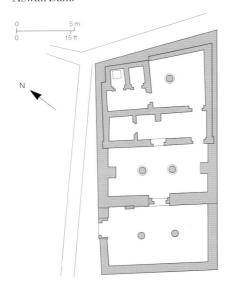

*(Right) The New Kingdom
temple of Khnum at Kumma
was moved to Khartoum.*

*(Far right) The temple
dedicated to Amun and to
local gods at Amara West.*

Semna

Another Middle Kingdom fortress site, Semna lay on the Nile's west bank at the southern side of the second cataract about 80 km (50 miles) south of Wadi Halfa. The area contained a temple of Senwosret III dedicated to the deified king and to the Nubian god Dedwen. It was renewed by Tuthmosis I and III and Hatshepsut, with later work also carried out by Taharqa. This temple is also now in Khartoum.

Amara West

About 250 km (155 miles) south of Wadi Halfa on the west bank of the Nile (because of the turn in the river here to the north) and close to the third cataract, a 19th-dynasty town at the site of Amara West supported a temple of Ramesses II. The temple was dedicated primarily to Amun and also to other local gods who were represented in subsidiary chapels. A number of interesting texts were inscribed in this temple including lists of Asiatic and African names and, on the sides of the temple entrance, duplicates of the Dream and Marriage Stelae of Ramesses II.

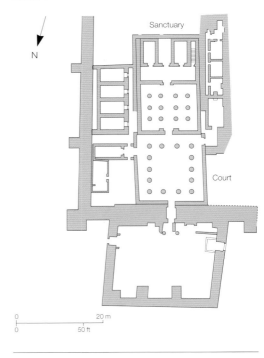

Sedeinga

Some 20 km (12.5 miles) south of Amara on the west bank of the Nile, this site held a small temple of Amenophis III. Apparently, Amenophis' great

*The ruins of the temple at
Sedeinga: it was dedicated to
Tiye, wife of Amenophis III,
perhaps as a deified form of
the solar aspect of Hathor.
Hathoric capitals and
depictions of Tiye as a
female sphinx can still be
seen at the site.*

royal wife Tiye was the focus of this temple,
perhaps as a form of Hathor; but the temple is now
destroyed.

Gebel Dosha

A few kilometres south of Sedeinga and on the
same bank of the Nile, the minor site of Gebel
Dosha received a small rock-cut chapel from Tuthmosis III.

Soleb

Just to the south of the third cataract on the Nile's
west bank, Soleb contains the remains of an important sandstone temple of Amenophis III. This
temple represents the southernmost major monument of the ambitious building programme of
Amenophis and was apparently paralleled by the
king's northernmost great monument at Athribis
(Tell Atrib) in the eastern Delta. Originally, Soleb

*(Below left) Gebel Dosha, a
small rock-cut chapel of New
Kingdom date, demonstrates
the huge variety of temple
forms found in Egypt.*

*(Below) The sandstone temple
of Amenophis III at Soleb is
one of the more important
sites in Upper Nubia.*

Soleb Temple, like the massive mortuary temple of Amenophis III at Thebes, was designed for the king by Amenophis son of Hapu and was dedicated to Amun-Re and the deified Amenophis III himself.

seems to have followed the standard plan of a peristyle court, hypostyle hall and sanctuary; but like Luxor Temple, Soleb was expanded, receiving a sun court and a kind of shortened colonnade at some time after the construction of the inner temple area. The temple was dedicated to Amun-Re residing in Soleb, and secondly to Nebmaatre, lord of Nubia – the deified Amenophis III himself – who was depicted as a god with the attributes of Amun and of a lunar deity. The decorative programme of the temple included scenes from the king's first Sed festival as well as important depictions of the ritual 'striking the doors' and 'illuminating the dais' which preceded the celebration of the king's jubilee. Symbolically, these and other representations indicate an interesting duality in the temple: that of Amun-Re as the 'solar eye' and Amenophis as the 'lunar eye' of Egyptian mythology. The lunar eye was also associated with the lioness-goddess Tefnut-Mehit (whose name refers to the full moon), and the two famous red granite lions which were installed here by Amenophis (later moved to Gebel Barkal and now in the British Museum) were probably intended to illustrate the symbolic connection between the king and the lunar deity.

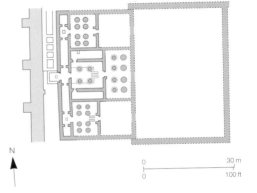

(Below) The three contiguous temples of Amun, Mut and Khonsu dedicated by Sethos I at Sesebi.

N

| 0 | 30 m |
| 0 | 100 ft |

icated to the Theban triad Amun, Mut and Khonsu dedicated by Sethos I.

Island of Argo

A small temple at this site near Tabo was built here by Taharqa in the 25th dynasty reusing New Kingdom blocks.

Sesebi

A New Kingdom town at this site, some 80 km (50 miles) to the south of Soleb, contained a temple of the Aten built by Akhenaten and a later temple ded-

Kawa

Several temples of Amun were built at this site, opposite Dongola on the east bank of the Nile, by Amenophis III, Tutankhamun, Taharqa and various Napatan and Meroitic kings. The temple of

Taharqa was important as it established a sanctuary of Amun alongside that at Gebel Barkal and thus created a second key site of Kushite worship.

Sanam

This site just south (here downstream) of Napata and Meroe contains the ruins of a 25th-dynasty temple of Amun-Re constructed by Taharqa.

Gebel Barkal

The southernmost major site of Egyptian temple building, Gebel Barkal is situated just below the region of the fourth cataract in the area of the ancient capitals of Napata and Meroe, about 400 km (249 miles) north of Khartoum. The site was an important river crossing on the overland route between Egypt and central Africa and includes several palaces and at least 13 temples.

Gebel Barkal was first described by European explorers in the 1820s. In 1916 excavation was begun by George A. Reisner for the Harvard-Boston Expedition, which cleared a number of buildings and assigned each of them a 100-number, prefaced by the letter B. From the 1970s to the present, further excavations have been accomplished by a team from the University of Rome, under the direction of Sergio Donadoni, and from the 1980s by another team from the Boston Museum of Fine Arts, under the direction of Timothy Kendall.

The Egyptians named Gebel Barkal 'the pure mountain' after the large sandstone butte, 74 m (243 ft) high, that stands at the location. The distinctive southern pinnacle of this butte may have had particular importance for them – possibly as a phallic symbol representing the regenerative powers of Amun, but also as it resembles, when viewed from the east, the royal Egyptian uraeus surmounted by the white crown. When viewed from the west, the same topographical feature resembles the divine serpent crowned with a sun disc. Timothy Kendall has shown that the small temples close to the western foot of the rock feature were dedicated to female deities normally associated with this latter form of the uraeus, while temple structures recently discovered on the eastern side seem to have been associated with the deities of the royal crowns.

(Above left) A granite statue of Amun in the form of a kneeling ram protecting king Taharqa, from the temple of Taharqa at Kawa.

(Above) Gebel Barkal reconstructed: the view looks east from temple B200, with some of the temples below the great sandstone butte around which the site developed.

(Below) Temple B700 at Gebel Barkal was Egyptian in its architecture and decoration. Although little remains today, 19th-century drawings helped in this reconstruction of the temple's entrance porch.

Oases and Outposts

The areas of Egyptian control beyond the Nile Valley were many, but scattered throughout the harsh desert terrain. The oases which dot the Libyan Desert to the west of the Nile were inhabited from Palaeolithic times and acted as vital staging points along important trade routes through much of Egyptian history. Temples were built at many of these sites for their permanent populations, and some, such as that of Hibis in the Kharga Oasis, were substantial monuments. To the east of Egypt proper the Sinai held similar, though smaller outposts of Egyptian civilization, usually associated with the mining that was carried out in that region; and various other peripheral sites along the North African and Levantine coasts held temples of Egyptian construction, often for the garrisons which were stationed in these far-flung regions. In total, these sites of the oases and outposts number in the hundreds, and only the most important can be included here.

THE OASES

Siwa

Siwa, one of the more remote of the western oases, is nevertheless the most famous due to the visit of Alexander the Great to this site in 331 BC in order to consult its oracle. A great wind-scoured depression some 17 m (55 ft) below sea level, the area of Siwa lies only 50 km (31 miles) from the present Libyan border. The depression is some 80 km (49.75 miles) long and varies from 3 to almost 30 km (2–18.5 miles) wide. It was here that a great oracle of Ammon (perhaps not originally related to the Egyptian god Amun) was located, and several Egyptian temples were constructed as its fame grew. In the course of the predations of Egypt by the Persian king Cambyses in 525–522 BC, he despatched an army of 50,000 men to destroy the oracle at Siwa. The army vanished in the desert, however, doubtless serving to increase considerably the prestige of the oracle. Some 200 years later, Alexander the Great visited Siwa, at which time Amun declared him to be his son – the divine recognition preceding his formal crowning as king of Egypt at Memphis. Alexander's visit to Siwa doubtless further enhanced the site's reputation, although by Roman times its fame had begun to decline.

At Aghurmi in the central oasis region, some 4 km (2.5 miles) from the modern town, a temple dating to the 26th dynasty and Ptolemaic Period is presumed to be the temple visited by Alexander. The structure stands at the edge of a rock bluff and contains a small forecourt, vestibule and sanctuary. A narrow corridor to the right of the sanctuary may have been used by the priests who represented the oracle. The decoration is simple but of interest as it depicts both the Egyptian king Amasis II (26th dynasty) and the governor of Siwa offering to the gods on different walls, showing the elevated position of the latter in this remote location.

At Umm el-Ubeida a little to the south of Aghurmi, a small, later temple was built by Nectanebo II, though this was damaged by an earthquake and blasted apart for its stone in the 19th century. A number of other small, usually undecorated temples were built at other sites around the oasis.

The famed 'Temple of the Oracle' (right) which Alexander the Great is said to have visited in 331 BC sits atop the rock of Aghurmi at Siwa. Following his visit to Siwa Alexander was depicted with the horns of Ammon on this silver tetradrachm (below).

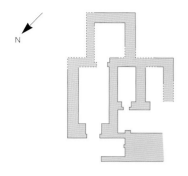

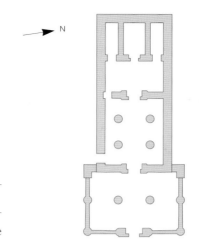

Bahariya

The Bahariya depression lies between Siwa and the Nile Valley and a little to the south. At el-Qasr el-Bahariya, at the northern end of the depression, there is a ruined temple of the 26th dynasty. To the west are four chapels constructed by Apries, including one of the few known dedicated to the household god Bes. The decorations show the king presenting offerings along with the local governor. Some 16 km (10 miles) to the south of el-Qasr el-Bahariya, the site of Qasr Allam contains a small temple of Alexander the Great.

The complex is somewhat unusual, consisting of a double-chambered sanctuary area surrounded by a great wall. To the rear of the sanctuary stood two priests' houses, and the rest of the complex was made up of storage and service rooms.

el-Dakhla

In Arabic 'the inner one' (of the Dakhla and Kharga oases), el-Dakhla is situated some 350 km (217 miles) due west of Luxor, though the site is reached by way of the road from Asyut and el-Kharga. The site was inhabited in Palaeolithic times and there were Old Kingdom settlements here, yet few standing monuments remain. At Balat on the eastern side of the oasis there are ruins of a small temple of New Kingdom date, and at Ismant el-Kharab (ancient Kellis) a little further west stands a small Roman temple. This, the only known temple of the god Tutu, stood here until 1920 but is now ruined. At Mut el-Kharab, near the oasis' centre, are the scant remains of a destroyed temple of Amun's consort Mut, after which the locality is still named. To the northwest, el-Qasr el-Dakhla held a Graeco-Roman temple of Thoth, now buried under the houses of the village. The gate is visible as the entrance to a private house, and inscribed blocks from the structure may be seen in the walls of other homes. Deir el-Hagar, a few kilometres west of el-Qasr el-Dakhla at the end of the oasis, holds the more substantial ruins of a Roman period stone temple dating to the reigns of the emperors Nero,

Vespasian, Titus and Domitian. Although unrestored, this is the only temple with significantly surviving remains in the el-Dakhla area. The site of Ain Amur, almost midway between the Dakhla and Kharga oases, has the remains of a small temple of the Roman period. The monuments of this area have been the subject of ongoing study by an international Egyptological expedition including scholars of Canadian, Australian and other nationalities.

el-Kharga

In Arabic 'the outer one' (of the Dakhla and Kharga oases), Kharga oasis lies some 220 km (137 miles) to the south of Asyut. The depression is almost 100

(Far left) The plan of the temple of Amasis II at Siwa may reflect local architectural tradition in some of its elements.

(Left) The Roman temple of Deir el-Haggar in the Dakhla Oasis represents one of the more complete monuments of the area.

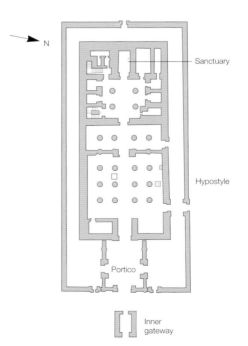

Sanctuary

Hypostyle

Portico

Inner gateway

The temple at Hibis is the largest and best-preserved temple of the Kharga Oasis, and also one of the finest examples of an Egyptian temple of the Persian period, though the outer elements were added in Graeco-Roman times.

235

km (62 miles) long and was inhabited from prehistoric times. Several ancient texts show that a temple of Amun-Re was built here in New Kingdom times, but nothing of this has been found. The known temples of the area all date to the Persian period and beyond.

Hibis – the Egyptian Hebet, 'the plough' – located just over 2 km (1.25 miles) to the north of the modern city of Kharga, is the site of the famous and well-preserved temple of Amun. Although the foundations may have been begun in the 25th dynasty, the walls were decorated by the Persian king Darius, who is usually credited with building them. The temple also received additions in the reign of Nectanebo II (the colonnade) and in Ptolemaic times. Many aspects of the temple's plan, construction and decoration are unusual. Built from the speckled local limestone, in ancient times a lake surrounded the temple, though this has now disappeared. A sphinx-lined approach leads through a series of gateways to a colonnade, peristyle court, hypostyle hall and sanctuary. As in many of the Graeco-Roman temples, the roof contains areas dedicated to Osiris, with scenes depicting the burial of the god. Many of the temple's representations are distinctive, not only for their rather bold style but also for a number of themes such as the catalogue of deities represented in the sanctuary, and in the hypostyle hall a winged figure of Seth overcoming the serpent Apophis, regarded by some art histori-

ans as a precursor of the motif of St George and the dragon. The temple was excavated and restored by New York's Metropolitan Museum of Art earlier this century but has suffered from a locally rising water table. The structure has recently undergone repairs by the Egyptian Antiquities Service and is currently scheduled for removal to another site. Its many graffiti (p. 47) have been studied by Eugene Cruz-Uribe.

To the south of Kharga, various other sites contain the remains of smaller temples. At Kom el-Nadura, about 2 km (1.25 miles) to the southeast of Hibis temple, on a fairly visible hill, are the scant remains of a stone temple of the Roman period

(Below) The hypostyle hall of Kharga's temple of Hibis contains a number of palm-capital columns of rather squat proportions.

(Below right) A relief from Hibis temple depicting lettuce being offered to the god Min – who was often venerated in desert and oasis shrines.

The temple of Amun at Hibis is approached through a series of gateways – including the inner gate of Darius I – which leads to the temple's portico and hypostyle hall.

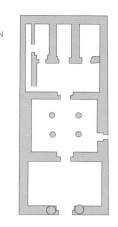

N

The temple of Amun, Mut and Khonsu at el-Ghueida.

(reign of Antoninus Pius) with outlying mud-brick structures. At Qasr el-Ghueida – some 25 km (15.5 miles) south of el-Kharga – there are moderately substantial remains of a temple dedicated to the Theban triad of Amun, Mut and Khonsu. The structure was perhaps begun in the 25th dynasty and received decoration from Darius I but was completed in Ptolemaic times. As with most of the temples in this area, the sanctuary is stone-built with surrounding areas of the temple being constructed of mud-brick. At Qasr Zaiyan (Greek Tchonemyris) – about 30 km (18.5 miles) south of el-Kharga – there is a temple of Amun from the Ptolemaic and Roman periods often attributed to Antoninus Pius. Much of the outer, mud-brick pylon with its stone gateway survives along with

The south entrance of the ruined temple of Nadura.

(Below) The temple of Amun at Qasr Zaiyan.

Notable for its supposed historical associations ('King Solomon's Mines') as well as its temple remains, this area to the north of the Gulf of Aqaba – about 25 km (15.5 miles) from Eilat – was the site of extensive Egyptian copper mining. In addition to an early Semitic sanctuary, a temple of Hathor was discovered here by Beno Rothenberg in 1969. Inscriptions covering a period of 150 years – from the reign of Sethos I to that of Ramesses V – show the height of the cult activity at the site. Thoroughly a product of its exotic desert environment, the temple contained a number of hybrid Egyptian and local features; and an impressive copper serpent with a gilded head was found in the fourth and last stratum of the temple remains.

(Above) The decorated exterior rear wall of the sanctuary, the temple of Qasr Douch in the el-Kharga basin.

The plan of the small temple of Qasr Douch: the outer walls are of mud-brick, the inner sanctuary is of stone.

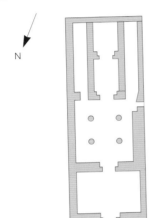

N

sections of the inner mud-brick walls and the stone sanctuary. At the southern end of the oasis – about 85 km (53 miles) south of el-Kharga – the area of Qasr Douch (the ancient Kysis) contains a temple of Serapis and Isis dated to the 19th year of Nerva Trajanus (AD 177). The partly decorated inner stone structure survives, along with sizeable sections of the outer, brick-built chambers and walls.

THE SINAI

Egyptian activity in the Sinai is known from Early Dynastic times, and the area was explored and worked for its mineral deposits, especially those of turquoise and copper, from the Old to the New Kingdoms. Although many sites with evidence of Egyptian presence are known, only a few temples were built here, the most important at Serabit el-Khadim. Apart from the major gods of the Egyptian pantheon, the most important deities honoured in these outpost temples were Hathor, 'Lady of Turquoise', long associated with the Sinai, and Sopdu, lord of the eastern desert.

(Above) A rock engraving depicting Ramesses III offering to Hathor at Timna.

(Above left) A faience votive mask of Hathor from Timna.

(Left) The Hathor temple at Timna, discovered by Beno Rothenberg in 1969, was constructed beneath an overhanging rock of cultic significance.

Serabit el-Khadim

Located inland from a point about half way down the western coast of the peninsula, about 10 km (6.25 miles) north of the Wadi Mughara, Serabit el-Khadim was the most important site of Egyptian activity in the Sinai and contained an unusual complex of sanctuaries and shrines. These were dedicated primarily to Hathor, patron goddess of the copper and turquoise miners. The earliest part of the main Hathor temple, which is rock-cut with a fronting court and portico, dates to the beginning of the 12th dynasty; and this core area was extended in the New Kingdom by Hatshepsut, Tuthmosis III and Amenophis III. The temple is particularly unusual in its plan and in the way it angles from its earliest, rock-cut niches and turns to the west into the curiously elongated building which makes up the later areas of the complex. On the north side of the temple is a shrine of the kings venerated in the locality, which was founded by Amenemhet III, and a wall containing numerous stelae. A smaller shrine dedicated to the god of the eastern desert, Sopdu, was built a little to the south of the Hathor temple. Flinders Petrie worked at the site of Serabit el-Khadim in 1905, and it was here that he found the 'proto-Sinaitic' script which is believed to be an early precursor of the alphabet.

The remains of the temple of Hathor at Serabit el-Khadim, the most important site of Egyptian activity in the Sìnai, with several of the temple's stelae which remain standing. Sopdu, the god of the eastern desert, and Thoth were also worshipped at this site, along with several deified kings.

The unusually elongated temple complex at Serabit el-Khadim was extended from its original rock-cut niches through a series of later structures.

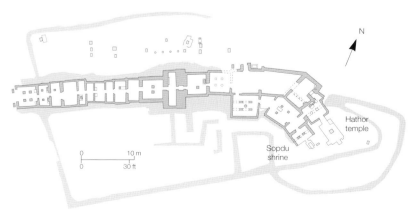

Hathor temple

Sopdu shrine

0   10 m
0   30 ft

N

Epilogue: Exploration and Conservation Today

Modern exploration

Despite the common perception that the glory days of Egyptian discovery are in the past, unrecognized or hidden temples continue to be discovered in Egypt (see for example Thoth Hill, p. 172 or Abydos, p. 144) and, perhaps more importantly, Egyptologists are continually discovering new things about the temples which have long stood in full view. Egypt has itself an increasing number of trained archaeological scholars now working in this area and, as with other monuments, the Egyptian government also allows and encourages international participation in the study and restoration of its ancient temples.

Organizations such as the Egypt Exploration Society continue to do excellent work in organizing and supporting research in Egypt and a number of universities and museums around the world sponsor field expeditions which regularly conduct research at Egyptian sites. The German Institute of Archaeology has done much work at temple sites such as Elephantine and Gurna, as has the Franco-Egyptian Mission at Karnak. In only the last few years the remains of the oldest known Egyptian temple have been explored at Hierakonpolis (p. 204), and completely unknown 'layers' of temples have been exposed at sites such as Elephantine (p. 211) and elsewhere. While excavation continues at many sites – and many more remain to be fully explored – an even more pressing need in many cases is that of full recording of the temple monuments. The University of Chicago's Oriental Institute – the oldest continuously running field expedition in the Middle East – provides an excellent example of this kind of

(Below) A Hungarian team excavate within the brick temple on Thoth Hill, Thebes.

(Above) Reconstruction work on the ninth pylon at Karnak by the Franco-Egyptian Mission.

ongoing research through its Egyptian headquarters, Chicago House, on the east bank of the Nile at Luxor. Since 1924, in addition to several tombs, Chicago House teams have documented large portions of Karnak Temple, Luxor Temple, and all the reliefs and inscriptions of the temple of Ramesses III at Medinet Habu. Recording any one of these temples is a gargantuan task, but the Oriental Institute's Epigraphic Survey has produced highly accurate drawings of the inscriptions and relief scenes on these temples through many years of patient effort. As a result of this research, numerous folio volumes have been published on temples of the Theban area.

The 'Chicago House method' of recording temple texts and representations consists of first taking a photograph of an area of wall or other feature that is being studied. An artist then draws, in pencil, the various details on to the photograph at the wall itself in order to eliminate accidental marks or damage. Later, the lines are retraced in ink and the photographic emulsion is bleached away leaving only the drawing. Finally, this carefully produced drawing is checked, by scholars, against the original surface. Other expeditions use somewhat different methods of tracing and recording the original images but all strive to meet the exacting standards necessary for the truly accurate recording of temple scenes.

While only one of the many academic and other institutions now conducting research and recording in Egypt's temples, the goals and methods of Chicago House show some of the concerns and methodologies of modern study of the ancient religious sites.

The re-erection of ancient columns on new bases, as well as other reconstruction work, has been accomplished at the Small Aten Temple at el-Amarna by a team led by British Egyptologist Barry Kemp. Here a column is being assembled from panels of glass-fibre reinforced concrete welded to an inner iron framework. The panels are casts taken from moulds based on fragments of ancient columns at the site.

The Epigraphic Survey

Epigraphic Survey of the Oriental Institute of the University of Chicago, Luxor, 1924–present:

Field Directors:

Harold H. Nelson (1924–1948)*
(with a gap 1940–1946, World War II – Chicago House closed)
Richard A. Parker (1948–1949)
George R. Hughes (1949–1958)
John A. Wilson (Acting, 1958/1959)
George R. Hughes (1959–1964)
Charles F. Nims (1964–1972)
Edward F. Wente (1972/1973)
Kent R. Weeks (1973–1976)
Charles C. Van Siclen, III (Acting, 1976/1977)
Lanny D. Bell (1977–1989)
Peter F. Dorman (1989–1997)
W. Raymond Johnson, Jr. (1997–current)

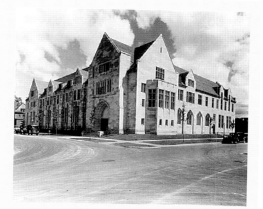

The Oriental Institute of the University of Chicago, home base of the Epigraphic Survey.

* Also Architectural Survey of the Oriental Institute in Luxor: Field Director: Uvo Holscher (1927–1933)

Egyptian Temples Abroad

In acknowledgment of the help given to UNESCO by various nations in dismantling and moving many of
the temples of Nubia to preserve them from the rising waters created by the Aswan High Dam, the Egyptian
government graciously presented a number of the smaller Nubian temples to other countries.

Temple	Element	New Site	City	Country
Debod	temple	City Park	Madrid	Spain
Dendur	temple	Metropolitan Museum of Art	New York	USA
el-Lessiya	rock-cut temple	Museo Egizio	Turin	Italy
Kalabsha	gateway	Ägyptisches Museum	Berlin	Germany
Taffa	temple	Rijksmuseum van Oudheden	Leiden	Netherlands

Restoration and conservation

Given the vast number of temples existing throughout Egypt in various degrees of preservation, the
conservation of these monuments may be seen as
an urgent though almost impossibly large task.
Many temples survive only partially and many of
those that have survived are being destroyed
through human encroachment, rising water tables,
air pollution and many other aspects of modern civilization. Accurate recording of existing temples –
as described above – is a vital step towards conservation, but in many cases physical restoration,
strengthening and even relocation is necessary to
protect the fragile heritage of the ancient monuments. The Egyptian government has committed
resources to this task, but it is bigger than can real-
istically be handled by one nation and has become a
matter of international involvement.

The relocation of Egyptian temples at the time
of the construction of the High Dam at Aswan in
the 1960s is a prime example of this. Dams had
been built to span the Nile beginning as early
as 1898, but the High Dam, due to its size and
location, threatened to submerge many of the
ancient temples of southern Egypt forever. Many
were saved by a massive campaign mounted by the
United Nations in 1960. A number of monuments,
such as the temples of Abu Simbel and Kalabsha,
were dismantled through the efforts of UNESCO
and reassembled on new sites beyond the final
reach of the rising waters of Lake Nasser. Other,
smaller temples were dismantled and transported
much further distances to foreign countries as gifts
from the Egyptian government.

Conservation of temples *in situ* is not always a
simple matter to achieve, however. For a number of
years the temple at Hibis in the Kharga Oasis, for
example, has been earmarked to be dismantled and
moved to a nearby site on higher ground in order to
protect the structure from the rising ground water
that is destroying its foundation. Unfortunately,
although the deterioration of the temple was first
noticed some 40 years ago, efforts to correct the
problem have so far been unsuccessful or simply
unemployed.

The work of conservation and restoration also
goes far beyond the moving of standing temple
structures, however. Sandstone blocks discovered
in 1923 at the site of ancient Coptos (p. 151) by the
archaeologist Dows Dunham working for the
Museum of Fine Arts, Boston, were given to the
museum by Egypt and were displayed until 1995 in
two sections as part of a wall and a gateway. In the
last few years, the blocks were recognized by Egyptologists Nancy Thomas and Diana Wolfe Larkin to
be part of a single structure and have now been
reassembled as a partially complete gateway 5.2 m
(17 ft) high and weighing 24 tons. After the removal
of embedded dirt and grime, much of the original
paint, and even gold leaf, has come to light; and the
reconstructed temple gateway is now the second
largest Egyptian structure in the United States,
after the temple of Dendur in the Metropolitan
Museum of Art in New York.

In the case of some ancient temples, there is very
little that remains to be restored. At many sites,
hardly anything above ground level has survived
where almost all the fine stonework was robbed for
use in later building elsewhere and much of the
mud brickwork was dug away for fertilizer for the
fields. But even in such cases seemingly impossible
things can be done. At el-Amarna, for example,
where just this situation prevails in the temples of
the heretic king Akhenaten, Barry Kemp is currently rebuilding, in modern materials, and as
accurately as possible, some of the features of the
ancient structures.

Both at el-Amarna and at Saqqara, where
Franco–Egyptian teams have long worked at the
reconstruction of nearly destroyed buildings, and
in many other areas in Egypt, modern reconstruction is one way in which the ancient religious sites
can be made to live again. But these efforts are
hardly for esoteric or sentimental reasons – the
story of the Egyptian temple is one which has been
considerably enriched and illuminated by ongoing
conservation and reconstruction as well as discovery and research. Inevitably, it is as we conserve the
temples of Egypt that we come to understand them
better.

*(Opposite) Small stone talatat
blocks from the dismantled
temples of Akhenaten were
packed within the cores of
pylons constructed by later
Egyptian kings at the Great
Temple of Amun at Karnak.
Here,* talatat *are seen prior
to removal from Karnak's
ninth pylon.*

Visiting the Temples

While it is beyond the scope of this small section to suggest detailed itineraries or choices among Egypt's many hundreds of temple sites, some general recommendations can be made in terms of key sites and preparing to visit them.

Key sites

The temples of Egypt's very earliest historical periods are, without exception, no longer standing and most of these structures are now covered over or confined within controlled archaeological sites with little to see. It is with the Old Kingdom monuments that temples first become accessible to the visitor, though these structures are mainly limited to the pyramid complexes of Middle Egypt. For the Middle Kingdom it is more difficult to find viewable remains of standing structures, though the reconstructed barque shrine of Senwosret I at Karnak provides an accessible example of some of the exquisite stone carving produced in this period.

With the New Kingdom the situation changes, and several of the finest temples from this period have survived in relatively intact condition, though none is complete. Most cluster in the area of ancient Thebes – modern Luxor – and many of these monuments provide superlative examples of the developed temple form. On the east bank, Luxor Temple, while anomalous in certain respects, is relatively well preserved and provides a manageable introduction before attempting the vast Amun temple of Karnak. Karnak itself requires years to explore all of its vastness, but its sheer size shows something of the power of this and other large temple institutions. On the Theban west bank the New Kingdom royal mortuary temple is represented by over a dozen examples in various states of preservation. While the terraced temple of Hatshepsut at Deir el-Bahri best represents the rock-cut type of structure, the mortuary temple of Ramesses III at Medinet Habu provides a near complete example of the free-standing temple which may be compared with the remaining mortuary structures of Ramesses II (the Ramesseum) and the less visited temple of Sethos I.

In areas other than Thebes, the cenotaph of Sethos I at Abydos represents one of the finest New Kingdom mortuary temples in Egypt; and the temples of Abu Simbel are the most impressive of the rock-cut type. The temples of the Late Period have not generally survived, though that of Hibis, if somewhat off the regular tourist routes, provides a relatively complete example from that era. From the Graeco-Roman Period a good many temples survive; and those of Edfu, Kom Ombo, Philae and Dendera are all fine examples of the later temple style.

Outside the Nile Valley, the temples of most of the western oases are relatively accessible, though many involve considerable drives through long stretches of desert. Beyond the borders of Egypt proper, the temples of Nubia – while not inexpensive to visit – are now easier to see than in the past.

Apart from Abu Simbel, which has regularly scheduled air flights from Cairo and Luxor, the temples of Lower Nubia may now be seen by way of boat cruises which circle Lake Nasser, stopping at the sites where most of the relocated temples of the area are now situated.

Planning ahead

In attempting to come to understand Egyptian temples through actual visits, it is important to remember that temples of the same period are often very different in plan and in their state of preservation, so that preparation of a limited itinerary needs to be done in conjunction with study of a book such as the present one in order to balance temple types and remaining features. For example, the pylons and outer courts of the mortuary temple of Ramesses III at Medinet Habu are very well preserved, though the inner halls and sanctuary areas have not fared so well. This is the opposite of the situation in the temple of Sethos I at Abydos where the outer pylons and courts are destroyed but the inner temple stands in quite magnificent condition. Only by visiting both sites or similar ones can a real sense of the appearance of the New Kingdom mortuary temple be achieved.

It is usually advantageous – especially if visiting monuments for the first time – to study their plans and read a basic description of their features ahead of any visit, as many temples are quite maze-like and it is easy to miss important areas. It also helps to plan to visit sites according to the light – not just for the purposes of photography, but also to get the best views of the monuments and their decorations. Usually the best light for viewing temple walls with outside exposures is that of early morning or late afternoon when angled light and soft shadows place texts and representations in clear relief.

Tickets may be purchased at the entrances of most major temples (photography usually requires an extra pass), but those for monuments in remote areas often have to be purchased ahead at the nearest major site or antiquities office. Some sites also need special government permissions or escorts in order to visit them, and it is usually a good idea to inform others as to one's destination and expected time of return when visiting the more remote temples in desert areas.

Equipment

Beyond the requisite wide-brimmed hat, water bottle, and usual travel and touring equipment, good maps or knowledgeable local guides are needed in order to get to some of the more remote temples away from the regular tourist routes. Tickets must also often be obtained in advance as mentioned above.

Visits to such sites should not be made without ample water and other basic supplies, depending on the location involved. There are many times when a flashlight is extremely valuable both for use in darkened passages and chambers and in adding light to deeply shadowed areas of wall decoration – which can be difficult to see or photograph when they are close to brightly lit areas. For detailed study, small, lightweight binoculars can also be useful in looking at texts and representations high on the walls of larger temples and for scanning distant structures.

For photography a wide range of films is often needed – 100, 400, and 800 or 1000 ISO speeds may all be used in photographing a single temple. A range of lenses – or a wide-ranging zoom lens – is also useful as most temples present everything from finely detailed closeups to wide panoramic views. Polarizing and other filters are often especially valuable in controlling the large amount of reflected light found in association with outer wall surfaces.

(Below) Modern visitors to the temple of Karnak.

245

Further Reading

Abbreviations

AAWLM *Abhandlungen der Akademie der Wissenschaften und der Literatur in Mainz*
ÄAT *Ägypten und Altes Testament*
ÄF *Äyptologisches Forschungen*
AH *Aegyptiaca Helvetica*
ASAE *Annales du Service des Antiquités de l'Égypte*
BdÉ *Bibliothèque d'Étude*
BIFAO *Bulletin de l'Institut français d'archéologie orientale*
BRL *Bulletin of the John Rylands Library*
BSFE *Bulletin de la Société Française d'Égyptologie*
CdÉ *Chronique d'Égypte*
EES *Egypt Exploration Society*
GM *Göttinger Miszellen*
HÄB *Hildesheimer ägyptologische Beiträge*
JARCE *Journal of the American Research Center in Egypt*
JEA *Journal of Egyptian Archaeology*
JNES *Journal of Near Eastern Studies*
JSSEA *Journal of the Society for the Study of Egyptian Antiquities*
KMT *KMT: A Modern Journal of Ancient Egypt*
LÄ Helck, W. and E. Otto (eds), *Lexikon der Ägyptologie* (Wiesbaden, 1975–)
MAS *Münchner Ägyptologische Studien*
MDAIK *Mitteilungen des Deutschen Archäologischen Instituts, Abteilung Kairo*
NARCE *Newsletter of the American Research Center in Egypt*
NAWG *Nachrichten von der Akademie der Wissenschaften zu Göttingen*
OIP *Oriental Institute Publications (Chicago)*
OLA *Orientalia Lovaniensia Analecta*
OLP *Orientalia Lovaniensia Periodica*
PÄ *Probleme der Ägyptologie*
PMMA *Publications of the Metropolitan Museum of Art Egyptian Expedition*
RAIN *Royal Anthropological Institute News*
SAK *Studien zur altägyptischen Kultur*
SO *Studia Orientalia*
ZÄS *Zeitschrift fur Ägyptische Sprache und Altertumskunde*

INTRODUCTION

Chronology

Dates used throughout the book mainly follow the chronological table from: Baines, J. and J. Málek, *Atlas of Ancient Egypt* (Oxford and New York, 1980), 36–7.

Temple, Land and Cosmos

Arnold, D., *Die Tempel Ägyptens: Götterwohnungen Kultstätten, Baudenkmäler* (Zürich, 1992)
Quirke, S. (ed.), *The Temple in Ancient Egypt: New Discoveries and Recent Research* (London, 1997)
Shafer, B. (ed.), *Temples of Ancient Egypt* (Ithaca, 1997)
Snape, S., *Egyptian Temples* (Princes Risborough, 1996)
Spencer, P., *The Egyptian Temple: A Lexicographical Study* (London, 1984)

I HOUSES OF ETERNITY

Temple Origins

Adams, B. and K. Cialowicz, *Protodynastic Egypt* (Princes Risborough, 1997)
Brinks, J., *Die Entwicklung der königlichen Grabanlagen des Alten Reiches. Eine strukturelle und historische Analyse altägyptischer Architektur*, HÄB 10 (Hildesheim, 1979)
Fairservis, W.A., *The Hierakonpolis Project. Season January to March 1978. Excavation of the Temple Area on the Kom el Gemuwia* (Poughkeepsie, 1983)
Hoffman, M.A., *Egypt Before the Pharaohs: The Prehistoric Foundations of Egyptian Civilization* (Austin, 1979)
Holmes, D.L., 'Chipped Stone-Working Craftsmen, Hierakonpolis and the Rise of Civilization in Egypt'. In R. Friedman and B. Adams (eds), *The Followers of Horus: Studies Dedicated to Michael Allen Hoffman* (Oxford, 1992), pp. 37–44
Kemp, B., *Ancient Egypt: Anatomy of a Civilization* (London and New York, 1989)
O'Connor, D., 'The Status of Early Egyptian Temples: An Alternate Theory'. In R. Friedman and B. Adams (eds), *The Followers of Horus: Studies Dedicated to Michael Allen Hoffman* (Oxford, 1992), pp. 83–98
Williams, B., 'Narmer and the Coptos Colossi', *JARCE* 25 (1988), pp. 35–59

Old and Middle Kingdom Development

(See individual temple entries in Part V)
Arnold, D., 'Totentempel II', *LÄ* VI (1985), c. 699–706
Goedicke, H., 'Cult-Temple and "State" during the Old Kingdom in Egypt'. In E. Lipinski (ed.), *State and Temple Economy in the Ancient Near East*, vol. 1 (Leuven, 1978), pp. 113–31
Lehner, M., *The Complete Pyramids* (London and New York, 1997)
Stadelmann, R., 'Taltempel', *LÄ* VI (1985), c. 189–94
—'Totentempel I', *LÄ* VI (1985), c. 694–9

New Kingdom Temples

(See individual temple entries in Part V)
Arnold, D., *Wandbild und Raumfunktion in ägyptischen Tempeln des Neuen Reiches* (Berlin, 1962)
Barguet, P., *Le Temple d'Amon Ré à Karnak. Essai d'exégèse* (Cairo, 1962)
Bell, L., 'Luxor Temple and the Cult of the Royal ka', *JNES* 44:4 (1985), pp. 251–94
Brand, P., *The Monuments of Seti I and their Historical Significance: Epigraphic, Art Historical and Historical Analysis*, Ph.D. Dissertation (Toronto, 1998)
Murnane, W.J., *United with Eternity: A Concise Guide to the Monuments of Medinet Habu* (Chicago and Cairo, 1980)
Mysliwiec, K., *Eighteenth Dynasty Before the Amarna Period* (Iconography of Religions, 16: Egypt, 5) (Leiden, 1985)
Stadelmann, R., 'Totentempel III', *LÄ* VI (1985), c. 706–11

A Glorious Decline

(See also individual temple entries in Part V)
Arnold, D., *Temples of the Lost Pharaohs* (Oxford, 1999)
Ball, J., *Egypt in the Classical Geographers* (Cairo, 1942)
Bell, H.I., *Cults and Creeds in Graeco-Roman Egypt* (New York, 1953; repr., Chicago, 1975)
Dunand, F., 'Les syncrétismes dans la religion de l'Égypte romaine'. In F. Dunand and P. Lévêque, *Les syncrétismes dans les religions de l'antiquité* (Leiden, 1975), pp. 152–85
Evans, J.A.S., 'A Social and Economic History of an Egyptian Temple in the Graeco-Roman Period', *Yale Classical Studies*, No. 17 (New Haven, 1961), pp. 149–283
Kákosy, L., 'Temples and Funerary Beliefs in the Graeco-Roman Egypt'. In *L'Égyptologie en 1979*, 1 (1982), pp. 117–27
Winter, E., *Untersuchungen zu den ägyptischen Tempelreliefs der griechisch-römischen Zeit* (Vienna, 1968)

The Christian and Islamic Periods

Bernard, Y., 'L'Égypte: d'Amon à Allah', *Archéologia* 214 (1986), pp. 60–7
Brandon, S.G.F., 'The Life-Giving Significance of Lustration in the Osirian Mortuary Ritual and in Primitive Christian Baptism'. In *Proceedings of the XIth International Congress of the International Association for the History of Religions, 2: Guilt or Pollution and Rites of Purification* (Leiden, 1968), pp. 52–3
Griggs, C.W., *Early Egyptian Christianity: From its Origins to 451 C.E.* (Coptic Studies, 2) (Leiden, 1991)
Leclant, J., 'Histoire de la diffusion des cultes égyptiens', *Annuaire, École Pratique des Hautes Études, V section: Sciences religieuses* 84 (1975–76)

Early Travellers and Modern Rediscovery

Clayton, P., *The Rediscovery of Ancient Egypt* (London and New York, 1982)
David, R., *Discovering Ancient Egypt* (New York, 1993)
Dawson, W.R., E. Uphill and M.L. Bierbrier, *Who Was Who in Egyptology* (London, 3rd ed., 1995)
Fagan, B.M., *The Rape of the Nile* (New York, 1975)
Greener, L., *The Discovery of Egypt* (New York, 1966)
James, T.G.H. (ed.), *Excavating in Egypt: The Egypt Exploration Society 1882–1982* (Chicago, 1982)
Jomard, E.F., *Description de l'Égypte* (Paris, 1809–28)
Kaiser, W., *75 Jahre Deutsches Archäologisches Institut Kairo 1907–1982* (Mainz, 1982)
Sievernich, G. and H. Budde, *Europa und der*

Orient: 800–1900 (Berlin, 1989)
Thomas, N., *The American Discovery of Ancient Egypt* (Los Angeles, 1996)

II BUILDINGS FIT FOR GODS

Selecting the Sacred Space
Posener, G., 'Sur l'orientation et l'ordre des points cardinaux chez les Égyptiens', *NAWG* 2 (1965), pp. 69–78
Vittmann, G., 'Orientierung', *LÄ* IV (1982), c. 607–9
Vörös, G. and R. Pudleiner, 'Preliminary Report of the Excavations at Thoth Hill, Thebes: The pre-11th dynasty temple and the western building (season 1996–1997)', *MDAIK* 54 (1998), pp. 335–40
Wells, R., 'Sothis and the Satet Temple on Elephantine: A Direct Connection', *SAK* 12 (1985), pp. 255–302
Žába, Z., *L'Orientation Astronomique dans l'Ancienne Égypte, et la Précession de l'Axe du Monde* (Prague, 1953)

Rituals of Foundation
Blackman, A.M. and H.W. Fairman, 'The Consecration of an Egyptian Temple according to the Use of Edfu', *JEA* 32 (1947), pp. 75–91
Engelbach, R., 'A Foundation Scene of the Second Dynasty', *JEA* 20 (1934), pp. 183–4
Helck, W., 'Tempelbenennungen', *LÄ* VI (1986), c. 363–5
Montet, P., 'Le rituel de fondation des temples', *Comptes-Rendus de l'Academie des Inscriptions et Belles-Lettres* (1960), pp. 172–9
Weinstein, J., *Foundation Deposits in Ancient Egypt* (Ann Arbor, 1973)
Zibelius-Chen, K., 'Tempelgründung', *LÄ* VI (1986), c. 385–6

Building Techniques
Arnold, D., *Building in Egypt: Pharaonic Stone Masonry* (New York and Oxford, 1991)
—*Lexikon der ägyptischen Baukunst* (Munich, 1994)
Clarke, S. and R. Engelbach, *Ancient Egyptian Construction and Architecture* (London, 1930)
Klemm, D. and R., *Steine der Pharaonen* (Munich, 1981)
Lucas, A. and J.R. Harris, *Ancient Egyptian Materials and Industries* (London, 4th. ed., 1962)
Said, R., *The Geology of Egypt* (Brookfield, VT, 1990)
Spencer, A.J., *Brick Architecture in Ancient Egypt* (Warminster, 1979)

Decorating the 'God's House'
Arnold, D., *Wandbild und Raumfunktion in ägyptischen Tempeln des Neuen Reiches* (Berlin, 1962)
Gundlach, R., 'Tempelrelief', *LÄ* VI (1986), c. 407–11
Jaksch, H., *Farbpigmente aus Wandmalereien altägyptischer Gräber und Tempel*, Univ. dissertation (Heidelberg, 1985)
Kurth, D. (ed.), *Ägyptologische Tempeltagung Systeme und Programme der ägyptischen Tempeldekoration* (ÄAT 33.1) (Wiesbaden, 1995)
Mysliwiec, K., *Eighteenth Dynasty Before the Amarna Period* (Iconography of Religions, 16: Egypt, 5) (Leiden, 1985)

Niwinski, A., 'Untersuchungen zur ägyptischen religiösen Ikonographie der 21. Dynastie, 1: Towards the Religious Iconography of the 21st Dynasty', *GM* 49 (1981), pp. 47–59
Wilkinson, R., 'The Turned Bow in Egyptian Iconography', *Varia Aegyptiaca* 4:2 (1988), pp. 181–7
—'The Turned Bow as a Gesture of Surrender in Egyptian Art', *JSSEA* XVII:3 (1991), pp. 128–33
Winter, E., *Untersuchungen zu den ägyptischen Tempelreliefs der griechisch-romischen Zeit* (Vienna, 1968)

Graffiti
Edgerton, W.F., *Medinet Habu Graffiti Facsimiles* (OIP 36) (Chicago, 1937)
Thissen, H. J., 'Graffiti', *LÄ* II (1977), c. 880–2

Growth, Enhancement and Change
Andrews, C.A.R., 'Some Temple Accounts (P.BM 10225)'. In C. Eyre (ed.) *The Unbroken Reed: Studies in Honour of A.F. Shore* (EES Occasional Publications, 11) (London, 1994), pp. 25–34
Bleiberg, E., 'The Redistributive Economy in New Kingdom Egypt: An Examination of *b3kw(t)*', *JARCE* 25 (1988), pp. 157–68
Epigraphic Survey, *The Temple of Khonsu, 1: Scenes of King Herihor in the Court* (Chicago, 1979)
Evans, J.A.S., 'A Social and Economic History of an Egyptian Temple in the Graeco-Roman Period', *Yale Classical Studies*, No. 17 (New Haven, 1961), pp. 149–283
Haring, B.J.J., *Divine Households: Administrative and Economic Aspects of the New Kingdom Royal Memorial Temples in Western Thebes* (Leiden, 1997)
Helck, W., 'Tempelwirtschaft', *LÄ* VI (1986), c. 414–20
—'Usurpator', 'Usurpierung', *LÄ* VI (1986), c. 904–05, 905–06
Spalinger, A., 'Some Revisions of Temple Endowments in the New Kingdom', *JARCE* 28 (1991), pp. 21–40

III WORLDS WITHIN WORLDS

General
Gundlach, R. and M. Rochholz (eds), *Ägyptische Tempel-Struktur, Funktion und Programm* (HÄB 37) (Hildesheim, 1994)
Helck, W., 'Tempeldarstellungen', *LÄ* VI (1986), c. 377–9
Spencer, P., *The Egyptian Temple: A Lexicographical Study* (London, 1984)

The Temple Entrance
Coche-Zivie, C.M., 'Sphinx', *LÄ* V (1984), c. 1139–47
Derchin, P., 'Réflexions sur la décoration des pylônes', *BSFE* 46 (1966), p. 17ff.
Habachi, L., *The Obelisks of Egypt* (Cairo, 1984)
Spencer, A.J., *Brick Architecture in Ancient Egypt* (Warminster, 1979)

The Outer Courts
Arnold, D., *Die Tempel Ägyptens: Gotterwohnungen Kultstätten, Baudenkmäler* (Zürich, 1992)
— 'Tempelarchitektur', *LÄ* VI (1986), c. 359–63
El-Saghir, M., *The Discovery of the Statuary Cachette of Luxor Temple* (Mainz, 1991)

Gundlach, R. and M. Rochholz, *Ägyptische Tempel: Struktur, Funktion und Programm* (HÄB 37) (Hildesheim, 1994)
Jarosi, P. and D. Arnold, 'Säule', *LÄ* V (1984), c. 343–8

The Inner Halls and Sanctuaries
Arnold, D., *Wandbild und Raumfunktion in ägyptischen Tempeln des Neuen Reiches* (Berlin, 1962)
—'Hypostyle Halls of the Old and Middle Kingdoms'. In P. der Manuelian and R. Freed (eds), *Studies in Honour of William Kelly Simpson*, 2 vols (Boston, 1996), pp. 39–54
—'Kapitell', *LÄ* III (1980), c. 323–7
Grothoff, T., *Die Tornamen der ägyptischen Tempel* (Aachen, 1996)
Jarosi, P, and D. Arnold, 'Säule', *LÄ* V (1984), c. 343–8
Müller, M., 'Schrein', *LÄ* V (1984), c. 709–12

Other Temple Structures
Daumas, F., *Les mammisis des temples égyptiens* (Annales de l'Université de Lyon, 3ieme série, 32) (Paris, 1958)
—'Geburtshaus', *LÄ* II (1977), c. 462–75
Ghalioungui, P., *The House of Life, Per Ankh* (Amsterdam, 1973)
Gessler-Lohr, B., *Die heiligen Seen ägyptischer Tempel* (HÄB 21) (Hildesheim, 1983)
Jaritz, H., 'Nilmesser', *LÄ* IV (1982), c. 496–8
Philips, A.K., 'Observation on the Alleged New Kingdom Sanatorium at Deir el-Bahari', *GM* 89 (1986), pp. 77–83

Temple Symbolism
Allen, J.P., *Genesis in Egypt: The Philosophy of Ancient Egyptian Creation Accounts*, Yale Egyptological Studies 2 (New Haven, 1988)
Baines, J., '*Bnbn*: Mythological and Linguistic Notes', *Orientalia* 39 (1970), pp. 399–404
—'Temple Symbolism', *RAIN* 15 (1976), pp. 3, 10–15
Brovarski, E., 'The Doors of Heaven', *Orientalia* 46 (1977), pp. 107–15
Brunner, H., 'Die Sonnenbahn in ägyptischen Tempeln'. In *Archäologie und Altes Testament: Festschrift fur Kurt Galling* (Tubingen, 1970), pp. 27–34
Graefe, E., 'Der Sonnenaufgang zwischen den Pylonturmen', *OLP* 14 (1983), pp. 55–79
Hoffmeier, J.K., 'The Use of Basalt in Floors of Old Kingdom Pyramid Temples', *JARCE* XXX (1993), pp. 117–24
Hornung, E., *Idea into Image* (New York, 1992)
Reymond, E.A.E., *The Mythical Origin of the Egyptian Temple* (Manchester, 1969)
Ringgren, H., 'Light and Darkness in ancient Egyptian Religion'. In *Liber Amicorum: Studies in honor of C.J. Bleeker* (Leiden, 1969), pp. 140–50
Saleh, A.A., 'The So-called "Primeval Hill" and Other Related Elevations in Ancient Egyptian Mythology', *MDAIK* 25 (1969), pp. 110–20
Wilkinson, R.H., *Symbol and Magic in Egyptian Art* (London and New York, 1994)
— 'Symbolism', *The Oxford Encyclopedia of Ancient Egypt* (Oxford, 2000)

IV BETWEEN HEAVEN AND EARTH

The Egyptian Gods and their Cults
There is a vast literature in this area. All that can be done here is to mention some general works and a few which relate to specific issues covered in the text.

Assmann, J., *Egyptian Solar Religion in the New Kingdom: Re, Amun and the Crisis of Polytheism* (Tr. A. Alcock, London, 1994)

Baines, J., "'Greatest God' or Category of Gods?', *GM* (1983), pp. 13–28

Cerny, J., *Ancient Egyptian Religion* (Westport, CT, 1979)

David, R., *A Guide to the Religious Ritual at Abydos* (Warminster, 1981)

Giveon, R., 'New Material Concerning Canaanite Gods in Egypt'. In *Proceedings of the Ninth World Congress of Jewish Studies, Jerusalem, 1985* (Jerusalem, 1986), pp. 1–4

Goedicke, H., 'God', *JSSEA* 16 (1986), pp. 57–62

Hart, G., *A Dictionary of Egyptian Gods and Goddesses* (London, 1986)

Hoffmeier, J.K., *Sacred in the Vocabulary of Ancient Egypt: The term dsr, with special reference to Dynasties I–XX* (Göttingen, 1985)

Hornung, E., *Conceptions of God in Ancient Egypt: The One and the Many* (Tr. J. Baines, Ithaca, 1982; London, 1983)

Morenz, S., *Egyptian Religion* (Tr. A.E. Keep, London and Ithaca, 1973)

Mysliwiec, K., 'Amon, Atun and Aton: The Evolution of Heliopolitan Influences in Thebes'. In *L'Egyptologie in 1979, 2: Axes priorities de recherches* (Cairo, 1983), pp. 285–9

Quirke, S., *Ancient Egyptian Religion* (London, 1992)

Redford, D.B., 'The Sun-Disc in Akhenaten's Program: Its Worship and Antecedents', *JARCE* 13 (1976), pp. 47–61

Shorter, A.W., *Egyptian Gods: A Handbook* (Boston, 1981)

Silverman, D.P., 'Divinity and Deities in Ancient Egypt'. In B.E. Shafer (ed.), *Religion in Ancient Egypt: Gods, Myths, and Personal Practice* (Ithaca and London, 1991)

te Velde, H., 'Some Remarks on the Structure of Egyptian Divine Triads', *JEA* 57 (1971), pp. 80–6

Watterson, B., *The Gods of Ancient Egypt* (London, 1984; repr. Gloucestershire, 1996)

The Role of the King
Assmann, J., *Der König als Sonnenpriester: Kosmographischer Begeisttext zur kulttischen Sonnenhymnik in thebanischen Tempeln und Gräben* (MDAIK, Ägyptologische Reihe, 7) (Glückstadt, 1970)

Barta, W., *Aufbau und Bedeutung der altägyptischen Opferformel* (ÄF, 24) (Glückstadt, 1968)

Bell, L., *Mythology and Iconography of Divine Kingship in Ancient Egypt* (Chicago, 1994)

Frankfort, H., *Kingship and the Gods* (Chicago, 1978)

Hoffmeier, J.K. 'The King as God's Son in Egypt and Israel', *JSSEA* XXIV (1994), pp. 23–38

Posener, G., *De la divinité du pharaon* (Paris, 1960)

Quaegebeur, J. (ed.), *Ritual and Sacrifice in the Ancient Near East* (Leuven, 1993)

Spiegelberg, W., *Der demotische Text der Priesterdekrete von Kanopus und Memphis (Rosettana) mit den hieroglyphischen und griechischen Fassungen und deutscher Übersetzung* (Heidelberg, 1922; repr. 1990)

Teeter, E., *The Presentation of Maat: The Iconography and Theology of an Ancient Egyptian Offering Ritual* (Chicago, 1990)

Wildung, D., *Ni-user-Ré Sonnenkönig – Sonnengott* (Munich, 1984)

Priests and Temple Personnel
Another area for which there exists a copious literature. The following represents only a small selection of general works and selected detailed studies.

Altenmüller-Kesting, B., *Reinigungsriten im ägyptischen Kult* (Hamburg, 1968)

Blackman, A.M., *Gods, Priests and Men: Studies in the Religion of Pharaonic Egypt* (London, 1992; 2nd ed. London, 1995)

Brovarski, E., 'Tempelpersonal I', *LÄ* VI (1986), c. 387–401

Bryan, B.M., 'Non-royal women's titles in the 18th Dynasty', *NARCE* (1984)

Fisher, H.G., 'Priesterin', *LÄ* IV (Wiesbaden, 1982), c. 1100–5

Galvin, M., *Priestesses of Hathor in the Old Kingdom and the 1st Intermediate Period* (Ann Arbor, 1981)

—'The Hereditary Status of the Titles of the Cult of Hathor', *JEA* 70 (1984), pp. 42–9

Johnson, J., 'The Role of the Egyptian Priesthood in Ptolemaic Egypt'. In L.H. Lesko (ed.) *Egyptological Studies in Honour of Richard A. Parker* (Hanover, NH, 1986), pp. 70–84

Kees, H., *Die Hohenpriester des Amun von Karnak von Herihor bis zum Ende der Äthiopenzeit* (PÄ, 4) (Leiden, 1964)

Lesko, B.S. (ed.), *Women's Earliest Records from Ancient Egypt and Western Asia* (Atlanta, 1989)

Martin-Pardey, E., 'Tempelpersonal II', *LÄ* VI (1986), c. 401–7

Moursi, Mohamed I., *Die Hohenpriester des Sonnengottes von der Frühzeit Ägyptens bis zum Ende des Neuen Reiches* (MÄS 26) (Munich, 1972)

Naguib, S.-A., *Le Clerge féminin d'Amon Thebain à la 21e Dynastie* (Leuven, 1990)

Robins, G., 'The god's wife of Amun in the 18th dynasty in Egypt'. In A. Cameron and A. Kuhrt (eds), *Images of Women in Antiquity* (London and Canberra, 1983), pp. 65–78

—*Women in Ancient Egypt* (London and Cambridge, MA, 1993)

Sauneron, S., *The Priests of Ancient Egypt* (New York, 1960)

Ward, W.A., *Essays on Feminine Titles of the Middle Kingdom and Related Subjects* (Beirut, 1986)

Temple Feasts and Festivals
Altenmüller, H., 'Feste', *LÄ* II (1977), c. 171–91

Assmann, J., *Ägyptische Hymnen und Gebete* (Bibliothek der Alten Welt: Der Alte Orient) (Zurich and Munich, 1975)

Blackman, A. M., 'The Significance of Incense and Libations', *ZÄS* 50 (1912), pp. 69–75

Bleeker, C.J., *Egyptian Festivals: Enactments of Religious Renewal* (Studies in the History of

Religions, Supplements to Numen, XIII) (Leiden, 1967)

Dittmar, J., *Blumen und Blumensträusse als Opfergabe im alten Ägypten* (MÄS, 43) (Munich, 1986)

Grimm, A., *Die altägyptischen Festkalender in den Tempeln der griechisch-römischen Epoche* (ÄAT, 15) (Wiesbaden, 1994)

Husson, C., *L'Offrande du miroir dans les temples égyptiens d'époque gréco-romaine* (Lyon, 1977)

Poo, M.-C., *Wine and Wine Offerings in the Religion of Ancient Egypt* (London, 1995)

Radwan, A., 'The 'nh-Vessel and its Ritual Function'. In *Fs Mokhtar* 2 (Cairo, 1985), pp. 211–17

Ryhiner, M.-L., *L'offrande du Lotus dans les temples égyptiens de l'époque tardive* (Rites égyptiens, 6) (Brussels, 1986)

—*Altägyptische Festdaten* (AAWLM, 10) (Wiesbaden, 1950)

Schott, S., *Das schöne Fest vom Wüstentale: Festbräuche einer Totenstadt* (AAWLM, 11) (Wiesbaden, 1953)

— *Ritual und Mythe im altägyptischen Kult* (Studium Generale, 8) (Berlin,1955)

Smith, G.E., 'Incense and Libations', *BRL* 4 (1921), pp. 191–262

Wiebach, S., 'Die Begegnung von Lebenden und Verstorbenen im Rahmen der thebanischen Talfestes', *SAK* 13 (1986), pp. 263–91

Wild, R.A., *Water in the Cultic Worship of Isis and Sarapis* (Études preliminaires aux religions orientales dans l'empire romain, 87) (Leiden, 1981)

Yeivin, S., 'Canaanite Ritual Vessels in Egyptian Cultic Practices', *JEA* 62 (1976), pp. 110–14.

The Role of the Common People in Worship
Baines, J., 'Practical Religion and Piety', *JEA* 73 (1987), pp. 79–98

—'Society, Morality and Religious Practice'. In B.E. Shafer (ed.), *Religion in Ancient Egypt: Gods, Myths, and Personal Practice* (Ithaca, 1991)

Pinch, G., *Votive Offerings to Hathor* (Oxford, 1993)

V TEMPLES OF GODS AND KINGS

It is impossible to give here even a representative bibliography for all the hundreds of individual temples throughout Egypt. The reader is referred for each geographic area to the relevant section of B. Porter and R.L.B. Moss, *Topographical Bibliography of Ancient Egyptian Hieroglyphical Texts, Reliefs, and Paintings* I–VII (Oxford, 1927–51; 2nd rev. ed., Oxford, 1964–). The citations given here are mainly for standard works on major temples and for works on temples discovered or studied since the publication of the *Topographical Bibliography*.

The following general guides to Egypt may also be found useful:

Baines, J. and J. Málek, *Atlas of Ancient Egypt* (Oxford and New York, 1980)

Bard, K. (ed.), *Encyclopedia of the Archaeology of Ancient Egypt* (New York, 1999)

Murnane, W., *The Penguin Guide to Ancient Egypt* (Harmondsworth, 1983; rev. ed. 1996)

Shaw, I. and P. Nicholson, *The British Museum Dictionary of Ancient Egypt* (London, 1995)

The Delta: From the Mediterranean to Memphis

Bietak, M., *Tell el-Dab'a II* (Vienna, 1975)

de Meulenaere, H. and P. MacKay, *Mendes II* (Warminster, 1976)

el-Sayed, R., *Documents relatifs à Saïs et ses divinités* (Cairo, 1975)

Fraser, P.M., *Ptolemaic Alexandria*, 3 vols (Oxford, 1972)

Habachi, L., *Tell Basta* (Cairo, 1957)

Hansen, D.P., 'Excavations at Tell el-Rub'a', *JARCE* VI (1967), pp. 5–16

Hogarth, D.G., H.L. Lorimer and C.C. Edgar, 'Naukratis, 1903', *Journal of Hellenic Studies* XXV (1905), pp. 105–36

Montet, P., *Les Enigmes de Tanis* (Paris, 1952)

Naville, É., *The Shrine of Saft el Henneh and the Land of Goshen 1885* (London, 1887)

Petrie, W.M.F., *Tanis II, Nebesheh (Am) and Defenneh (Tahpanhes)* (London, 1888)

Porter, B. and R.L.B. Moss, *Topographical Bibliography of Ancient Egyptian Hieroglyphical Texts, Reliefs, and Paintings*, vol. IV (2nd rev. ed., Oxford, 1964–)

Steindorff, G., 'Reliefs from the Temples of Sebennytos and Iseion in American Collections', *Journal of the Walters Art Gallery* VII–VIII (1944–45), pp. 38–59

Uphill, E.P., *The Temple of Per Ramesses* (Warminster, 1984)

Middle Egypt: From Memphis to Asyut

Anthes, R. et al., *Mit Rabineh 1955 and 1956* (Philadelphia, 1959, 1965)

Arnold, D., 'Das Labyrinth und seine Vorbilder', *MDAIK* 35 (1979), pp. 1–9

Boak, A.E.R. (ed.), *Karanis, The Temples, Coin Hoards, Botanical and Zoological Reports, Seasons 1924–31* (New York, 1933)

Edel, E. and S. Wenig, *Die Jahreszeitenreliefs aus dem Sonnenheiligtum des Königs Ne-user-Re* (Berlin, 1974)

el-Sayed Mahmud, A., *A New Temple for Hathor at Memphis* (Wiltshire, 1978)

Fakhry, A., *The Monuments of Sneferu at Dahshur*, 2 vols (Cairo, 1959–61)

Holthoer, R. and R. Ahlqvist, 'The "Roman Temple" at Tehna el-Gebel', *SO* 43:7 (1974)

Lauer, J.P., *Saqqara: The Royal Cemetery of Memphis* (London, 1976)

Lauer, J.P. and J. Leclant, *Le temple haut du complexe funéraire du roi Téti* (Cairo, 1972)

Naville, É., *Ahnas el Medineh (Heracleopolis Magna)* (London, 1894)

Newberry, P.E., F.L. Griffith et al., *Beni Hasan*, 4 vols. (London, 1893–1900)

Peet, T.E., C.L. Woolley, J.D.S. Pendlebury et al., *The City of Akhenaten*, 3 vols (London, 1923, 1933, 1951)

Petrie, W.M.F. et al., *Memphis*, 4 vols (London, 1909–13)

Petrie, W.M.F. and E. Mackay, *Heliopolis, Kafr Ammar and Shurafa* (London, 1915)

Porter, B. and R.L.B. Moss, *Topographical Bibliography of Ancient Egyptian Hieroglyphical Texts, Reliefs, and Paintings*, vol. IV (2nd rev. ed., Oxford, 1964–)

Ranke, H., *Koptische Friedhofe bei Karara und der Amontempel Scheschonks I bei el Hibe* (Berlin and Leipzig, 1926)

Reisner, G., *Mycerinus: The Temples of the Third Pyramid at Giza* (Cambridge, MA, 1931)

Ricke, H. et al., *Das Sonnenheiligtum des Königs Userkaf*, 2 vols. (Cairo, 1965; Wiesbaden, 1969)

Roeder, G., *Hermopolis 1929–1939* (Hildesheim, 1959)

Rübsam, W.J.R., *Götter und Külte in Faijum während der griechisch-römisch-byzantinischen Zeit* (Bonn, 1974)

Spencer, A.J., *Excavations at el-Ashmunein* (London, 1989)

Zivie, A.P., *Hermopolis et le nome de l'Ibis* (Cairo, 1975)

Northern Upper Egypt: From Asyut to Thebes

Bakry, H.S.K., 'The Discovery of a Temple of Sobk in Upper Egypt', *MDAIK* 27 (1971), pp. 131–46

Bisson de la Roque, F. and J.J. Clére et al., *Rapport sur les fouilles de Medamoud (1925–32)* (Cairo, 1926–36)

Calverly, A.M. et al., *The Temple of King Sethos I at Abydos*, vols I–IV (London and Chicago, 1933–38)

Chassinat, E. and F. Daumas, *Le Temple de Dendara*, I– (Cairo, 1934–)

Daumas, F., *Dendara et le temple d'Hathor* (Cairo, 1969)

David, A.R., *A Guide to the Religious Ritual at Abydos* (Warminster, 1981)

Fischer, H.G., *Dendera in the Third Millennium B.C.* (New York, 1968)

Frankfort, H., *The Cenotaph of Seti I at Abydos* (EES Memoirs 39) (London, 1933)

Mariette, A., *Denderah*, 4 vols (Paris, 1870–73)

—*Abydos*, 2 vols (Paris, 1869–80)

Petrie, W.M.F., *Athribis* (London, 1908)

—*Koptos* (London, 1896)

—*The Royal Tombs of the First Dynasty/Earliest Dynasties* (London, 1900–01)

Porter, B. and R.L.B. Moss, *Topographical Bibliography of Ancient Egyptian Hieroglyphical Texts, Reliefs, and Paintings*, vol. VI (2nd rev. ed., Oxford, 1964–)

Wegner, J.W., *The Mortuary Complex of Senwosret III: A Study of Middle Kingdom State Activity and the Cult of Osiris at Abydos*. Ph.D. dissertation (Philadelphia, 1996)

The Temples of Thebes

East Bank

Barguet, P., *Le Temple d'Amon Ré à Karnak. Essai d'exégése* (Cairo, 1962)

Bell, L., 'Luxor Temple and the Cult of the Royal *ka*', *JNES* 44:4 (1985), pp. 251–94

Brunner, H., *Die Südlichen Räume des Tempels von Luxor* (Mainz, 1977)

Dorman, P. and B.M. Bryan (eds) *Sacred Space and Sacred Function in Ancient Thebes* (Chicago, 2007)

Epigraphic Survey, *The Temple of Khonsu*, 2 vols (OIP 100, 103) (Chicago, 1979, 1981)

Epigraphic Survey, *Reliefs and Inscriptions at Karnak*, 4 vols (OIP 23, 25, 74, 107) (Chicago, 1936–1986)

Epigraphic Survey, *Reliefs and Inscriptions at Luxor Temple*, 2 vols (OIP 112, 116) (Chicago, 1994, 1998)

Gayet, A., *Le Temple de Louxor* (Cairo, 1894)

Golvin, J.-C. and J.-C. Goyon, *Karnak, Ägypten: Anatomie eines Tempels* (Tübingen, 1990)

Helck, W., 'Ritualszenen in Karnak', *MDAIK* 23 (1968), pp 117–37

Murnane, W.J., 'False-doors and Cult Practices Inside Luxor Temple'. In *Fs Mokhtar* 2 (Cairo, 1986), pp. 135–48

Nelson, H.H. (artist); W.J. Murnane (ed.), *The Great Hypostyle Hall at Karnak, Vol. 1, Pt. 1: The Wall Reliefs* (Chicago, 1981)

Osing, J., 'Die Ritualszenen auf der Umfassungsmauer Ramses' II. in Karnak', *Or* 39 (1970), pp. 159–69

Porter, B. and R.L.B. Moss, *Topographical Bibliography of Ancient Egyptian Hieroglyphical Texts, Reliefs, and Paintings*, Vol. II (2nd rev. ed., Oxford, 1964–)

Traunecker, C., 'Les rites de l'eau à Karnak d'après les textes de la rampe de Taharqa', *BIFAO* 72 (1972), pp. 195–236

—*La chapelle d'Achôris à Karnak* (Paris, 1995)

Wit, C. de, *Les inscriptions de temple d'Opet, à Karnak* (Biblioteca Aegyptiaca 11) (Brussels, 1958)

West Bank

Arnold, D., *Der Tempel des Königs Mentuhotep von Deir el-Bahari, Vol. I: Architektur und Deutung; Vol. II: Die Wandreleifs des Sanktuares'*, *MDAIK* (Mainz, 1974–81)

Epigraphic Survey, *Medinet Habu*, 8 vols (Chicago, 1930–70)

Karkowski, J., 'Studies on the Decoration of the Eastern Wall of the Vestibule of Re-Horakhty in Hatshepsut's Temple at Deir el-Bahri', *Études et Travaux* 9 (1976), pp. 67–80

Lipinska, J., *Deir El-Bahari: The Temple of Tuthmosis III*, 4 vols (Warsaw, 1977)

Murnane, W.J., *United with Eternity: A Concise Guide to the Monuments of Medinet Habu* (Chicago and Cairo, 1980)

Naville, É., *The Temple of Deir el Bahari*, 6 vols (London, 1894–1908)

Nims, C.F., 'Ramesseum Sources of Medinet Habu Reliefs'. In J.H. Johnson and E.F. Wente (eds), *Studies in Honor of George R. Hughes, January 12, 1977* (Chicago, 1976)

Oriental Institute, University of Chicago, *Medinet-Habu*, vols. I–VIII (Chicago, 1930–70)

Osing, J., *Der Tempel Sethos' I. in Gurna. Die Reliefs und Inschriften*, I– (Mainz, 1977–)

Petrie, W.M.F., *Six Temples at Thebes* (London, 1897)

Porter, B. and R.L.B. Moss, *Topographical Bibliography of Ancient Egyptian Hieroglyphical Texts, Reliefs, and Paintings*, Vol. II (2nd rev. ed., Oxford, 1964–)

Vörös, G. and R. Pudleiner, 'Preliminary Report of the Excavations at Thoth Hill, Thebes: The pre-11th dynasty temple and the western building (season 1996–1997)', *MDAIK* 54 (1998), pp. 335–40

—'Preliminary Report of the Excavations at Thoth Hill, Thebes: The temple of Montuhotep Sankhkara', *MDAIK* 53 (1997), pp. 283–7

Wysocki, Z., et al., *The Temple of Queen Hatshepsut: Results of the Investigations and Conservation Works of the Polish–Egyptian Archaeological and Preservation Mission, Deir el-Bahri*, vols 1–3 (Warsaw, 1980–85)

Zivie, C.M., *Le Temple de Deir Chelouit. III. Inscription du Naos* (Cairo, 1986)

Southern Upper Egypt: From Thebes to Aswan

Adams, B., *Ancient Hierakonpolis*, with *Supplement* (Warminster, 1974)

Bisson de la Roque, F., *Tôd (1934 à 1936)* (Cairo, 1937)

Bresciani, E. and S. Pernigotti, *Assuan. Il tempio tolemaico di Isi. I blocchi decorati e iscritti* (Pisa, 1978)

Caminos, R.A. and T.G.H. James, *Gebel es-Silsilah*, I– (London, 1963–)

Cauville, S., *Essai sur la théologie du temple d'Horus à Edfou* (BdE, 102) (Cairo, 1987)

de Rochemonteix, M. and E. Chassinat, *Le Temple d'Edfou*, 14 vols (Paris, 1892; Cairo, 1918–)

de Morgan, J. et al., *Kom Ombos*, 2 vols (Vienna, 1909)

Derchain, P., *Elkab*, Vol. I: *Les Monuments religieux à l'entrée de l'Ouady Hellal* (Brussels, 1971)

Downes, D., *The Excavations at Esna 1905–1906* (Warminster, 1974)

Edel, E., *Die Felsengräber der Qubbet el-Hawa bei Assuan*, I– (Wiesbaden, 1967–)

Fairservis, W.A., Jr. et al., 'Preliminary report on the first two seasons at Hierakonpolis', *JARCE* 9 (1971–72), pp. 7–68

Germond, P., *Les invocations à la bonne année au temple d'Edfou* (AH, 11) (Geneva, 1986)

Jaritz, H., *Elephantine III: Die Terrassen Vor Den Tempeln Des Chnum Und Der Satet: Architektur Und Deutung* (Berlin, 1980)

Junker, H. and E. Winter, *Philä*, I– (Vienna, 1958–)

Labrique, F., *Stylistique et théologie à Edfou: Le rituel de l'offrande de la campagne; Étude de la composition* (OLA, 51) (Leuven, 1992)

Lyons, H.G., *A Report on the Island and Temples of Philae* (London, 1897)

Meeks, D., *Le grand texte des donations au temple d'Edfou* (Cairo, 1972)

Mond, R. and O.H. Myers, *Temples of Armant: A Preliminary Survey* (London, 1940)

Porter, B. and R.L.B. Moss, *Topographical Bibliography of Ancient Egyptian Hieroglyphical Texts, Reliefs, and Paintings*, vols V, VI (2nd rev. ed., Oxford, 1964–)

Quibell, J.E. (vol. II with F.W. Green), *Hierakonpolis*, 2 vols (London, 1900, 1902)

Reymond. E.A.E., 'Worship of the Ancestor Gods at Edfou', *CdE* 38, 75 (1963), pp. 49–70

Sauneron, S., *Esna*, I– (Cairo, 1959–)

— *Les fêtes réligieuses d'Esna aux derniers siècles du paganisme* (Esna, vol. 5) (Cairo, 1962)

Sauneron, S. and H. Stierlin, *Die letzten Tempel Ägyptens. Edfu und Philae* (Zürich, 1978)

Zabakar, L.V., 'Adaptation of Ancient Egyptian Texts to the Temple Ritual at Philae', *JEA* 66 (1980), pp. 127–36

Nubia: From Aswan to Gebel Barkal

Aldred, C., *The Temple of Dendur* (New York, 1978)

—'The Temple of Dendur', *Metropolitan Museum of Art Bulletin* XXXVI:1 (Summer, 1978)

Almagro, M., *El templo de Debod* (Madrid, 1971)

Blackman, A.M., *The Temple of Derr* (Cairo, 1913)

Caminos, R.A., *The New Kingdom Temples of Buhen*, 2 vols. (EES Archaeological Survey of Egypt 33) (London, 1974)

Curto, S., *Il tempio di Ellesija* (Turin, 1970)

Fairman, H.W., 'Preliminary Report on the Excavations at Sesebi (Sudla) and 'Amarah West, Anglo-Egyptian Sudan, 1937–8', *JEA* 24 (1938), pp. 151–6

Gauthier, H., *Le Temple de Ouadi es-Seboud* (Cairo, 1912)

—*Le Temple d'Amada* (Cairo, 1913–26)

Hinkel, F.W., *The Archaeological Map of the Sudan* (Berlin, 1977)

Kendall, T., *The Gebel Barkal Temples 1989–90: A Progress Report on the Work of the Museum of Fine Arts, Boston, Sudan Mission* (Geneva, 1990)

—'Kings of the sacred mountain: Napata and the Kushite twenty-fifth dynasty of Egypt'. In D. Wildung (ed.), *Sudan: Ancient Kingdoms of the Nile* (Paris and New York, 1997)

Knudstad, J., 'Serra East and Dorginarti: A Preliminary Report on the 1963–64 Excavations of the University of Chicago Oriental Institute Sudan Expedition, *Kush* 14 (1966), pp. 165–86

MacAdam, M.F.L., *The Temples of Kawa*, 2 vols (London, 1949–55)

Porter, B. and R.L.B. Moss, T*opographical Bibliography of Ancient Egyptian Hieroglyphical Texts, Reliefs, and Paintings*, vol. VII (2nd rev. ed., Oxford, 1964–)

Reisner, G., 'Inscribed Monuments from Gebel Barkal', *ZÄS* 6 (1931), pp. 76–100

Ricke, H., G.R. Hughes and E.F. Wente, *The Beit el-Wali Temple of Ramesses II* (Chicago, 1967)

Roede, G. and W. Ruppel, *Der Tempel von Dakke*, 3 vols (Cairo, 1913–30)

Schneider, H.D., *Taffeh: Rond de wederopbouw van een Nubische tempel* (The Hague, 1979)

Siegler, K.G., *Kalabsha: Architektur und Baugeschichte des Tempels* (Berlin, 1970)

Smith, H., *Preliminary Reports of the Egypt Exploration Society Nubian Survey* (Cairo, 1962)

Steindorff, G., *Aniba*, 2 vols (Glückstadt, 1935–37)

The Desert Temples: Oases and Outposts

Fakhry, A., 'Oase', *LÄ* IV (1982), c. 541

—*The Oases of Egypt*, 2 vols (Cairo, 1973–74)

Gardiner, A.H. et al., *The Inscriptions of Sinai*, 2 vols. (London, 1952–55)

Giveon, R. 'Tempel, ägyptische, in Kanaan', *LÄ* VI (1986), c. 357–8

Kaper, O.E., *Temples and Gods in Roman Dakhleh: Studies in the Indigenous Cults of an Egyptian Oasis* (Groningen, 1997)

Rothenberg, B. (ed.), *The Egyptian Mining Temple at Timna* (London, 1988)

Wimmer, S., 'Egyptian Temples in Canaan and Sinai'. In S. Israelit-Groll (ed.), *Studies in Egyptology Presented to Miriam Lichtheim* (Jerusalem, 1990)

Winlock, H., *The Temple of Hibis in el Khargeh Oasis* (PMMA 13) (New York, 1941)

Epilogue: Exploration and Conservation Today

Bell, L., B. Fishman and W.J. Murnane, 'The Epigraphic Survey (Chicago House)', *NARCE* 118 (1982), pp. 3–23, and 119 (1982), pp. 5–13

der Manuelian, P., 'Digital Epigraphy: An Approach to Streamlining Egyptological Epigraphic Method', *JARCE* 35 (1998), pp. 97–114

Gammal, M. Hassan el, *Luxor, Egypt: Balancing archeological preservation and economic development*. Ph.D. dissertation (Philadelphia, 1991)

Quirke, S. (ed.), *The Temple in Egypt: New Discoveries and Recent Research* (London, 1997)

Traunecker, C., 'Aperçu sur les dégradations des grès dans les temples de Karnak', *Cahiers de Karnak* 5 (1970–72), pp. 119–30

Illustration Credits

Abbreviations:
a-above; b-below; c-centre; l-left; r-right; t-top
AKG London/Photo: Erich Lessing 42a
Cyril Aldred 126–7
Archivio White Star: M. Bertinetti 59a; G. Veggi, 61br, 178–9
Donald Bailey 56b, 234br
Bibliothèque Nationale, Paris 103l
British Museum, London 74, 85c, 90ar, 91br, 93ar, 107bl, 110c, 180
Photo: Harry Burton, courtesy Metropolitan Museum of Art, New York 86bl
Cairo Museum 63b, 64cr, 82br, 90bl, 99br, 121bl, 126bl, 203br
Peter Clayton 46–7, 75ar, 83a, 90–1, 134al, 139b, 171a, 208a, 234bl
Cleveland Museum of Art 97l
Eugene Cruz-Uribe 236–7, 237b, 238t
Courtesy of the Archive of the Czech Institute of Egyptology, Prague 26b, 75al, 109ar, 110t, 124r, 138b, 171b, 236br
Martin Davies 219a
Aidan Dodson 85t, 116bl, 123ar, 123c, 128b, 129b,130b, 130–1, 134–5, 140l, 143a, 217tr
Egypt Exploration Society 105b, 105c, 106br; photo: Barry Kemp 241a
Dina Faltings/Anja Stoll 104–5
© Chr. Favard-Meeks 27l, 104br
Werner Forman Archive/The Egyptian Museum, Cairo 112r, 128t
Photo: Francis Frith, courtesy The Collection of the Center for Creative Photography, University of Arizona 33r
German Archaeological Institute, Cairo 27r
M. Girodias 83b
Heidi Grassley © Thames & Hudson Ltd., London 6-7, 8, 14–15, 28, 34–5, 44bl, 44br, 52-3, 55a, 58a, 62a, 63al, 64b, 67r, 69r, 71l, 76–7, 80–1, 115t, 118a, 118b, 119, 120br, 121ar, 122a, 122b, 125b, 126a,131br,135a, 149b, 168, 175, 183, 188–9, 203al, 204, 206a, 206br, 207al, 207ar, 209, 210al, 210ar, 214a, 215a, 224, 225, 226
Griffith Institute, Ashmolean Museum, Oxford 33l
Richard Harwood 136, 136–7, 179t, 180–1, 187a, 187b, 188–9, 189, 201, 236bl, 236–7, 237c
Photo: Hirmer 12–13, 23ar, 45ar, 62b, 127br, 147br, 159, 166, 203ar
George Johnson 151ar, 194–5, 202br, 206bl, 212b, 227
Könemann Verlagsgesellschaft mbH, Köln/photo: Andrea Jemolo 112l, 151b, 168–9
Kurt Lange 18al
Image © 1999 by Learning Sites Inc.; reprinted with permission (archaeological data and interpretation by Timothy Kendall) 233ar, 233br
Jürgen Liepe, Berlin 84–5, 165t, 176c, 177a, 197c
Louvre, Paris 94l
Metropolitan Museum of Art, New York: Gift of George F. Baker 1891, 30l; Michael Duigan 133a
Museum of Fine Arts, Boston 141t
Paul Nicholson 55b, 73bl, 89ar, 91a, 107ar
David O'Connor 19b
Oriental Institute, Chicago 199a, 241b
Robert Partridge, Ancient Egypt Picture Library 23al, 94r, 172b, 179br, 190, 212a, 216, 222a, 222b
John Ross 7, 9, 29, 46al, 57, 59b, 63ar, 64al, 65b, 66, 75br, 78b, 79, 100–1, 165t, 170b, 194, 214b, 243, 244–5
Photos courtesy of Beno Rothenburg 238c, 238–9, 239l
Royal Scottish Museum, Edinburgh 87b
Alberto Siliotti, Image Service by Geodia 49, 98, 108–9
William Schenck 69t, 88, 92–3, 93b, 96, 109br, 145b, 150br, 177cl, 192, 208b, 218, 239ar
Albert Shoucair 124–5, 127ar,
Hourig Sourouzian, Cairo 108
Jeffrey Spencer 19a, 39a, 106a
Jeremy Stafford-Deitsch 152l, 155, 156al, 156br, 157, 158b, 163a, 169br, 184, 185, 200l, 200r, 202a, 205, 207br, 211b, 219br, 220-21, 221
Courtesy of Gyösö Vörös 173
Joachim Willeitner, Munich 97r
Derek Welsby 231a, 231bl, 231br, 232a, 233al
Fred Wendorf 16l
Richard Wilkinson 17a, 37a, 43b, 44–5, 45b, 47, 51, 54l, 60, 67l, 68, 69bl, 70a, 71r, 72, 76ar, 77, 89b, 99bl, 99a,113, 114-5, 115ar, 115br, 118–19, 141br, 143b, 144, 145a, 146–7, 147ar, 148l, 148r, 153a, 153br, 156–7, 158a, 160, 161, 162, 163b, 167, 169a, 170a, 176b, 177br, 186a, 195a, 195b, 196, 197a, 197b, 198al, 198b, 199b, 217bl, 217br, 218–19, 240a

Drawings and maps
James Bruce Travels to Discover the Source of the Nile, 1768–73, 31br
Judi Burkhardt 24, 43, 54r, 58, 61ar, 73, 165
From Champollion & Rossellini Monuments of Egypt & Nubia, 46b, 228
After David O'Connor 18b
From Vivant Denon Voyages, 1802, 139a
Description de l'Égypte, 1809, 4–5, 31t, 31c, 142b, 150ar
Courtesy Egypt Exploration Society 93al
B. Garfi after A. Fakhry, The Monuments of Sneferu at Dahshur II, Cairo 1963. By kind permission of Barry Kemp, 50
From Janssen, Atlas, 1619, 102
From B. Kemp Anatomy of a Civilization, CUP, 76al, 110br
Jean-Claude Golvin, courtesy of Éditions Errance 41b, 28–9, 56a, 65a, 67a, 70b, 95br,138a, 182–3
From Lamy Egyptian Mysteries, London & New York, 82, 84al, 96-7, 150al
From M. Lehner Complete Pyramids, London & New York, 1997, 19c (George Taylor), 21, 90al, 125r, 131tr
Ernst Weidenbach from C.R. Lepsius Denkmäler, 1849–59, 174
Frederick Ludwig Norden Voyages d'Egypte et de Nubie, 1755, 31bl,
After J.D.S. Pendlebury The City of Akhenaton, Part III, Vol. 2, 1951, 78a
Geoff Penna 177cr
Richard Pococke A Description of the East, and Some Other Countries, 1743–5, 30r
David Roberts Egypt and Nubia 1846–50, title page, 32b, 213b, 215b,
Searight Collection, London 103r
Noelle Soren 38b, 39c, 41a, 42, 68, 89
Tracy Wellman after W. Murnane, United with Eternity, Chicago/Cairo 1980, 38l
After Fred Wendorf 16r
Philip Winton 10–11, 17b, 20–1, 22b, 23bl, 24–5, 26a, 36t, 36b, 37b (courtesy of Gyösö Vörös), 38–9, 40, 48, 61al (after Jean-Claude Golvin), 95al, 104bl (after Christine Favard-Meeks), 104c, 107c, 109cl, 110bl, 111, 112a, 113a, 114, 116t, 116br, 116–17, 117, 119al, 119ar, 120a, 120bl, 121r, 121br, 122ar, 123bl, 123al, 124l, 125l, 126, 126–7, 128cl, 128cr, 129c, 131tl, 130r, 131c, 131bl, 132tl, 132c, 133c, 134b, 135b, 137a, 137c, 143, 139c, 140r, 140–1, 143l, 144r, 145al, 146 (after Jean-Claude Golvin), 147bl, 149t, 152r, 153bl, 154, 155t, 172, 173c, 175t, 178, 181, 182t, 186br, 187bl, 188, 189t, 191t, 191c, 192b, 193t, 193b, 201t, 202bl, 205t, 209c, 211a, 213a, 217al, 220a, 221a, 223a, 223b, 227a, 229, 230, 232c, 235, 237t, 238c, 239b.

Acknowledgments

I would like to acknowledge a number of my Egyptological colleagues who kindly shared their research, supplied information, illustrations and contacts, or, in some cases, offered comments on sections of this book for which they had particular knowledge. Drs Eugene Cruz-Uribe, James Hoffmeier, Timothy Kendall, Jiro Kondo and Gay Robins all deserve mention in this regard – as does Charles Jones who supplied helpful information, along with Lyla Brock, Diane Flores, Suzanne Onstine and Shang-Ying Shih. Special thanks are also due to Dr Stephen Quirke for reading the tyescript and offering a number of helpful suggestions and insights from his own work. I also gratefully acknowledge Egypt's Supreme Council of Antiquities for allowing my own continued study and archaeological research in Egypt, and special thanks go to Drs Gaballa Ali Gaballa, Muhammad Sughayr and Muhammad Nasr as well as Sabry el-Aziz, Muhammad el-Bialy, and the local inspectors who have facilitated my work in Egypt or with whom I have enjoyed profitable discussions and professional interaction over the years and in the course of this book's completion.

The project was fortunate in being able to draw from the work of a number of excellent photographers and I would particularly like to thank George Johnson in this regard and also my good friend and Expedition photographer, Dick Harwood, who contributed a number of his own personal photographs. Other sources of illustrations and information were Donald Bailey, Peter Clayton, Aidan Dodson, Christine Favard-Meeks, the Czech Institute of Egyptology, Prague, Ulrich Hartung, Jack Herron, Barry Kemp, Paul Nicholson, David O'Connor, Bob Partridge, Donald and Susan Redford, Beno Rothenburg, Donald Saunders, Will Schenck, Jeffrey Spencer, Gyözö Vörös and Derek Welsby.

I was also privileged to have the help of talented artists including my friends Judi Burkhardt and Noelle Soren who prepared a number of the line drawings for the book.

I am also very grateful to all the publisher's editorial, picture research, design and production staff who brought this project to completion.

Finally, but in actuality above all, I would like to acknowledge the kind help of my wife Anna – both for her patience with the author, and for her help in getting the ms. prepared during an extremely busy time.

Index

Page numbers in *italics* refer to illustrations